Statistical Methods for Organizational Research

Statistical Methods for Organizational Research is an accessibly written textbook explaining the ideas underpinning descriptive and inferential statistics in organizational research. Acting as much more than a theoretical reference tool, the book guides readers, a step at a time, through the stages of successful data analysis.

Covering everything from introductory descriptive statistics to advanced inferential techniques such as ANOVA, multiple and logistic regression and factor analysis, this is one of the most comprehensive textbooks available. Dealing with more than statistical techniques, it focuses on conceptual issues, such as the distinction between statistical and practical significance, statistical power and the importance of effect sizes.

Using examples that are directly relevant to organizational research it includes practical advice on topics such as the size of samples required in research studies, using and interpreting *SPSS* and writing up results.

In helping readers to develop a sound understanding of statistical methods rather than focusing on complex formulas and computations, this engaging textbook is appropriate for readers of all ability levels — from those who wish to refresh their knowledge to those new to the subject area.

Chris Dewberry lectures in Organizational Psychology at Birkbeck, University of London.

Statistical Methods for Organizational Research

Theory and practice

Chris Dewberry

Routledge
Taylor & Francis Group

LONDON AND NEW YORK

First published 2004
by Routledge
2 Park Square, Milton Park, Abingdon, Oxon OX14 4RN

Simultaneously published in the USA and Canada
by Routledge
270 Madison Ave, New York, NY 10016

Routledge is an imprint of the Taylor & Francis Group

© 2004 Chris Dewberry

Typeset in Perpetua and Bell Gothic by
Florence Production Ltd, Stoodleigh, Devon
Printed and bound in Great Britain by
TJ International Ltd, Padstow, Cornwall

British Library Cataloguing in Publication Data
A catalogue record for this book is available from the British Library

Library of Congress Cataloging in Publication Data
Dewberry, Chris.
    Statistical methods for organizational research/by Chris Dewberry.
        p. cm.
    Includes bibliographical references and index.
    1. Organization–Research–Statistical methods.   I. Title.
    HD30.4.D484 2004
    302.3′5′015195–dc22   2003026278

ISBN 0–415–33424–1 (hbk)
ISBN 0–415–33425–X (pbk)

For my mum, my dad
and Lynne

Contents

CONTENTS

Illustrations

FIGURES

TABLES

Foreword

Many people wishing to carry out or interpret organizational research have neither the time nor, perhaps, the mathematical background and aptitude, to get to grips with the complex algebra underpinning statistical methods. In writing this book I have, therefore, tried to convey ideas with everyday language rather than with mathematical formulae and computations. In taking this approach there is, of course, a danger that things will be over-simplified, and that the reader will be left with no more than a very superficial understanding of the discipline of statistics. I hope that this is not the case here: the intention has been to explain statistical ideas simply but not simplistically.

Two central aims of this text are to enable readers to use statistical methods to help answer questions which are important to organizations, and to share these answers with others. To do so, it is necessary to know not only how to carry out a given technique, but also how to interpret the results it produces, and how to communicate this information to others with clarity. Therefore, I have placed emphasis not only on how to carry out a range of statistical techniques using *SPSS*, a widely used software package, but also on how to make sense of the results, and how to write them up in a way that others familiar with statistical methods will understand.

In dealing with inferential statistics, the part of the discipline concerned with examining associations and differences and with generalizing research findings, I have placed considerable emphasis on the importance of examining effect sizes as well as on statistical significance. Statistical significance is essentially concerned with whether it is possible to generalize associations or differences found in research data. For example, if you carry out research on 30 people in an organization, and find an association between their job satisfaction and their job commitment, statistical significance will indicate the confidence with which you can generalize these findings and say 'job commitment and job satisfaction are associated, not only in the people I collected data on, but in others too'. While the concept of statistical significance lies at the heart of statistical analysis, it can lead to some pitfalls. One such potential pitfall, considered in this book, is the danger that statistical significance can be interpreted to mean the same thing as practical significance. Statistically significant findings may be of practical significance, but this is not necessarily the case. A second is that finding that two variables are associated, or that they have different averages, does not tell you anything about the strength of that association, or about the size of the difference in averages. The interpretation of statistically significant findings should always be combined with an examination of the amount of association present, or the size of the difference found. It is here that effect sizes, which are specifically designed to express the size of associations or differences, are so useful, and I have, therefore, placed emphasis on the importance of using them when interpreting and reporting findings.

My awareness of the critical importance of effect sizes when interpreting research results was originally raised by the seminal work of Jacob Cohen, a man who has also influenced this text in another way. Thanks to the work of Cohen and others, I have been able to provide tables indicating the sample sizes necessary to use the various statistical techniques covered in the book. Providing such tables in textbooks on applied statistics is unusual. While people applying for grants to carry out organizational research are often required to justify the sample sizes they intend to use by providing the results of power analysis, this subject is rarely covered in general applied texts such as this one. It seems to me that this is wrong: anyone carrying out research which leads to the use of inferential statistics should be aware of the close relationship between sample sizes, power and the likelihood of obtaining statistically significant findings. While the sample size tables presented in this book are less detailed than those set out in texts and computer software dedicated to power analysis, they should nevertheless provide the reader with a helpful guide to the size of the sample that he or she will need to successfully carry out a piece of organizational research.

For those who are completely new to statistics, and who wish to learn about both the principles of the subject and how to carry out analyses, I suggest that you work through Chapter 1 on descriptive statistics, carry out the practical exercises in Chapter 4, and then read through Chapters 2 and 3 on the principles and mechanics of inferential statistics. You will then be in a position to use Chapters 5 and 6 to analyse data, interpret the results, and write these up clearly. Those who have some familiarity with the statistical analysis, but who feel a little rusty, might also benefit from this approach, particularly because, as I have explained, the book covers some principles and ideas that are given relatively little treatment in many traditional textbooks on applied statistics. Those carrying out statistical analysis on a regular basis are unlikely to need advice on which aspects of the book, if any, they may benefit from consulting.

THE PRESENTATION OF NULL HYPOTHESIS SIGNIFICANCE TESTING IN THIS TEXT

During the last 50 years, the analysis and interpretation of quantitative research data in a variety of disciplines, including organizational research, has become almost synonymous with null hypothesis significance testing. Textbooks designed to explain statistical methods to people involved in research are usually made up of technique after technique, each designed to evaluate the 'statistical significance' of one variety of research data or another. In many ways, this is not surprising. Researchers want to know what they can conclude from their data, and on the surface statistical significance provides a clear basis for discriminating between findings which should be taken seriously and those which should not. The importance of significance testing is heightened further by the tendency of scientific journals to use the .05 significance level as one of the criteria with which to evaluate whether or not the results of a research study are worthy of publication.

However, in recent years particularly, the utility of null hypothesis significance testing has been seriously questioned (Anderson *et al.* 2000; Carver 1978; Cohen 1994; Nester 1996). Of the various criticisms that have been made, perhaps the most telling are the following four. First, statistical significance does not tell us what we want to know – whether or not our research hypothesis is correct. Instead, it tells us only that if our null hypothesis is true there is a particular likelihood that we would obtain data with a differ-ence (or association) as large as that which we have found in our research (Cohen 1994). To take an example, imagine that we suspect that in some large organization, on average men are being paid more than women. To examine this supposition, we take a random sample of the salaries of men and women who work there, observe that the mean salary of the sampled men is higher than the mean salary of the sampled women, carry out a *t*-test, and obtain a significance level of .04. What we would like this finding to confirm is whether or not we can safely conclude that women in the organization earn less than men. Unfortunately however, all we can conclude is that if men and women earn the same amount in the organization there is only a 4 per cent chance that we would find a difference between the salaries of men and women sampled as large as we have found, or larger. Indeed, from a Bayesian perspective even this conclusion is open to doubt (Berger 2003).

The second problem is that generally when we carry out a null hypothesis significance test we want to find out whether the difference or association we have found is of practical or theoretical importance, something we should sit up and take notice of. The difficulty is that statistical significance, at least when taken alone, cannot verify the importance of our findings in this way. Statistical significance does not mean the same thing as practical or theoretical importance. Statistical significance informs us that we would be unlikely to obtain a difference (or association) as large as the one we have found (or larger) if the null hypoth-esis that there is absolutely no association or difference between populations, not even the tiniest difference, is correct. It does not tell us any more than that (Cohen 1994). To know whether a difference is important from a practical or theoretical point of view we need to consider the context of the research, and what a difference or association as large as the one we have found actually means in this context. A statistically significant result may or may not have theoretical or practical importance; such importance is not conveyed by that presence of statistical significance alone, and indeed there is no guarantee that a difference or association that does not reach the .05 level of significance is not practically or theoret-ically very important.

The third criticism is that in many of the contexts in which tests of statistical significance are applied, they are able to do no more than confirm what we almost certainly already know. To use again the example of the salaries of men and women in a large organization, would we really expect the mean salaries of all the men and all the women to be *precisely* the same before we carry out our research? Or to put this slightly differently, is it really the case that all we are interested in is whether there is any difference at all, however small, between the mean salaries of men and women in the organization? From this standpoint, carrying out a test of statistical significance, a test which provides evidence about the like-lihood of obtaining the data we have collected if there is absolutely no difference whatsoever between the mean salaries of men and women in the organization, may seem a somewhat futile exercise. So a null hypothesis significance test indicates that we would be unlikely to obtain a difference between the salaries of men and women as large as we have found in our sample data if there is no difference at all between the salaries of men and women in the organization. 'So what?' we might reply, 'we were almost 100% certain before starting the research that the mean salaries of men and women in the organization wouldn't be absolutely identical anyway'.

Fourth, the likelihood of obtaining statistical significance in a research study is greatly influenced by the sample size used (Cohen 1988). In research utilizing very large samples, even very small associations and differences in the sample data are likely to be statistically significant, leading to a danger of making a great deal of something which from a practical or theoretical standpoint is of little consequence. Conversely, research in which very small samples are used is unlikely to yield differences (or associations) which are statistically significant even if large differences (or associations) exist between the populations being sampled.

These concerns about null hypothesis significance testing are further intensified when we consider that statisticians do not agree among themselves on how statistical significance should be reported, or even whether it should be reported at all. Non-advanced statistical textbooks often present the logic as uncontroversial, a set of rules that are as solid and dependable as a rock. In fact statistics, like every other scholarly discipline, has always been characterized by debate and disagreement. Ronald Fisher (1925, 1935, 1955), who developed much of the initial logic and techniques for significance testing, argued that it should involve an examination of the data obtained in relation to the null hypothesis, and that the smaller the p value, the stronger the evidence against the null hypothesis. Jerzy Neyman and Egon Pearson (Neyman 1961, 1977; Neyman and Pearson 1933) argued, contrary to Fisher, that not only null hypotheses but also alternative hypotheses are necessary in significance testing. Furthermore, unlike Fisher, they took very seriously the frequentist principle that in the repeated practical use of a statistical procedure, the long-run actual error should not be greater than (and ideally should equal) the long-run average reported error (Berger 2003). For Neyman and Pearson, the implication of this is that the critical value of p should be chosen *in advance* of the research, and in reporting findings both Type I and Type II error probabilities should be given. Fisher disagreed with this, but as Gigerenzer (1993) points out, statistical textbooks have tended to paper over the controversy, and to present the Fisher and Neyman and Pearson positions in a hybrid form that fails to acknowledge the philosophical differences between them and the implications of these differences for the practice of significance testing.

Furthermore, it is not only differences between the Fisher and Neyman and Pearson schools of thought that are relevant here. The Bayesian approach, named after the sixteenth-century English dissenting minister who formulated its underlying principle (Bayes 1763) and now widely associated with the work of Jeffreys (1961) is attracting increasing attention. The Bayesian approach, unlike the other two, is designed to estimate the probability that the null hypothesis is correct, given the research data, and it differs critically from them in requiring researchers to estimate the probability that the null hypothesis is correct *before* collecting research data as well as after collecting it. While there has recently been an effort to integrate the approach of Fisher with the approach of Neyman and Pearson, this is currently an area of considerable controversy among statisticians (Berger 2003).

All of this leaves the writer of a statistical text designed to help people analyse, interpret, and report the results of research carried out in organizations, with several issues to carefully consider. Should the text follow the usual approach of presenting a hybrid of the Fisher and Neyman and Pearson schools or, as Gigerenzer (1993) suggests, present these approaches separately and thereby familiarize the reader with the philosophical and practical differences of opinion surrounding significance testing? Should the text seek to cover Bayesian methods as well as the more traditionally covered ones? And what should be done to make the reader aware of the limitations and problems associated with significance testing, and to help him or her analyse and interpret research data productively and efficiently in the light of these limitations?

After some thought I decided to take a pragmatic approach to these issues, based on four principal assumptions. First, people carrying out research in organizations should be aware of the limitations of significance testing, and so far as it is possible techniques which can help to overcome these limitations should be provided. Second, it is almost inevitable that those carrying out research in organizations will use statistical packages such as *SPSS* to analyse their data, and it therefore makes little sense to include in this book complex statistical techniques that are not presently incorporated in such packages. Third, to those people for whom the book is principally aimed, those without an advanced understanding of mathematics and statistics, it is better to present the principles developed by Fisher and Neyman and Pearson as a single coherent body than to present two opposing schools of thought and leave the reader with a deep sense of uncertainty about who is right and what he or she should do in the light of this when analysing, interpreting and reporting data. Fourth, academic journals act as gate-keepers to what is acceptable and unacceptable in the application and reporting of statistical methods of data analysis, and it would not be helpful to either aspiring or established researchers to suggest approaches to data analysis and reporting likely to be rejected by such journals.

In the light of these considerations I have omitted Bayesian approaches as they are neither available in *SPSS,* the software package chosen for this book, nor are they commonly reported in journal articles. Undoubtedly, proponents of the Bayesian approach to statistics have strong arguments, and interesting developments are taking place in this area (Berger 2003) but the applications of their approach are currently in a period of development and would benefit from application in statistical software that can be used by researchers who are not expert mathematicians.

When discussing null hypothesis significance testing in the book I, like most other textbook writers, present a hybrid form of the Fisher and Neyman and Pearson approaches, for example suggesting that researchers report exact p values (in line with Fisher) but making the reader aware of both the null and alternative hypotheses, type I and type II errors, and the probability of making a type II error through a discussion of power analysis and by drawing attention to necessary sample sizes in relation to each statistical technique (in line with Neyman and Pearson). I have done so principally because I believe that for people who wish to learn about and use inferential statistical methods it is better to try to provide a single, coherent, comprehensive and well-informed account than to provide two or more separate and competing accounts, leaving the reader to struggle with the differences between them and what the practical implications of these differences might be.

Nevertheless, the reader who wishes to pursue these issues will almost certainly find the very readable article by Gigerenzer (1993) both illuminating and thought provoking.

Finally, I have generally followed the practical recommendations made by the American Psychological Association (Wilkinson and the Task Force on Statistical Inference 1999) which was set up partly to comment on significance testing in psychology in the light of the issues raised by Cohen (1994). These recommendations have the benefit of moving emphasis away from a slave-like and unthinking emphasis on null hypothesis significance testing to a more thoughtful and informed appreciation of what a particular set of data actually means. Furthermore, some of the steps that they recommend, such as habitually reporting effect sizes as well as significance levels, go a considerable way to counteract the limitations inherent in the null hypothesis significance test. The overall view of the Task Force was that despite the strong criticisms of significance testing it should not be abandoned altogether. Rather, significance testing should be used in an informed way, and when the results of significance tests are reported this information should always be supplemented with other information such as means, standard deviations and effect sizes. This is the approach used in this book.

Acknowledgements

I would like to thank Anne Howarth for her editorial work on an earlier draft of this book, Sarah Moore, Rachel Crookes and Francesca Poynter for their editorial work on the final draft, Neil Conway for his helpful suggestions on the presentation of the material on structural equation modelling, and Philip Dewe for his support and encouragement throughout the project. I would also like to thank my family and all my friends for everything.

The material in this book has been adapted and developed from material originally produced for the MScs and Postgraduate Diplomas in Organizational Psychology and Human Resource Management by distance learning offered by the University of London External programme (www.londonexternal.ac.uk).

Part I

Descriptive and inferential statistics

Chapter 1

Descriptive statistics

There is virtually no limit to the research that can be carried out on organizations. Areas as diverse as culture change, the factors associated with job satisfaction, team performance, marketing, organizational effectiveness, fairness, accounting practices and strategic management can be examined with a variety of research perspectives and using a broad range of research techniques. Very often this research involves measurement and, with it, the use of numbers. For example, it is possible to measure the job satisfaction of nurses and doctors by asking them how many aspects of the job they are happy with, or to measure the performance of hospitals by measuring how long patients take to recover from operations. With numerical measurement it is possible to collect information about large and representative samples of people, teams or organizations, and use this to look for important differences or associations between things, to make valuable predictions and to simplify complex relationships. By analysing and interpreting such numerical data, ideas can be confirmed or refuted, unexpected relationships can be discovered, theories can be developed and tested, and practical recommendations can be made. Numerical analysis is, therefore, of central importance to organizational research, and at the heart of numerical analysis is the discipline of statistics.

Statistics can be divided into two areas:

- descriptive;
- inferential.

Descriptive statistics is concerned with *describing* numbers and the relationships between them. Very often the intention is to capture the essence of the numbers, to summarize them in such a way as to render them as easy as possible to understand and digest. The second area, inferential statistics, is concerned with *analysing* numbers and drawing conclusions from them. Basically, this involves collecting a relatively small set of numbers (for example, those referring to the job commitment of 30 employees in a car manufacturing plant) and using them to make guesses about a larger set of numbers that the researcher is interested in (for example, the job commitment of everyone in the car manufacturing plant). Let's begin by examining fundamental elements of descriptive statistics.

The numbers collected in quantitative research are referred to as data. So if you collect the ages of five people:

—   Ruth: 35 years
—   John: 42 years
—   Julie: 57 years
—   Andy: 27 years
—   Jill: 33 years

the ages of these five people constitute your **data**. Each particular number, such as the 35 years of Ruth, is referred to as a **data point**. So here you have one set of data and five data points: 35, 42, 57, 27 and 33. Data can be collected from anything – rivers, shirts, carpets, clocks, mice – anything at all can provide us with numerical information. In organizational research, data are usually collected about individuals working in organizations (e.g. the appraisal ratings of 20 different employees), about collections of people (e.g. the number of units sold by 20 different sales teams), about organizations themselves (e.g. the share price of 100 companies), and about their products (e.g. the number of defective radios produced by an electrical manufacturer). In this book, for the sake of consistency, the focus is on individuals working in organizations. In other words, the unit of analysis is people, and it is assumed to be individual people that data are collected on. However, it should be borne in mind that the ideas and principles to be explained can, equally, be applied to other units of analysis such as teams, organizations and the goods and services that organizations produce.

As already explained, the data we collect about people can concern a variety of different things, such as their well-being, their job performance, their age and so on. Each of these is referred to as a **variable**. A variable is simply something that is measurable and that varies. So age is a variable because we can measure it and not everyone is exactly the same age.

Data come in one of two different types: categorical and continuous.

CATEGORICAL DATA

Using categorical data, as the name suggests, involves placing things in a limited number of categories. Usually in organizational research these 'things' are people, and typical categories include gender and level of seniority. So if we say that we have 34 women and 10 men in an organization, we are referring to categorical data because people are being placed in either one of two categories.

In principle, many different types of categories can be used to classify people. Categories are used for the colour of eyes (green-eyed people, blue-eyed people, brown-eyed people etc.), for the region of the country where people live, or all sorts of other things. In organizational research, categories such as gender and level of seniority tend to be selected because these are thought to be the most important. Sometimes the categories exist before the research begins, and gender and level of seniority are examples of this. At other times categories are created during the course of the research. For example, a questionnaire might ask managers to indicate whether they agree or disagree that the organization should be

Table 1.1 *Age and gender of five people, with gender coded 0 and 1*

Name	Age	Gender
Ruth	35	1
John	42	0
Julie	57	1
Andy	27	0
Jill	33	1

re-structured. Those agreeing and disagreeing can be viewed as two different categories of people. Whatever categories are chosen, they are normally qualitatively different from each other: men are qualitatively different from women because we cannot reduce all the differences between them to a small number of dimensions such as how tall they are, how socially perceptive they are, or how extroverted they are.

Because, nowadays, computers are usually used to analyse data, and computer programs designed for statistical analysis are much better at dealing with numbers than with words, categorical data are usually represented numerically. So, instead of telling a computer that someone is 'male' or 'female', we may tell it that the person has a value of 0 or a value of 1 for gender, and that a 0 for gender indicates that they are male whereas a 1 indicates that they are female. You could represent the information about the five people mentioned earlier in the way shown in Table 1.1.

In Table 1.1, we have assigned the number 1 to females and 0 to males. The coding is arbitrary – the fact that 1 is greater than 0 does not mean that females are greater than males – we might just as well have coded males as 1 and females as 0. The important thing is that we have a numerical code that indicates which category people are in: in this case the female category or the male category. It is because these numbers simply indicate which category someone is in, and do not imply that one category is somehow greater than another, that we know we are dealing with categorical data.

Another example would be the classification of employees according to the part of the country they work in: North, South, East or West. If you counted the number of employees working in these regions and found the following:

- North: 156
- South: 27
- East: 43
- West: 92

you would have categorical data. As with the gender data considered earlier you know that they are categorical because the information you have about each person does not suggest that they are greater than someone else in some way, but merely that they belong to a different category.

Let's say you decided to code people according to the region they work in as follows:

- North: 0
- South: 1
- East: 2
- West: 3

Table 1.2 *The regions in which people work, coded 0 to 3*

Case	Region
1	1
2	3
3	2
4	0
5	0
6	3
7	1
8	1
9	2
10	1

You might then find that the first 10 people you found out about were as shown in Table 1.2. Note that here a 'case' is simply a numerical label given to a particular person in order to identify them. So the first person you have information about is labelled case number 1, the second is labelled case number 2, and so on. In most organizational research, data are collected from people and so each case refers to a particular person as it does in this example. However, this is not always true. For example, sometimes **cases**, the things that we collect data on, may be physical entities such as machines or, at other times, each case might be a different organization. In this book, for the sake of consistency, and because it is the typical situation in organizational research, cases refer to people.

With categorical data you must always remember that a number is being used to specify which category a case belongs in rather than to indicate anything about whether it is, in any sense, greater than, or less than, another case. If you look at the information in Table 1.2, you will, for example, see that the region of case 2 is 3, whereas the region of case 9 is 2. This does not mean that case 2 is in any way 'greater than' case 3: it merely means that, according to the codes given, case 2 comes from the West whereas case 9 comes from the East.

Describing and summarizing categorical data

Having established what categorical data are, we can now consider how such data can best be described and summarized. A very helpful way is to represent the number of people in each category as **relative proportions**. So, if there are 10 men and 10 women in a survey we indicate that the proportions of men and women are equal. Proportions are usually expressed as **percentages**. Information about the number of cases in each category, and the relative proportion of cases in each category, can be shown in a simple table such as Table 1.3.

Knowing that about 40 per cent of the people are men and about 60 per cent are women makes it easier to get a picture of their relative proportions than just knowing that 15 are men and 22 are women. Similarly, Table 1.4 shows how the proportion of people from each of the four regions considered earlier could be presented.

Table 1.4 shows, again, the percentages make it easier to appreciate the proportion of people in each region than the simple numbers do. So you might not notice that about half of the employees work in the North unless

Table 1.3 *The frequency and percentage of men and women surveyed*

	Number	Percentage
Men	15	40.5
Women	22	59.5

Table 1.4 *The frequency and percentage of people working in four regions*

Region	Number	Percentage
North	156	49.1
South	27	8.5
East	43	13.5
West	92	28.9

you expressed this information in terms of the percentage of cases in each category as well as the number of cases in each category.

Another useful way of presenting information about proportions is with a graph, and a useful graph for categorical data is the **pie chart**. A pie chart is shown in Figure 1.1.

Figure 1.1 clearly shows the relative proportion of people from the four regions and, arguably, has more immediate impact on someone interested in this information than Table 1.4 in which the same information is presented in numerical form.

Another way of representing categorical data graphically is with a **bar chart**. An example of a bar chart is shown in Figure 1.2. It is based on the data used in the pie chart, but here the number of cases in each category is represented by the height of each bar. While it does not convey the relative proportions of the number of people in the four regions as clearly as the pie chart, it does enable us to compare the numbers of people in each region more easily. This illustrates the important point that the choice of a graph must be driven by the information that the writer is trying to communicate to the reader.

So far in this chapter you have been looking at how to describe information about just one categorical variable at a time. However, we often wish to examine the relationship between two categorical variables. Imagine that you were interested not only in the number of employees working in each region of the country, but whether this was related to the gender of employees. You can set out information about both region and gender simultaneously in what is called a **contingency table** such as that shown in Table 1.5. In presenting information in a contingency table, it is often helpful to include percentage information too (see Table 1.6).

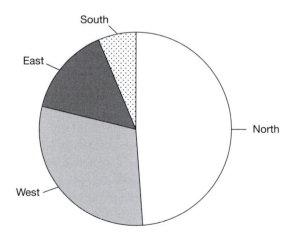

Figure 1.1 *The proportion of people working in four regions*

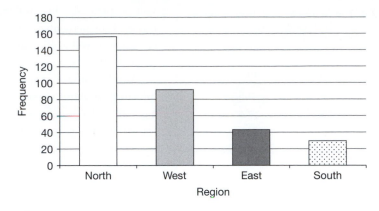

Figure 1.2 *The number of people working in four regions*

Table 1.5 *The regions in which people work, and their gender*

	Males	Females
North	26	130
South	14	13
East	31	12
West	22	70

Table 1.6 *Breakdown of the region in which people work, and their gender: frequencies and percentages*

	Male		Female	
	Number	Percentage	Number	Percentage
North	26	28.0	130	57.8
South	14	15.0	13	5.8
East	31	33.3	12	5.3
West	22	23.7	70	31.1

In Table 1.6 the proportion of males who are working in each region can be compared with the proportion of females working in each region. Presenting information in this way can draw attention to potentially interesting relationships. For example, here, the fact that the proportion of males working in the East is about six times as high as the proportion of females working in the East may be important.

CONTINUOUS DATA

Whereas categorical data involve variables which refer to different categories or classes, continuous data involve variables which vary on a continuous dimension. Occupation is a categorical variable because people are either in one occupational type or another. Age, on the other hand, is a continuous variable because we are not simply in one age category or another, we all exist at some point along a continuum of age, from the moment we are born to the moment we die. So, someone who is 26 years old lies on an age dimension at point 26. Another critical difference between categorical and continuous data is that it is possible to get a 'score' on a continuous dimension which is greater than, or less than, that scored by someone else. A person who is 36 years old has a greater age (and therefore a greater 'score') than someone who is 26. Similarly, John may have higher-rated job perform-ance than Jim, and Mary may have greater well-being than Sally. Here, job performance and well-being, like age, are regarded as continuous rather than categorical variables, and each case has a score on a particular variable or dimension.

Sometimes continuous scales (like categorical ones) are present before research begins. For example, we may wish to measure how much people are paid and how old they are, and in these cases convenient continuous measurement scales are probably already available in the form of annual salary, and age expressed in years or months. However, at other times it is necessary to develop a scale specifically to measure a continuous dimension of research interest. For example, a common way of obtaining continuous data in organizational research is with a **Likert scale** (named after the psychologist who proposed it). A Likert scale consists of a series of written statements that express a clearly favourable, or unfavourable, attitude towards something. Respondents have to indicate how much they agree or disagree with each statement, usually in terms of whether they strongly disagree, disagree, are uncertain, agree, or strongly agree. For example, you might measure well-being very crudely with the following scale which is based on a single statement.

■   I am very happy with my life:

☐   Strongly agree
☐   Agree
☐   Uncertain
☐   Disagree
☐   Strongly disagree

You can then allocate scores to this scale as follows:

5   Strongly agree
4   Agree
3   Uncertain
2   Disagree
1   Strongly disagree

If 10 people complete the scale they might obtain scores like those shown in Table 1.7.

Table 1.7 *Ten well-being scores*

Case	Well-being
1	5
2	3
3	2
4	3
5	3
6	3
7	4
8	4
9	5
10	1

On a scale of 1 to 9, how positive
do you feel about your manager?

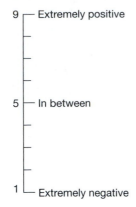

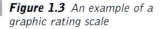

Figure 1.3 *An example of a graphic rating scale*

In your view, how effective is the
new marketing programme?

☐ Not at all effective

☐ Not very effective

☐ In between

☐ Quite effective

☐ Very effective

Figure 1.4 *An example of an itemized rating scale*

Other common methods of constructing measurement scales in organizational research are the graphic rating scale where someone is asked to mark a point on a line which corresponds to their view (see Figure 1.3), and the itemized rating scale in which the respondent is asked to indicate which of several response categories they agree with (see Figure 1.4). As with Likert scales, answers to these can be allocated a score. So, in Figure 1.3 a respondent would probably receive a score of 1 if they indicated that they felt 'extremely negative' about their manager, 5 if they indicated that they felt 'in between', 8 if they felt one point less than 'extremely positive', etc. Similarly, in Figure 1.4 they might receive a score of 1 if they indicated that the marketing programme was not at all effective, 2 if it was quite effective, etc.

An interesting feature of the Likert scale, the graphic scale and the itemized rating scale is that while people can only obtain a limited range of scores on each (e.g. 1, 2, 3, 4 or 5) the data obtained from them are treated as continuous. The reason is that it is assumed that the underlying dimension being measured is continuous. For example, in Figure 1.2 the underlying dimension measured by the Likert scale, well-being, is assumed to be continuous because, in principle, someone can have anything from zero well-being to the maximum possible level of well-being. This illustrates that it is important to distinguish between the nature of the variable being measured and the scale used to measure it. For example, weight (a variable) may be measured in kilograms or pounds (two different measurement scales). In the same way, the extent to which a manager is committed might be measured by counting the number of times she works late over a six-month period, or asking her to indicate on a questionnaire whether she is uncommitted, slightly committed, moderately committed or highly committed to the organization (again, two different measurement scales).

Stevens (1946) made a widely cited distinction between four different types of measurement scale: nominal, ordinal, interval and ratio. A nominal scale is used to measure categorical variables. So, if the categorical variable is type of manager, and the scale used to measure it is whether someone is a junior manager, a middle manager, or a senior manager, we would refer to this as a nominal scale.

Ordinal, interval and ratio scales are used for continuous variables. An ordinal scale is one in which the points on the scale are not equal distances apart. For example, imagine that the variable is job performance, and it is measured with a scale with the following points: poor job performance, very good job performance and excellent job performance. Here, the interval between poor job performance and very good job performance is quite large whereas the interval between very good and excellent performance is relatively small. The intervals between each pair of points are therefore not equal in this case, and for this reason it is referred to as an ordinal scale. Now consider a quite different example, the centigrade scale used to measure the variable of temperature. Here, the interval between each pair of points on the scale is equal: the difference in temperature between 10 degrees centigrade and 11 degrees centigrade is the same as the difference between 11 degrees and 12 degrees. When the intervals between the points on a scale are equal, we refer to it as an interval scale.

Finally, there is the ratio scale. The ratio scale has the same properties as the interval scale, but it also has an additional property: an absolute zero. The centigrade measure of temperature is not a ratio scale because zero degrees centigrade does not mean that there is zero temperature; it is just the point at which water freezes. With a ratio scale the points have equal intervals and zero really does mean zero. In an organizational context it is not uncommon to find ratio scales. For example, when annual salary is measured in the local currency this is a ratio scale because having a salary of, say, zero dollars a year would actually mean earning nothing at all.

The distinction between nominal, ordinal, interval and ratio scales is often presented as being very important for applied statistics. In particular, it is suggested that when choosing a statistical test, the researcher should carefully consider which of Stevens' four measurement scales has been used to collect the data (Stevens 1951). For example, texts may recommend that the ubiquitous t-test (to be discussed in Chapter 4), should only be used with data obtained from interval or ratio measurement scales. However, this was a controversial issue among statisticians from the outset, with Stevens' argument criticized almost as soon as he had made it by Lord (1953). Velleman and Wilkinson (1993) provide an interesting review of the issue, and conclude that while the distinction between categorical and continuous variables is vital, the rigid application of Stevens' four measurement scales is not. This position, that measurement scales are not of critical importance when choosing statistical tests, also endorsed by Howell (1997), will be adopted in this book as well.

However, there are three qualifications to this. First, ignoring the distinction between Stevens' scales of measurement does not imply that we can also ignore the distinction between categorical and continuous data. On the contrary, being able to differentiate between categorical and continuous data is vital. Second, playing down the importance of measurement scales in the process of deciding which type of statistical technique to use does not imply that measurement scales should be dismissed when research is planned, or when research findings are interpreted. When designing research it is certainly good practice to try to measure continuous variables with the best scale possible, with ratio scales being better than interval ones, interval scales better than ordinal, and ordinal scales with reasonably equal distances between points better than ordinal scales with gross variations in the differences between points, such as a 3-point rating scale of 'absolutely disagree', 'strongly disagree' and 'absolutely agree'. And when interpreting research findings a researcher should always actively interpret the results of the analysis, and critically examine them, in the light of both what the variables are (e.g. well-being or job satisfaction) and

11

the way they have been measured (e.g. with a set of questions which require responses which are measured on a Likert scale). Without such active and thoughtful interpretation, meaningless and potentially harmful conclusions can be drawn. For example, if the job performance of two people in a department is rated as excellent and the other two as extremely poor, it is not sensible to use this information to grade the performance of the department as mediocre.

Having discussed measurement scales in a little detail, let's turn to ways in which continuous data can be summarized.

Summarizing continuous data

When a researcher has collected data on a continuous variable in an organization (e.g. the age of employees in years) he or she will want to get an impression of the overall nature of this data; to summarize the data in a way that will make it easy to digest and understand. The two pieces of information that are most often used to achieve this are central tendency and dispersion.

Measures of central tendency

Central tendency is concerned with expressing information not about the extremes of continuous data but about the central part of it. So, if information is collected about the age of all the people who work in a large organization, measures of central tendency are designed to tell you not about the very oldest or the very youngest employees, but about where the ages in the centre of this range tend to be. There are three ways of measuring central tendency:

- the mode;
- the median;
- the mean.

THE MODE
The mode is simply the number that occurs most frequently. So, in Table 1.7 the mode is 3 because there are more 3s than any other single number.

THE MEDIAN
The median is the figure obtained by placing all of the numbers in rank order, and finding the one that falls half-way from the smallest number to the largest. In Table 1.8 the data points relating to well-being have been rank ordered.

Now that, in Table 1.8, the numbers are sorted from the lowest to the highest, you can identify the one that comes half-way up. It is case number 5, because there are five cases below this case, and another five above it. So the median is the score for case number five, which is 3.

In the above situation, working out the median is very straightforward because, as there is an odd number of cases (11), one case will always appear half-way up the rank order.

Table 1.8 *Rank-ordered well-being scores*

Rank order	Case	Well-being score
1	10	1
2	3	2
3	11	2
4	2	3
5	4	3
6	5	3
7	6	3
8	7	4
9	8	4
10	1	5
11	9	5

Table 1.9 *Ten well-being scores*

Case	Well-being score
1	5
2	1
3	5
4	3
5	2
6	3
7	2
8	4
9	5
10	1

However, if there is an even number of cases this does not apply. For example, if there had been 10 cases here instead of 11, there would not be a case half-way up the rank order. To get round this problem, and obtain the median with an even number of cases, add together the two numbers closest to the middle of the rank order, and divide by two.

So, if there are 10 rank-ordered cases, the fifth highest has a score of 3, and the sixth highest has a score of 4, the median is:

3 + 4 divided by 2 = 3.5

THE MEAN

The last way of presenting information about central tendency is the mean. The mean is the figure that people usually refer to as 'the average', and you are almost certainly familiar with it already. If you have a 10-year-old, an 11-year-old, and a 12-year-old child, what is their average age? It is the sort of thing you probably learned early on at school, and the answer, as of course you know, is obtained by adding all the scores together and dividing by the number of scores:

10 + 11 + 12 = 33,

and

33 divided by 3 is 11

So, 11 is the mean age of the three children.

How measures of central tendency are used

The most widely used ways of presenting information about central tendency are the median and the mean. The mode is not used very much because as it is only based on one figure – the one which occurs most frequently – it often gives a misleading picture of the central tendency of the data. For example, imagine that you obtained the information shown in Table 1.9, on the well-being of 10 employees, using a Likert scale. Here, the mode would be 5 because there are more 5s than any other score. But to say that the central tendency of the data is 5 gives a misleading impression. In fact, 5 is an extreme score, and if you consider this data you will probably agree that the central tendency actually seems to be closer to 3 than to 5.

The median is normally better than the mode at capturing the central tendency of the data. Here the median would be 3 (i.e. the fifth highest score is 3, the sixth highest is also 3 and 3 + 3 divided by 2 = 3), and this clearly does represent the central tendency of the data better than the mode of 5.

The mean has an advantage over the median and the mode in that the values of all the data points contribute to it directly. However, there are circumstances in which the median can nevertheless be a better measure of central tendency than the mean. This occurs when the data contain some extreme scores, or 'outliers'. Consider the data set in Table 1.10, which shows the ages of 10 staff.

The median age of the staff in Table 1.10 is 22.5, and this fairly represents the central tendency of the staff who are mostly in their early twenties. But the mean is 29.2 – inflated by the two older people in their sixties. So in cases like this, where there are some extreme scores, the median gives a better impression of central tendency than the mean.

One of the reasons why measures of central tendency are helpful is that they can be used to summarize information about a great deal of data in a highly concentrated and efficient way. Imagine that you collect information about the ages of 2,000 employees. In this case scrutinizing so many numbers would be virtually impossible. But by indicating that the mean age is 43.7 you immediately get an impression of the central tendency of this data. Even when you only have information about a small number of people, measures of central tendency can be very helpful. Let's say you were to run two training programmes, one using training method A, and one using training method B. You are interested in which of these programmes is more effective, so you train 30 people using one programme, and another 30 people using the other. You then measure how much each person has learnt using a continuous scale, with 0 indicating that they have learnt nothing, and 100 indicating that they have learnt everything perfectly. You could then use the median or mean amount learnt by the people trained with each method to

Table 1.10 *The ages of 10 staff*

Case	Age
1	23
2	22
3	62
4	18
5	64
6	22
7	19
8	20
9	21
10	21

make a direct comparison between the amount learnt in the two training programmes. Comparing the amount learnt with the two methods would be far more difficult if you did not use a measure of central tendency, and instead tried to compare the 30 individual scores obtained with one training method with the 30 obtained from the other one.

Measures of dispersion

As well as summarizing continuous data with measures of central tendency, it is also helpful to provide summary information about the dispersion of the scores – how spread out they are. How can you measure dispersion? In fact, there are several ways to do it.

THE RANGE

The first, and simplest method, is known as the range. The range is simply obtained by subtracting the smallest score from the largest one. Thus:

– the range for Department A is 46 − 44 = 2;
– the range for Department B is 65 − 25 = 40.

This gives a straightforward and clearly understandable measure of the extent to which data on a continuous dimension are dispersed. However, the range is not always a good measure of dispersion. If you collect information about the ages of people in Departments C and D you might find the following:

– Department C: 25, 26, 27, 45, 63, 64, 65;
– Department D: 25, 43, 44, 45, 46, 47, 65.

Here the range is the same in both cases: 40 years, but the ages in Department C are generally more spread out than the ages in Department D. What is needed to get round this problem is a measure of dispersion that does more than simply reflect how spread out the largest and smallest scores are and which prevents extreme scores from having a disproportionate influence. In fact, there is a measure of dispersion which has these properties: the inter-quartile range.

THE INTER-QUARTILE RANGE

The inter-quartile range is actually quite closely related to the median. Imagine that you collect data about the salaries of all 1,001 people who work in a large organization. If you rank-order these salaries from the lowest to the highest, and then choose the salary that is half-way between the lowest and the highest, what would this be called? You will no doubt remember that this would be the median salary.

Another way to think about the median is that it occurs 50 per cent of the way up the range of data when they are ordered from the lowest to the highest. It is for this reason that the median can also be called the 50th percentile. To understand what **percentiles** are, imagine that you have collected information about the salary of all 7,000 people who work in a financial organization. George Brown, an employee at the company, earns $37,000 a year, and you want to know how this salary compares to everyone else who works there. To create percentiles, all 7,000 salaries are rank-ordered and then divided into 100 equal portions. The highest salary in each portion is known as a percentile. So the 1st percentile is the value that only 1 per cent of the salaries fall at or below, and the 61st percentile is the value that 61 per cent of the salaries fall at or below. If George Brown's salary of $37,000 falls at the 75th percentile, we know that 75 per cent of the people at the company earn the same or less than he does, and that 25 per cent earn more.

The inter-quartile range is obtained by subtracting the salary for the 25th percentile (one-quarter of the way from the lowest to the highest salary) from the 75th percentile (three-quarters of the way from the lowest to the highest salary). Put slightly differently, the inter-quartile range refers to the range of the 50 per cent of the data points that are closest to the median when the data are rank-ordered. So if you say that the inter-quartile range for salary is $13,000, you mean that the 50 per cent of the data you have collected that is closest to the median of that data has a range of $13,000.

Unlike the range, the inter-quartile range, of course, is not affected by extreme outliers (an outlier is a data point with an extremely high value or an extremely low value compared with the majority of other data points). If the organization in question were the software company Microsoft, and one of the people paid a salary were its founder, Bill Gates, the astronomical amount that he earned from the company would make the range between the smallest salary and the highest (his own) extremely large. This would be misleading, because it would suggest that the salaries are far more dispersed than they actually are. However, if you take the inter-quartile range, Bill Gates' salary no longer comes into the equation because, being outside the middle 50 per cent of the salary range, his earnings would be excluded.

However, the inter-quartile range does have a disadvantage. Let's say you know that the data you have collected on a variable have a median of 56.3 and an inter-quartile range of 8.3. You now know that the middle 50 per cent of the data are roughly between the low 50s and about 60. But what about the other 50 per cent of the data that are below the 25th percentile and above the 75th percentile? How spread out are they? The inter-quartile range tells you nothing about this at all. One way of dealing with this problem is to provide the inter-quartile range and the range together. So you might report that the median salary is $35,000, the inter-quartile range is $6,200, and the range is $18,700. This would give a better impression of the overall dispersion of the data than just providing the range or the inter-quartile range alone.

THE VARIANCE

Neither the range nor the inter-quartile range is directly affected by all of the data points measured on a variable. For example, the range is not influenced at all by the data point that is next to the highest value, and the inter-quartile range is not affected by any points other than the 25th and 75th percentiles. You can argue that a better measure of dispersion would be one which took account of how spread out *all* of the scores you have measured are.

One such measure is the variance. The formula for the variance of a sample is:

$$\frac{\sum(x - \overline{x})^2}{n}$$

Table 1.11
Ten job-performance ratings

Name of employee	Performance rating
Bill	1
Sam	6
June	3
Tony	5
Ruth	2
Heather	4
Mary	3
Frank	5
Robin	7
Jim	2

Table 1.12
Computing the variance

Name of employee	Performance rating	$x - \bar{x}$	$(x - \bar{x})^2$
Bill	1	−2.8	7.84
Sam	6	2.2	4.84
June	3	−0.8	0.64
Tony	5	1.2	1.44
Ruth	2	−1.8	3.24
Heather	4	0.2	0.04
Mary	3	−0.8	0.64
Frank	5	1.2	1.44
Robin	7	3.2	10.24
Jim	2	−1.8	3.24

Although we will not be concerned with statistical formulae in this book, it is helpful to make an exception here and to have a look at this one. The formula for the variance is essentially a set of instructions. It is telling you that you should:

1   take each data point (referred to as x) and subtract from it the mean of the data points (the convention is to refer to the mean with an x with a bar on top);
2   square the result, and add this to all the other data points to which you have done the same thing (Σ is the Greek letter sigma, and in statistics it is used as an instruction to add up some numbers);
3   divide by n, the number of data points.

This will be come clearer if we take a concrete example. Say that you have asked managers to rate the performance of 10 employees on a 7-point scale, and the results are as shown in Table 1.11. If you want to find the variance of the data in Table 1.11, the first thing you need to establish is the mean, which is 3.8. The next steps are shown in Table 1.12.

In Table 1.12 we have first taken each performance rating and subtracted it from the mean performance rating (for example, the mean is 3.8, so Bill's rating of 1, minus 3.8 is equal to −2.8, Sam's is 6 − 3.8 which is 2.2, etc.). This effectively gives a figure representing the difference between each person's rating and the mean of all of their ratings. We have then squared these difference scores. So Bill's difference score of −2.8, when squared, comes to 7.84. Similarly Sam's difference score of 2.2, when squared, comes to 4.84.

The next thing the formula asks us to do is to add up the result: $\Sigma(x - \bar{x})^2$ where Σ means 'add up'.

So add together all the square difference scores from Bill's 7.84 down to Jim's 3.24 and the result is 33.60.

17

Now we are nearly there! The formula for the variance was:

$$\frac{\sum(x - \bar{x})^2}{n}$$

So, the last thing to do is to divide the total of the squared differences from the mean, 33.60, by n. This n, which stands for number, refers to the number of performance ratings we are dealing with (in this case 10). So 33.60 divided by 10 is 3.36, and we can therefore report that the variance = 3.36.

You will be delighted to know that equipped with a statistical program such as *SPSS* you will not have to do all of these computations yourself every time you want to work out the variance. This is done very quickly and easily by such programs. But it is worth going through this step-by-step in the way that we have done so that you can understand what is happening, and why the variance does constitute a measure of dispersion.

To understand this, take a look at what the variance formula is doing. It is, in fact, asking us to first of all take each score and find its difference from the mean of the scores. So if there is very little dispersion in the scores, it makes sense that all of the scores will be very close to the mean, and these difference scores will be very low. However, if the scores are highly dispersed (imagine, for example, that the scores are 976, 13, 531 and 117) the differences from the mean (in this case 409.25) will be very large (566.75, −396.25, 121.75, −292.25). Now, you could simply get a measure of how dispersed the scores are by adding up these difference scores. But the trouble is that if you did so the plus and minus signs would cancel each other out. So if you add together 566.75, −396.25, 121.75 and −292.25 the answer is . . . 0! This suggests that there is no dispersion at all between the numbers, which is clearly absurd. However, if you square the difference scores before adding them up you get rid of the minus signs (because a minus multiplied by a minus is a plus). By using the squared differences from the mean, rather than the actual differences from the mean, you get round this problem.

The last thing you do in finding the variance is to divide the sum of the squared difference scores by the number of scores. In doing so you are finding, if you think about it, *the average of the squared differences of the scores from the mean score*. If each squared difference from the mean represents how far a given score is from the mean, the variance is effectively the average of all these differences across all cases. You should now see the logic behind the variance. It represents the average of the squared differences between a set of scores and the mean of these scores. The more dispersed the scores are, the further they will be from their mean, and the greater the variance will be.

As mentioned earlier, the variance has a clear advantage over the range and the inter-quartile range as a measure of dispersion in that it is directly influenced by all of the scores. That is, all of the scores are actually used in the computation of the variance, whereas in the case of the range only the highest and lowest scores are used, and in the case of the inter-quartile range only the 25th and 75th percentile scores are used.

However, a problem with the variance is that it doesn't give a figure which seems to sensibly reflect the amount of variation between the scores. For example, let's look again at the case in which there are four scores of 976, 13, 531 and 117. We compute the variance of these scores and find that the answer is 192,817.60! This, I think you will agree, seems very odd. The range of this data is 963, and yet we are being told that the dispersion is approaching 200,000! So the variance doesn't give a very sensible impression of the amount of dispersion in the data, and it is for this reason that instead of reporting the variance we usually report the standard deviation.

THE STANDARD DEVIATION

The standard deviation is directly related to the variance. In fact, it is simply the square root of the variance. The formula for the standard deviation of a sample is:

$$\sqrt{\frac{\sum(x - \bar{x})^2}{n}}$$

So, you do the same computations that you did for the variance, but this time you find the square root of the result. In the case of 976, 13, 531 and 117, this turns out to be 439.11. This, as I'm sure you will agree, gives you a far better impression of the amount of dispersion in this simple set of data than the variance of over 192,000.

So why bother talking about the variance at all? Well, we have looked at the variance in some detail because it is at the heart of a great deal of the inferential statistics that we shall move on to in later chapters. The variance, although it is not good at giving a sensible intuitive impression of how dispersed the data are, does have some very important mathematical properties which allow it to be used in many sorts of useful inferential statistical methods. So having an idea of how it is calculated, and what it represents, is very helpful in understanding most inferential statistical methods. As well as this, looking at the variance closely does allow us to appreciate how it works as a means of calculating the amount of dispersion in a set of scores.

Another helpful way of representing data collected on a continuous variable is the **frequency distribution**. To produce a frequency distribution, the data are grouped into categories according to their magnitude. For example, the ages of people who work in an organization might be divided into 18–25 year olds, 26–35s, 36–45s, 46–55s, 56–65s and over 65s. This information could be presented as in Table 1.13.

In addition, the cumulative frequency might also be shown. The **cumulative frequency**, shown in Table 1.14, provides information about the total number of cases in a particular class added to the number of cases in all lower classes. As well as the frequency and cumulative frequency, we might also present the **relative frequency** and **cumulative relative frequency**. The relative frequency and cumulative relative frequency are generally expressed as percentages as in Table 1.15.

The useful thing about the cumulative frequency distribution and the cumulative relative frequency distribution is that they provide instant information

Table 1.13 *The frequency of different age groups in an organization*

Age	Frequency
18–25	24
26–35	38
36–45	49
46–55	43
56–65	29
Over 65	5

Table 1.14 *The frequency and cumulative frequency of different age groups in an organization*

Age	Frequency	Cumulative frequency
18–25	24	24
26–35	38	62
36–45	49	111
46–55	43	154
56–65	29	183
Over 65	5	188

about the number (or percentage) of people with scores lower than a particular cut-off point. For example, Table 1.14 shows that 62 people are less than 36 years old, and Table 1.15 indicates 82 per cent are less than 56 years old.

When we considered categorical data, it was suggested that these could be presented graphically, and that pie and bar charts are particularly useful ways of doing this. In the case of continuous data, representing information graphically is also very helpful, and this is usually done with a **histogram**. A histogram is very similar to a bar chart. The main difference is that a bar chart is designed to represent the number of scores in discrete categories (for example, the number of people in several different ethnic groups, or the number of people working for different departments). Consequently, each bar on the graph is separated. Histograms are designed for continuous data, but nevertheless represent it, like bar charts, in the form of bars. The way that this is achieved is by grouping the data (as in Table 1.15) and then using the height of each bar to indicate the number of people in each group.

A histogram is shown in Figure 1.5. The data on which it is based represent the performance of 2,008 people on a training course, and each bar shows the number of people obtaining a score in a 20-point range. As you can see, the plot of the data forms a clearly defined shape, and this is referred to as the frequency distribution. In this case the shape is

Table 1.15 *The frequency, relative frequency and cumulative relative frequency of different age groups in an organization*

Age	Frequency	Percentage	Cumulative percentage
18–25	24	13	13
26–35	38	20	33
36–45	49	26	59
46–55	43	23	82
56–65	29	15	97
Over 65	5	3	100

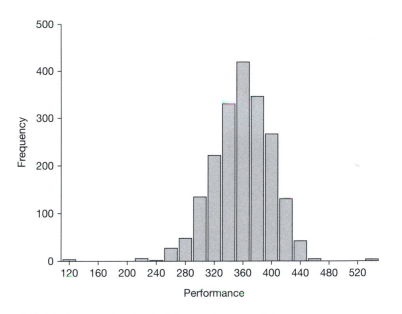

Figure 1.5 *A histogram showing training performance data*

roughly symmetrical, and looks a little like an inverted 'u'. The shape of a distribution is very important because it can tell you a great deal about the nature of the data. You can tell from this distribution that the bulk of the trainees scored between 300 and 420 points, and that the mean score was probably somewhere around 360 points. Furthermore, as you move away from the mean score, fewer and fewer trainees appear. So while more than 100 trainees obtained scores in 10-point bands close to the 360, only a handful obtained scores in 10-point bands below 280 and above 440. What's more, as the number of people appearing in these bands decreases, it does so roughly symmetrically on both sides of the mean.

However, it is not always the case that histograms are symmetrical on both sides of the mean. The histogram in Figure 1.6 shows the distribution of the ages of trainees. Here, there is a distinct tail trailing off towards the right. Because this distribution is not symmetrical, it is said to be a **skewed distribution**. When the 'tail' of the skew is towards the *larger* scores (as it is here towards the older trainees), it is referred to as a *positive* skew. Sometimes, however, you get the reverse effect, and the tail of the skew is off to the left towards the lower numbers. Such a distribution is shown in Figure 1.7. Finally, Figure 1.8 shows what is known as a **bimodal distribution**. A bimodal distribution looks like two symmetrical or skewed distributions placed side by side. It is called bimodal because there are two distribution peaks (i.e. modes) rather than one.

As well as histograms, frequency distributions are also often presented as **line drawings** or more technically **frequency polygons**. Instead of showing the number of cases in a category with a bar, a frequency polygon shows this with a single point. When these points are joined together they give good indication of the shape of a distribution. A frequency polygon is shown in Figure 1.9.

21

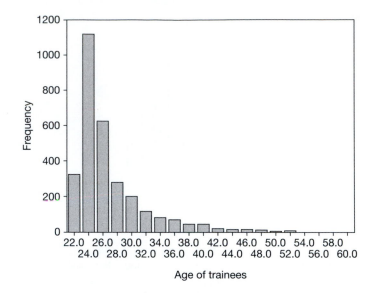

Figure 1.6 A positively skewed distribution

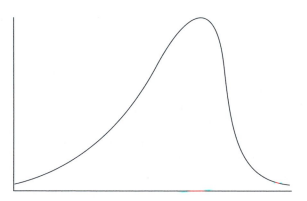

Figure 1.7 A negatively skewed distribution

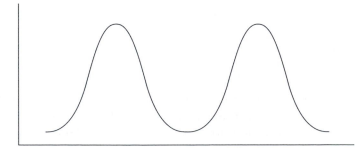

Figure 1.8 A bimodal distribution

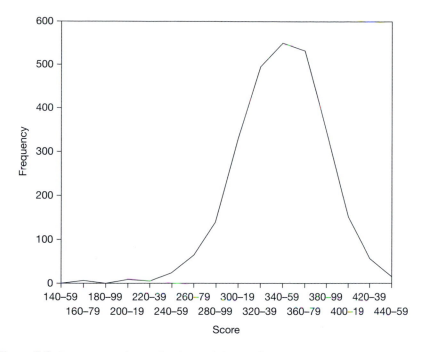

Figure 1.9 *Frequency polygon showing training performance*

Reporting measures of central tendency and of dispersion

In this chapter, three ways of measuring the central tendency of continuous data have been introduced: the mode, median and mean. And we have four ways of measuring the dispersion of continuous data: the range, inter-quartile range, variance and standard deviation. The methods most commonly reported in journal articles are the mean and median for central tendency, and the standard deviation for dispersion.

The mean and median are favoured ways of presenting information about central tendency because, in almost all circumstances, they convey more useful information than the mode. Remember, the mode is based on only one consideration: which data point is most common in a variable? The median and mean have the advantage of being influenced by all the data points, not just one. The mean is the measure of central tendency of choice if the distribution of the data is reasonably symmetrical and there are no extreme outliers because every data value contributes to the calculation of the mean. However, if the distribution is heavily skewed (positively or negatively), and/or there is one or more extreme outlier in the data, the median is generally better because it is more resistant than the mean to the effects of outliers and skew.

The standard deviation is usually chosen as the way of presenting information about the dispersion of continuous data because, like the mean, it is influenced by the value of every data point. However, like the mean, extreme scores can distort it. Look again at the ages of staff which, because of the presence of extreme scores, produced a distorted mean. They are shown in Table 1.16.

Table 1.16 *The ages of 10 staff (reproduced from Table 1.10)*

Case	Age
1	23
2	22
3	62
4	18
5	64
6	22
7	19
8	20
9	21
10	21

Here, as you saw when this example was first discussed, the two people in their sixties distort the mean, raising it to 29.2 when the median is only 22.5. The same thing happens to the standard deviation. This works out at 16.93 for these 10 ages. This does not seem very sensible – the 10 people here are mostly in their early twenties and there are generally only two or three years of age difference between them. But the two extreme ages provided by the two people in their sixties inflate the standard deviation very considerably. To illustrate this further, let's look at what happens to the standard deviation if you replace the two people in their sixties with two people aged 23 and 21. This brings down the standard deviation of the 10 scores from 16.93 to only 1.55! So you get a very large reduction in the standard deviation by eliminating the two extreme scores.

The implication of this is important. The standard deviation is, when used in the right circumstances, a good measure of dispersion. But if there are one or more extreme scores in the set of data you are dealing with, the standard deviation (and the variance) is highly vulnerable in that it can lead to the impression that there is considerably more dispersion in the data than there actually is for the bulk of the scores.

If several means (or medians) and standard deviations are reported simultaneously, they are usually presented as in Table 1.17.

A feature of the data presented in Table 1.17 is that, with the exception of salary, the figures are given to two decimal places. Decisions about the number of decimal places to give when reporting data generally depend on two factors: accuracy and precision. Accuracy simply refers to how accurately something is measured. We might measure the length of a steel rod roughly by casually placing a tape against it, or accurately by using a very sensitive electronic instrument. Precision refers to the exactness with which we report a

Table 1.17 *Age, length of service, absence, salary, well-being and performance: means and standard deviations*

	Mean	Standard deviation
Age	37.24	6.84
Length of service	6.73	2.13
Absence (days)	31.38	6.24
Salary	$61,013	$9,275
Well-being	4.24	2.12
Performance	16.78	3.75

measurement. So we could report the length of a steel rod roughly to the nearest metre, or highly precisely to perhaps 50 decimal places. A high degree of precision tends to suggest a high level of accuracy: if you are told that the average length of three steel rods is 5.66666667 metres, this probably suggests to you that each rod has been very accurately measured. However, it might be that the length of the rods has only been very roughly estimated, to the nearest metre. If this rough and ready measurement indicates that the rods are 7, 4 and 6 metres long, the mean of these three figures to eight decimal places turns out to be 5.66666667. However, this high level of precision clearly gives a very misleading indication of the (poor) level of accuracy. In organizational research, and the social sciences generally, it is rarely possible to measure things with the high level of accuracy often found in the physical sciences. So the convention is to give figures to no more than two decimal places. Because statistical software packages such as *SPSS* often provide highly precise output, when reporting the results of statistical analyses it is often necessary to truncate the number of decimal places they present. So if an *SPSS* report of the mean job satisfaction of 10 people measured on a 7-point scale was 5.48676, a researcher would normally present this figure as 5.49.

Returning to ways of summarizing data, there is one last method that is worthy of discussion even though it is not used a great deal in practice. It is known as the **5-point summary** and it consists of providing five pieces of critical information about a continuous variable. These are the lowest value (known as the lower extreme), the highest value (called the highest extreme), the median value, the 25th percentile (called the lower fourth), and the 75th percentile (called the upper fourth). The 25th percentile is called the lower fourth because it cuts off the lowest 25 per cent of the data. That is, the data points between the lower fourth and the lower extreme represent one fourth of the data, the fourth with the lowest values. Similarly, the 75th percentile cuts off the highest fourth of the data. This is made clearer with an example. Imagine that you are provided with a 5-point summary of the ages of people who work in an oil refinery:

Age of oil refinery staff

Highest extreme:	62
Upper fourth:	51
Median:	38
Lower fourth:	30
Lowest extreme:	18

These five pieces of information provide a great deal of information about central tendency and dispersion of the data. The median of 38 is a good measure of central tendency, but more than this we can see that the 50 per cent of the oil refinery workers who are closest to the median age are between 30 and 51 years old. In relation to the dispersion of the ages of the oil refinery employees, we can see that the ages range from as low as 18 to as high as 62 (yielding a range of 44 years), but that the 50 per cent of the workers with ages closest to the mean have an age range of only 21 years. The 5-point summary can be used for any distribution shape, and when there are extreme outliers. Furthermore,

25

as I imagine you will agree, it provides more intuitively helpful information than just, as is typical, providing the information that the oil refinery workers had a mean age of 38 years with a standard deviation of 8.7 years. It gives us a feel for the data that is lacking when only the mean and standard deviation are given.

There are probably three reasons why the 5-point summary, despite its applicability in a wide range of situations, and its ability to provide an excellent feel for the data, is not used more frequently in academic journals. The first is that five numbers are required to describe the data whereas when the mean and standard deviation are used there are just two. When there is a considerable amount of data to present, use of the 5-point summary may significantly increase the length of the results section of an article. The second reason is that a variety of widely used statistical tests are designed to examine differences between means rather than differences between medians, and do so by using information about the variance (which, as explained earlier, is directly related to the standard deviation). If statistical tests are examining differences between means, it does seem appropriate to state what those means are. The third reason is convention: presenting the mean and standard deviation happens to be the conventional way of doing things. It may not always be the best way, but it is the way most people are familiar with.

Nevertheless, the 5-point summary is a good way of summarizing continuous data, and providing you have enough space and are presenting to people who are familiar with it, it can be recommended. Certainly, the use of statistical tests which examine differences in means need not be an obstacle, as it is a simple matter to report the 5-point summary when the data are described and then to give the means and standard deviations as well when the test results are reported.

This completes the material on descriptive statistics. In Chapter 2 we will move on to examine inferential statistical analysis. However, if you do not have experience of using statistical software to carry out the various descriptive techniques discussed here in Chapter 1, and you have access to *SPSS*, you will probably find it helpful to work through the practical exercises in Chapter 4 before you begin Chapter 2.

SUMMARY

- Statistics can be divided into two areas: descriptive and inferential.
- The data collected in quantitative research can be categorical or continuous.
- When people are coded on a categorical dimension, they are placed in a finite number of qualitatively different categories (for example, males and females).
- Categorical data are usually presented in a table showing the frequency and percentage of people in each category, and can be displayed graphically in a pie chart or a bar chart.
- Contingency tables are used to present information about the distribution of people across two categorical dimensions (such as gender and ethnicity).
- With continuous data, someone can obtain a score which is higher or lower than the score obtained by someone else.

■ Measures of the central tendency of continuous data are the mode, median and mean. The median and the mean are used most often.

■ Measures of the dispersion of continuous data are the range, the inter-quartile range, the variance and the standard deviation. The standard deviation is used most often.

■ Continuous data can be placed in categories according to their magnitudes and then presented as frequencies, cumulative frequencies, percentages and cumulative percentages.

■ Continuous data can also be presented graphically in a histogram or a frequency polygon.

■ When continuous data are plotted in a histogram or frequency polygon, a shape known as a frequency distribution is formed.

■ Frequency distributions can be symmetrical, have a positive or a negative skew, or be bimodal.

■ The 5-point summary is an under-used but effective way of describing the distribution of data on a continuous variable.

QUESTIONS

(Answers to all questions can be found on pages 332–3.)

1 What is a variable?

2 Are the following data categorical or continuous?

Department	Number of employees
Marketing	45
Sales	63
Finance	34

3 Name two types of chart that are useful for presenting categorical data.

4 What sort of table is used to present information about two categorical variables simultaneously?

5 Name three measures of central tendency. Which is used least often and why?

6 Name four measures of dispersion.

7 Name a measure of central tendency and a measure of dispersion that may provide a misleading indication of the nature of the data measured on a continuous variable if there are one or more extreme outliers.

8 What is the relation between the variance and the standard deviation?

9   Identify the following frequency distributions:

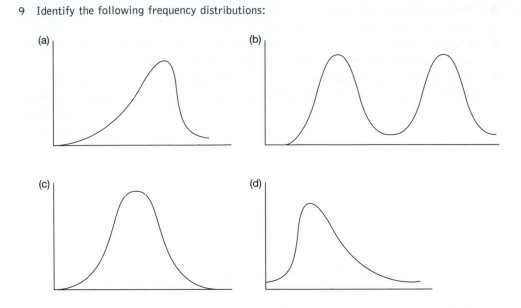

10   What are the components of a 5-point summary?

Chapter 2

The principles of inferential statistics

Descriptive statistical techniques are very useful, but ultimately they only summarize and communicate the information contained in our samples. Very often we wish to go beyond these samples. For example, instead of only being able to say that, on average, the 50 employees in an organizational attitude survey have high levels of job satisfaction, we might want to generalize this finding, and say something about the average job satisfaction in the organization as a whole. With inferential statistical analysis this is made possible, and the purpose of this chapter is to introduce some of the main principles on which inferential statistical analysis is based. The first part of the chapter introduces samples, populations and probability, and the second part is concerned with associations, differences, statistical significance, effect sizes and statistical power.

SAMPLES

In order to carry out organizational research it is necessary to decide on the sample of people to include in your study. For example, if you wish to study the effect of part-time contracts on the job commitment of women in China who are in their twenties, it would clearly make sense to use a sample of women in this age group living in China in your research. That is, women who are 20 to 29 years old and in part-time jobs might constitute your sample.

In inferential statistics we also talk about samples. But here we do not actually mean a sample of people. In the context of inferential statistics, a sample refers not to a sample of people, but to a sample of numbers. To understand what this means, stay with the example of research on part-time workers. Let's say that from each of the women in their twenties whom you involve in your research, you measure job commitment on a scale of one to seven, where one equals very low job commitment and seven equals very high job commitment. And let's also say that you obtain the results shown in Table 2.1.

So, in Table 2.1 you have data on the job commitment of 12 women who work part-time and are in their twenties, with the first getting a job-commitment score of 4, the second a score of 3, and so on. From a statistical point of view, the job-commitment scores collected here represent a sample. The numbers 4, 3, 1, 6, 4, 6, 2, 3, 2, 3, 5, 4 are a sample of scores from the population of scores that you really want to know about. The

Table 2.1 *The job commitment of 12 people*

Case	Commitment
1	4
2	3
3	1
4	6
5	4
6	6
7	2
8	3
9	2
10	3
11	5
12	4

population of scores you really want to know about is the job-commitment scores of *all* Chinese women in their twenties who are in part-time work. If there are, say, 3,500,245 women in their twenties in China who work part-time, you could, in principle at least, have obtained all 3,500,245 job-commitment scores. If you had done so, you would have the population of job-commitment scores of women in their twenties who work part-time in China. However, it is very unlikely that you would ever be in a position to obtain the job-commitment scores of all the women you are interested in – getting the population of scores you want to know about is, in most cases, simply impractical. So, instead of this you take a sample of scores – 12 in the example used here – and use this sample to estimate the scores you would have obtained if you had collected all 3,500,245 job-commitment scores you really want to know about.

POPULATIONS

As you can see, a statistical sample refers not to a sample of people but to a sample of numbers that are obtained from people (or from anything else that is being researched). These numbers vary on each of the variables we are interested in measuring in our research – such as age, salary, job performance and aggressiveness. Each sample of numbers is drawn from a population of numbers and, generally speaking, it is the population of numbers, and not the sample, that you really want to know about. If you want to carry out research on the job satisfaction of people in Mexico, you cannot measure the job satisfaction of all working people in that country. So, instead, you take perhaps 1,000 Mexican people, measure their job commitment (to obtain your statistical sample), and use this to estimate what you want to know about the job-satisfaction scores of all working Mexican people (the statistical population in which you are interested).

And what is it that you will want to know about the population? Usually it is the information that was discussed in Chapter 1. In the case of categorical variables it is the proportions of cases that fall into certain categories (e.g. the proportion of all Mexicans who are male and female), and in the case of a continuous variable such as job satisfaction it is the central tendency and the dispersion of scores (e.g. the mean or median job-satisfaction scores of Mexican people, and the standard deviation of the job-satisfaction scores of Mexican people). These vital pieces of information can tell you a great deal that can help you in your research. So, if you were interested in comparing the job satisfaction of the French, Australians and Mexicans, having the mean job-satisfaction scores of people from these three countries would clearly be extremely useful.

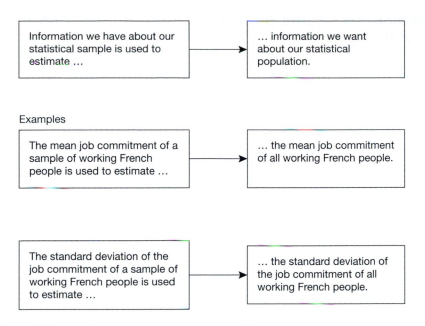

Figure 2.1 *Generalizing from samples to populations*

The problem is that while you might want to compare the job satisfaction of all French, Australian and Mexican people (three statistical populations) you are only likely to have information about the job-satisfaction scores of a sample of French, Australian and Mexican people (three statistical samples). Therefore, what you need to do is to use the information that you obtain about your statistical samples to estimate what you want to know about your statistical populations. This is illustrated in Figure 2.1.

In Figure 2.1, the mean and standard deviation of the job-commitment scores of the population of interest have been inferred from the mean and standard deviation of the known sample of job-commitment scores. You have entered the realm of inferential statistics.

QUESTIONS ABOUT INFERENTIAL STATISTICS

As you read this, some doubts and concerns about this practice may be occurring to you. For example, you may be wondering:

■ how you can possibly know for sure that the mean of the sample is the same as the mean of the population;
■ how big your statistical sample needs to be before you know that it is a perfect estimate of the population.

Consider each of these issues in turn.

Do the mean and standard deviation of a sample accurately reflect those of the population?

How can you know that the mean of your sample, or the standard deviation of your sample, is an accurate estimate of the population mean, and population standard deviation? Is it not the case that you might find the mean job commitment of a sample of 20 Mexican people but that it may actually be a really poor estimate of the mean job commitment of all Mexicans? The answer to this is that you never know for certain that the information about the central tendency and dispersion of your sample (these are technically known as **sample statistics**) are actually accurate estimates of the central tendency and dispersion of your population (known as **population parameters**). Instead, all you can work out is the probability that the sample statistics are good estimates of the population parameters. That is, the only way you can be sure of the mean job commitment of all working Mexican people is to measure the job commitment of all working Mexican people and then find the mean of these scores. If you don't measure the job commitment of all these people, all you can possibly do is *estimate* this population mean. The single best way to do this is by using the mean job-commitment scores obtained from a representative sample of Mexican people. A representative sample of Mexicans is one that does not systematically exclude any particular types of Mexicans, such as women, or people who live outside cities.

So, the conclusions drawn from inferential statistical methods are, in a very fundamental sense, not certainties and truths but estimates and probabilities. However, if the right steps are taken, not just statistically, but also more generally in the research process, these estimates and probabilities will be based on good-quality information, and founded on tried and tested logic. Therefore, they should prove extremely helpful in the process of developing good theories and sound knowledge.

How large a sample?

The second question raised was how large does a sample have to be before you can be sure that it provides a perfect estimate of a population parameter such as the population mean? Well, having read the section above, you will appreciate that actually this is not a very good question to ask. You never know with certainty that you have a perfect estimate of a population parameter such as the mean of the population, from a sample statistic such as the mean of the sample. The best you can hope for is that you know the probability that your estimate of a sample statistic (such as the mean of a sample) is within a certain range of the mean of a population parameter (such as the mean of the population).

PROBABILITY AND CONFIDENCE INTERVALS

This information about the probability that a sample statistic (e.g. the mean of a sample of Mexican people on job commitment) is a good estimate of a population parameter (i.e. the mean job commitment of all working Mexicans) is expressed using **confidence intervals**. With confidence intervals, you specify how confident you want to be of knowing the range of values that a population mean might fall within. Most commonly the 95 per cent confidence interval is specified. That is, based on your sample data, you estimate, with 95 per cent confidence, the lowest and highest values that the population mean might actually have.

To understand the concept of a confidence interval, look back at the data in Table 2.1, giving 12 job-commitment scores.

The mean and the 95 per cent confidence interval for this commitment data turn out to be:

- mean – 3.58
- 95 per cent confidence interval
  - lower: 2.59
  - upper: 4.58

How this confidence interval is worked out will be explained in Chapter 3; for the time being it is sufficient to accept that it can be done. The sample mean, which is the best estimate you have of the population mean, is 3.58, and the confidence interval tells you that you can be 95 per cent confident that the population mean is actually no lower than 2.59 and no higher than 4.58. Using inferential statistical methods, you can't be sure that the sample mean is the same as the population mean, but you can be 95 per cent confident that the population mean lies somewhere between 2.59 and 4.58. This is equivalent to saying that, in actual fact, the population mean may be lower than 2.59, or it might be higher than 4.58, but there is only a 5 per cent chance of this.

Obviously, you would like the confidence interval to be as small as possible. It is not much use knowing that you can be 95 per cent confident that the mean level of job commitment of nurses is somewhere between 1.5 and 6.5 on a 7-point scale! It would be much better to know that you can be 95 per cent confident that you have a small range of scores – say, ranging only from 3.57 to 3.59 – within which your population mean actually falls.

There are two factors that determine the size of the confidence interval of the mean. They are:

- the sample size;
- the sample variance.

This is actually common sense, if you think about it.

Imagine that you wanted to estimate the mean salary of people working for a large multinational organization. You take two random samples of people who work for the organization, and ask them their salaries. One sample consists of five people, and the other of 100 people. The mean salary in the small sample turns out to be $41,000, and in the large sample it is $52,000. Which of the two samples do you think would be more likely to have given you an accurate estimate of the mean salary of everyone who works for the organization?

Your intuition, like formal statistical theory, will tell you that the larger sample is more likely to give you a good estimate of the mean population in the whole organization.

Table 2.2 The job-commitment scores of people in two organizations

Organization A	Organization B
5	1
5	8
5	10
6	3
6	5
5	6
5	8
6	2
6	9
6	3
Mean = 5.50	Mean = 5.50
Standard deviation = 0.53	Standard deviation = 3.17

Table 2.3 The confidence intervals for job commitment in two organizations

	95% confidence interval	
	Lower	Upper
Organization A	5.12	5.88
Organization B	3.23	7.77

So, the 95 per cent confidence interval for the larger sample will almost certainly cover a smaller range than the 95 per cent confidence interval for the smaller sample. Put slightly differently, you can be more confident that the large sample provides you with an accurate estimate of the population mean than that a small sample does.

The other factor that affects the size of the confidence interval is the amount of variation in the data. Imagine that you go into two organizations and collect information from 10 people in each about their job commitment, measured on a 7-point scale. The results are shown in Table 2.2.

As you can see in Table 2.2, the mean job-commitment score is 5.5 for both organizations. But which mean do you think is more likely to give you an accurate estimate of the mean of all the people in each organization? Which would you be more confident in? Again, statistical theory is probably in line with your common sense or intuition here. The confidence intervals for these two sets of data are shown in Table 2.3.

In Table 2.3, you can see that the confidence interval for Organization A, where the variation in the job-performance scores was relatively small, is less wide than the confidence interval for Organization B, where the dispersion of the scores was considerably greater. To summarize, therefore, the extent to which you can be confident that a sample statistic such as the mean is an accurate estimate of its equivalent population parameter depends on the size of the sample and the amount of variation in the data. The larger the sample, and the smaller the amount of variation in the scores within the sample, the more confident you can be that your sample statistic (the thing you know about) is a good estimate of the population parameter (the thing you want to know about).

Confidence intervals for categorical data

As well as obtaining the confidence intervals for continuous data, you can also do it for categorical data. Imagine you wish to know the proportion of women in a large organization who smoke. You take a sample of 20 women, and find that eight of them smoke. This suggests that 40 per cent of women in the organization are smokers. However, because you have only a sample of women, you can't be sure that the proportion of women in the organization as a whole who smoke is exactly 40 per cent. Nevertheless, you can obtain the 95 per cent confidence interval for this, which turns out to be 19 per cent to 61 per cent. So, given that you have found that 40 per cent of your sample of 20 women smoke, you can be 95 per cent confident that the actual number of women who smoke in the organization is no less than 19 per cent and no more than 61 per cent.

As with continuous data, the range of values in the confidence interval for categorical data is reduced if you increase the sample size. This is because the larger the sample, the more confident you can be that the proportion of your sample that has a particular characteristic is a good estimate of the proportion of the population that has that characteristic. If instead of finding that eight out of a sample of 20 women smoke, you find that 40 out of a sample of 100 women smoke, the 95 per cent confidence interval this time works out as 30 per cent to 50 per cent. Whereas the range of the confidence interval based on a sample size of only 20 was 42 points (61 per cent minus 19 per cent), the range of this interval based on a sample size of 100 is reduced to only 20 points (50 per cent minus 30 per cent). Once again you can be more confident in the accuracy of your sample statistic if it is based on a large sample than if it is based on a small one.

ASSOCIATIONS AND DIFFERENCES IN INFERENTIAL STATISTICS

In the first part of this chapter you have looked at statistical theory concerned with the issue of how you can generalize from statistical samples to statistical populations. In some research this may be all you want to do. You may be interested in identifying the levels of job commitment in an organization, or the ethnic mix of the people there. To do so you can take a random sample of, say, 50 people, and measure their job-commitment levels, or take 30 people at random and note their ethnicity. You can then use this information to estimate the mean job-commitment level, or the proportion of people from different ethnic groups, in the organization as a whole.

In the case of surveys such as this, all you may wish to do is to provide information about the central tendency and dispersion of the continuous data in your sample (for example, the mean, confidence interval of the mean, and the standard deviation of well-being levels), or the frequencies of categories of categorical data (for example, the proportion of men and of women). These may be the only reasons for conducting the survey.

However, in analytical research you will wish to go beyond merely describing the data in your samples, and beyond using your sample statistics to estimate population parameters. For example, you may, in addition, want to:

- examine relationships between different variables;
- try to predict scores on one variable from the scores on one or more others;

■ see if the central tendency of a variable is greater for one group of people than another.

Broadly speaking, this is achieved by focusing on two sorts of relationships: associations and differences.

Associations

Associations occur between variables. While the nature of these associations can, in principle, be very complex, in practice most widely used statistical techniques assume that these relationships are relatively simple. We will focus on the possible associations between two continuous variables. Such associations can be positive, or negative, or there can be no association at all. Examples of each of these three types of relationship are shown in Tables 2.4, 2.5 and 2.6. In each table the well-being and job commitment of five employees is shown. Both of these variables are measured on scales ranging from 1 to 5. So the first person in Table 2.4 scored 5 for well-being and 5 for job commitment, the second scored 4 for well-being and 3 for job commitment and so on.

You would say that there is a positive association between well-being and job commitment in the data presented in Table 2.4 because, quite clearly, having a relatively high well-being score is associated with receiving a relatively high job-commitment score. And,

Table 2.4 *A positive association between well-being and job commitment*

Case	Well-being	Job commitment
1	5	5
2	4	3
3	3	4
4	2	2
5	1	1

Table 2.5 *A negative association between well-being and job commitment*

Case	Well-being	Job commitment
1	5	1
2	4	2
3	3	3
4	2	4
5	1	5

Table 2.6 *No association between well-being and job commitment*

Case	Well-being	Job commitment
1	5	5
2	4	1
3	3	2
4	2	3
5	1	4

of course, the converse is also true, low well-being is associated with low commitment. In Table 2.5 there is a negative or inverse relationship between well-being and job commitment. Here, the higher the well-being score, the lower the job-commitment score tends to be. Finally, in Table 2.6 there is no association at all between well-being and job commitment. We cannot say that higher well-being is associated with higher job commitment, nor can we say that higher well-being is associated with lower job commitment: the variables are not associated at all.

Differences

Having considered associations, you can now move on to the issue of differences. In the case of categorical data, researchers are generally interested in differences between proportions. In Table 2.7 the contingency table presented in Chapter 1 (Table 1.6) is reproduced. It shows the numbers and proportions of males working in four regions and the numbers (and proportions) of females working in those four regions. You might be interested in examining whether the proportion of men working in each of the four regions is different from the proportion of women working in each of the regions.

In the case of continuous variables, you will usually be interested in differences in central tendency. Tables 2.8 and 2.9 give the scores for the well-being of men and women, again measured on a 5-point scale. In Table 2.8 the mean well-being score for men, 4.2, is higher than the mean well-being score for women, 2.8. Therefore, there is a difference in the central tendency of the well-being scores of the men and women. However, in Table 2.9 the mean score is 4.0 both for men and for women, and there is no difference in central tendency in this case.

It is worth noting that while with continuous variables you will usually be interested in differences in *central tendencies* of various variables, it is also possible to examine whether differences exist in their *dispersion* (for example, are the well-being scores of men more dispersed than those of women?).

You can examine associations between both categorical and continuous variables, and you can also examine differences between both categorical variables (in relation to proportions) and continuous ones (in relation to central tendency, and sometimes dispersion). The analysis of associations and differences lies at the heart of many inferential statistical methods and, as you will see later, statistical packages like *SPSS* contain a variety of powerful and

Table 2.7 Breakdown of the region in which people work and their gender: frequencies and percentages (reproduced from Table 1.6)

	Male		Female	
	Number	Percentage	Number	Percentage
North	26	28.0	130	57.8
South	14	15.1	13	5.8
East	31	33.3	12	5.3
West	22	23.7	70	31.1

Table 2.8 *Male and female well-being scores with a difference in central tendency*

Well-being	
Men	Women
5	4
4	1
5	2
3	3
4	4
Mean = 4.2	Mean = 2.8

Table 2.9 *Male and female well-being scores with no difference in central tendency*

Well-being	
Men	Women
4	2
4	5
5	4
3	5
4	4
Mean = 4.0	Mean = 4.0

sophisticated statistical techniques to examine associations and differences in great detail, and under a variety of circumstances. However, before moving on to discuss these techniques, we will first of all examine some of the core theoretical ideas on which they are based. Armed with an understanding of these ideas, you will be in a much better position to understand what the techniques are doing, and how the results they produce should be interpreted.

RESEARCH HYPOTHESES AND INFERENTIAL STATISTICS

When people use inferential statistics they are usually concerned with testing hypotheses. That is, they want to know whether something that they are interested in is true or not. Examples of hypotheses that might be tested in organizational research are:

- Training method A results in people retaining more job-relevant information than training method B.
- A particular measure of intelligence predicts how well people will perform their jobs at work.
- People who believe that they have chosen their careers experience more job satisfaction than people who believe they have had no choice over their careers.

In each case, the stated hypothesis implies that something is true when it might not be true. For example, the hypothesis that:

Training method A results in people retaining more job-relevant information than training method B

can be contrasted with the hypothesis that

Training method A does *not* result in people retaining more job-relevant information than training method B.

The second of these two is known as the **null hypothesis**. The null hypothesis is usually a statement that there is no association between two or more statistical populations, or that there is no difference between the central tendency (or dispersion) of two or more statistical populations. So, if you take the other two examples of research hypotheses in organization research shown above, the implicit null hypotheses would be:

- A particular method of intelligence does *not* predict how well people will perform their jobs at work.
- People who believe that they have chosen their careers do *not* experience more job satisfaction than people who believe they have had no choice over their careers.

The null hypothesis is always paired with an **alternative hypothesis**. This alternative hypothesis is the one that the researcher *really* wants to test. So, using our training example it is:

> Training method A *does* result in people retaining more job-relevant information than training method B.

When researchers write about their work in academic journals they do not tend to state the null hypothesis, instead, they just present the alternative one. However, it is very important to recognize that *every* alternative hypothesis *must* be paired with a corresponding null hypothesis, because it is the null hypothesis which is tested with inferential statistics. So, if a null hypothesis is not explicitly stated, it must still be there in the background, and the meaning of it must be clear.

How can you use inferential statistical methods to investigate whether each of these null hypotheses should be accepted because it is true, or whether it is false and, therefore, the corresponding alternative hypothesis should be accepted instead? To understand this, you first need to be clear about a fundamental point:

> A null hypothesis is a statement about the nature of the population, not the nature of the sample.

When you state the null hypothesis that there is no difference between the mean salary of men and the mean salary of women, you are claiming that if you were to measure the salary of an infinite number of men, and the salary of an infinite number of women, there would be absolutely no difference at all between these two means. So, if you worked out the mean salary of an infinite number of men very precisely to, say, 1,000 decimal places, and then worked out the mean salary of an infinite number of women to 1,000 decimal places also, these two means would be *exactly* the same. It is these population means, and these population means alone, that you are referring to in your null hypothesis.

In the same way, if you propose the null hypothesis that there is no association between salary and job commitment, you are making a statement about whether, if you were to sample an infinite number of people, you would find some association, however slight, between how much people earn and their job commitment. If there is even the smallest relationship between job commitment and salary, the null hypothesis is false.

SIGNIFICANCE TESTING

Now, given that you know that the null hypothesis is a statement about the statistical population, how can you know whether to accept it or reject it? How can you know that there is absolutely no difference between the means of two statistical populations, or that there is no association at all between two or more variables in the populations you are interested in? The only way to search for an answer to these questions is to examine the characteristics of your statistical samples. For example, imagine that your null hypothesis is that there is no difference in the mean well-being of men and women, and that to try to find out whether this is true you collect information about the well-being of 100 men and 100 women. The mean and standard deviation of the sample data are shown in Table 2.10.

Table 2.10 *The well-being of 100 men and 100 women*

	Well-being	
	Mean	Standard deviation
Men	4.13	0.11
Women	4.17	0.18

The sample means are different in Table 2.10 for men and women. But remember that your null hypothesis does not concern the sample data, but is a statement about the statistical populations from which the sample data have been drawn. It may well be that there is no difference between the mean well-being of all men and the mean well-being of all women, but that the difference you have found in your two samples is due to chance. After all, if the mean well-being score of all men is exactly 4.15, you would not necessarily obtain a mean of exactly 4.15 if you just measured the well-being of a sample of 100 men – as explained on page 32, sample statistics are only estimates of population parameters. As a consequence, if you took several random samples of men, with 100 men in each sample, you would probably find that sometimes the sample mean would be over 4.15, and sometimes it would be less than 4.15.

Let's return to the case of a sample of 100 men and 100 women. Here are the null and alternative hypotheses.

- *Null hypothesis*: There is no difference between the mean well-being of men and the mean well-being of women.
- *Alternative hypothesis*: There is a difference between the mean well-being of men and the mean well-being of women.

As a researcher, what you really want to find out here is whether the alternative hypothesis is true. However, statistical tests cannot directly tell you whether the alternative hypothesis is true or not. What they do, instead, is to tell you how likely you would be to obtain research data with a difference between means (or an association) as large as the one you have found if the null hypothesis that there is no difference (or no association) between the populations is true. This is explained more fully in the next section on statistical significance.

What is meant by statistical significance?

We are now in a position to examine what is meant by statistical significance. Look again at the sample data in Table 2.10. In this case what a test of statistical significance would ask is this:

> If the null hypothesis is true, what is the probability that you would obtain a difference between the two sample means as large as this?

Let's say that, using inferential statistical methods to analyse your data, you find that if the null hypothesis is true, only one time in 1,000 would you obtain a difference in the means as large as the one you have in Table 2.10. On the basis of this finding you can quite sensibly argue that since this is so unlikely you should probably accept the alternative hypothesis instead. That is, you accept the alternative hypothesis that the population of well-being scores for men and the population of well-being scores for women have different means. Put more simply, the mean well-being of men and the mean well-being of women are different.

But what if you find that if the null hypothesis is true, then one time in every three you would, by chance, find a difference between means as large as that in your sample data? In this case it would surely be more sensible to conclude that actually getting this result by chance alone if the null hypothesis is true is not very unlikely at all. Therefore, instead of rejecting the null hypothesis and accepting the alternative one, you should simply accept the null hypothesis.

While this example has dealt with differences between means, it is also possible to use significance tests to examine the null hypothesis that there is no **association** between variables and, in so doing, to test the alternative hypothesis that the variables are associated.

The logic of significance testing can be summarized as follows:

1   Tests of statistical significance are usually concerned with whether there is an association between populations, or whether there is a difference in the central tendency of populations.
2   They work by examining the probability that the null hypothesis is false. The null hypothesis is normally that there is no association between the populations, or that there is no difference in the central tendency of the populations.
3   If a test of statistical significance indicates that if the null hypothesis is correct there is still a sizeable chance that we would obtain a difference (or association) as large as the one we have found in our research, we *accept* the null hypothesis and reject the alternative hypothesis.

41

4   If a test of statistical significance indicates that if the null hypothesis is correct there is only a relatively small chance that we would obtain a difference (or association) as large as the one we have found in our research, we *reject* the null hypothesis and accept the alternative one.

What statistical tests do is to tell you the probability that you would get a difference between variables as large as the one you have found in your sample data, *if the null hypothesis is true*. Or they tell you the probability you would get an association between variables as large as the one you have found in your sample data, *if the null hypothesis is true*. What you then have to do is to decide, on the basis of this information, whether to accept or reject the null hypothesis. How do you do this? There is a convention that is generally accepted in research, not only in organizational research but in many other research areas as well. It is as follows:

If the statistical test tells you that the probability that . . .

1   if the null hypothesis is true

2   you would have obtained a difference (or association) in your sample data as large as the one you have found

3   less frequently than 5 per cent of the time by chance

. . . it makes reasonable sense to reject the null hypothesis.

This is because you are being told that you would be unlikely to obtain the difference (or association) you have found in your data if the null hypothesis is true. Given that this is the case, you say that the difference (or association) found in your sample data is 'statistically significant'.

But, if the statistical test tells you that the probability that . . .

1   if the null hypothesis is true

2   you would have obtained a difference (or association) in your sample data as large as the one you have found

3   5 per cent or more of the time by chance (5 per cent of the time, 10 per cent of the time, 50 per cent of the time, etc.)

. . . it makes sense to accept the null hypothesis.

This is because you are being told that you would be quite likely to obtain the difference you have found in your data if the null hypothesis is true. In this case you say that the difference you have found in your sample data is not statistically significant.

The probability that you will obtain a statistically significant result partly depends on the level of significance used. In this book, for the sake of simplicity, and because it is the widely used convention, we have always referred to the 5 per cent or .05 level of significance. In fact, significance is sometimes set at .01 (or even .001). If the null hypothesis is true you are, by definition, more likely to obtain significance at the 5 per cent level than at the 1 per cent level.

Why, you may ask, is the level of significance set at the 5 per cent or .05 level? Surely it would be safer to set it much higher than this. If we want to be certain that the null hypothesis is false and the alternative hypothesis is true, why not say 'I am only willing to reject the null hypothesis and accept the alternative hypothesis if I would only obtain a difference as large as the one I have in my data (if the null hypothesis is true) 1 time in 10,000 by chance'? This way we could be very sure that we have not accepted the alternative hypothesis when we should have accepted the null hypothesis instead. The reason that very high significance levels like this are not used is that while dealing quite effectively with one problem it introduces a new one. The problem that is dealt with, called a **Type I error**, is the danger of rejecting the null hypothesis when it should be accepted. We make a Type I error when there is actually no difference (or association) between populations but we wrongly conclude from our sample data that such a difference (or association) is there. For example, if there is no difference between the job commitment of employees working in sales and marketing, but we measure the job commitment of 20 sales and marketing people and from this incorrectly conclude that those in sales are more committed than those working in marketing (or vice versa), we are making a Type I error. If we reduce the level required for statistical significance from .05 to, say, .001, the likelihood of making a Type I error is reduced. The trouble is that if we do this the probability of making a **Type II error**, that is accepting the null hypothesis when it is actually false, increases. The .05 level of significance is generally chosen not because it is perfect, but because it represents a reasonable trade-off between (1) the danger of making a Type I error, which is particularly likely to occur if we set the significance level too high (e.g. .10); and (2) the danger of making a Type II error, which is prone to happen if we set the significance level too low (e.g. .0001).

All statistical significance tests provide information about how unlikely the differences or associations you have found in your sample data are if the null hypothesis is true. And they do so with what is called a p, or probability, value. For example if you use the t-test, which is the most commonly used statistical test for examining whether two samples of continuous data are drawn from populations with the same means, SPSS will provide you with information about the p value of the result. If you obtain a p value of 0.03, this means that the probability of finding a difference between the sample means as large as the one you found is 3 in 100. Shown in Table 2.11 are some examples of p values for differences between means, and how they should be interpreted.

The way to decide whether the result is statistically significant or not is to ask whether the p value is less than 0.05. This is because, as discussed above, the convention is to reject the null hypothesis and accept the alternative hypothesis if the difference (or association) you find, or a bigger one, would occur by chance less than 5 per cent of the time if the null hypothesis is true.

Table 2.11 *Interpreting p values for the differences between means*

p value	Interpretation	Statistically significant?
0.023	The probability of obtaining a difference between the sample means as big as this if the null hypothesis is true, is 23 in 1,000	Yes
0.049	The probability of obtaining a difference between the sample means as big as this if the null hypothesis is true, is 49 in 1,000	Yes
0.1	The probability of obtaining a difference between the sample means as big as this if the null hypothesis is true, is 1 in 10	No
0.0001	The probability of obtaining a difference between the sample means as big as this if the null hypothesis is true, is 1 in 10,000	Yes
0.05	The probability of obtaining a difference between the sample means as big as this if the null hypothesis is true, is 5 in 100 (one time in 20)	No

So, if the *p* value is less than 0.05 you can claim to have a statistically significant result, reject the null hypothesis and accept the alternative hypothesis. However, if the *p* value is 0.05 or over, you have to say that your result is not statistically significant and accept the null hypothesis.

EFFECT SIZE

So far in this chapter we have looked at the logic behind tests of statistical significance. As explained earlier, these are used to test the null hypotheses that there is no association between populations or that there is no difference in the central tendency (or dispersion) of populations. What these tests do *not* tell us is the size or extent of any such associations or differences. So if we are interested in whether training programme A is more effective than training programme B, a statistical test of significance can be helpful, but if we want to know how much more effective one training programme is than the other, the test will not provide any help. If we want to know the size of differences in central tendency, or the strength of the associations, we need information about effect sizes. An **effect size** is simply a measure of how big an association or a difference is.

You can refer to effect sizes in relation to:

■ samples (for example, how strong is the association between age and salary in a sample of 250 Polish employees?);
■ populations (for example, how strong is the association between age and salary in Polish employees?).

Effect sizes are very important. For example, when you carry out research into the effectiveness of a training programme, you are not necessarily interested in whether one training programme is marginally better than another, but whether one training programme is substantially better than another. And when you are interested in whether there is an association between the extroversion of sales people and their sales figures, you are not necessarily interested in whether there is a very small association between them, but a substantial one.

But don't you already have an answer to the question of whether an association or difference is important and significant – the idea of statistical significance? Is it not the case that a statistically significant difference is also a practically important difference? The answer is, no. Statistical significance does not mean that you have a substantial association, or a substantial difference – an association or difference which is big, practically important, and always worth taking notice of and doing something about. To understand why this is so, recall what you mean when you say that something is statistically significant.

Statistical significance at the .05 probability level means that an association (or difference) you have found in your sample data would occur less than 1 time in 20 by chance, if the null hypothesis is true.

Can you find that your association or difference is statistically significant if there is only a small association or a small difference? That is, can you obtain statistical significance if the effect size you have found is small and, from a practical point of view, insubstantial and uninteresting? The answer is, yes. *This is because the chance of obtaining a statistically significant result depends not just on the population effect size, but also on the sample size you have used in your research (and, as mentioned earlier, on the significance level adopted).* With two very small samples of the salaries of men and women, you are unlikely to find that the difference between the means of the two samples is statistically significant even if there is actually a very big difference in the mean salaries of men and women (i.e. a big population effect size). And conversely, if you take two very large samples of men and women, you are likely to find that even if the difference in the salaries of men and women is very small indeed, you will still obtain a statistically significant result.

Some examples

- A correlation is a measure of the strength of association between two variables. The strength of correlation varies from 0 (no association at all between the variables) to 1 (for a perfect positive association) or −1 (for a perfect negative correlation). So a correlation of 0.1 is very weak, and one of 0.9 is very strong. If the correlation between gender and salary is actually 0.1, this would mean that there is a very weak association between how much people earn and whether they are male and female. However, if you sampled 1,000 men and women you would have a very good chance of finding that the association between salary and gender is statistically significant even though, at 0.1, it is very weak.
- Someone might try to sell your organization a psychometric test to use in selection. They might have data to show that the correlation between the score that people

obtain on the test and their job performance is statistically significant. This would imply that the test is worth buying since it will helpfully predict job applicants who will perform well or perform badly at work. However, if the sample size used to examine the association between the test scores and job performance was very large (say 1,000 or more) this would be likely to be statistically significant even if the actual correlation between the test scores and job performance is very small (say about 0.1).

Small effect sizes can also be important

Sometimes a small effect size is very important. Imagine that a researcher found a way of improving the performance of staff by just 1 per cent with no disadvantage to the staff and at no cost to the organization. The effect size here is small, but because a 1 per cent increase in performance would be very useful to the organization, and very attractive if it entailed no concomitant costs, the research finding would be important. What this shows is that it is not simply whether a finding is statistically significant that matters, nor even whether the effect size is large or small. What matters is statistical significance, and the size of the effect, in the general context of the research.

> You should consider statistical significance in the context of sample size, and you should consider effect size in the context of the theoretical implications and practical applications of the research findings.

What all this means is that:

1   you should treat the notion of statistical significance with caution;
2   when interpreting the results of statistical analysis, you should be aware of the sample sizes used, and the effects these are likely to have on the chance of obtaining statistically significant results;
3   the larger the sample size, the more likely that you will obtain a statistically significant association or difference, if one exists;
4   when examining research findings you should consider effect sizes as well as statistical significance;
5   you should consider effect sizes in the context of the possible implications and practical applications of research findings – although large effects are generally more desirable than small ones, in some contexts a small effect can be important.

Reporting the size of an effect

Finally, if you are to report the size of an effect, how can this be done most effectively? A variety of effect size measures have been suggested, covering all the major forms of association and difference. However, only some are used with any regularity, and it is these that we will focus on here.

The effect size for the association between two continuous variables

For the association between two continuous variables, the correlation coefficient is an excellent measure of effect size. The correlation coefficient will be dealt with in some detail in Chapter 6 but, as we have seen, the correlation coefficient may range between 0 if there is no association between two variables, to 1 if there is a perfect positive relation between them, and −1 if there is a perfect negative relation between them. In organizational research, and social science research generally, a small effect is viewed as a correlation of about 0.1 (or −0.1 for a negative correlation), a medium effect is a correlation of about 0.3 (−0.3), and a large effect would be a correlation of 0.5 (−0.5) or more (Cohen and Cohen 1975).

Effect size for the difference between two means

For the difference between two means, the effect size used is referred to as 'd'. It is obtained by taking the difference between two means and dividing by the standard deviation of the scores on which they are based. So, if the mean performance for women is 22.7, the mean performance for men is 13.4, and the standard deviation of the performance of all of the men and women is 14.5, the effect size of this difference between the means is:

$$(22.7 - 13.4)/14.5 = 0.64$$

For the social sciences and organizational research, a small effect is viewed as a d of about 0.2, a medium effect as about 0.5, and a large effect as 0.8 or more (Cohen 1988). So, in this case, the difference between the performance of men and women has a medium to large effect size.

STATISTICAL POWER

By now it should be clear that the reason we carry out tests of statistical significance is because we wish to examine the likelihood that we would generate data with a difference between means (or a strength of association) as great as we have found in our research if the null hypothesis is true. We do this because if we find that we would be quite likely to obtain such a difference or association if the null hypothesis (e.g. there is no difference in the job performance of men and women) is true, we can infer that the alternative hypothesis (e.g. there is a difference in the job performance of men and women) is likely to be false. Conversely, if we find that the difference between means, or the strength of association, we find in our research data is sufficiently large that it would be very unlikely to occur by chance if the null hypothesis is true, we can infer that our alternative hypothesis, the hypothesis we are really interested in (i.e. that men and women do not have the same level of job performance), is likely to be true.

The ability of statistical tests to demonstrate that a difference or association of a particular magnitude would be unlikely if the null hypothesis is true, *under circumstances in which the null hypothesis is actually false*, is referred to as **statistical power**. The more statistical power that you have in your research study; the more likely you are to get the evidence you are looking for if your research hypothesis is actually true. In a sense, statistical power is comparable to Sherlock Holmes' magnifying glass; the more powerful the glass the more likely he is to detect fingerprints on the murder weapon if they are there. Similarly, the more statistical power you have the more likely you are to obtain evidence for the alternative hypothesis if it is true.

Power analysis is dealt with in excellent, though quite technical, texts by Cohen (1988) and Bausell and Li (2002). Briefly, statistical power depends on four factors: the significance level adopted in the study (e.g. is the .05 or the .01 level of significance adopted?), the effect size of the association between the populations (or difference in the means of the populations) you are trying to detect and, most important of all, the sample size used in the study. Basically, as you increase the required significance level (say from .001 to .05), as the size of the effect increases, and as the size of the sample increases, so there is a concomitant increase in statistical power. The reverse is also true of course; by decreasing the required level of significance, and reducing the effect size and the sample size, the amount of power to find evidence for the alternative hypothesis, if it is true, diminishes.

What then, are the implications of this? Perhaps the most important implication is that it is possible to identify a variety of strategies for increasing statistical power. Bausell and Li (2002) discuss 11 such strategies, and three of the key ones are as follows. First, adopting the .05 significance level, as is the convention, will give you more statistical power than adopting a more stringent level of significance such as .01. However, as discussed earlier, as the significance level is reduced, so the probability of making a Type I error (accepting the null hypothesis when it should be rejected) increases. So there is only a relatively small amount of scope here for increasing power.

A second step that can be taken to improve power is to increase the population effect size. In fact, this is easier to achieve than is often assumed. If your study is well planned, you use good control measures to minimize the effect of extraneous variables affecting your data, and you use methods of measurement (e.g. questionnaires) that are well designed and which do a very good job of measuring just the variable you are interested in, you can markedly increase the population effect size. For example, if you are examining whether training method A provides better training than training method B, designing a good study by taking such steps as ensuring that how much people learn from the two methods is assessed on the same day, at the same time, and in similar conditions, and employing a good measure of how much they have learnt, will boost the effect size of the difference between your measure of how much people have learnt if, indeed, there really is a difference. This is interesting, not least because it brings together the statistical ideas of power and effect size, and the methodological idea of designing a good piece of research.

A third way of increasing statistical power is increasing your sample size. In fact, this has a very marked effect on power. For example, if a t-test is being used to examine whether there is a difference in the mean of two populations, the effect size, d, is 1.00, and the significance level adopted is .05, increasing the sample size from 10 to 40 people will increase the power from only 55 per cent (i.e. not much better than a 50–50 chance of obtaining a p value of less than .05 if the null hypothesis is false) to 99 per cent (i.e. an excellent chance of obtaining a p value of less than .05 if the null hypothesis is false). However, we must be careful here. Recall that in the discussion of the concepts of statistical significance and effect sizes it was pointed out that with a very large sample it is possible to obtain a statistically significant result even if the effect size is very small. Hopefully you will now see why: both effect size and sample size influence power, and if the sample size is big enough you can detect differences and associations between populations even if these associations and differences are very small indeed and, from a practical point of view, insignificant. So, a large sample size is a good thing in that it will give you more power to detect a difference between the means of two populations if such a difference actually exists (or an association between two populations if such an association actually exists), but dangerous in that it will enable you to achieve statistical significance even if the population effect size is very small. Therefore, with big sample sizes it is particularly important to check the effect size using the correlation coefficient (for associations), or *d* (for differences between means), before making too much of what you have found.

Finally, a most helpful fact about power analysis is that as power can be exactly determined from a knowledge of significance level, effect size and sample size, so it is possible to determine the sample size that is required in a study if we know about the other three variables: the significance level to be adopted, the population effect size, and the required power. For example, we can say that for a correlation, if you expect a medium population effect size of .3, you adopt the .05 significance level, and you are prepared to accept that you will have an 80 per cent chance of rejecting the null hypothesis if it is false (i.e. a power of 80 per cent), you will require a sample size of exactly 85 people. In the later chapters, the way in which power analysis can be used to determine necessary sample sizes for various types of statistical analysis has been used to provide indications of the sample sizes you will need in your research to get a reasonable chance of finding evidence for your research hypotheses.

Armed with this information, you can effectively answer one of the most common questions that researchers ask: 'How many people do I need to include in my study?'. There is one snag however. In order to work out the sample size you will require in your study you need to estimate the population effect size, and this raises the thorny issue of how you can possibly estimate the population effect size *before* you have done the study. After all, getting a good estimate of the population effect size is probably a considerable part of the reason for doing the study in the first place!

In fact, there are three ways that you can estimate the effect size before you run your research. The first is to carry out a small-scale pilot study, using the same measures, types of people, and testing conditions that you intend to use in the study proper, and use the results you obtain from this to estimate the effect size.

> *Example*: You are interested in whether there is an association between the salaries and job satisfaction. To estimate the effect size between these variables you carry out a small-scale pilot study, measuring the salaries and job satisfaction of 30 employees. You obtain a correlation coefficient of .24. You use the correlation of .24 as an estimate of the effect size of the population when calculating the sample size you will need in your subsequent full-scale study. Note that it is essential that the data obtained in the pilot study are not included in the analysis of the data from the full-scale study.

49

The second way of estimating effect sizes is to carry out a review of published studies which are similar to the one you are proposing to carry out (i.e. ones which used the same measurement scales you intend to use, were carried out in an environment similar to the one you plan to use in your own study, and involved similar people) and to use the effect size found in these as a guide to what you can expect in your own study.

> *Example*: You wish to investigate whether the conscientiousness of train drivers, as measured with a personality questionnaire, is associated with the extent to which they are punctual. You examine the literature and find two studies that seem relevant. One examined the relationship between the conscientiousness of lorry drivers and the number of times they arrived late for work over a six-month period. The other was concerned with the relationship between the conscientiousness of junior managers and, again, measured the number of times they arrived late for work over a six-month period. The correlation between conscientiousness and punctuality was .33 in the first study and .53 in the second study. You average these and predict an effect size of .43 in your own study.
>
> In fact, the increased use of meta-analyses (see Chapter 6) is making the task of establishing effect sizes in this way easier than it used to be. Meta-analyses are analyses of the average results obtained across a large number of studies when a particular issue is investigated. If you can find a meta-analysis that examines issues similar to the one you intend to study yourself, it can be a very useful source of effect size estimates.

The third method for estimating effect sizes is the simplest. The idea is simply to adopt a medium effect size, that is one which has been found to be the average across many studies carried out in the social sciences. As explained earlier, a medium effect size for differences between means is a *d* of .5 and the medium effect size for correlations is .3 (Cohen 1988; Bausell and Li 2002).

GENERALIZATION, CONFIDENCE AND CAUSALITY

If you carry out a piece of research and obtain evidence that the difference between variable means, or the association between variables, is statistically significant, what are the implications of this? In the final section of this chapter we will examine the important issue of how you should interpret statistically significant differences and associations and, in particular, the extent to which it is appropriate to generalize your findings, how confident you can be that your findings are true, when it is safe to assume that the associations and differences you have found have causal relationships.

Imagine that you carry out a piece of cross-sectional research on the relation between pay and well-being in a large organization. You obtain two main findings. First, there is a correlation between how much people earn and how happy they feel. Second, the mean level of happiness of people in the top two grades of the organization is higher than that of the people in the bottom two grades. Three important questions may now occur to you:

1   To what extent can you generalize your findings beyond the sample of people, the organization, and the setting you have used in your study?
2   To what extent should you have confidence in your findings?
3   Can you claim that you have found evidence of a causal relationship (e.g. that being in the top two grades causes people to be happier than being in the bottom two grades)?

The first issue concerns generalization: under what circumstances is it appropriate to generalize findings beyond the sample of people, organization and setting you have collected data on? This issue is closely connected with research design, an area that is not covered in this book, but on which there are many readable texts such as those by Collis and Hussey (2003) and Saunders *et al.* (2002). Assuming that you have a good working knowledge of research design, let's return to the fictitious study outlined above. If you were to obtain the results outlined above, would you be in a position to claim that for people in general, salaries and well-being are positively associated, and that people in the top grades of organizations will be happier than those in the lowest grades? Or, in contrast, is it only appropriate to claim that it is likely that the association and difference you have found cannot be generalized beyond the people, organization and setting in which you collected your data?

Unfortunately, this question cannot be answered by carrying out a statistical analysis of your existing data. While inferential statistical analysis can be carried out on your data to examine the extent to which the association and difference found can be generalized to the populations of numbers you have sampled from, it cannot tell you anything about populations of numbers you *haven't* sampled from. So, if you are to generalize your findings, the question is whether the population of numbers you have sampled from would also be found if you obtained data from people, organizations and settings other than those used in your study.

There is no simple, formulaic, answer to this question. Instead, you need to actively think about the research design, carefully considering the extent to which it may or may not be appropriate to generalize your findings to people, organizations and settings beyond those examined in your research study. For example, a very tentative answer to the question of the extent to which you can generalize your findings can be obtained by posing the question: 'Are there any reasons to suspect that the statistically significant association or difference, and effect sizes, I have found in my study would be different if I carried out the research again with other participants, organizations, or settings?'. If the answer to this question is yes (and in organizational research it very often is), very considerable caution should be shown in generalizing the findings. If the answer is no, you may tentatively conclude that it *may* be possible to generalize the findings to other people, organizations and settings. However, the only way to gain a substantial degree of confidence in the extent to which your findings can be generalized in this way is to carry out the research again, carefully and appropriately sampling from whatever people, organizations and settings you wish to generalize your results to.

The second issue concerns the level of confidence we can have in our research findings. This is something about which there is some controversy in statistics (e.g. Cohen 1994; Gigerenzer 1993), but I will draw attention here to two factors with which I believe most

51

statisticians would agree. The first is that the smaller the p value obtained from a statistical analysis, the more confident we can be that the null hypothesis is false (Fisher 1925), and therefore that the alternative hypothesis is true. The second is that if more than one research study is carried out to examine the same thing, the greater the proportion of these studies which obtain statistical significance, and the lower the p values obtained across these studies, the more confident we can be that the null hypothesis is false.

Incidentally, in relation to confidence, it is not at all unusual for the inexperienced researcher to claim that by finding a statistically significant association or difference between two variables they have 'proved' something. So a naïve researcher might believe that the statistically significant difference between the happiness of people in the top two grades and the bottom two grades proves that in the organization studied people in the most senior positions are happier than those in the bottom two grades. Such a claim is misleading and wrong. Remember that statistical significance merely indicates that, if the null hypothesis is true, the probability of finding an association (or difference) between variables as large as the one found in the data is less than 5 per cent. If statistical significance is attained, this does not mean that the existence of the association or difference between populations has been 'proved'. Proof is a word used in law courts rather than in science. Instead, we should more cautiously claim only that we have found evidence that the variables in question *may* be associated, or that we have found evidence that means of the variables *may* be different. To claim that something has been proved implies that there is certainty about it, and, as explained earlier, inferential statistics is concerned with establishing probabilities and like-lihoods rather than certainties.

The final issue is causality. In what circumstances can you claim that one variable causes changes in another? For example, in this case could you claim that you have shown that, at least in the organization you studied, changes in pay cause changes in happiness, or being in the top two grades in an organization causes people to be happier than if they are in the bottom two grades? This question often causes considerable confusion. One reason for this is that it is often incorrectly assumed that statistical tests of association (e.g. the statistical significance of a correlation coefficient) do not, and cannot, inform us about causality, whereas tests of difference (e.g. the t-test) can do so.

In fact, whether or not we can infer that one or more variables has a causal effect on another has nothing to do with whether we are examining associations or differences, nor does it depend on the particular statistical test used to analyse the data. In order to answer the question of whether a change in one variable has a causal effect on another variable we need to examine the research design from which the data have been produced. If it is the case that a carefully controlled experimental study has been carried out, and the only possible explanation for variation in variable x is variation in variable z, it is appropriate to infer that variable z is having a causal effect on variable x. However, if there are any explanations for the variation in variable x other than the variation in variable z, we cannot claim that such a causal relationship exists.

Let's take an example to illustrate this point. Imagine that you are a researcher who has developed a medicine to reduce blood pressure in people suffering from hypertension. In a double blind study (in which neither the patient nor the researcher is aware of the dosage), 100 people suffering from influenza are given a placebo pill not containing any of the medicine, a pill containing 1 mg of the medicine, a pill containing 5 mg, or a pill containing 10 mg. Which of these pills they receive is random, and they are all given the pills at the same time and in the same environment. One week later their blood pressure is measured, and a statistically significant correlation of −.6 is found between the amount of the drug they received and their blood pressure. In these circumstances, because an experimental design has been used, and steps have been taken to eliminate the influence of all critical extraneous variables, it would be acceptable to tentatively conclude that the medicine caused a reduction in blood pressure.

However, such carefully controlled experimental designs are very rare in research carried out in organizations. Much more common is the type of situation proposed in this section in which a researcher finds that there is an association between high pay and happiness, or a difference in the happiness of people in higher grades and lower ones. In these circumstances it is certainly not the case that the only explanation for the variation in pay levels is variation in happiness (or vice versa). In fact, it is possible that pay levels are having a causal effect on happiness, happiness is somehow having a causal effect on pay levels, or some other variable or variables is influencing both happiness and pay levels. Consequently, all we can say in this case is that there is a relationship between pay and happiness. The question of *why* this relationship exists cannot be answered with the data obtained here.

SUMMARY

In this chapter we have covered many of the key ideas and principles underpinning inferential statistics. An awareness of these ideas is helpful not only when carrying out your own statistical analysis, but also when interpreting research findings reported by others. For example, being aware that when an association or difference is statistically significant this does not *necessarily* indicate that it is of practical significance, and that effect sizes are of critical importance when considering research findings, will prove valuable whatever the particular inferential statistical technique you are using or reading about. However, what has not been covered here is how all this is done: how are confidence intervals worked out, and how can we use sampled data to infer that the probability that two populations' means are different is less than, or greater than, 5 per cent? This is covered in the next chapter.

- It is important to distinguish between a sample of people and a statistical sample of numbers, or scores, obtained from these people.
- We are usually interested in inferring information about a statistical population of numbers from the statistical sample of numbers. Commonly, you infer population parameters such as the population mean and population standard deviation from sample statistics such as the sample mean and sample standard deviation.
- In research, a statistical sample of numbers is collected on whatever variable the researchers are interested in (such as job commitment, age or job performance). So you often want to know about the population mean and standard deviation of a variable such as

job commitment, and you estimate this from the mean and standard deviation of a sample of job-commitment scores.

■ You can never be sure that you have accurate estimates of population parameters from sample statistics because inferential statistics is based on probabilities rather than certainties.

■ A confidence interval indicates that, with a specified level of confidence (e.g. 95 per cent), a population parameter falls somewhere between two specific values. For example, a 95 per cent confidence interval of 4.7–5.3 for the well-being of Spanish waiters means that we can be 95 per cent confident that the well-being of Spanish waiters falls between these two values.

■ For continuous data, the less variation in the variable, and the larger the sample, the smaller the confidence interval will be.

■ For categorical data, the larger the sample, the smaller the confidence interval will be.

■ Often in organizational research you are interested in the associations between categorical or continuous variables, or in the differences in the central tendencies of continuous variables.

■ Null hypotheses and alternative hypotheses are statements made about statistical populations you wish to know about rather than the statistical samples you do know about.

■ Statistical tests tell you the probability that you would obtain a difference (or association) between variables as large as the one you have found in your sample data, *if the null hypothesis is true*.

■ If the probability is less than 0.05 (5 per cent) that you would obtain a difference (or association) between variables as large as the one you have found in your sample data, *if the null hypothesis is true*, the convention is to reject the null hypothesis and accept the alternative hypothesis. In these circumstances the finding is said to be statistically significant.

■ There is an important distinction between statistical significance, on the one hand, and theoretical or practical importance, on the other.

■ When considering the theoretical and practical importance of quantitative research findings, you should consider not only whether an association or difference is statistically significant but, also, the relevant effect sizes.

■ Common measures of effect size are the correlation coefficient (for the degree of association between two continuous variables) and *d* (for the amount of difference between the means of two variables).

■ If there is a real association or difference between populations, you are more likely to obtain statistical significance with large samples than with small samples.

■ Whether an effect size is large enough to be important needs to be considered in the context of the theoretical implications and practical applications of the research.

■ Power analysis makes it possible to establish the likelihood that a null hypothesis will be rejected if it is false. This likelihood is derived from information about the estimated population effect size, the significance level adopted in the study, and the sample size used.

■ Power analysis can also be used to identify the sample size required in a research study. In this case, information is required about the significance level to be adopted and the level of power required. It is also necessary to estimate the population effect size by carrying out a pilot study, examining the research literature for relevant studies carried out in the past, or adopting the effect sizes found to be typical in the social sciences.

■ In considering the extent to which the results of a research study can be generalized beyond the participants, organizations and settings used in that study, an attempt should be made to actively think of reasons why generalization may or may not be possible. The only way to gain a substantial degree of confidence in such generalization is to carry out the research again with other people and organizations, and in other settings.

■ The lower the *p* value obtained in a test of significance, the more confident we can be that the null hypothesis is false. Also, the greater the proportion of research studies carried out to examine an association or difference which produce statistically significant findings (and the lower the *p* levels obtained across these studies), the more confident we can be that the null hypothesis is false. Claims that statistically significant findings 'prove' that particular associations and differences exist are incorrect and should be avoided.

■ If it is the case that a carefully controlled experimental study has been carried out, and the only possible explanation for variation in variable *x* is variation in variable *z*, it is appropriate to infer that variable *z* is having a causal affect on variable *x*. However, if there are any explanations for the variation in variable *x* other than the variation in variable *z*, we cannot claim that such a causal relationship exists.

QUESTIONS

1   In inferential statistics do we generalize from samples to (a) larger samples or (b) populations?

2   Which of the following is true?

   (a)   If we have good sample statistics we can determine the values of population parameters with exactness and certainty.

   (b)   When estimates of population parameters are based on sample statistics we cannot be sure they are correct.

3   Which of the following correctly describes a confidence interval?

   (a)   An estimate of the range of values within which a population parameter falls at a given level of probability.

   (b)   An estimate of how confident we can be in a sample statistic.

4   What two factors determine the size of the confidence interval for a mean?

5   Which of these do inferential statistical methods make it possible to test directly?

   (a)   The alternative hypothesis.

   (b)   The null hypothesis.

6 Is the null hypothesis a statement about (a) the nature of the population or (b) the nature of the sample?

7 Why is .05 commonly chosen as the cut-off value for statistical significance?

   (a) It provides a reasonable compromise between the probabilities of making type I and type II errors.
   (b) It provides a trade-off between the probabilities that the null hypothesis and the alternative hypothesis are correct.

8 Statistical significance tells us whether a difference between two means is important from a practical point of view. True or false?

9 Name a widely used measure of the effect size of an association, and a widely used measure of the effect size of the difference between two means.

10 How is *d* worked out?

11 What are the conventions in organizational research for (a) small, medium and large correlations, and (b) small, medium and large differences between means?

12 What is statistical power and what factors determine the amount of statistical power that is present?

Chapter 3

The mechanics of inferential statistics

In Chapter 2 some key principles underpinning inferential statistics were introduced. When these ideas were explained, it was at times necessary to simply accept that certain steps can be taken. *How* these steps can be taken was not discussed. For example, it was stated that it is possible to use sample data to calculate confidence intervals which specify, with a particular degree of certainty (e.g. 95 per cent), the range of values within which a population mean (for continuous data) and a population proportion (for categorical data) will fall. So, we might measure the well-being of 50 Californian hospital nurses and calculate that the 95 per cent confidence interval for the mean well-being of all Californian hospital nurses on a 5-point scale is between 3.2 and 3.8. We don't know for sure what the mean well-being of Californian nurses is, but based on our sample data we can be 95 per cent confident that this mean lies somewhere between 3.2 and 3.8 on our measurement scale. Chapter 2 also explained that statistical tests can be used to test research hypotheses such as 'there is an association between how much people earn and their well-being', and 'using an appraisal system increases job performance'. However, again no account was given as to *how* this can be done.

In this chapter we will put these omissions right by examining some of the mechanics by which inferential statistical methods work. The intention is not to provide an in-depth coverage of the specific logic and mathematical equations underpinning most statistical methods: for the reader who wishes to delve more deeply into the mathematical principles underlying inferential statistical analysis there are many good textbooks dealing with this. Here, the aim is more modest: to provide an insight into the basic mechanisms by which most widely used inferential statistical techniques work. This discussion of the mechanics of inferential statistics will begin by focusing on frequency distributions.

THE NORMAL DISTRIBUTION

At the heart of the process by which inferential statistics works is the frequency distribution, so we will begin by briefly revisiting the material on frequency distributions covered in Chapter 1. There it was shown that histograms or frequency polygons can be used to depict the shape of a frequency distribution. A histogram showing the performance of people on a training programme is shown in Figure 3.1.

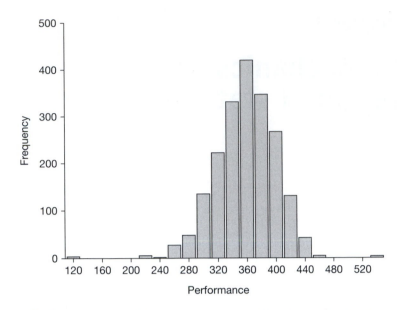

Figure 3.1 *The frequency distribution of a measure of training performance*

As you can see, the distribution shown in Figure 3.1 has a particular shape. It is roughly symmetrical, with most people getting a performance score of around 360. As we move from left to right, away from the score of 360, fewer and fewer people appear, with only a very small number getting scores of over 480. In the same way, as we move away from the central tendency of about 360 from right to left, fewer and fewer people appear, with hardly any getting scores lower than 200.

Why do you think that this sample of scores has this particular shape? Why is it not a completely different shape? To answer this question the trick is to remember the critical point that this is a *sample* of scores. In this case, it represents the scores we have obtained from about 2,000 trainees. It does not represent the scores obtained by an infinite number of trainees. So, now consider that it was somehow possible to collect an infinite number of training performance scores from people like those whose scores appear in the sample data. What distribution shape would you expect this infinite number of scores to have, based on what you can see about the distribution of the sample data in Figure 3.1?

I hope you will agree that the shape of the distribution of the infinite number of perform- ance scores would probably be similar to the shape shown in Figure 3.1. That is, the shape of the distribution of a large sample of training performance scores is likely to reflect the shape of the distribution it is drawn from, the statistical population. If the statistical popu- lation is negatively skewed, and you draw a large sample of scores from it, the shape of this sample distribution is likely to be negatively skewed too. In the same way, a large sample drawn from a positively skewed population of scores is likely to be positively skewed, and a large sample drawn from a symmetrical distribution is likely to be at least roughly symmetrical itself.

From the point of view of inferential statistics this would be a relatively trivial point if

58

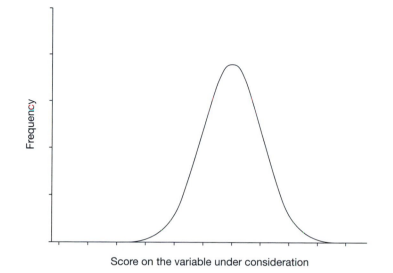

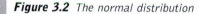

Figure 3.2 *The normal distribution*

it were not for one thing: there is a great deal of evidence that the shape of the distributions of the populations of many things in the world has a particular distribution shape which
statisticians call the **normal distribution**. It doesn't matter whether we are dealing with
things as diverse as the height of women in inches, the number of hours that electric lights
last before they fail, or the job performance of junior managers in a large organization, the
distribution of these variables probably closely approximates the shape shown in Figure 3.2.
By assuming that populations of scores on all sorts of continuous variables are normally
distributed (i.e. distributed according to the precise mathematical definition of the normal
distribution), statisticians have been able to develop a large number of powerful and
extremely useful statistical techniques.

THE RELATIONSHIP BETWEEN DISTRIBUTIONS AND PROPORTIONS

Having considered the normal distribution, we will now examine the relationship between
the shape of any distribution and the proportion of scores that fall within a particular area
within it. To explain this idea, it will help to take a concrete example. Imagine a large
school with a playground that is exactly rectangular in shape. The teachers at the school ask
all of the teenagers at the school to stand in the playground. The smallest teenagers are
positioned to the extreme left of the playground, and the taller the teenagers are the further
to the right they are asked to stand, with the very tallest teenagers at the extreme right of
the playground. The distribution of the teenagers within the playground is shown in Figure
3.3a. Imagine that a chalk line is drawn on the playground, three-quarters of the way from
the left to the right as in Figure 3.3b. If a teenager called John is standing directly over the
line, what proportion of the teenagers are short, or shorter, than he is?

59

(a)

(b)

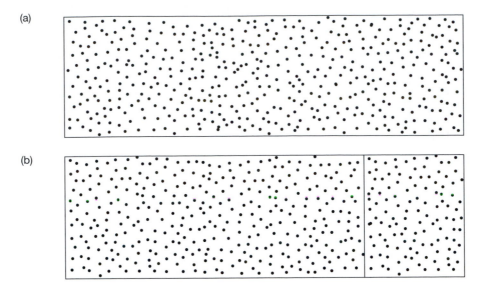

Figure 3.3 *(a) A playground in which teenagers are positioned so that the shortest are to the left and the tallest to the right; (b) As (a) but with a chalk line drawn three-quarters of the way from the left to the right*

The answer, as you may have worked out for yourself, is that 75 per cent of the teenagers to the left of the chalk line would be as short or shorter than John. If the teenagers gradually increase in height from left to right, and the line bisects a point 75 per cent of the way from left to right of the rectangle, then it follows that 75 per cent would be as short, or shorter than the teenagers to the right of the chalk line. In the same way, if the chalk line was drawn one-quarter of the way from the left of the playground, 25 per cent of the teenagers would be shorter than one standing on this new chalk line.

We can work this out because we know two things. The first is that the teenagers in the playground are distributed in such a way that their height systematically increases from left to right. The second is that we know that if we draw a line 75 per cent of the way to the right of a rectangle as in Figure 3.3b, exactly 75 per cent of the area of the rectangle will be to the left of the line, and exactly 25 per cent will be to the right. If we were not dealing with a regular shape like a rectangle, this would no longer follow. For example, imagine that the playground was laid out not in the regular shape of a rectangle, but in the shape of a bell as shown in Figure 3.4. Let's say a chalk line was drawn 75 per cent of the way from the left to the right of this bell-shaped playground. What proportion of the teenagers would be as short or shorter than Wendy, a girl standing on this new line? To try to answer this question, it may help you to draw the line on Figure 3.4.

The answer is that you can't tell what proportion of the teenagers standing in the bell-shaped playground would be as short or shorter than those standing to the right of the new line, and the reason you can't is that you don't know the precise percentage of the area of this playground that lies to the right of the chalk line. With the rectangular playground you know that 75 per cent of the playground was to the left of the line, and that therefore 75 per cent of the teenagers would be as short, or shorter, than those standing on the line.

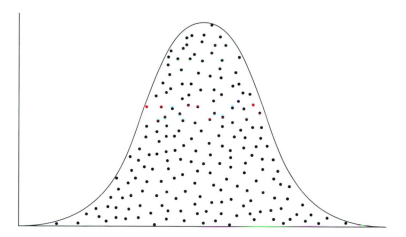

Figure 3.4 *A bell-shaped playground in which the height of teenagers increases from left to right*

But in the case of the bell-shaped playground you don't know the proportion of the playground that is to the left of the chalk line, and so you don't know the proportion of the teenagers who would be shorter than Wendy, the girl standing on it.

Ok, but let's say that a teacher asked a mathematician to calculate the proportion of the playground to the right of the chalk line drawn on the bell-shaped playground and that she worked out that 85.3 per cent of the playground area lies to the left of it. Are you now in a position to work out what proportion of teenagers would be shorter than those to the right of the chalk line? The answer this time is, yes. Because you know the teenagers are distributed according to their heights, with taller and taller teenagers standing further and further towards the right, and because you know that 85.3 per cent of the playground lies to the left of the line, you can rightly conclude that 85.3 per cent of the teenagers in the bell-shaped playground are as short or shorter than Wendy.

What has all this got to do with the normal distribution? Well, the answer is, quite a lot. We can talk of the bell-shaped playground as having a distribution and the teenagers standing in it are distributed according to two factors. The first factor is that the taller they are the further to the right they stand. The second factor is the shape of the playground. It is the combination of these two factors that distributes the teenagers in a particular position from left to right and, in turn, it is this distribution of the teenagers which allows us to work out what proportion of them are shorter than those standing to the right of the chalk line. If we take the normal distribution (which has a shape just like the bell-shaped playground) we can use the same principle to work out the proportion of that distribution that is to the right (or the left) of a line drawn through it in exactly the same way that we did with the line drawn through the bell-shaped playground. In fact, the chalk line drawn on the playground in Figure 3.4 is just like a line drawn on a normal distribution.

A knowledge of the area of the playground to the left of the chalk line in Figure 3.4 provided us with information about the proportion of teenagers as short, or shorter, than one standing on the line. In just the same way, a knowledge of the area of a normal distribution

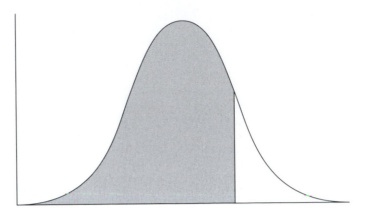

Figure 3.5 *The proportion of scores below a vertical line drawn on the normal distribution*

to the left of any vertical line drawn through it tells us the proportion of scores which are the same or smaller than those on which that line falls. This is shown in Figure 3.5.

THE MEAN, THE STANDARD DEVIATION AND *Z* SCORES

Having clarified the relation between proportions of scores and the normal distribution, we will leave the discussion of distributions for a moment, and recall some of the descriptive statistics covered in Chapter 1. In Chapter 1, two very important descriptive statistics were introduced: the mean and standard deviation. The mean is a measure of central tendency, and the standard deviation is a measure of dispersion. Let's imagine that you are able to measure the ages of all the employees in an electricity generating company, and you calculate that the mean age of employees is 40 years old, and the standard deviation of their ages is 5 years. If this were the case you could say that someone who is 45 years old has an age which is one **standard deviation above the mean**. This is because the mean of 40 plus the standard deviation of 5 equals 45 and, therefore, 45 is one standard deviation above the mean. In the same way, we can say that someone who is 50 years old has an age two standard deviations above the mean, someone who is 55 years old has an age three standard deviations above the mean, and someone who is 30 years old has an age two **standard deviations below the mean**. A simple way to work this out is to take a particular employee's age, subtract the mean age of everyone in the electricity generating company, and divide by the standard deviation of their ages. So, if John is 45, 45 minus 40 (the mean age) divided by 5 (the standard deviation) equals 1, and we can say that John has an age which is one standard deviation above the mean. Similarly, if Robert is 30 years old then:

$$(30 - 40)/5 = -2 \text{ standard deviations.}$$

Therefore, we can say that Robert's age is two standard deviations *below* the mean. Basically what we have done here is to calculate the number of standard deviation units that the ages of John and Robert are from the mean of all the people in the organization.

This idea can be applied to anything we measure. So, if the mean salary paid in an organization is $40,647, the standard deviation of all the salaries in the organization is $3,375, and Tom is paid $44,500, then Tom's salary is:

($44,500 − $40,647)/$3375 = 1.14 standard deviation units *above* the mean.

And if the average diameter of pebbles on a beach is 2.47 inches, the standard deviation of the diameter of all the pebbles on the beach is .23 inches, and you pick up a pebble which is 2.13 inches in diameter, then the pebble you have in your hand is:

(2.13 − 2.47)/.23 = 1.48 standard deviation units *below* the mean.

In statistics, the technical name for the figure we have been working out here is a **z score**. A z score tells us the number of standard deviation units a particular score is from the mean of all the scores we know about on a dimension. The formula for a z score is exactly the one that we have been using. That is,

z score = $(x - \bar{x})/\text{SD}$

where x is the score obtained by a particular case, $\bar{x}$ is the mean of all the cases, and SD is the standard deviation of all the cases. When a z score is positive it tells us the number of standard deviation units that a score falls above the mean, and when it is negative it tells us the number of standard deviation units that a score falls below the mean.

Z SCORES AND THE NORMAL DISTRIBUTION

Armed with our knowledge of what z scores are, we are now in a position to draw together all of the things discussed so far in this chapter. We have agreed that if we draw a line through a normal distribution we can work out the proportion of people (or objects) with scores *the same or less than* those on that line. We also agreed that we can also work out the proportion with scores *greater than* those on the line. Now, in the normal distribution, z scores dictate the position of these vertical lines. A z score of 0 is always in the centre of the distribution, a z score one standard deviation above the mean is always in the position shown in Figure 3.6, and one drawn two standard deviations below the mean is always in the position shown in Figure 3.7.

Because we can work out the percentage of a distribution that lies above (or below) a vertical line drawn through the distribution, it follows that we can position a line any number of z scores (i.e. standard deviation units) we like from the mean, and work out the percentage of the distribution with scores equal to, or less than, that point. So we can work out the percentage of cases with z scores equal to or less than 1.00, the percentage with z scores equal to, or less than, −1.36, and the percentage equal to or less than any other number of z score units. Using some complex algebra, this is exactly what statisticians have done, and the results of their labour can be seen in Tables 3.1 and 3.2. Table 3.1

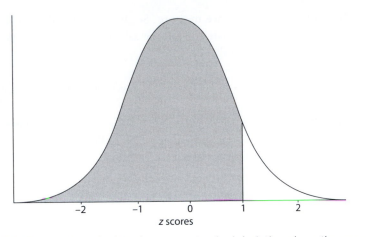

Figure 3.6 *The position of a line drawn one standard deviation above the mean on a normal distribution*

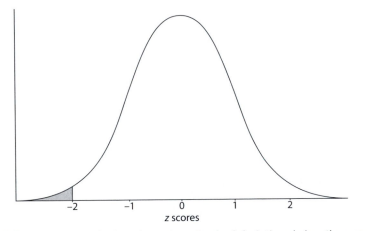

Figure 3.7 *The position of a line drawn two standard deviations below the mean on a normal distribution*

shows the percentages for positive *z* scores (where we are dealing with the number of standard deviation units above the mean), and Table 3.2 shows the percentages for negative *z* scores (where we are dealing with the number of standard deviation units below the mean).

To use the tables:

1   Decide on which table to use. If the *z* score is positive use Table 3.1, and if it is negative use Table 3.2.
2   Look up the *z* score to one decimal place (e.g. 0.1 or 1.6) in the first column of the table.
3   Look up the second decimal place of the *z* score in the first row of the table (e.g. for 0.14, the 4 is looked up in the first row).

Where the column and the row meet, the percentage of the distribution that is the same or less than a particular score is given. Let's illustrate this with an example.

Table 3.1 *Percentages for positive z scores*

Z	Second digit of z									
	0.00	0.01	0.02	0.03	0.04	0.05	0.06	0.07	0.08	0.09
0.0	50.0	50.4	50.8	51.2	51.6	52.0	52.4	52.8	53.2	53.6
0.1	54.0	54.4	54.8	55.2	55.6	56.0	56.4	56.8	57.1	57.5
0.2	57.9	58.3	58.7	59.1	59.5	59.9	60.3	60.6	61.0	61.4
0.3	61.8	62.2	62.6	62.9	63.3	63.7	64.1	64.4	64.8	65.2
0.4	65.5	65.9	66.3	66.6	67.0	67.4	67.7	68.1	68.4	68.8
0.5	69.2	69.5	69.9	70.2	70.5	70.9	71.2	71.6	71.9	72.2
0.6	72.6	72.9	73.2	73.6	73.9	74.2	74.5	74.9	75.2	75.5
0.7	75.8	76.1	76.4	76.7	77.0	77.3	77.6	77.9	78.2	78.5
0.8	78.8	79.1	79.4	79.7	80.0	80.2	80.5	80.8	81.1	81.3
0.9	81.6	81.9	82.1	82.4	82.6	82.9	83.2	83.4	83.7	83.9
1.0	84.1	84.4	84.6	84.9	85.1	85.3	85.5	85.8	86.0	86.2
1.1	86.4	86.7	86.9	87.1	87.3	87.5	87.7	87.9	88.1	88.3
1.2	88.5	88.7	88.9	89.1	89.3	89.4	89.6	89.8	90.0	90.2
1.3	90.3	90.5	90.7	90.8	91.0	91.2	91.3	91.5	91.6	91.8
1.4	91.9	92.1	92.2	92.4	92.5	92.7	92.8	92.9	93.1	93.2
1.5	93.3	93.5	93.6	93.7	93.8	93.9	94.1	94.2	94.3	94.4
1.6	94.5	94.6	94.7	94.8	95.0	95.1	95.2	95.3	95.4	95.5
1.7	95.5	95.6	95.7	95.8	95.9	96.0	96.1	96.2	96.3	96.3
1.8	96.4	96.5	96.6	96.6	96.7	96.8	96.9	96.9	97.0	97.1
1.9	97.1	97.2	97.3	97.3	97.4	97.4	97.5	97.6	97.6	97.7
2.0	97.7	97.8	97.8	97.9	97.9	98.0	98.0	98.1	98.1	98.2
2.1	98.2	98.3	98.3	98.3	98.4	98.4	98.5	98.5	98.5	98.6
2.2	98.6	98.6	98.7	98.7	98.8	98.8	98.8	98.8	98.9	98.9
2.3	98.9	99.0	99.0	99.0	99.0	99.1	99.1	99.1	99.1	99.2
2.4	99.2	99.2	99.2	99.3	99.3	99.3	99.3	99.3	99.3	99.4
2.5	99.4	99.4	99.4	99.4	99.5	99.5	99.5	99.5	99.5	99.5
2.6	99.5	99.6	99.6	99.6	99.6	99.6	99.6	99.6	99.6	99.6
2.7	99.7	99.7	99.7	99.7	99.7	99.7	99.7	99.7	99.7	99.7
2.8	99.7	99.8	99.8	99.8	99.8	99.8	99.8	99.8	99.8	99.8
2.9	99.8	99.8	99.8	99.8	99.8	99.8	99.9	99.9	99.9	99.9
3.0	99.9	99.9	99.9	99.9	99.9	99.9	99.9	99.9	99.9	99.9
3.1	99.9	99.9	99.9	99.9	99.9	99.9	99.9	99.9	99.9	99.9
3.2	99.9	99.9	99.9	99.9	99.9	99.9	99.9	99.9	99.9	99.9
3.3	99.9	99.9	99.9	99.9	99.9	99.9	99.9	99.9	99.9	99.9
3.4	99.9	99.9	99.9	99.9	99.9	99.9	99.9	99.9	99.9	99.9
3.5	99.9	99.9	99.9	99.9	99.9	99.9	99.9	99.9	99.9	99.9

Table 3.2 *Percentages for negative z scores*

Z	Second digit of z									
	0.00	0.01	0.02	0.03	0.04	0.05	0.06	0.07	0.08	0.09
−3.5	0.1	0.1	0.1	0.1	0.1	0.1	0.1	0.1	0.1	0.1
−3.4	0.1	0.1	0.1	0.1	0.1	0.1	0.1	0.1	0.1	0.1
−3.3	0.1	0.1	0.1	0.1	0.1	0.1	0.1	0.1	0.1	0.1
−3.2	0.1	0.1	0.1	0.1	0.1	0.1	0.1	0.1	0.1	0.1
−3.1	0.1	0.1	0.1	0.1	0.1	0.1	0.1	0.1	0.1	0.1
−3.0	0.1	0.1	0.1	0.1	0.1	0.1	0.1	0.1	0.1	0.1
−2.9	0.2	0.2	0.2	0.2	0.2	0.2	0.2	0.2	0.1	0.1
−2.8	0.3	0.3	0.2	0.2	0.2	0.2	0.2	0.2	0.2	0.2
−2.7	0.4	0.3	0.3	0.3	0.3	0.3	0.3	0.3	0.3	0.3
−2.6	0.5	0.5	0.4	0.4	0.4	0.4	0.4	0.4	0.4	0.4
−2.5	0.6	0.6	0.6	0.6	0.6	0.5	0.5	0.5	0.5	0.5
−2.4	0.8	0.8	0.8	0.8	0.7	0.7	0.7	0.7	0.7	0.6
−2.3	1.1	1.0	1.0	1.0	1.0	0.9	0.9	0.9	0.9	0.8
−2.2	1.4	1.4	1.3	1.3	1.3	1.2	1.2	1.2	1.1	1.1
−2.1	1.8	1.7	1.7	1.7	1.6	1.6	1.5	1.5	1.5	1.4
−2.0	2.3	2.2	2.2	2.1	2.1	2.0	2.0	1.9	1.9	1.8
−1.9	2.9	2.8	2.7	2.7	2.6	2.6	2.5	2.4	2.4	2.3
−1.8	3.6	3.5	3.4	3.4	3.3	3.2	3.1	3.1	3.0	2.9
−1.7	4.5	4.4	4.3	4.2	4.1	4.0	3.9	3.8	3.8	3.7
−1.6	5.5	5.4	5.3	5.2	5.1	5.0	4.9	4.8	4.7	4.6
−1.5	6.7	6.6	6.4	6.3	6.2	6.1	5.9	5.8	5.7	5.6
−1.4	8.1	7.9	7.8	7.6	7.5	7.4	7.2	7.1	6.9	6.8
−1.3	9.7	9.5	9.3	9.2	9.0	8.9	8.7	8.5	8.4	8.2
−1.2	11.5	11.3	11.1	10.9	10.8	10.6	10.4	10.2	10.0	9.9
−1.1	13.6	13.4	13.1	12.9	12.7	12.5	12.3	12.1	11.9	11.7
−1.0	15.9	15.6	15.4	15.2	14.9	14.7	14.5	14.2	14.0	13.8
−0.9	18.4	18.1	17.9	17.6	17.4	17.1	16.9	16.6	16.4	16.1
−0.8	21.2	20.9	20.6	20.3	20.1	19.8	19.5	19.2	18.9	18.7
−0.7	24.2	23.9	23.6	23.3	23.0	22.7	22.4	22.1	21.8	21.5
−0.6	27.4	27.1	26.8	26.4	26.1	25.8	25.5	25.1	24.8	24.5
−0.5	30.9	30.5	30.2	29.8	29.5	29.1	28.8	28.4	28.1	27.8
−0.4	34.5	34.1	33.7	33.4	33.0	32.6	32.3	31.9	31.6	31.2
−0.3	38.2	37.8	37.5	37.1	36.7	36.3	35.9	35.6	35.2	34.8
−0.2	42.1	41.7	41.3	40.9	40.5	40.1	39.7	39.4	39.0	38.6
−0.1	46.0	45.6	45.2	44.8	44.4	44.0	43.6	43.3	42.9	42.5
−0.0	50.0	49.6	49.2	48.8	48.4	48.0	47.6	47.2	46.8	46.4

Sally works in a large manufacturing organization, earning $43,450 a year. The mean salary in the organization is $39,386, and the standard deviation of the salaries in the organization is $5,563. Therefore, the z score for Sally's salary is:

(43450 − 39386)/5563 = 0.73 standard deviation units above the mean.

If we are willing to assume that the salaries in the organization that Sally works for are normally distributed, we are now in a position to see what percentage of these salaries are less than Sally's. To do this we look up the z score of 0.73 in Table 3.1 and find that the percentage figure given is 76.7. So we can infer that 76.7 per cent of the employees in Sally's company earn the same or less than she does. And, of course, this implies that the remaining 23.3 per cent must earn more than Sally. Critically, it has only been possible to work out that 76.7 per cent of the employees earn the same as or less than Sally, and 23.3 per cent earn more, because we have assumed that the distribution of salaries in the organization as a whole is normally distributed. If the distribution of salaries is some other shape, the figures given in Table 3.1 would be incorrect, and the percentages we took from the table would, therefore, be incorrect also. However, if the distribution of salaries, while not being perfectly normally distributed is nevertheless reasonably close to a normal distribution, the figures in Table 3.1 won't be too far out.

Although the example above has involved salaries, the same logic can be used for anything else you care to measure: job satisfaction, extroversion, intelligence, age, anything. As long as you are willing to assume that the population of any of these variables has a normal distribution, and as long as you have a good estimate of the mean and the standard deviation of that population, you can take any one person's score, convert it to a z score, and then use Table 3.1 or 3.2 to find the percentage of people in the population who have a score which is: (a) the same or less; or (b) greater.

This is possible because when we are dealing with a normal distribution there is a strict relationship between four factors: a given raw score, the z score, the mean of the

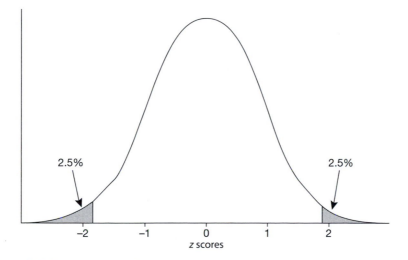

Figure 3.8 *The proportion of z scores below −1.96 and above 1.96*

distribution, and the standard deviation of the distribution. It is because of this strict relationship that we are able to find the z score when we know the raw score, the mean and the standard deviation. But the implication is that we can find out about *any* one of these four pieces of information if we know the other three. This is of great importance in inferential statistics because it allows us to establish certain critical raw scores as long as we know the mean, the standard deviation and the z score. To get an insight into why this is the case, look up the percentages for the following z scores: -1.96 and 1.96. You will see that the percentage of the distribution with scores the same as or less than these are 2.50 per cent and 97.5 per cent respectively. So 2.5 per cent of the scores are the same as or less than 1.96, and 2.5 per cent are greater than 1.96 (see Figure 3.8). This means that the remaining z scores, those between -1.96 and 1.96, make up 95 per cent of the distribution. Another way to put this is that if the population of scores on a continuous variable such as job satisfaction has a normal distribution, when the scores are converted to z scores, 95 per cent of them will be between -1.96 and 1.96. Armed with this knowledge it is easy to work out, on any normally distributed variable, the two values between which 95 per cent of the scores will fall. To find the lower value, that is the value below which 2.5 per cent of the scores fall, we take the mean score and subtract 1.96 units of standard deviation. So, if the mean age of people in an organization is 44.2 years, and the standard deviation is 7.8 years, the lower value is:

$$44.2 - (1.96 \times 7.8) = 28.91$$

And to find the higher value, the value above which 2.5 per cent of the scores fall, we take the mean score and add 1.96 units of standard deviation. So:

$$44.2 + (1.96 \times 7.8) = 59.49$$

As long as we are willing to assume that the ages of the people in the organization have a normal distribution, and as long as we are confident that the mean age is 44.2 and the standard deviation of the ages is 7.8, we can conclude that 95 per cent of employees will be between 28.91 and 59.49 years old. What's more, we can say that 2.5 per cent will be equal to or less than 28.91 years old, and 2.5 per cent will be over 59.49 years old.

THE SAMPLING DISTRIBUTION OF MEANS, THE STANDARD ERROR, THE CENTRAL LIMIT THEOREM AND CONFIDENCE INTERVALS

We are now in a position to examine how confidence intervals can be worked out. In doing so, we will focus on the confidence interval of the mean as this is the one which is most commonly used. The confidence interval for the mean of a sample tells you, with a particular level of confidence (e.g. 95 per cent confidence), the range of scores that the population mean will lie between. For example, you might measure the job satisfaction of 50 people in a very large organization and find that the mean job satisfaction level is 3.27 on a 7-point scale, and that the standard deviation of the 50 sampled job-satisfaction scores is 1.24. You know that your estimate of the mean job satisfaction of all the people in the organization, based on the sample of 50 scores, is 3.27. However, you are also aware that if you had put different people in your sample, their mean score may not have been exactly 3.27. What you want to know is the range of possible mean scores that the job satisfaction of all the people in the organization might lie within. You are willing to adopt the 95 per cent confidence level. In other words you want to be able to say, 'I have estimated the mean job satisfaction level in the organization to be 3.27. This may be somewhat inaccurate because it is based on a sample of only 50 scores, but I am 95 per cent confident that the job satisfaction of all employees is no less than *a* and no greater than *b*'.

The question is, how do we work out what *a* and *b* are? Well if you have followed the logic so far in this chapter, it is not too difficult. The first point to be aware of is that it is possible to take not just one sample of scores from a population, but many of them. For example, rather than taking just one sample of 50 job-satisfaction scores from a large organization, we could, in principle, take a million such samples of 50 job-satisfaction scores. If we did so we could also work out the mean of each of the samples, ending up with a million sample means. The million means would not all be the same of course, some would be greater than others because sometimes, by chance, we might sample 50 relatively high job-satisfaction scores and at other times 50 relatively low job-satisfaction scores. This being the case we can easily plot the frequency distribution of these means in just the same way that we plotted the frequency distribution of scores obtained from individuals in Chapter 1. The resulting distribution is known as **the sampling distribution of means**.

Let's imagine for a moment that you have somehow obtained the sampling distribution of the means for 50 job-satisfaction scores. This distribution is shown in Figure 3.9. Let's also imagine that the mean of this distribution is 5.0, and that 95 per cent of the means fall between 4.5 and 5.5. In these circumstances, you could say that if someone took just one sample of 50 job-satisfaction scores and worked out the mean score, this *might* be less than 4.5, and it *might* be more than 5.5, but this would only happen 5 per cent of the

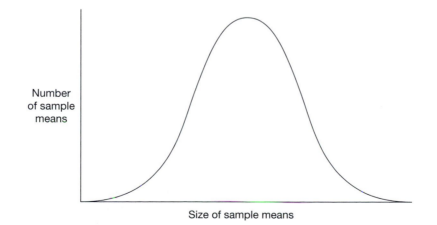

Number of sample means

Size of sample means

Figure 3.9 *The distribution of the sample means of 50 job-satisfaction scores*

69

time. The remaining 95 per cent of the time, a single sample of 50 job-satisfaction scores would have a mean somewhere between 4.5 and 5.5. To put this slightly differently, we could be 95 per cent confident that any one sample would have a mean somewhere between 4.5 and 5.5.

Now, recall that if we are dealing with a normal distribution, 95 per cent of it falls between z scores (i.e. standard deviation units) of -1.96 and $+1.96$. Another way of saying this is that 95 per cent of a normally distributed set of scores will have z scores between -1.96 and $+1.96$. So, if we assume for a moment that a set of the sample means is normally distributed, that the mean of these sample means is 5.0, and that they have a standard deviation of 0.255, it follows that 2.5 per cent of the sample means will be above the sample mean plus 1.96 standard deviation units, and 2.5 per cent will be below the sample mean minus 1.96 standard deviation units. So:

$$5 + (1.96 \times 0.255) = 5.5$$

and

$$5 - (1.96 \times 0.255) = 4.5.$$

What this shows is that as long as the distribution of sample means is normal *with just two pieces of information* we can work out the range within which the mean of a single sample will fall 95 per cent of the time. These two pieces of information are: (a) the mean of the sample means; and (b) the standard deviation of the sample means, otherwise called the **standard error**. In the case of this example this range is 4.5 to 5.5.

This is all very well, but generally speaking we are not in a position to take large numbers of samples from a population so as to find out the mean and standard deviation of these sample means. On the contrary, we usually only take one sample. So, how can we use the information contained in just one sample to estimate not just the mean of the population, but also the 95 per cent confidence interval for that mean? The answer is that we make use of one of the most important theorems in the discipline of inferential statistics, the **central limit theorem**. The central limit theorem states that:

> given a population with a mean of x and a variance of y, the distribution of sample means will have:

- a mean equal to the population mean;
- a standard deviation equal to the standard deviation of the population divided by the square root of the number of people sampled;
- a distribution shape close to the normal distribution (as long as 30 or more cases are sampled).

The central limit theorem also states that:

> the shape of the distribution of sample means will approach the normal distribution as the size of the sample increases, *and this will occur even if the population is not normally distributed*.

The implication of the central limit theorem, here, is that if we obtain the job-satisfaction scores of 40 employees, and find that this sample of scores has a mean of 5.34 and a standard deviation of 1.13, we can estimate the distribution of sample means to have:

- a standard deviation of $SD/\sqrt{n} = 1.13/\sqrt{40} = 0.18$
- a distribution which approaches the normal distribution.

Therefore, the central limit theorem has enabled us to estimate the standard error (i.e. the standard deviation of the distribution of sample means), with the information we get *with just one sample*. If we combine this with the assumption that the mean of the sample will approximate the mean of the sample means, we now have an estimate of both the mean of the sample means and their standard error. Furthermore, because the central limit theorem tells us that the distribution of sample means is normal, we can work out the sample mean we would expect to find 95 per cent of the time using the simple method outlined earlier.

Upper 95 per cent confidence limit = 5.34 + (1.96 × 0.18) = 5.99

and

Lower 95 per cent confidence limit = 5.34 − (1.96 × 0.18) = 4.69

Therefore, we can conclude that, based on our sample of 50 job-satisfaction scores, our best estimate of the mean of the population of job-satisfaction scores from which we have sampled is 5.34 and that, with 95 per cent confidence, the population mean is somewhere between 4.69 and 5.99. That is, we have worked out the 95 per cent confidence interval of the mean.

SIGNIFICANCE TESTS

The mechanics underlying significance tests is very similar to that underlying the computation of confidence intervals. Recall that significance tests are used to estimate the probability that a difference, or association, as large as that we have found in our sample data would have occurred if the null hypothesis is true. The null hypothesis is that there is no difference (or association) between two or more samples. For example, the null hypothesis might be that there is no difference in the job satisfaction of men and the job satisfaction of women. We examine this by measuring the job satisfaction of, say, 50 men and 50 women, and we might find that the mean scores are 5.45 and 6.21 respectively. What we want to know is how likely we would be to obtain a difference between the sample means as large as this if the null hypothesis that there is no difference in the job satisfaction of men and women is true.

The way this is done, and this applies to all significance tests and not just those that might be used in this particular circumstance, is to compute what is called a test statistic. A test statistic is a value that reflects the size of the difference, or the strength of the association, that we have found in our sample data. In the case of this particular example, the test statistic that would probably be computed is called t, and the formula that would be used to do this would be:

$$t = \frac{\bar{X}_1 - \bar{X}_2}{\sqrt{\left(\frac{\left(\sum X_1^2 - \frac{(\sum X_1)^2}{N_1}\right) + \left(\sum X_2^2 - \frac{(\sum X_2)^2}{N_2}\right)}{N_1 + N_2 - 2}\right)\left(\frac{1}{N_1} + \frac{1}{N_2}\right)}}.$$

This rather intimidating formula basically states the following:

> t is equal to the difference between the two sample means divided by an estimate of the standard error of the difference between the sample means we would expect to find if we took many pairs of samples when the null hypothesis is true.

If the null hypothesis is true, and we take many pairs of sample means and work out the value of t, it will sometimes be relatively large (when by chance we take two samples which turn out to have quite different means) and sometimes very small or even zero. If we plot the distribution of these values, we can work out the probability of getting a t value as high as, say 0.17 or 1.49, or anything else. In fact, as with all test statistics, the exact shape of this distribution depends on the number of uncertain parameters on which the particular test statistic is based, a value known as the **degrees of freedom**. We will not consider the concept of degrees of freedom in detail here because it is one of the most elusive ideas associated with inferential statistics. Suffice it to say that the degrees of freedom for a particular test statistic can always be worked out quite simply from a formula provided by statisticians. In the case of the t statistic computed here, the degrees of freedom are obtained by adding together the number of scores in the two samples and subtracting two (i.e. $50 + 50 - 2 = 98$). In other circumstances the number of degrees of freedom are calculated differently.

Because statisticians have worked out the sampling distribution of all test statistics when the null hypothesis is true (and have done so for all degrees of freedom), it is possible to find the proportion of times that we would obtain a test statistic value as high as, say 3.4 or 5.9, or anything else, when the null hypothesis is true. In the case of the t statistic used here, with 98 degrees of freedom, the sampling distribution indicates that only 5 per cent of the time would we get a t value as high as 1.984. If we work out the value of the t statistic for our two samples of 50 job-satisfaction scores, and it turns out to be 1.984, we can conclude that the null hypothesis that there is no difference in the job satisfaction of men and women *may* be true, but if it is true we would only obtain a difference between the scores as large as the one we found in our research 5 per cent of the time. If the *t* value is greater than 1.984, we can conclude that if the null hypothesis is true we would find a difference between the scores as large as the one we found in our research even less than 5 per cent of the time. In these circumstances, as explained in Chapter 2, the convention is to reject this null hypothesis, and accept the alternative hypothesis instead.

In this example, the test statistic called *t* has been used but, as will be clear in Chapters 5 and 6, other test statistics are also employed, common ones being χ^2 (often written as chi square and pronounced kye square), and *F*. Each of these test statistics has a different distribution shape when the null hypothesis is true, and in each case this shape also depends on the degrees of freedom. However, the logic underlying the use of any of these test statistics is always the same:

1   Work out the value of the test statistic for the sample data collected in the research.
2   Consult the known distribution for that test statistic for particular degrees of freedom when the null hypothesis is true.
3   If the probability of obtaining a test statistic as large as that computed from the sample data is less than a pre-agreed cut-off value, which in practice is almost always .05 or 5 per cent, accept the null hypothesis.
4   If the probability of obtaining a test statistic as large as that computed from the sample data is greater than the pre-agreed cut-off value, reject the null hypothesis and accept the alternative hypothesis.

Finally, some of these test statistics are sensitive to the direction of the difference or association between scores whereas others are not. For example, if the means of two samples, A and B, are compared, it may be that the mean of sample A is greater than the mean of sample B, or vice versa. The *t* statistic is sensitive to this, and it will work out to be a positive number (e.g. *t* = 1.27) if the mean of the first sample is greater than the second, and a minus number (e.g. *t* = −1.27) if the mean of the second sample is greater than the first. Other test statistics, such as *F*, which is often used to examine whether there is a difference between the means of three or more samples, are not directional. The greater the difference between the means of three samples of scores the greater the *F* statistic will be (assuming that the standard deviations don't change) irrespective of which means are higher or lower.

Generally speaking, whether or not a test statistic is sensitive to the direction of a difference or association is unimportant in practice. The one exception to this rule is in relation to what are called one- and two-tailed tests of statistical significance. One-tailed tests, which can only be used with test statistics which are sensitive to the direction of an association or difference, are more powerful than two-tailed tests. That is, you are more likely to be able to reject the null hypothesis if it is true with a one-tailed test than with a two-tailed test. One-tailed tests may be used when: (a) you are able to predict the direction of an association or difference before you collect your data; and (b) if, should you obtain a test statistic large enough to reach statistical significance, you are willing to treat it as non-significant if it is in the opposite direction to the one you predicted. As most researchers are interested in the significance of associations and differences even if they are in the opposite direction to the one predicted, one-tailed tests are generally inappropriate, and they will not be used in this book.

In this chapter it has only been possible to provide a brief introduction to the mechanics of inferential statistics. If you are interested in learning more, and have a good basic grounding in algebra, you may find it useful to read the text by Howell (2002). Although Howell's book is aimed at psychologists, it includes most of the statistical methods used by people carrying out organizational research.

SUMMARY

- We can use the shape of the distribution of a sample to infer the likely shape of the distribution of the population from which it is drawn.
- The larger the sample, the more likely the distribution shape of the sample will reflect the distribution shape of the population from which it is drawn.
- We can work out the percentage of scores that falls: (a) at or below; and (b) above, a vertical line drawn through a normal distribution.
- Units of standard deviation above or below the mean are called z scores, and because a particular z score is always in the same position on the normal distribution, it is possible to work out the percentage of cases that are: (a) the same as or less; or (b) above, a particular z score.
- In a normal distribution 95 per cent of all z scores fall between -1.96 and 1.96, 2.5 per cent fall below -1.96, and 2.5 per cent fall above 1.96.
- In principle, it is possible to take a very large number of samples of a given size from a population, and plot the frequency distribution of the means of these samples.
- The central limit theorem states that the mean of samples drawn from a population will have a mean equal to the population mean, and a standard deviation equal to the standard deviation of a given sample divided by the square root of the number of people sampled. It also states that the sample means will be normally distributed (even if the distribution of the population is not).
- The implication of the central limit theorem is that we can establish the standard deviation of the sample means (the standard error) with the information contained in just one sample.
- If we assume that the mean of a sample approximates the mean of the population, and that the distribution of sample means is normal, and that we have a good estimate of the standard error, we can work out the 95 per cent confidence interval for the mean of the sample.
- Statistical tests are concerned with whether or not a null hypothesis is true.
- Statistical tests utilize test statistics. For example, the t statistic can be computed from the information in two samples when we wish to know whether these samples are drawn from

two populations with different means. Test statistics have known distributions when the null hypothesis is true.

■ If the test statistic computed from one or more samples falls within a range expected 95 per cent of the time when the null hypothesis is true, we normally conclude that the association or difference with which that statistic is concerned is not statistically significant.

■ If the test statistic computed from one or more samples falls outside the range expected 95 per cent of the time when the null hypothesis is true, we normally conclude that the association or difference with which that statistic is concerned is statistically significant. This means that the null hypothesis might be true, but if it is we would obtain a difference or association as large as the one we have found less than 5 per cent of the time.

QUESTIONS

1   The shape of the distribution of a large sample is likely to be approximately the same as the shape of the distribution of the population from which it has been drawn. True or false?

2   A sample of appraisal scores has a mean of 6.35 and a standard deviation of 1.27. What score is: (a) one standard deviation above the mean; (b) two standard deviations below the mean?

3   Assuming that the distribution of male employees' appraisal scores in an organization is normally distributed, and that the mean appraisal score of men is 5.92 with a standard deviation of 1.35, what proportion of male employees would you expect to: (a) have an appraisal score of over 6.00; (b) have an appraisal score of 5.00 or less?

4   If the ages of people in an organization are normally distributed, what proportion would obtain z scores of: (a) over 1.96; (b) -1.96 or less?

5   What is the sampling distribution of means?

6   According to the central limit theorem, which of the following is true:

Given a population with a mean of x and a variance of y, the distribution of sample means will have:

(a) a standard deviation equal to the standard deviation of the population divided by the square root of the number of people sampled;

(b) a mean equal to the mean of the population divided by the number of people sampled.

7   We can expect the mean of a population to fall within $+$ and -1.96 standard errors of the sample mean as long as the sample is of reasonable size (i.e. about 30 cases). True or false?

75

8   If we obtain a test statistic of 1.83 from our data (with 30 degrees of freedom), and find that the probability of obtaining this if the null hypothesis is true is .04, and we have adopted the .05 significance level, should we:

(a) accept the null hypothesis and reject the alternative hypothesis;
(b) reject the null hypothesis and accept the alternative hypothesis?

Chapter 4

An introduction
to *SPSS*

The purpose of this chapter is to familiarize you with the basics of using *SPSS*, including how to enter data, how to specify the type of data analysis you require, and how to read the output. These things cannot be taught very successfully in the abstract. Therefore, the idea is that you read this material while actually running *SPSS* on a computer.

GETTING STARTED

Start *SPSS* by double-clicking on the *SPSS* icon on your desktop. When *SPSS* has started running see the Data Editor page, which looks like a spreadsheet. This is shown in Figure 4.1. Assuming that you are collecting data on people, each row of white squares on this 'spreadsheet' is for the data you have obtained on a particular person. If you were collecting data on, say, organizations, each row of white squares would contain information on a particular organization instead. For the sake of consistency, and because it is generally the case in organizational research, we will assume that the data are collected on people. So, if the first person you have collected data on is someone called Jim, you will place the information you have on Jim in the first row of white boxes or 'cells'. Running along the top of the white cells are grey boxes marked *var*, which stands for variable. If you have information about Jim on two variables (e.g. his age and his salary) you enter each of these in a specific column: the first column for his age, and the second for his salary.

All this is best explained with a simple example. Let's say that you give a questionnaire to 10 people in an insurance company. The questionnaire simply asks them to specify their gender and to indicate on a 5-point scale what their current level of well-being is. Of course, in reality you would be unlikely to collect information about such a small number of people, ask them about such a small number of things, or measure their well-being with a single question! But for the purposes of demonstrating how *SPSS* works, this simple set of data, shown in Table 4.1, will be fine.

When the questionnaires are returned to you, you number each one: 1 for the first, 2 for the second etc. This is good practice, because it will later allow you to identify which questionnaire is which. The first questionnaire returned is from a male with a well-being score of 3, the second from a female with a well-being score of 5 and so on as is shown in the table.

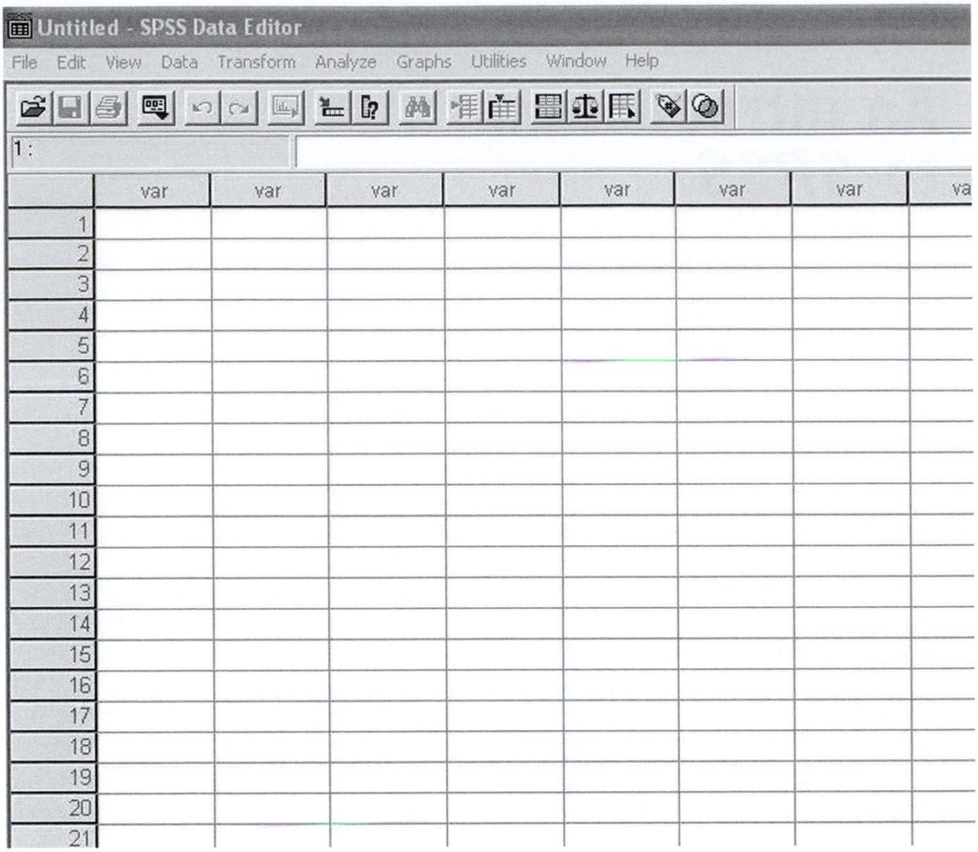

Figure 4.1 *The SPSS Data Editor page*

What you need to do is to enter this information in the *SPSS* Data Editor, and then request the analysis of the data that you wish to be carried out. To do this there are three basic steps:

1   define the variables;
2   enter the data;
3   run the analysis.

We will go through each of these in turn.

Table 4.1 *The gender and well-being of 10 people*

Case	Gender	Well-being
1	Male	3
2	Female	5
3	Male	2
4	Female	3
5	Male	8
6	Male	Missing data
7	Male	2
8	Female	4
9	Male	3
10	Female	1

DEFINING VARIABLES

The first step is to tell the data editor what variables you wish to enter information about. At the bottom of the Data Editor page, you will see a tab with the words *Data View*. Next to this you should see another tab *Variable View*. The *Data View* that you are currently in allows you to enter data. But before doing so you need to go into *Variable View* in order to indicate the details of the variables you have.

> ➤ Click on **Variable View**.

Now you should see a page very similar to the one in the *Data View*, but this time the columns are headed *Name*, *Type*, *Width* etc. (see Figure 4.2).

What you are going to do here is to tell the data editor that you have three variables, and provide information about the nature of these variables. The first variable from Table 4.1 is 'case' (i.e. the number allocated to each respondent that we wrote on the questionnaire).

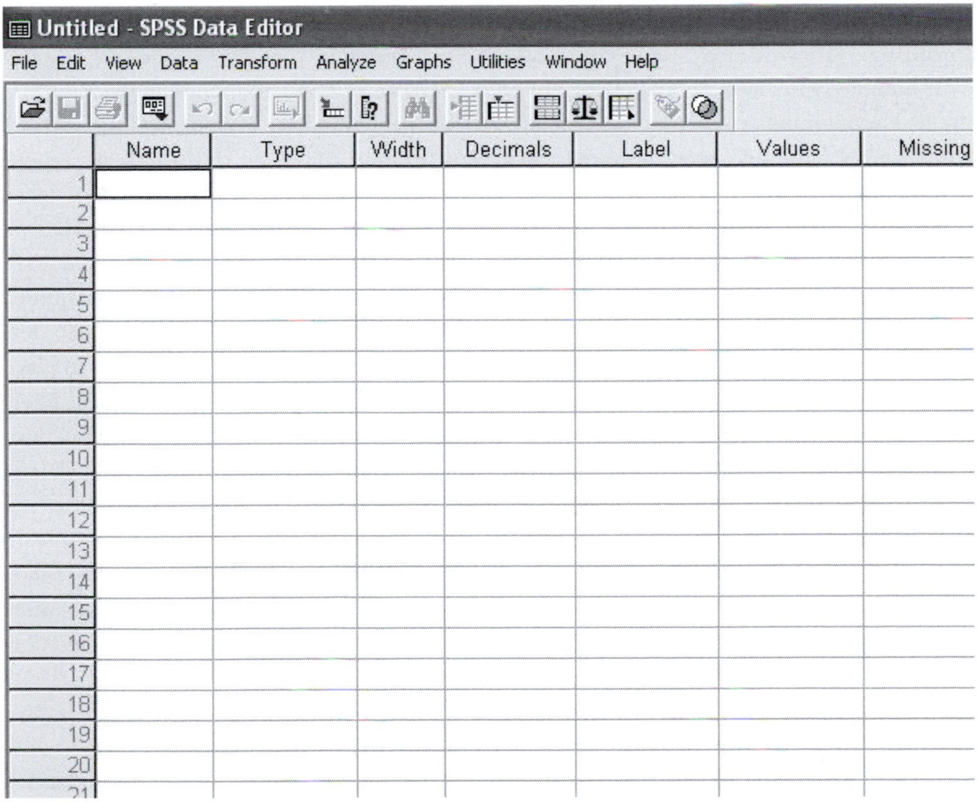

Figure 4.2 *The* SPSS *Variable View page*

➤ Position your cursor on the cell in row number 1, under the column labelled **Name**.

➤ Left-click on your mouse, type the word 'case', and press **Return** on your keyboard (**Return** is the key which starts a new line). The *Variable View* should now look like Figure 4.3.

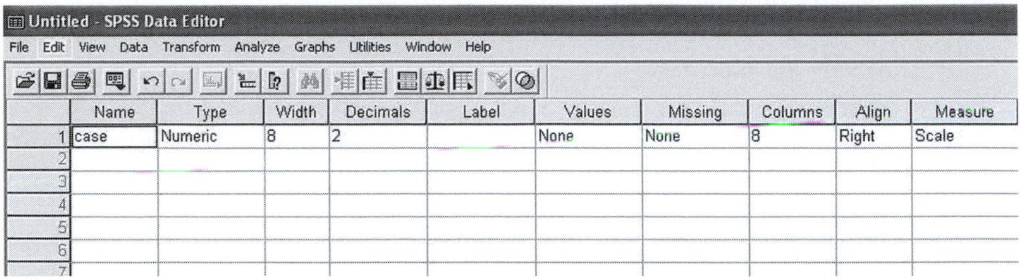

Figure 4.3 *The* SPSS Variable View *page after the variable 'case' has been entered*

What you have done is to tell *SPSS* that the first variable is called 'case'. You don't have to call this variable 'case' — you could call it, say, 'respnum', an abbreviation of respondent number. However, in all versions of *SPSS for Windows* up to and including version 11, the maximum number of characters that any variable name can have is eight, and the variable name cannot have any spaces between characters. So, you could not call it either 'respondentnumber' because this has over eight characters, or 'resp num' because an illegal space is used. If you are using *SPSS* version 12 you are not limited to eight characters here.

You have now told the data editor that you have a variable called 'case'. You may have noticed that when you pressed *Return* various information was placed in the other columns. In the second column, *Type*, you will see the word *Numeric* and a grey box with three dots on it. On the *Width* column you will see the number 8 and so on. You don't need to place information in all of these columns, so we'll just deal with the columns you are most likely to use. There is one column, *Label*, in which it is always a good idea to place information. *Label* allows you to give the variable a name that you will always understand. As explained earlier, the maximum number of characters that you can give a variable is eight (unless you are using *SPSS* version 12), but in *Label* you can have as many as 256 characters if you want to. This is often helpful because it is easy to forget that an abbreviation like 'respnum' refers to respondent number. It is also good practice because *SPSS* output, on which the results of your analyses are printed, usually shows the variable label rather than the variable name (with its maximum of eight characters).

➤ Type the word 'Case' in the top cell of the column **Label**.

➤ Now enter the second variable, 'gender', by clicking on the cell in the second row in the column labelled **Name** (that is directly under the word 'case' that you have already typed in). Here type the word 'gender' and press **Return**.

You have now told the data editor your second variable refers to gender.

> ➤ Now type 'Gender' in the **Label** column.

The gender variable is slightly more complicated than the case variable. The reason for this is that gender is a categorical variable with two possible values: male and female. Therefore, you need to tell the data editor that you are dealing with the two categories of male and female. To do this:

> ➤ Click on the cell in the second row under the column **Values**. A small grey box with three dots on it should appear.
> ➤ Click on this small grey box and a dialog box headed **Value Labels** will appear.

You are going to use this to tell the data editor that you are going to code males as the number 0, and females as the number 1. The reason for using the codes 0 and 1 rather than just typing in male for a man and female for a woman is that *SPSS* works far better with data in a numerical form than it does with words.

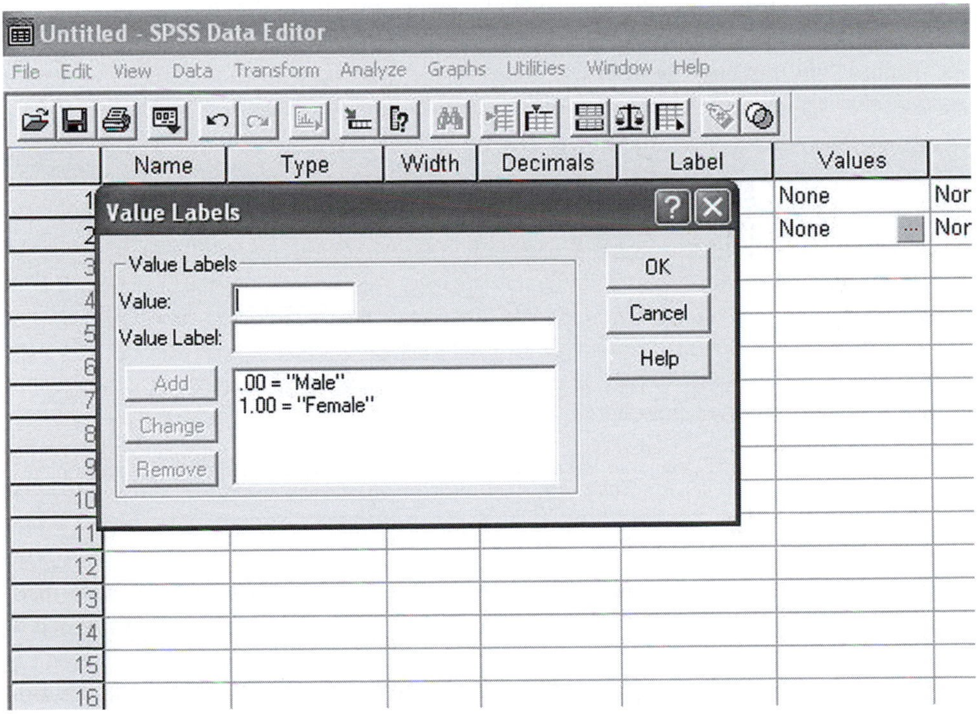

Figure 4.4 SPSS Variable View: *entering value label information*

- ➢ Click on the white box to the right of **Value** and type the number 0.
- ➢ Click on the white area next to **Value Label** and type 'male'.
- ➢ Click on the button under these called **Add**.

You should see that the *Value* and *Value Label* boxes are now empty and that in the box underneath the following has appeared: *.00 = 'Male'*. This is an instruction to the data editor that for the variable gender, '0' refers to males.

Repeat these three steps, this time entering '1' in *Value*, and 'female' in *Value Label*, and again clicking on *Add*. Now in the box you should also see *1.00 = 'Female'* (see Figure 4.4).

- ➢ Finally, click on the **OK** button on the dialog box and you will be returned to the main **Variable View** page.

Well done, you have now told the data editor that you have two variables, number and gender, and that gender is coded 0 for males and 1 for females. You are now ready to enter the final variable, well-being.

- ➢ Type 'wellbe' in the third cell under the column labelled **Name** and press **Return**.
- ➢ Type 'Well-being' under the **Label** column and press **Return**.

The page should now look as shown in Figure 4.5

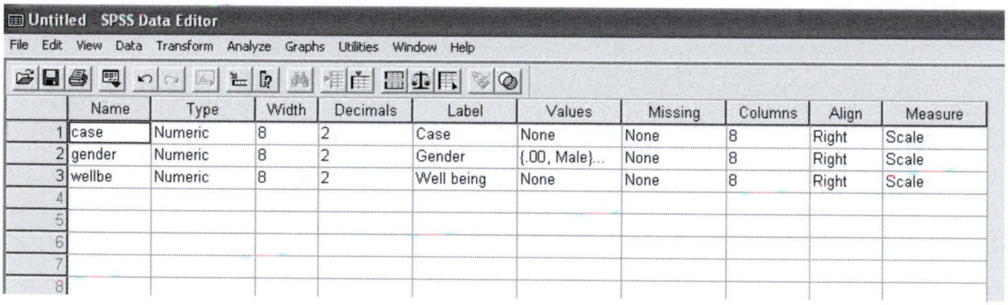
Untitled - SPSS Data Editor
File Edit View Data Transform Analyze Graphs Utilities Window Help
Name Type Width Decimals Label Values Missing Columns Align Measure
1 case Numeric 8 2 Case None None 8 Right Scale
2 gender Numeric 8 2 Gender {.00, Male}... None 8 Right Scale
3 wellbe Numeric 8 2 Well being None None 8 Right Scale
4
5
6
7
8

Figure 4.5 *The* SPSS Variable View *after the case, gender and well-being variables have been entered*

That's it! You have now completed the job of telling the data editor that you have three variables, 'case', 'gender' and 'wellbe', that gender is coded 0 for males and 1 for females, and that the labels of these variables are 'Case', 'Gender' and 'Well-being'.

Whenever you wish to enter variables into *SPSS* in future, you can do so using exactly the same steps. You can call the variables anything you like (as long as the name has no more than eight characters, unless you are using *SPSS* version 12 where this limit on the number of characters is no longer in force), label them whatever you like and code the values of categorical variables in any way you like.

ENTERING DATA

> ➤ Return to the *Data View* by clicking on the tab called **Data View** at the bottom left of the page.

You will see that the first three columns have now been labelled *case*, *gender* and *wellbe*. You are now ready to enter your data.

> ➤ Begin by clicking on the cell in the first row under **case** and typing in '1' and pressing **Return**.

You will see that the number 1.00 appears. This is your case number one.

> ➤ Now click on the first cell under the column labelled **gender**.

If you look at Table 4.1, you will see that this first person is a male. Since you are coding males as 0, you need to enter a 0 here.

> ➤ This time, instead of pressing Return after typing in the 0, press the right arrow on your keyboard.

This has the advantage of positioning the cursor in the correct position for your next piece of data – the first row under the column headed *wellbe*. The table shows that the first respondent obtained a score of 3 for well-being:

> ➤ Enter a 3 in this cell (followed by pressing the right arrow as usual).

You have now entered all of the data for case number 1, as shown in Figure 4.6.

> ➤ Click on the cell in which you intend to enter the next piece of data, enter it, and carry on like this until you have entered the data for all 10 cases.

Remember to code the males as 0 and the females as 1, and don't worry if you make a mistake, it is very simple to correct it by clicking on the cell with the incorrect data and typing the correction in. When you get to case number six, you will see that there is missing data for well-being. This is quite common in real research. For example, a respondent may fail to fill in a questionnaire properly, or you may not be able to read their writing. This is easy to deal with; all you need to do is leave the relevant cell alone, and you will know that it contains missing data because there will be a small dot in it. When you have finished, the page should look as shown in Figure 4.7.

> ➤ Save the file by clicking on **File** at the top left of the page, then **Save** on the drop-down options. In the white box next to **File Name** type the words 'Exercise 1 data', and click on the **Save** button.

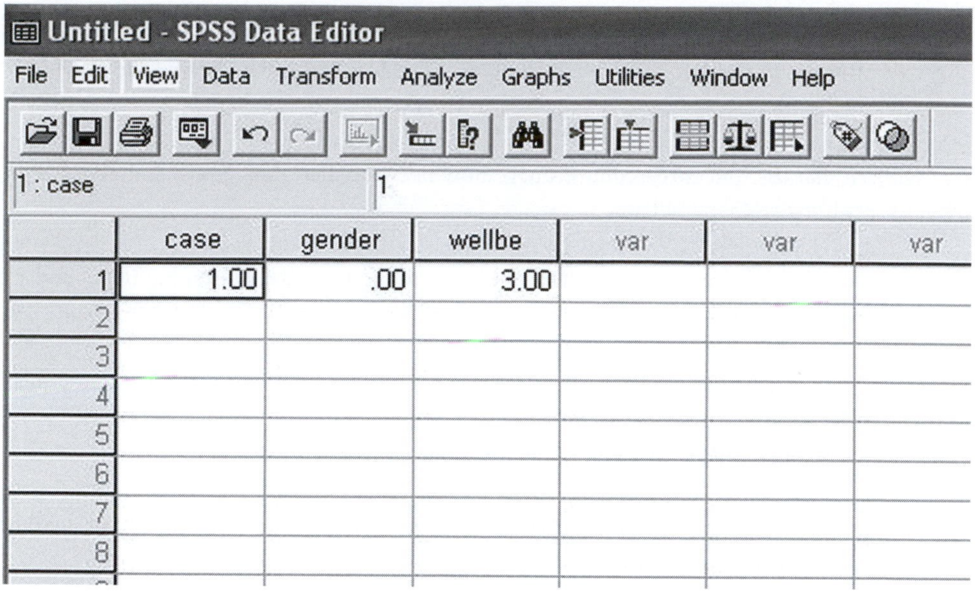

	case	gender	wellbe	var	var	var
1	1.00	.00	3.00			
2						
3						
4						
5						
6						
7						
8						

Figure 4.6 *The* SPSS Data View *after the data on the first case have been entered*

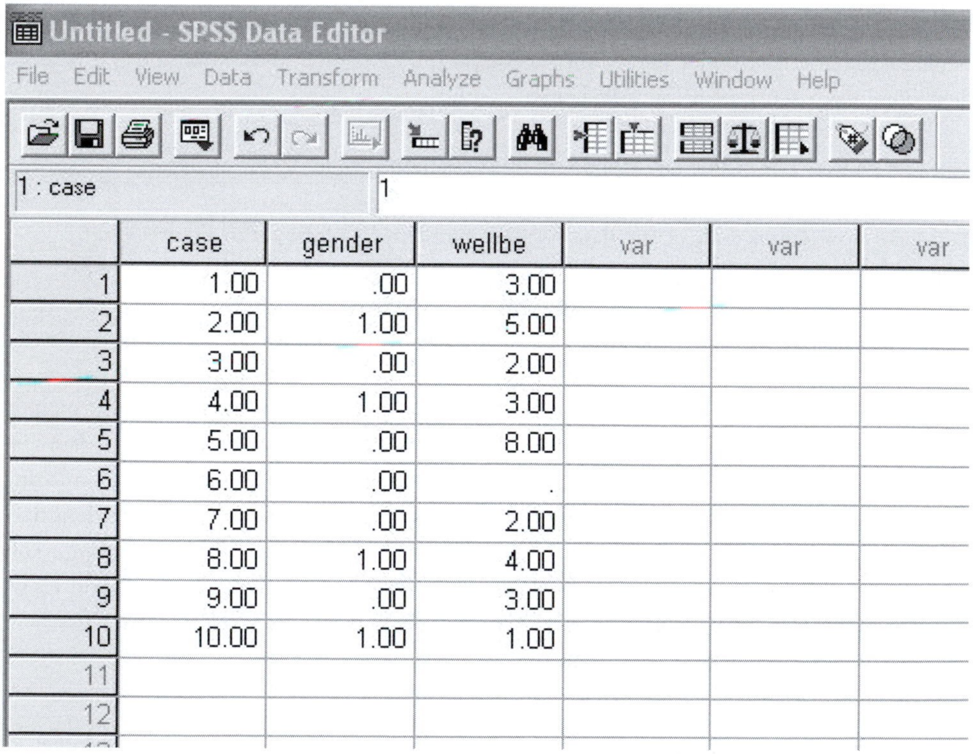

	case	gender	wellbe	var	var	var
1	1.00	.00	3.00			
2	2.00	1.00	5.00			
3	3.00	.00	2.00			
4	4.00	1.00	3.00			
5	5.00	.00	8.00			
6	6.00	.00	.			
7	7.00	.00	2.00			
8	8.00	1.00	4.00			
9	9.00	.00	3.00			
10	10.00	1.00	1.00			
11						
12						

Figure 4.7 *The* SPSS Data View *after data on 10 cases have been entered*

You have now saved your first data file. If you wish, you can leave this session now by clicking on *File* and then *Exit*. When you return later you will need to run *SPSS* again and then retrieve the data file you have saved by clicking on *File*, then *Open*, then selecting *Data . . .*, navigating to your file in the dialog box, highlighting it by clicking on it, and then clicking on the *Open* button. Otherwise, continue straight on to the next section, requesting data analysis.

REQUESTING DATA ANALYSIS

You are now in a position to use *SPSS* to generate some useful tables and graphs on the data entered. You have two variables of interest here: the categorical variable of gender and the continuous variable of well-being. You are going to produce a frequency table, pie chart and bar chart for gender. And for well-being you will produce a table containing a variety of useful information, including the number of cases, the minimum value, maximum value, median, mean and standard deviation. You'll also produce a histogram for well-being.

Before explaining how to do this, a little more background on *SPSS* will be provided. In *SPSS* there are essentially three types of page:

■ the Data Editor page which has both a *Data View* and the *Variable View*. You have already worked with this;
■ the Syntax page;
■ the Output page.

The Data Editor page is used to input data and to specify the characteristics of this data such as what the values of a given categorical variable refer to. It can also be used to request data analyses. This is achieved by using the pull-down menus at the top of the page. For example, if you click on *Analyze* at the top of the *Data View* you will see several options for analysing data.

The Syntax page can be used instead of the pull-down menus to give *SPSS* detailed instructions for carrying out data analyses, and it has the advantage that you can save the instructions written on the syntax page just like any other computer file. However, the disadvantage with using the syntax page is that the instructions have to be very precise and it is, therefore, best suited to someone relatively experienced in the use of *SPSS*. Therefore, in this book we will almost exclusively use the pull-down menus to request analyses.

The third type of *SPSS* page, the Output page, opens automatically when you request data analysis with the pull-down menus (or the syntax page). It is here that *SPSS* places the results of data analyses. Output pages can be saved just as the information in the Data Editor and Syntax pages can. However, they are often simply viewed on the monitor or, more frequently, printed out instead. It is in the Output page that you will find the tables, graphs and other statistical output from your analyses.

This will all become clearer with an example. Let's start by requesting some frequency information on the categorical variable *gender*. To do this:

➢ Click on **Analyze**.
➢ Click on **Descriptive Statistics**.

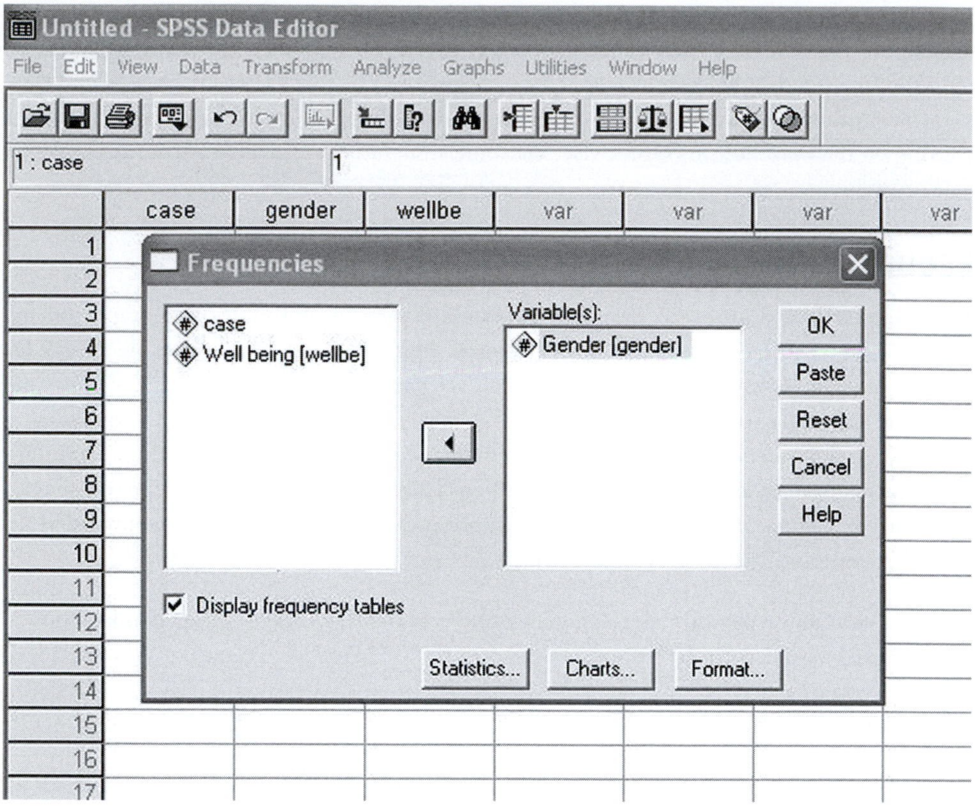

Figure 4.8 *Specifying the variable or variables to be analysed in* SPSS *Frequencies*

- ➢ Click on **Frequencies** . . . .
- ➢ A dialog box will open. In the white rectangle to the left hand side of the box you will see your three variables.
- ➢ Click on **Gender** and then on the small black triangle to the left of the white rectangle headed **Variable(s)**. The gender variable will be moved into the variables box as in Figure 4.8.
- ➢ Click on the **Charts** . . . button at the bottom of the dialog box to open another smaller dialog box that you can use to request a pie chart and a bar chart of the data in the gender variable.
- ➢ Click on the **Bar Charts** radio button.
- ➢ Click on **Continue**. The small dialog box will disappear.
- ➢ Click on **OK**.

You will find that the following Output page automatically opens with the results of the analyses you have requested. You can toggle between this and the Data Editor page by clicking on *Window* at the top of the screen and then whichever of the two pages you want to see. For the time being, let's stay with the Output page, shown in Figure 4.9.

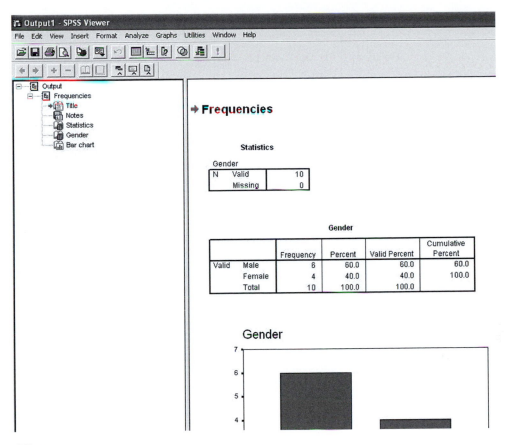

Figure 4.9 *The* SPSS *Output page for the* Frequencies *analysis of gender*

Note that the page in Figure 4.9 is divided vertically into two parts. To the right are the tables, graphs, results etc. that you have requested. You can scroll up and down through these by clicking on and dragging the bar on the extreme right. On the left hand side of the page are a series of labelled icons. Each icon refers to a particular component of the results output. You can go to the table or graph you want by clicking on one of these. For example, if you click on the *Bar chart* icon you will see that the bar chart is displayed on the left hand side of the screen.

The results you have produced are shown below. They are annotated here to indicate what various parts of the output mean. Annotations are used in the same way throughout Chapters 5 and 6.

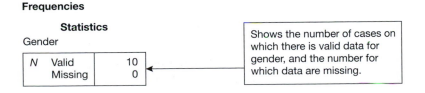

Frequencies

Statistics

Gender

N	Valid	10
	Missing	0

Shows the number of cases on which there is valid data for gender, and the number for which data are missing.

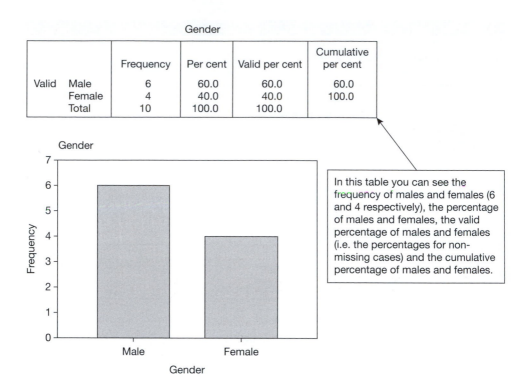

Gender

		Frequency	Per cent	Valid per cent	Cumulative per cent
Valid	Male	6	60.0	60.0	60.0
	Female	4	40.0	40.0	100.0
	Total	10	100.0	100.0	

In this table you can see the frequency of males and females (6 and 4 respectively), the percentage of males and females, the valid percentage of males and females (i.e. the percentages for non-missing cases) and the cumulative percentage of males and females.

It is possible to copy any of these components of the *SPSS* output in Word. For example, to copy the bar chart:

> ➢ Click on the **Bar chart icon** to highlight it.
> ➢ Click on **Edit** (top left of screen).
> ➢ Click on **Copy objects**.
> ➢ Open a page in Word and on this click on **Edit** and then **Paste**.

The bar chart will be pasted into Word. If you have any problems seeing the chart after you have pasted it into Word, try repeating the above process but this time in *SPSS* click on *Copy* instead of *Copy objects*. You can resize this if you want to. If you click on it you will see that a rectangle appears around it with a small black square at each corner and half way along each side. Place your cursor on the bottom right corner of this rectangle and a small line with arrows at each end will appear. Click on this and it will change to a small cross. By holding down the left button on your mouse and dragging the cross down and to the right or up and to the left you can adjust the size of the chart on the page.

OK, return to the *SPSS* Data Editor page. We will now request some detailed information on the continuous variable, well-being. To do so:

> ➢ Click on **Analyze**.
> ➢ Click on **Descriptive Statistics**.
> ➢ Click on **Explore**.

A dialog box will open. As you can see, it is laid out in a similar way to the *Frequencies* dialog box that you have already used, with the variables listed in the white rectangle to the left hand side.

> Click on **Well-being** and then on the small black triangle to the left of the box headed **Dependent List**. The *well-being* variable will be moved into the **Dependent List** box as in Figure 4.10.
> Click on **OK**.

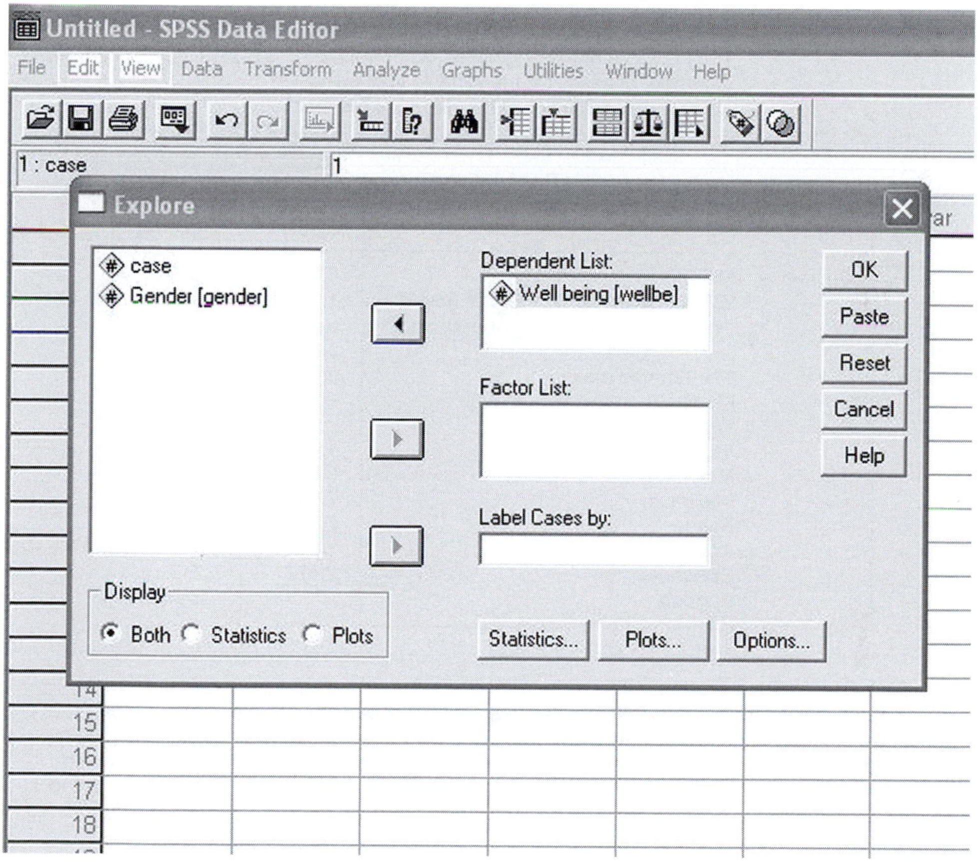

Figure 4.10 *Specifying the variable or variables to be analysed in* SPSS Explore

The following output will be produced.

Explore

Case processing summary

	Cases					
	Valid		Missing		Total	
	N	Per cent	N	Per cent	N	Per cent
Well-being	9	90.0%	1	10.0%	10	100.0%

This table shows the number of valid cases, the number of missing cases, and the total number of cases for the variable Well being. The missing case is, of course, case number 6.

Descriptives

			Statistic	Std error
Well-being	Mean		3.4444	.68943
	95% confidence interval for mean	Lower bound	1.8546	
		Upper bound	5.0343	
			3.3272	
	5% trimmed mean		3.0000	
	Median		4.278	
	Variance		2.06828	
	Std deviation		1.00	
	Minimum		8.00	
	Maximum		7.00	
	Range		2.5	
	Interquartile range		1.409	
	Skewness		2.472	.717
	Kurtosis			1.400

This is a very helpful table because it provides a great deal of summary information on the continuous variable in question. As you can see, much of the descriptive information outlined in Chapter 1 is provided: the mean, median, variance, standard deviation, range and inter-quartile range. In addition, the 95% confidence interval and standard error, discussed in Chapters 2 and 3, are also produced.

The 5% trimmed mean is the mean recalculated after the 5% most extreme data points, those furthest from it, are excluded. A comparison of the mean and the 5% trimmed mean is useful for checking that a few extreme values are not distorting the mean. If these two values are very different this suggests that such extreme values do exist and the data should be carefully checked. It is likely that the extreme cases concerned will be specified in the box and whiskers plot below.

The skewness value is a numerical indication of how skewed the data are, and kurtosis refers to how flat or peaked the frequency distribution is. However, these figures are not used much in practice because most researchers prefer to examine the shape of the frequency distribution by eye when it is plotted on a graph.

Well-being

```
Well-being Stem-and-Leaf Plot

Frequency     Stem &   Leaf

 1.00          1 .  0
 2.00          2 .  00
 3.00          3 .  0000
 1.00          4 .  0
 1.00          5 .  0
 1.00 Extremes      (>=8.0)

Stem width:   1.00
Each leaf:    1 case(s)
```

This stem and leaf plot is a useful way of examining the shape of the frequency distribution, and is often used to check that the distribution is roughly symmetrical and normal in shape. The 'stem' gives the values of the data points, and each 'leaf' indicates the number of cases which obtained the value in question. For example, here it is clear that four people have scores of 3 because there are four 0's next to the stem of 3.

The stem and leaf plot is like a bar chart turned 90 degrees so that it is lying on its side, and the shape of the 'leaves' shows the shape of the distribution.

Well-being

This is called a 'box and whiskers' plot. The 'box' is the rectangular area in the centre of the graph and the 'whiskers' are the two horizontal lines connected to the box by vertical lines. In a box and whiskers plot the top and bottom of the box are drawn at the 25th and 75th percentiles respectively. The median is shown with the thick horizontal line (in this case it is 3).

A very useful feature of the box and whiskers plot is that it also shows outliers (defined as those data points more than 1.5 box-lengths above or below the box, marked with a circle) and extreme values (data points more than three box-lengths above or below the box and marked with a cross). Helpfully, the number of the *SPSS* Data Editor row in which this outlier or extreme value occurs is also shown. In this example, case 5 is shown to have an outlying value, and it would be worth checking this to make sure it is a correct and valid data point.

The upper and lower whiskers are drawn in line with the highest and lowest values that are not outliers. The way to interpret it is quite simple: the box shows the limits and range of those 50% of the data points closest to the median, and the whiskers show the limits and range of all the data points bar those which are especially large or small.

We have now produced a great deal of interesting information about gender and well-being by using just *Frequencies* and *Explore*. We will complete this chapter by producing two more graphs, a pie chart for gender and a histogram for well-being. To do this make sure you are in the *SPSS* Data Editor and then:

➢ Click on **Graphs**.
➢ Click on **Pie** . . . A small dialog box will appear.
➢ Click on **Define**. Another dialog box will appear with the variables in the white rectangle to the left.
➢ Click on **Gender** and then on the button with the small black triangle on it to the left of the white box headed **Define Slices by**. Gender will be moved into the **Define Slices by** box.
➢ Click on **OK**.

A pie chart for gender will appear in the Output page.

To generate a histogram for well-being, return to the Data Editor page and then:

➢ Click on **Graphs**.
➢ Click on **Histogram** . . . A dialog box will appear with the variables in the white rectangle to the left.
➢ Click on **Well-being** and then on the button with the small black triangle on it to the left of the white box headed **Variable**. *Well-being* will be moved into the **Variable** box.
➢ Click on **OK**.

A histogram for well-being will appear in the Output page.

As with the other *SPSS* output, these graphs can be examined, pasted into Word, printed out or saved along with the rest of the results of the analysis.

Well done! You have now carried out your first piece of *SPSS* data analysis, and in doing so have been through the four stages that are normally necessary whenever you intend to use *SPSS* to carry out your data analysis: defining variables, entering data, requesting data analysis and examining the output. This may all have seemed quite complicated and fiddly, but you will find that the steps you have used become second nature very quickly. What's more, these steps will be essentially the same now whatever type of data, and whatever type of data analysis, you wish to do.

The next step is for you to go through these stages on your own. Close down *SPSS* by clicking on *File* and then *Exit*. You will be asked whether you wish to save your data file and output files. You can do so if you wish but this is not necessary.

DATA ANALYSIS EXERCISE

Open *SPSS* again and you will see the Data Editor page.

In this exercise you will use *SPSS* to provide descriptive information on the data in Table 4.2. This table provides data on 15 people in an organization. Each person works in a particular department and has been given a score out of seven for job performance.

Table 4.2 *The job performance of 15 staff in three departments*

Case	Department	Performance
1	Finance	4
2	Production	6
3	Marketing	4
4	Finance	4
5	Production	5
6	Production	5
7	Marketing	3
8	Finance	7
9	Production	5
10	Production	4
11	Marketing	2
12	Marketing	1
13	Production	3
14	Finance	4
15	Marketing	5

Task 1

Your first task is to go through the steps of defining variables and entering the data. Don't forget that you will have to decide the variable names for department and perform-ance (remember, unless you are using *SPSS* version 12 you can't use these words as they are over eight characters long), and enter variable names for them. You will also have to decide on a numerical code for the types of department. If at any stage you can't remember what to do, refer to the instruc-tions given above for the first exercise.

Once you have your variables defined and your data entered you are in a position to analyse the data.

Task 2

Decide which type of analysis is appropriate and then produce descriptive statistics and graphs of these two variables. Remember that the data you have entered contain a categorical variable (i.e. department) and a continuous variable (performance).

When you have completed the tasks, you can check your output file against the results below, and then close *SPSS* by clicking on the cross at the top right of the screen.

Frequencies

Statistics

Department

N	Valid	15
	Missing	0

Department

		Frequency	Per cent	Valid per cent	Cumulative per cent
Valid	Finance	4	26.7	26.7	26.7
	Production	6	40.0	40.0	66.7
	Marketing	5	33.3	33.3	100.0
	Total	15	100.0	100.0	

Department

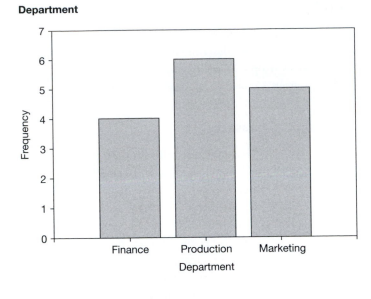

Graph

Explore

Case processing summary

	Cases					
	Valid		Missing		Total	
	N	Per cent	N	Per cent	N	Per cent
Performance	15	100.0%	0	.0%	15	100.0%

Descriptives

			Statistic	Std error
Performance	Mean		4.1333	.38873
	95% confidence	Lower bound	3.2996	
	interval for mean	Upper bound	4.9671	
	5% trimmed mean		4.1481	
	Median		4.0000	
	Variance		2.267	
	Std deviation		1.50555	
	Minimum		1.00	
	Maximum		7.00	
	Range		6.00	
	Interquartile range		2.0000	
	Skewness		−.259	.580
	Kurtosis		.558	1.121

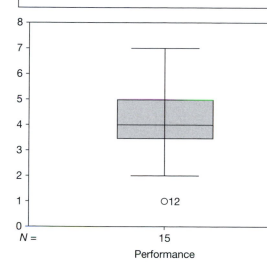

Performance

```
Performance Stem-and-Leaf Plot

Frequency        Stem & Leaf

 1.00 Extremes          (=<1.0)
 1.00            2 .  0
 2.00            3 .  00
 5.00            4 .  00000
 4.00            5 .  0000
 1.00            6 .  0
 1.00            7 .  0

 Stem width:      1.00
 Each leaf:       1 case(s)
```

Graph

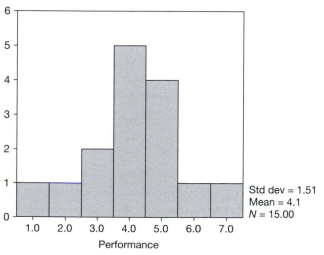

Std dev = 1.51
Mean = 4.1
N = 15.00

Performance

DATA TRANSFORMATION

Before data are analysed it is very often necessary to transform them in various ways. For example, you might have a variable indicating which of four age groups people are in (e.g. 16–20, 21–24, 25–30 and 31–34) and wish to create a new variable indicating which of two more general age groups they fall in (e.g. 16–24 and 25–34). Or you might have obtained Likert scale scores for people on five questions relating to happiness with career choice, and want to create a new variable in which you place the average of their score across these five questions.

SPSS provides several ways of transforming data, and this can be done either with the pull-down menus or with syntax files. If you are new to *SPSS* you may find the pull-down menus easier, but for those with some familiarity with it the syntax files are usually quicker and more efficient to use. In this section we will cover both approaches.

To explain how data transformation is achieved, we will use an example. Imagine that you design a questionnaire to measure how satisfied people are with their career. To keep things simple we will assume that this questionnaire contains just the following four items:

1   I am very happy with my current career
2   I wish I had chosen a different career
3   I never think I would be better off in a different career
4   I am convinced that I am in the wrong career

For each question, 10 respondents are asked to indicate whether they strongly agree, agree, are unsure, disagree, or strongly disagree. The responses to all questions are coded as follows:

> Strongly disagree = 1
> Disagree = 2
> Not sure = 3
> Agree = 4
> Strongly agree = 5

With the adoption of this coding system it is clear that questions 2 and 4 are negatively keyed, because here greater agreement (and therefore higher scores) indicates relatively higher *unhappiness* with career choice. The results are shown in Table 4.3.

Before analysing the questionnaire responses you wish to transform the variables in various ways. As explained below, the *Recode* and *Compute* commands are very useful for doing so.

RECODE

Recode is used when you wish to change the way in which a variable is coded. For example, you may have coded males as 1 and females as 2 and wish to change this coding to males = 0 and females = 1. In doing so you can choose to overwrite the original variable (in which case your original codings are permanently deleted), or you can opt to create a new variable containing the recoded version, leaving the original variable untouched.

Table 4.3 *The responses of 10 people to four career choice questions*

Case	Gender	cq1	cq2	cq3	cq4
1	1	3	2	2	1
2	2	4	2	4	1
3	2	5	1	4	1
4	2	1	5	2	4
5	1	2	3	1	4
6	1	3	4	3	2
7	2	5	2	4	3
8	1	3	3	4	2
9	2	4	5	5	4
10	1	5	1	5	3

In questionnaire surveys a common use of recoding occurs when questions with Likert scale responses are both positively and negatively keyed. For example, in developing a scale to measure how happy someone is with their career, the researcher may use four positively keyed questions (e.g. I am very content with the career path I have chosen) and four negatively keyed questions (e.g. I wish I had chosen a different career). If a 5-point Likert scale is used, and responses are coded 1 to 5 (e.g. strongly disagree = 1, disagree = 2, in between = 3, agree = 4, strongly agree = 5) it is necessary to recode the negatively keyed questions so that the greater the agreement the lower the score obtained (e.g. a response of 5 is recoded 1, 4 is recoded 2 etc.). Upon completion, higher scores will always indicate higher levels of happiness with career. It then becomes possible to combine the scores across all eight questions to obtain an overall score for happiness with career.

To do this, start *SPSS* if it is not already running, and then enter the data in Table 4.3 (see Figure 4.11) and then do the following:

> ➤ Click on **Transform**.
> ➤ Click on **Recode**.
> ➤ Click on **Into Different Variables**.

A dialog box will appear with your variables in the white box on the left hand side.

> ➤ Click on the first variable you wish to recode, (in this case 'cq2'), and then on the black triangle to the left of the box headed *Numeric Variable*[†] --> *Output Variable*. You will see that cq2--> ? appears in the large white rectangular box. You have now specified the variable you wish to have recoded, and the next step is to provide the name of the variable you wish to place the recoded version of 'cq2' in (referred to in *SPSS* as the output variable). On the left hand side of the dialog box you will see the heading *Output Variable*, and beneath this *Name* and *Label*.

[†] *Input Variable* in *SPSS* Version 12.

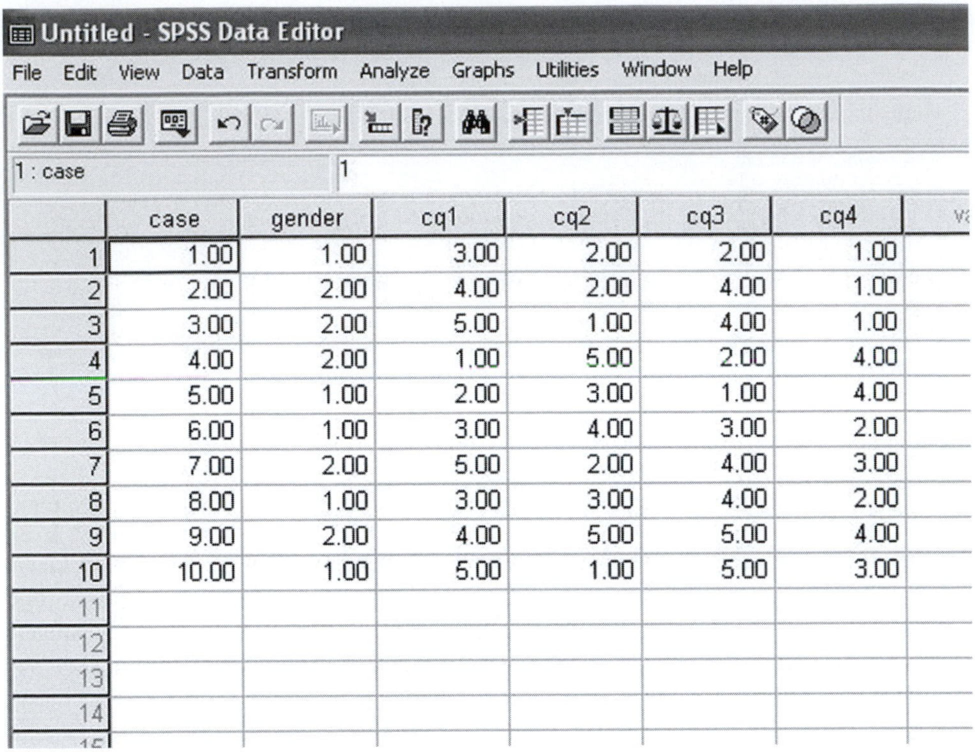

	case	gender	cq1	cq2	cq3	cq4
1	1.00	1.00	3.00	2.00	2.00	1.00
2	2.00	2.00	4.00	2.00	4.00	1.00
3	3.00	2.00	5.00	1.00	4.00	1.00
4	4.00	2.00	1.00	5.00	2.00	4.00
5	5.00	1.00	2.00	3.00	1.00	4.00
6	6.00	1.00	3.00	4.00	3.00	2.00
7	7.00	2.00	5.00	2.00	4.00	3.00
8	8.00	1.00	3.00	3.00	4.00	2.00
9	9.00	2.00	4.00	5.00	5.00	4.00
10	10.00	1.00	5.00	1.00	5.00	3.00
11						
12						
13						
14						

Figure 4.11 *Data entered for transformation*

In the small white box under *Name* type in the name you want to give the output variable. This name should be something which allows you to keep track of the fact that this new output variable is a recoded version of 'cq2'. Let's call it 'cq2rec' (meaning variable 'cq2' recoded) in this case.

➢ So type 'cq1rec' in the white box under *Name*. If you wish to, you can also give this variable a label, (perhaps 'Career question 2 recoded'), by typing this in the white box headed *Label*.

➢ Click on **Change**.

You will see that the output variable has been moved into the large white rectangle which now contains the following: cq2 --> cq2rec (see Figure 4.12).

The next step is to indicate the relationship between the values of the original variable (in this case 'cq2') and the new output variable (in this case 'cq1rec'). Here we wish to change the coding as follows: 5=1, 4=2, 3=3, 2=4, 1=5. This will ensure that the more people agree with the negatively keyed 'cq2' variable, the lower the score they will obtain, and the more they disagree with it, the higher the score they will obtain. To do this:

➢ Click on **Old and New Values**. A dialog box will appear. Click on the white circle to the left of **Value** under **Old Value** to highlight this, and then enter a 1 in the white rectangle to the right of **Value**.

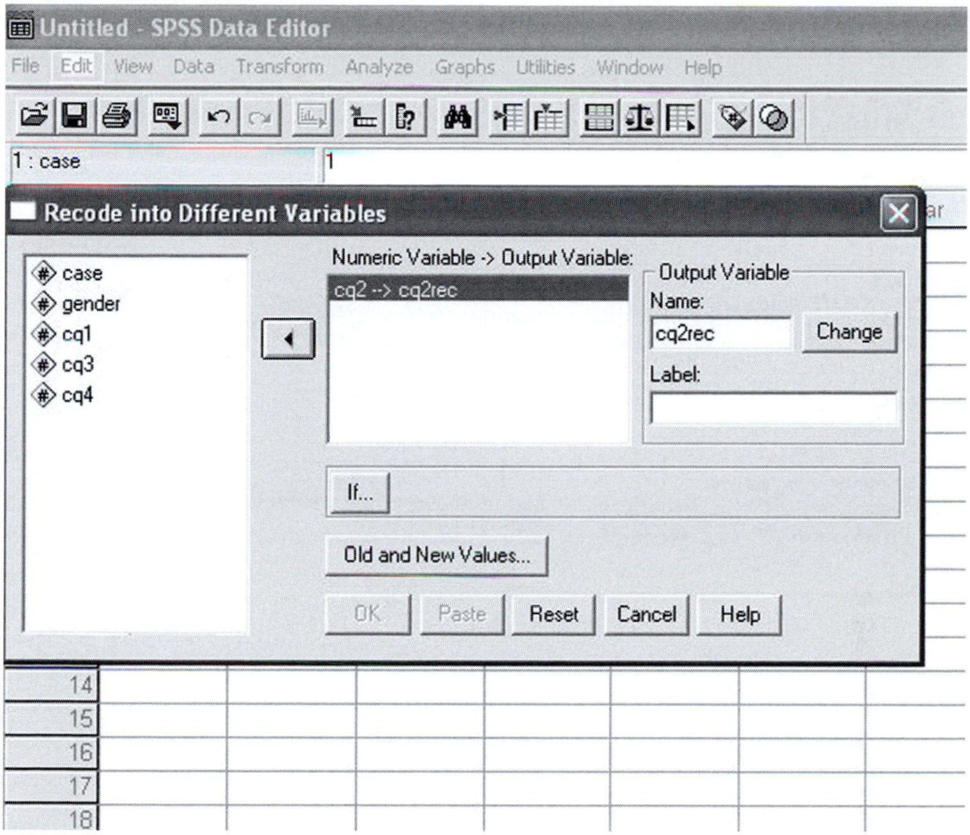

Figure 4.12 *Specifying variables for recoding*

We now need to give the value of the output variable when the original variable is coded in the way indicated under **Old Value, Value** (i.e. in this case 1). Here we want people who are coded 1 for 'cq2' to be coded as 5 for 'cqrec'. So we enter a 5 in the rectangular box to the right of **New Value, Value**.

➢ Click on **Add**. The coding of the value of the original variable (in this example 1 for 'cq2') is now linked to a code for the new variable (in this example 5 for 'cq2rec') in the white box headed *Old --> New*.
➢ You now need to repeat the previous two steps for each of the other recodings (i.e. 4=2, 3=3, 2=4 and 5=1). When you have finished, all five of the recodings should be seen in the white box headed *Old --> New* (see Figure 4.13).
➢ Click on **Continue**.
➢ Click on **OK**.

The new variable 'cq2rec' will be created. You can view this in *Data View*. Because in this example 'cq4' is also negatively keyed, you now need to go through the same procedure again to recode this, perhaps into a variable called 'cq4rec'.

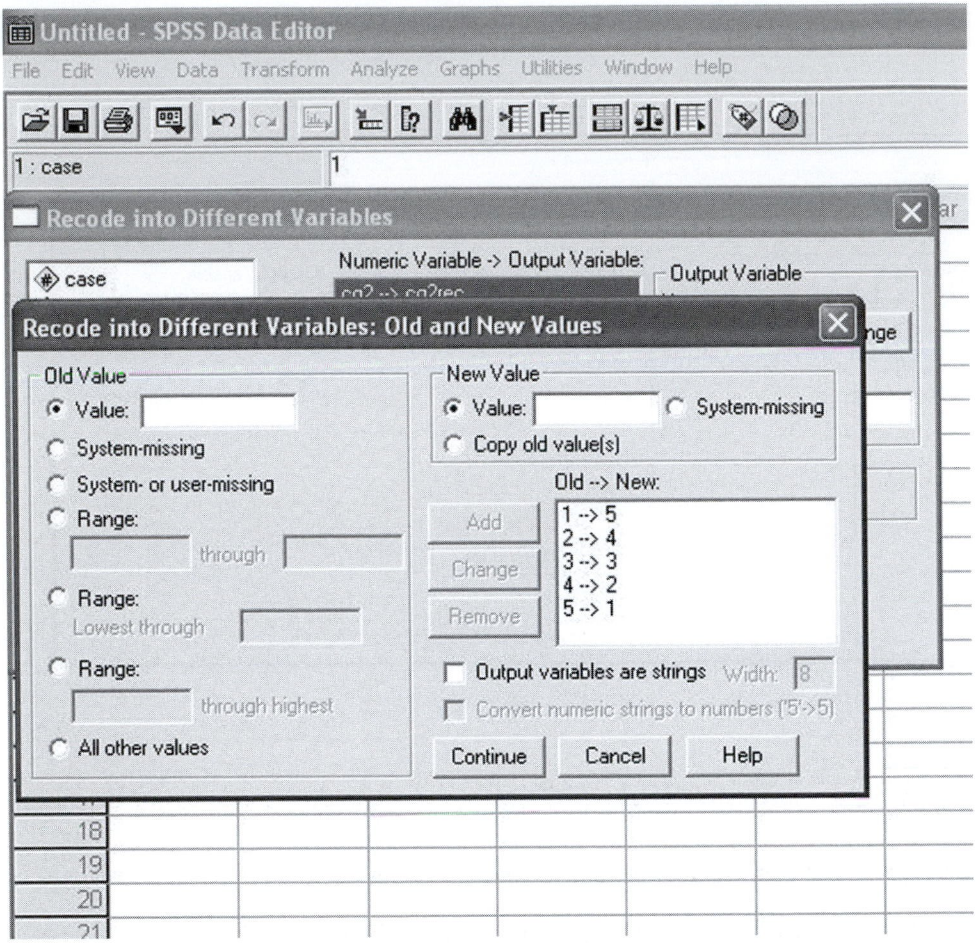

Figure 4.13 *Specifying old and new variables when recoding*

Sometimes you may wish to recode a variable only for some cases and not others. For example, you might want to recode the score that women get on a particular variable, but leave the score that men get on it intact. To do so you should follow the same procedure as that set out above for *Recode*, except that before clicking on *OK* (i.e. the last step) you should click on *If*. Here you can enter the name of the variable on which recoding depends and the value it should have if recoding is to go ahead. For example, if for some reason you only wanted 'cq2' to be recoded into 'cq2rec' for men, and not for women, you could enter gender = 1 in the *If* dialog box and then click on *Continue*. As a consequence of the command you have entered, the recoding would only take place for men.

COMPUTE

Another commonly used method for transforming data is the compute command. Compute is used when you want to create a new variable that results from some arithmetic function, a function usually involving existing variables. For example, having recoded 'cq2' and 'cq4', you are in a position to work out the mean score that each of the respondents has obtained across the four career happiness variables.

To do so:

➤ Click on **Transform**.
➤ Click on **Compute**.

A dialog box will appear. In the white box at the top left headed *Target Variable* write in the name of the new variable you wish to have created. In this example, because we are going to compute the mean score across the four career questions, we will type in 'careerav' (standing for career average). If you wish to give the newly created variable a label (in this case perhaps 'Mean career score') click on *Type & Label* and enter this in the white box next to *Label* and then press *Continue*.

Next you need to type in the expression that will create the new target variable. In this example we want to find the mean across the four questions so we enter:

(cq1 + cq2rec + cq3 + cq4rec)/4.

This indicates that the four career questions are to be added together and then divided by four to find the mean score (see Figure 4.14). If there had been six questions we would, of course, have divided by six. The brackets are used because by default *SPSS* carries out

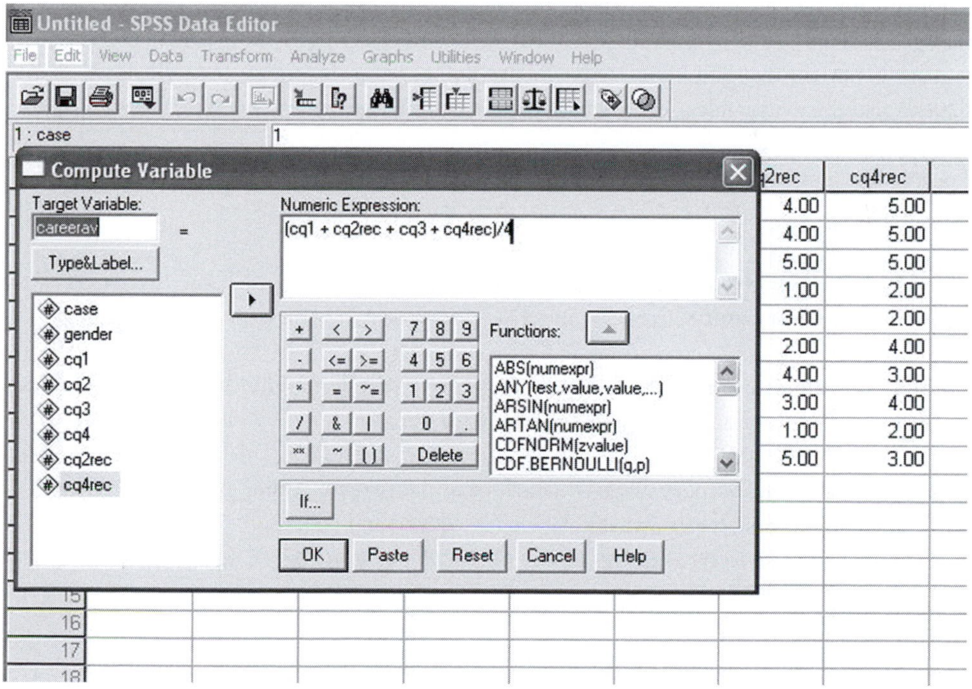

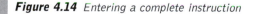

Figure 4.14 *Entering a complete instruction*

multiplications and divisions before additions and subtractions. When brackets are used, the computations inside the brackets are carried out first. You can either type this instruction in directly in the white box headed *Numeric Expression* or you can click on the variables as they appear in the white rectangle on the bottom left to transfer them across to the numeric expression box, and use the keypad to enter the brackets and + signs. Of course, if your intention was to compute some other score for the target variable, you would enter whatever numeric expression you wanted in order to do so.

> ➤ Click on **OK**.

The newly created variable of 'careerav' will be computed, and you can view it in *Data View*.

USING *SPSS* SYNTAX FILES

After some practice with *SPSS* you may find it easier to use syntax files as well as the pull-down menus. Syntax files are particularly efficient for data transformation, but they can also be used for many other purposes too. In fact, if while using this book you follow the various instructions for using statistical techniques, but instead of clicking on *OK* at the end of each set of instructions you click on *Paste* instead, you will find that the instructions that *SPSS* requires to carry out a particular technique will be automatically pasted into a syntax file.

A syntax file is just a blank space in which can be written the instructions that *SPSS* needs to carry out data transformations, statistical tests etc. As well as having these written in automatically by clicking on the *Paste* button, you can also type them in yourself. Beware though, that unless the commands are written absolutely perfectly they won't run. So unless you are confident that you know what you are doing, it is safer to use the pull-down menus than to use the syntax files, even if the former is more laborious and time consuming.

To create a new syntax file:

> ➤ Click on **File**.
> ➤ Click on **New**.
> ➤ Click on **Syntax**.

To carry out the data transformations which we have just done with the pull-down menus, you can get them done by typing in the following syntax:

*Create variables cq2rec cq4rec which have the reverse coding of cq2 and cq3 respectively and create variable labels for cq2rec and cq4rec.
Recode cq2 cq4 (1=5) (2=4) (3=3) (4=2) (5=1) into cq2rec cq4rec.
Execute.

Variable labels cq2rec 'Career question 2 recoded' cq4rec 'Career question 4 recoded'.
Execute.

*Now compute the average of cq1, cq2rec, cq3, and cq4rec.
Compute careerav = (cq1+cq2rec+cq3+cq4rec)/4.
Execute.

A few comments about this should help to make it clear. First, the lines beginning with an asterisk are not *SPSS* commands. Rather they are comments you can write to yourself about what you are asking *SPSS* to do. It is all too easy to type or paste in *SPSS* syntax, knowing exactly what you are doing at the time, and then return to the syntax file a few weeks later and be completely bemused by it. Therefore, it is always good practice to write in reminder comments.

Second, the comment lines must end with a full stop (period). In fact, this is also true of all *SPSS* syntax commands, the ones used here being Recode, Variable labels and Compute. Third, data transformation commands must be followed by an Execute command.

Once you have typed the commands in, and carefully checked that there are no mistakes, highlight the commands you want executed by left-clicking on your mouse and dragging it across all the commands to be carried out. Then click on the small black triangle at the top of the screen just to the right of the binoculars. The instructions will be carried out.

An advantage of syntax files is that they can be saved and used later (to save them now click on *File* and then *Save*, and to open them later click on *File and Open*). This can be very useful if you add some more data to your file and want the same transformations carried out again without having to spend time going through all the steps required to use the pull-down menus. The same also applies to carrying out statistical analyses: instead of repeatedly using the pull-down menus every time you enter additional data, you need only use the pull-down menus once, paste the instructions into a syntax file (by clicking on *Paste* instead of *OK*), save the syntax file, and then open and run the instructions again whenever you want to.

To practise carrying out data transformation, try recoding males as 0 and females as 1 using both the pull-down menus and a syntax file to do so.

Having completed this chapter, you are now familiar with the key procedures necessary to enter data, transform it where required and produce a variety of descriptive statistical analyses.

Part II

Methods of statistical analysis

INTRODUCTION

Many statistical techniques are available to analyse the results of organizational research. In Chapters 5 and 6 these techniques are introduced and instructions are provided on how to carry them out, and how to interpret and report the results they produce. However, before discussing these techniques, it is important to draw attention to a fundamentally important principle: both the design of a research study, and the statistical method used to analyse the data it produces, should be dictated, or at least highly influenced, by the research question or questions to which the researcher requires an answer. The good researcher should be clear about what he or she is trying to find out, should design research around that question (or questions), and should choose a particular statistical technique because it can help to provide an answer to that question (or questions).

This needs to be stressed because it is not uncommon for people to generate research data without a tightly defined research question, and then to say 'Okay, what statistical test should I use to analyse my data?'. This approach to research and data analysis invariably leads to disappointment. Before statistical analysis is even considered and, indeed, before a research study is designed, it is very important that the researcher clarifies his or her research questions, and is absolutely clear and focused about what he or she is trying to find out. When the research question(s) is absolutely clear, and the research is carefully designed in such a way that it is able to provide numerical data relevant to that question, the choice of statistical method is usually quite clear and straightforward. But when the research question is unfocused or even absent, the choice of statistical technique will be almost arbitrary; and in these circumstances it is unlikely that anything of much use will be found however complex and sophisticated the statistical analysis.

Having made this point, let's have a look at the nature of statistical methods used in organizational research. These methods generally take the form either of a specific statistical test of significance (such as a t-test), or of a more general technique in which tests of significance are usually involved (such as multiple regression). Although a large number of inferential statistical techniques have been developed over the years, those commonly used by organizational researchers fall into four basic categories. These are as follows.

1   Techniques for examining differences: it is possible to examine differences in the proportion of cases that fall into different categories. An example would be:

> Is the proportion of men who are accepted for jobs in engineering greater than the proportion of women accepted for jobs in engineering?

It is also possible to examine differences in the central tendency of continuous variables. An example would be:

> Is the job commitment of part-time staff less than the job commitment of full-time staff?

2   Techniques for examining associations between two variables: you can use these techniques to examine the strength and direction of the association between two continuous variables. An example of the sort of association you may wish to examine is:

> Is there an association between salary levels and job commitment and, if so, how strong is this association?

3   Techniques for examining how well scores on a variable can be predicted from scores on one or more other variables, and how much variation in a variable can be explained with one or more other variables. These techniques are based on associations between variables. Examples are:

> How well can you predict the job performance of employees if you know how conscientious they are and how committed they are?

> How much of the variation in the job performance of employees is explained by variation in their job commitment?

4   Techniques for identifying a small number of core theoretical variables underlying the relations between a larger number of directly measured variables, and examining whether specific constructs are being successfully measured by a questionnaire. Again, these techniques are based on associations. Examples include:

> Is there a set of core personality dimensions which underlie all of the specific ways in which people behave differently to each other?

> If you have developed a questionnaire to measure conscientiousness and commitment, do all items in the questionnaire clearly measure one of these two constructs?

Within each of these four categories, a very large number of techniques for use in specific circumstances have been developed. However, the aim here is only to cover those that you are most likely to use in your own research or find in journal articles. Chapter 5 will concentrate on the first of these four categories, differences. Chapter 6 will deal with associations, prediction and ways of identifying core theoretical variables and examining whether specific constructs are being successfully measured by a questionnaire.

As well as providing an introduction to a variety of techniques for analysing data, Chapters 5 and 6 also explain how to use *SPSS* to carry out these analyses, how to interpret the *SPSS* output and how to write up the results. For each statistical method there is a worked example.

If you have not carried out a particular analysis before, you may find it helpful to work through the example provided, using *SPSS* on your computer to reproduce the tables of data set out in this book.

When each type of statistical analysis is introduced, a table showing the size of the sample that will be required if it is to be used effectively is provided. The sample sizes have been computed from the information set out in the texts by Cohen (1988) and Bausell and Li (2002). These books, together with commercial software such as *nQuery Advisor* (www.statsol.ie/nquery/nquery.htm) and *Power and Precision* (www.power-analysis.com) make it possible to compute very exact sample sizes for a variety of statistical tests and methods, usually using information about three things: the required level of statistical significance (e.g. .05 or .01), the required power (e.g. 80 per cent or 90 per cent), and the effect size expected in the data to be produced by the research study. In practice, sample size calculations can be difficult, because while it is a relatively straightforward matter to choose the desired significance level and power for a study, determining the expected effect size is often problematic (see the discussion of how to estimate effect sizes on pages 49–50). Commonly, the researcher will have no more than an approximate estimate of the effect size that he or she expects to find and, as a consequence, it will only be possible to provide a rough estimate of the required sample size. In the sample size tables presented in the following two chapters, the somewhat rough and ready nature of most effect size estimates is reflected in the sample size figures given. The intention has not been to present exact sample sizes (e.g. 983 people will be required), and they have generally been rounded up slightly (e.g. from 983 to 1,000). With sample size analysis, as with other aspects of statistics, it is important to distinguish between accuracy and precision in presenting statistical information, and very precise sample sizes often suggest a misleadingly high level of accuracy in the estimated effect size. The reason for this is that, as explained above, most researchers do not have an exact and dependable estimate of the effect size they expect to find in the study they are about to carry out. If you *do* have a fairly precise and dependable estimate of the expected effect size, and obtaining a very accurate estimate of the sample size you will require in your study is important, refer to the texts by Bausell and Li (2002), or Cohen (1988), or to software such as *Nquery Advisor*, or *Power and Precision*. These provide detailed and precise sample size estimates (as well as making it possible to work out the power of a study with a known sample size). However, for those without very accurate and dependable effect size estimates, the tables presented here should prove helpful. Certainly, as you will see, they make it abundantly clear that with large effect sizes quite small sample sizes of 50 cases or less will often suffice, but that when small effects are present it is very likely that large samples of several hundred cases will be necessary. They also give a reasonable guide to a sensible sample size to use if you have no idea of the effect size you expect to find in your research study.

Chapter 5

Statistical methods for examining differences

This chapter covers eight commonly used techniques for examining differences. One of these is concerned with differences in proportions and the other seven with differences between means. As well as providing an introduction to these techniques, the way in which they can be carried out using *SPSS* will be explained. Furthermore, information about how to interpret the results of the *SPSS* output produced by the analyses, and how to write up the results of the analyses is provided.

DIFFERENCES IN PROPORTIONS

To examine whether the proportion of cases in one categorical dependent variable (e.g. gender) varies across the levels of a categorical independent variable (e.g. managers versus supervisors) the chi-square test is used.

DIFFERENCES IN CENTRAL TENDENCY

There are many statistical techniques for examining differences in central tendency, but some of the ones used most often by organizational psychologists are shown in Table 5.1. The various statistical techniques specified in this table have been developed for particular types of research design. Therefore, it is necessary to be familiar with some of the technical language used in research designs. The key concepts are briefly outlined below.

INDEPENDENT VARIABLES VERSUS DEPENDENT VARIABLES

In tests of difference, reference is normally made to independent and dependent variables. Independent variables are those that the researcher independently manipulates or contrasts in the research design, and the dependent variable is the variable upon which the outcome of this manipulation or contrast is measured. For example, the researcher may decide to compare the job performance of employees who have been through one of two training programmes. She decides to randomly allocate 100 employees either to training programme A or to programme B. Here, the manipulated independent variable is whether or not people have been on programme A or programme B, and the dependent variable, upon which the

Table 5.1 *Methods used to examine the statistical significance of differences in central tendency*

Number of independent variables	Number of levels of the independent variable	Independent samples versus paired samples or repeated measures	Statistical technique to use
One	Two	Independent samples	Independent samples *t*-test
One	Two	Paired samples or repeated measures	Paired samples *t*-test
One	Three or more	Independent samples	Independent samples one-way ANOVA
One	Three or more	Repeated measures	Repeated measures one-way ANOVA
Two or more	Two or more	Independent samples	Independent samples factorial ANOVA
Two or more	Two or more	Repeated measures	Repeated measures factorial ANOVA
Two or more	Two or more	One or more repeated measures and one or more independent samples	Mixed samples factorial ANOVA

outcome of this manipulation is measured, is job performance. Or the researcher may be interested in whether men and women differ in relation to their annual rate of absence. Here, the independent variable is gender (with males contrasted with females), and the dependent variable is the annual absence rate.

LEVELS OF THE INDEPENDENT VARIABLE

An independent variable is said to have two or more 'levels'. In organizational research, the independent variable is usually categorical (as against continuous), and each level represents a different category. Common examples are men versus women, and people who work in service-sector organizations versus those who work in manufacturing. Sometimes, these categorical variables have more than two levels. An example would be a study where the researcher wished to compare the well-being of people who work in marketing, people who work in finance and people who work in production. Here, there is one independent variable (type of department) with three levels (marketing, production and finance).

The various types of statistical techniques for examining differences set out in Table 5.1 differ in relation to the nature of the independent variables used: they involve independent or paired samples.

INDEPENDENT VARIABLES WITH INDEPENDENT SAMPLES

When the two or more levels of an independent variable refer to different groups of people, the independent variable can be said to have independent samples. So, if the independent variable is gender it will inevitably have independent samples because it will refer to a group of men and a group of women. Similarly, if one group of people has been trained, and a second group has not been trained, you again have an independent variable (training versus no training) with independent samples.

INDEPENDENT VARIABLES WITH RELATED SAMPLES

Independent variables are said to have related samples when you use a paired samples or a repeated measures design. In a paired samples design, people are deliberately matched as pairs on the basis that they have one or more critical features in common (such as gender and age). So, again, you might be interested in the effect of training on job performance, but instead of measuring the same people before and after training (a repeated measures design) you measure one group of people who have been trained, and another group who have not been trained, matching them on one or more critical variables which you believe will have a significant impact on their scores. For example, you might match the people according to their age and gender. In these circumstances if there is a male of 27 in the group who has been trained, you would match him with another 27-year-old male who has not been trained.

With a repeated measures design, each person is measured two or more times on the dependent variable, and this gives you several scores for each person. An example is the situation in which you measure the job performance of each person before and after training. The independent variable here is training, and it has two levels: before training and after training. It is a repeated measures design because the measurement of job performance is repeated on each person in the study – it is carried out once before training and is repeated after the training.

WHICH TEST?

When you have just one independent variable with two levels and independent samples (e.g. men versus women) use the **independent samples *t*-test**. With one independent variable with two levels and paired samples or repeated measures (e.g. the job satisfaction of employees measured before and after a training programme) use the **paired samples *t*-test**.

If you have one independent variable with three or more levels and independent samples (e.g. employees in finance, sales and production) use the **independent samples one-way ANOVA**. With one independent variable with three or more levels and repeated measures (e.g. the job satisfaction of employees measured before a training programme, immediately after the programme and one year later) use the **repeated measures one-way ANOVA**.

If you have more than one independent variable, each of these has two or more levels, and the samples are independent on all of the independent variables, use the **independent**

samples factorial ANOVA. If you have more than one independent variable, each of these has two or more levels, and you use repeated measures on all of the independent variables, use the **repeated measures factorial ANOVA**.

Finally, if you have more than one independent variable, each of these has two or more levels, and the samples are independent on one or more of the independent variables but you use repeated measures on one or more other independent variables, use the **mixed measures factorial ANOVA**. We will now consider each method in turn.

CHI-SQUARE TEST

When to use

The chi-square test is used when people have been measured on one categorical independent variable and one categorical dependent variable. For example, the independent variable might be gender and the dependent variable whether or not employees are promoted within two years of appointment. Each of these variables may have two or more categories. An example of a variable with two categories is gender (males and females), and an example of a variable with more than two categories might be level of seniority (e.g. senior manager, middle manager, junior manager). Before or during statistical analysis, the two variables are cast into a contingency table. Table 5.2 shows such a contingency table for the variables of gender and type of department (production versus human resources). Once in a contingency table, the combination of a particular row with a particular column is referred to as a cell. So Table 5.2 has four cells containing the values 25, 3, 75 and 9.

Technically, the chi-square test tells you whether the variable on the row (in this case, gender) is independent of the variable on the column (in this case, department). As such it is actually often viewed as a test of association rather than of difference. However, the chi-square test is easier to understand if it is viewed as a test of difference in proportions, and as it is equivalent to a direct test of proportions, this is not a problem.

Normally when the data are cast into a contingency table such as in Table 5.2, the question being asked is, 'does the proportion of people in each category of the dependent variable (e.g. the proportion of males and females) differ across each of the categories of the independent variable (e.g. production and finance)?'. If this is the case, it is helpful to place the independent variable in the rows of the contingency table, and the dependent variable in the columns. If you do this, and work out the proportion of cases in each row for each column in turn, as has been done in Table 5.2, it is easy to see the extent to which the proportions are similar. If you look at the first column in Table 5.2, production, the proportion of people in the two rows, representing men and women respectively, is 25 per cent and 75 per cent.

Table 5.2 *Men and women working in production and human resources departments: there is no difference in proportions across rows*

	Production	Human resources
Men	25	3
	(25%)	(25%)
Women	75	9
	(75%)	(75%)

Table 5.3 *Men and women working in production and human resources departments: there is a difference in proportions across rows*

	Production	Human resources
Men	20	9
	(20%)	(75%)
Women	80	3
	(80%)	(25%)

In the second column, human resources, although the frequency of cases is considerably less this time, the proportions of males and females are the same as in production (25 per cent males and 75 per cent females). The way chi-square works is to compute the number of cases you would expect in each cell if the null hypothesis is true, and compare this to the number that actually occurs in your data.

Because in Table 5.2 the proportions in each row are exactly the same in each column, there is no evidence in this case that the proportion of males and females differs across the production and finance departments. However, in Table 5.3 the situation is clearly different. Here, the proportions of men and women in the first column, production, are 20 per cent and 80 per cent respectively. In the second column, human resources, the proportion of males and females is different (75 per cent male and 25 per cent female).

We can think of the people in production and human resources shown in Table 5.3 as being two samples. A significant chi-square test indicates that the samples probably come from populations which have different proportions of people with the characteristic we are interested in (in this case, the 'characteristic' of being male or female).

It is possible to use the chi-square test on an unlimited number of categories within each variable. For example, in principle it could be used when the independent variable has 10 categories and the dependent variable has 15. However, if these data were placed in a contingency table, it would have 10 columns and 15 rows, resulting in a total of 150 cells. In these circumstances, if a difference were found between the proportion of people falling into the 10 columns across the 15 rows, the meaning of this would be almost impossible to interpret. In practice, therefore, chi-square is rarely used with a contingency table greater than 3 by 5 (one categorical variable has three categories and the other has five).

Examples

- An organization has three grades of seniority for managers. There is some concern that women are less likely to be represented in the more senior of the three grades. Here, therefore, the interest is in whether there is a statistically significant difference in the proportion of men and women across the three levels of seniority. The chi-square test is used to investigate this.

- An organization is concerned that women may be more likely to leave the organization than men. Chi-square is used to examine whether the proportion of men who have left the organization in the last year is significantly greater or less than the proportion of women who have left the organization in the past year.

Assumptions and requirements

The chi-square test is for categorical data. The main assumption of the chi-square test is that no case falls into more than one cell of the contingency table, so make sure that the design of the study producing the data you are analysing is such that no person can appear in more than one cell. For example, if the contingency table is based on two dichotomous variables: winners versus losers and men versus women, no man (or woman) should appear in both the winner category and the loser category.

Another requirement often cited is that no cells in the analysis should have expected frequencies of less than five. However, as Howell (1997, p. 152) points out, this convention is inconsistent with others, and there is no satisfactory basis for deciding which of these various conventions to follow. Furthermore, when total sample sizes are very small (e.g. less than 20) lack of statistical power is likely to be a much greater problem than the danger of violating distributional assumptions as a result of having insufficient expected cell sizes. For these reasons, if the recommended sample sizes shown below are followed, there should be no problem here.

The required sample size

Table 5.4 shows the sample sizes needed for 2 × 2, 2 × 3 and 2 × 4 contingency tables for small, medium and large effect sizes with a power of 80 per cent and a significance level of .05. If you wish to increase the power to 90 per cent, increase the sample sizes by 35 per cent.

The effect size for categorical data cast in a contingency table is referred to as w (Cohen 1988). You may wish to calculate w if you want to use the results of studies very similar to the one you have planned to estimate the sample size you will require in your own research, or if your intention is to use the results of a pilot study to estimate the sample size you will require. To do so either use the simple calculator available at www.dewberry-statistics.com or do it by hand as follows:

1 Draw the contingency table you expect to use in your research, labelling the rows and columns as appropriate.
2 Enter the figures in the cells from previous research findings, or from your pilot study.

Table 5.4 *The approximate sample sizes required for a chi-square test, assuming a power of 80% and a .05 significance level*

Effect size		Total sample size required for a particular contingency table		
	w	2 × 2	2 × 3	2 × 4
Small	0.1	785	965	1,100
Medium	0.3	90	110	120
Large	0.5	30	40	45

3   Work out the figure that would be *expected* in each cell if the null hypothesis is true. To do so, compute the total number of cases in each column, and then find the total number in each row. Next, calculate the total number of cases in all the cells of the table. Finally, to find out the number of cases expected in each cell if the null hypothesis is correct, multiply the column that each cell falls in by the row that it falls in and divide by the total number of cases.

4   Take each cell, subtract the value you entered in step 3 from the value you obtained with step 2, square the result, and divide this figure by the figure obtained in step 3.

5   To obtain w, add together the squared figures obtained in step 4 across all the cells, and then find the square root of the total.

Use Table 5.4 to find the nearest w to the one you have computed. For example, with a w of about .3, if you have a 2×2 contingency table and you expect a medium effect size, and are adopting the .05 significance level, you would need a sample size of about 90 to be 80 per cent certain of detecting a significant difference in the proportions, if one actually exists.

Table 5.5 *The gender of 20 employees working in two departments*

Case	Gender	Department
1	1	1
2	1	1
3	1	1
4	2	2
5	2	2
6	2	1
7	1	1
8	2	1
9	1	2
10	2	2
11	2	2
12	2	1
13	1	2
14	2	2
15	1	2
16	2	1
17	2	2
18	1	1
19	2	2
20	1	2

If you are not in a position to estimate the effect size, w, that you expect to find in your study, use the table to find the sample size you would require for a medium effect size.

A worked example

In this example, a researcher is interested in whether there is a difference in the proportion of males and females across two organizational departments: production and finance. So, here, the independent variable is whether people work in production or finance, and the dependent variable is their gender. To investigate the issue, the researcher randomly selects 20 employees and notes their gender and the department they work in. Gender is coded 1 for males and 2 for females, and department is coded 1 for production and 2 for finance. The data are shown in Table 5.5.

How to carry out a chi-square test using SPSS

Begin by entering your data in the *SPSS* Data Editor. Figure 5.1 shows what the data in Table 5.5 look like when they have been entered. The variable names used are 'gender' and 'dept' (for department). In this example I have used the *Variable View* in the data editor to enter full variable names for the variables 'gender' and 'dept' (not surprisingly calling them 'Gender' and 'Department'). The *Variable View* has also been used to enter the value labels of 1 for male and 2 for female, and 1 for production and 2 for finance.

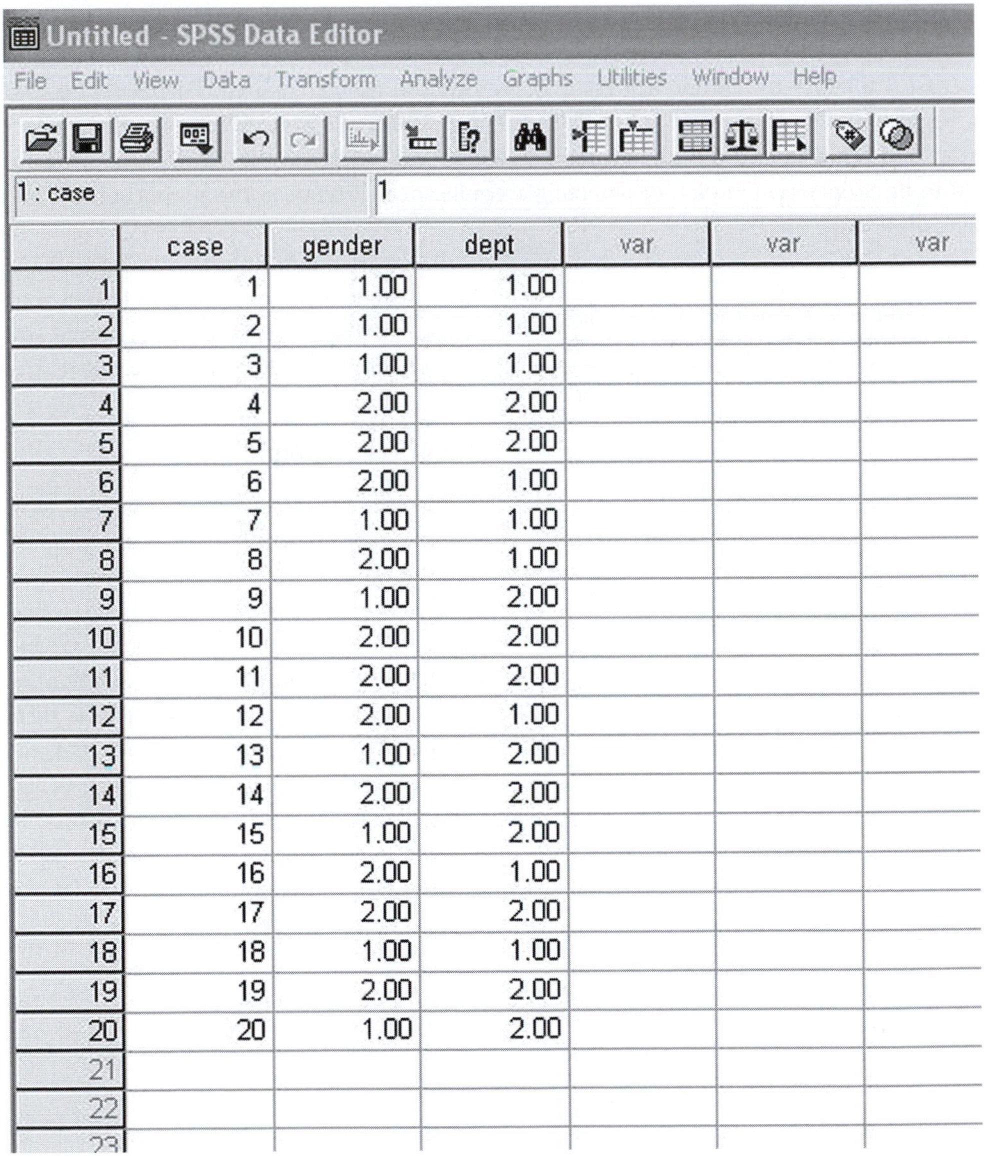

Untitled - SPSS Data Editor

File   Edit   View   Data   Transform   Analyze   Graphs   Utilities   Window   Help

1 : case   1

	case	gender	dept	var	var	var
1	1	1.00	1.00			
2	2	1.00	1.00			
3	3	1.00	1.00			
4	4	2.00	2.00			
5	5	2.00	2.00			
6	6	2.00	1.00			
7	7	1.00	1.00			
8	8	2.00	1.00			
9	9	1.00	2.00			
10	10	2.00	2.00			
11	11	2.00	2.00			
12	12	2.00	1.00			
13	13	1.00	2.00			
14	14	2.00	2.00			
15	15	1.00	2.00			
16	16	2.00	1.00			
17	17	2.00	2.00			
18	18	1.00	1.00			
19	19	2.00	2.00			
20	20	1.00	2.00			
21						
22						
23						

Figure 5.1 SPSS *Data Editor after chi-square data are entered*

To run the chi-square test:

➤ Click on **Analyze**.
➤ Click on **Descriptive Statistics**.
➤ Click on **Crosstabs**.
➤ A dialog box will open, with a list of your variables in the white rectangle on the left. Click on the independent variable, and then click on the small right arrow to the left of the white box headed **Column(s)**. This will move the independent variable into the **Column(s)** box (in this example 'department').
➤ Click on the dependent variable and then click on the small right arrow to the left of the white box headed **Row(s)** (see Figure 5.2) This will move the dependent variable into the rows box. In this example the dependent variable is gender.

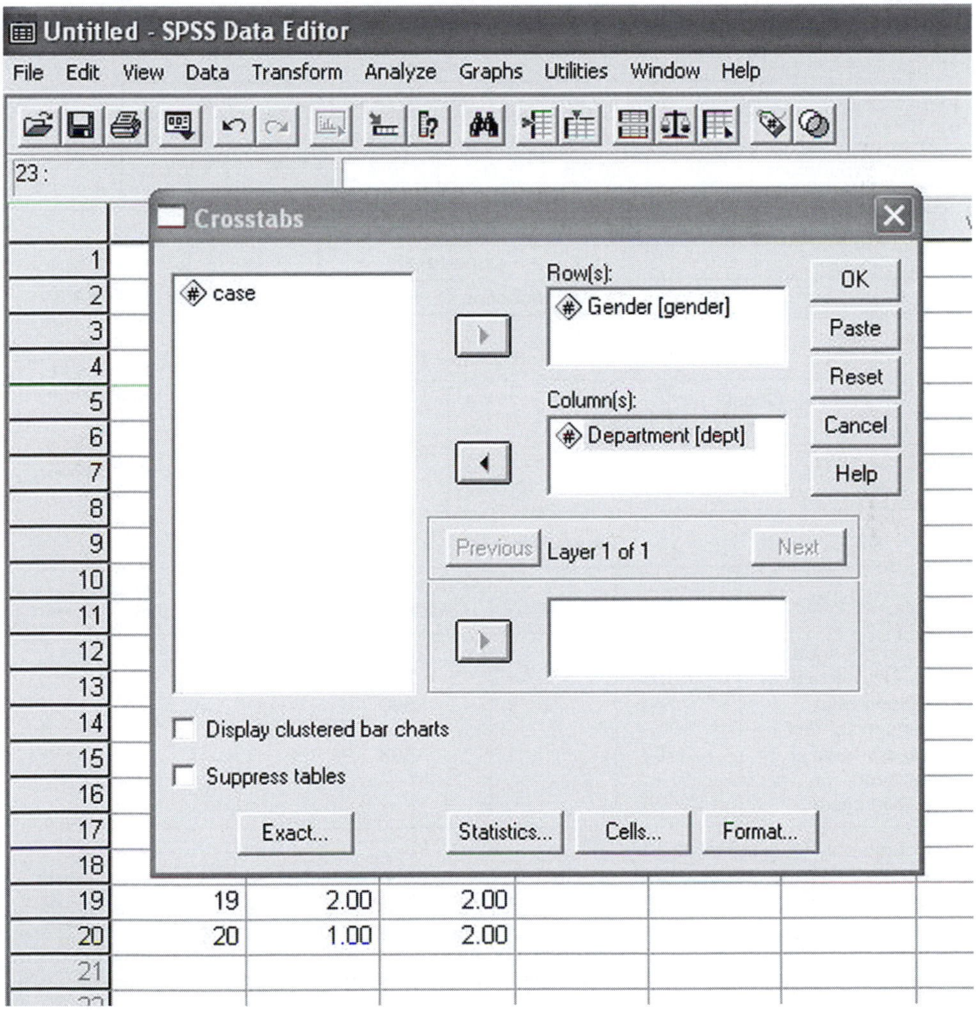

Figure 5.2 *Entering variables in* Crosstabs

➤ Click on **Statistics**.
➤ Click on the chi-square box. A tick will appear there.
➤ Click on **Continue**.
➤ Click on **Cells**.
➤ In the percentages area click on **Column**. A tick will appear.
➤ Click on **Continue**.
➤ Click on **OK**.

An output window will open with the results of the analysis as follows.

This table shows the total number of cases broken down by valid cases and missing cases.

Crosstabs

Case processing summary

	Cases					
	Valid		Missing		Total	
	N	Per cent	N	Per cent	N	Per cent
Gender* department	20	100.0%	0	.0%	20	100.0%

Gender* department crosstabulation

			Department		Total
			Production	Finance	
Gender	Male	Count	5	4	9
		% within department	55.6%	36.4%	45.0%
	Female	Count	4	7	11
		% within department	44.4%	63.6%	55.0%
Total		Count	9	11	20
		% within department	100.0%	100.0%	100.0%

This contingency table shows the number of cases in each cell, and the proportions within each column.

Chi-square tests

	Value	df	Asymp. sig. (2-sided)	Exact sig. (2-sided)	Exact sig. (1-sided)
Pearson chi-square	.737[b]	1	.391		
Continuity correction[a]	.165	1	.684		
Likelihood ratio	.740	1	.390		
Fisher's exact test				.653	.342
Linear-by-linear association	.700	1	.403		
N of valid cases	20				

[a] Computed only for a 2x2 table.
[b] 3 cells (75.0%) have expected count less than 5. The minimum expected count is 4.05.

Chi-square value.

Chi-square degree of freedom.

This is the probability of obtaining a difference in the proportions of males and females across the two departments as large as the one found here if the null hypothesis is true. Only if this figure is less than .05 can we say that the result is statistically significant.

How to report the results of a chi-square test

The results of this chi-square analysis might be reported as follows:

> Chi-square was used to examine whether the proportion of males and females varied across the production and finance departments. While 56 per cent of employees working in production are male, only 36 per cent of those working in finance are male. However, the difference between the proportion of men and of women in the finance and production departments is not statistically significant, chi-square $(1, N = 20) = 0.74$, $p = 0.39$.

Comments

- The figures given when reporting chi-square are, in turn: (1) the degrees of freedom; (2) the sample size (i.e. N); (3) the value of the chi-square test statistic; and (4) the probability value.
- If there had been a significant difference (i.e. the probability value had been less than .05) the last sentence would have been a little different. For example:

> There is a significant difference between the proportion of men and women in the finance and production departments, chi-square $(1, N = 20) = 9.90$, $p = 0.002$.

Interpretation

A non-significant chi-square indicates that, in the population from which we have sampled, the proportion of cases in each row does not differ across the columns. A significant chi-square indicates that, in the population from which we have sampled, the proportion of cases in each row does differ across the columns. Another way to express this is to say that when the value of chi-square is significant, for the populations from which you have sampled, the proportion of cases in each level of the dependent variable (e.g. men and women) differs across the levels of the independent variable (e.g. the production and finance departments), and when it is not significant the proportion of cases in each level of the dependent variable does not differ across the levels of the independent variable.

Whether the factor specified in the columns can be said to *cause* variations in the proportion of cases in each row, depends on the nature of the research. If a significant difference in proportions is found with a chi-square test, we can only infer that this is caused by the independent variable *if this is the only viable explanation*. In the example used here, it would clearly be absurd to claim that the department someone works in causes them to have a particular gender! In these circumstances, which are very common when chi-square analyses are carried out on data generated in organizational research, statistical significance merely tells us that the proportion of cases in each row are significantly different across the columns. It does not tell us *why* these proportions are different.

However, there are circumstances in which chi-square can be used to infer causality. Consider the situation in which 100 people with a rare disease are randomly divided into two groups. One group is given a drug designed to cure the disease, and the other is given a placebo, but otherwise there is no difference in the way they are treated. The proportion of people who recover from the illness is recorded. In this situation the only viable explanation for a statistically significant difference in the proportion of people given the cure who recover, and the proportion given the placebo who recover, is whether or not they were given the cure. In this type of very controlled research design therefore, where there is only one plausible explanation for a significant difference in proportions, chi-square can be used to infer the existence of a causal relationship between the independent and dependent variables. In all other situations a causal relationship between the independent and dependent variables cannot be inferred from a significant chi-square.

INDEPENDENT SAMPLES *t*-TEST

When to use

Use the independent samples *t*-test when you have one independent variable and one dependent variable. The independent variable specifies which of two groups people belong to (for example, males versus females, trained versus not trained), and the people in the two groups are different. You wish to know if there is a significant difference between the means of the two groups on the dependent variable.

Examples

- One group of managers is trained using an old method and another group with a new method. The job performance of the two groups is measured, and you wish to know if there is a significant difference between the mean job performance of the two groups. Therefore, job performance is the dependent variable, and the independent variable is whether managers have been trained on the old or the new method.
- You want to know whether there is a significant difference between the mean salaries of men and women in a financial organization. Here, the independent variable is males versus females, and the dependent variable is salary.

Assumptions and requirements

In ideal circumstances, the independent samples *t*-test is used with two samples drawn from normally distributed populations with the same variance. However, this *t*-test is a robust statistical technique and, in most circumstances, it stands up well to violations of these assumptions. Nevertheless, problems do arise when it is used with a combination of several different problems at once: populations with different variances, and severely non-normal distributions, and unequal sample sizes (Howell 1997). For this reason it is sensible to check the assumption that the population variances are equal and, if they are, use a slightly modified *t*-test which does not assume that the population variances are equal. Instructions for how to do this are given below, and this step should ensure that you do not draw unwarranted conclusions from the *t*-test results.

The required sample size

Table 5.6 shows the sample sizes required for small, medium and large effect sizes with a power of 80 per cent and a .05 significance level. The table indicates that if you wish to be 80 per cent certain of detecting a significant difference between the means of two populations, if such a difference exists, and the difference between the means has a medium effect size, you will require a sample of 130 cases, ideally with 65 cases in each of the two groups. To increase power to 90 per cent, increase the sample sizes by one-third. The relevant effect size for differences in means is d (see page 47). For information about how to establish the effect size you can expect in your study, see pages 49–50.

A worked example

In this example a researcher is interested in whether there is a difference in the well-being of men and women in an organization. He randomly selects 20 employees, notes their gender, and measures their well-being using a 10-point scale. Gender is coded 0 for males and 1 for females. The data are shown in Table 5.7.

How to carry out an independent samples t-test using SPSS

Begin by entering your data in the *SPSS* Data Editor. Figure 5.3 shows what the data in Table 5.7 look like when they have been entered. The variable names used are 'wellbe' (for well-being) and 'gender'. In this example I have used the *Variable View* in the data editor to enter full variable names for wellbe and gender (calling them 'Well-being' and 'Gender'). The *Variable View* has also been used to enter the value labels for gender of 0 for male and 1 for female.

Table 5.6 *The approximate sample sizes required for an independent samples t-test, assuming a power of 80% and a .05 significance level*

Effect size	d	Total sample size required
Small	0.2	800
Medium	0.5	130
Large	0.8	50

Table 5.7 *The gender and well-being scores of 20 people*

Case	Well-being	Gender
1	2	1
2	6	0
3	4	1
4	7	0
5	8	1
6	9	0
7	2	1
8	5	0
9	7	1
10	4	0
11	6	1
12	7	0
13	5	1
14	3	0
15	5	1
16	7	0
17	5	1
18	3	0
19	2	1
20	5	0

121

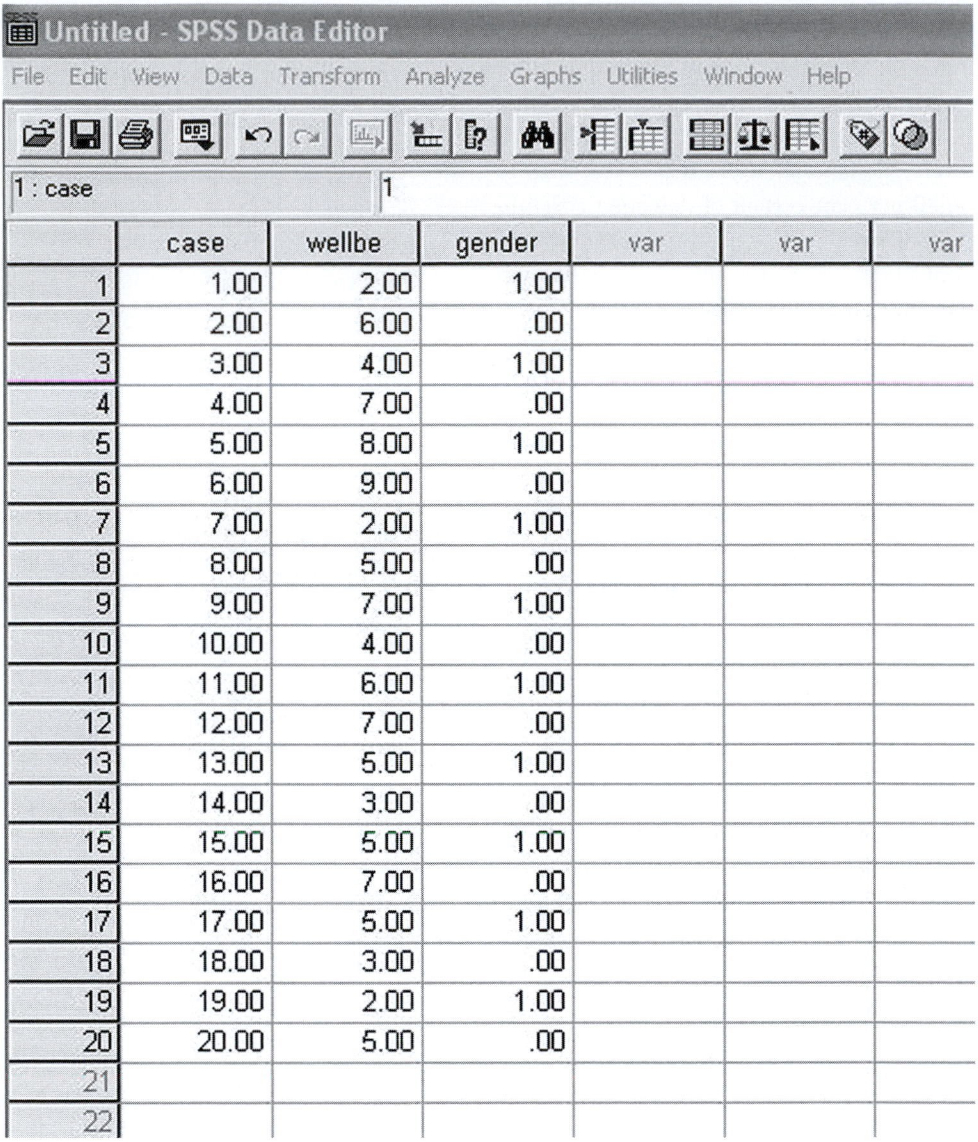
Untitled - SPSS Data Editor

File Edit View Data Transform Analyze Graphs Utilities Window Help

1 : case 1

	case	wellbe	gender	var	var	var
1	1.00	2.00	1.00			
2	2.00	6.00	.00			
3	3.00	4.00	1.00			
4	4.00	7.00	.00			
5	5.00	8.00	1.00			
6	6.00	9.00	.00			
7	7.00	2.00	1.00			
8	8.00	5.00	.00			
9	9.00	7.00	1.00			
10	10.00	4.00	.00			
11	11.00	6.00	1.00			
12	12.00	7.00	.00			
13	13.00	5.00	1.00			
14	14.00	3.00	.00			
15	15.00	5.00	1.00			
16	16.00	7.00	.00			
17	17.00	5.00	1.00			
18	18.00	3.00	.00			
19	19.00	2.00	1.00			
20	20.00	5.00	.00			
21						
22						

Figure 5.3 SPSS *Data Editor after independent samples* t*-test data are entered*

Next, run *Explore* in *SPSS*. To do this:

- ➢ Click on Analyze.
- ➢ Click on Descriptive Statistics.
- ➢ Click on Explore ....
- ➢ A dialog box will appear with the independent variable and the dependent variable in a white box on the left hand side. Click on the dependent variable

and then on the black triangle to the left of the white box headed **Dependent List**. The dependent variable will be moved across to the Dependent List box.

➢ Next, click on the independent variable and then on the black triangle to the left of the white box headed **Factor List**. The independent variable (in this example, gender) will be moved across to the Factor List box.

➢ Click on **OK**.

Output in the following form will appear.

Explore gender

Case processing summary

			Cases				
		Valid		Missing		Total	
Gender	*N*	Per cent	*N*	Per cent	*N*	Per cent	
Well-being Male	10	100.0%	0	.0%	10	100.0%
Female	10	100.0%	0	.0%	10	100.0%

Descriptives

Gender			Statistic	Std error
Well-being Male	Mean		5.6000	.61824
	95% confidence interval for mean	Lower bound	4.2014	
		Upper bound	6.9986	
	5% trimmed mean		5.5556	
	Median		5.5000	
	Variance		3.822	
	Std deviation		1.95505	
	Minimum		3.00	
	Maximum		9.00	
	Range		6.00	
	Interquartile range		3.2500	
	Skewness		.147	.687
	Kurtosis		−.703	1.334
Female	Mean		4.6000	.66999
	95% confidence interval for mean	Lower bound	3.0844	
		Upper bound	6.1156	
	5% trimmed mean		4.5556	
	Median		5.0000	
	Variance		4.489	
	Std deviation		2.11870	
	Minimum		2.00	
	Maximum		8.00	
	Range		6.00	
	Interquartile range		4.2500	
	Skewness		.046	.687
	Kurtosis		−1.004	1.334

Well-being

Stem-and-Leaf Plots

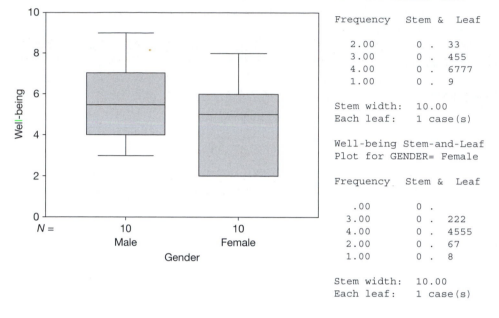

```
Well-being Stem-and-Leaf
Plot for GENDER= Male

Frequency   Stem &  Leaf

    2.00     0 .  33
    3.00     0 .  455
    4.00     0 .  6777
    1.00     0 .  9

Stem width:   10.00
Each leaf:    1 case(s)


Well-being Stem-and-Leaf
Plot for GENDER= Female

Frequency   Stem &  Leaf

     .00     0 .
    3.00     0 .  222
    4.00     0 .  4555
    2.00     0 .  67
    1.00     0 .  8

Stem width:   10.00
Each leaf:    1 case(s)
```

In the Table headed *Descriptives*, check that the minimum and maximum values given for your two variables seem correct, and in the box and whiskers plots look for any extreme scores. Details on how to do this are given on pages 90–1. If the minimum and maximum values are reasonable, and there are no outliers shown in the box and whiskers plot, follow the instructions below to perform the *t*-test.

If the minimum and maximum values don't look right, and/or there are outliers shown in the box and whiskers plot, check your data to make sure that the extreme values are not mistakes, and that from a research point of view it makes sense to include them in the analysis. If necessary, take steps to modify the data, and then run *Explore* again, repeating the process until you are confident that your data are sound. When you are confident that the data are acceptable, follow the instructions below to carry out the *t*-test.

In this example, the minimum and maximum values for both variables are reasonable, and there are no outliers shown in the box and whiskers plot, so we can proceed to the *t*-test straight away.

To run independent samples *t*-test:

> ➢ Click on **Analyze**.
> ➢ Click on **Compare Means**.
> ➢ Click on **Independent-Samples T Test . . . .**
> ➢ A dialog box will open with a list of your variables in the white rectangle on the left hand side. Click on the dependent variable and then click on the small black

arrow to the left of the white box headed **Test Variable(s)**. This will place the dependent variable (in this case well-being) in the box.

➤ Click on the independent variable and then click on the small black arrow to the left of the white box headed **Grouping Variable**. This will place the independent variable (in this case gender) in the box (see Figure 5.4).

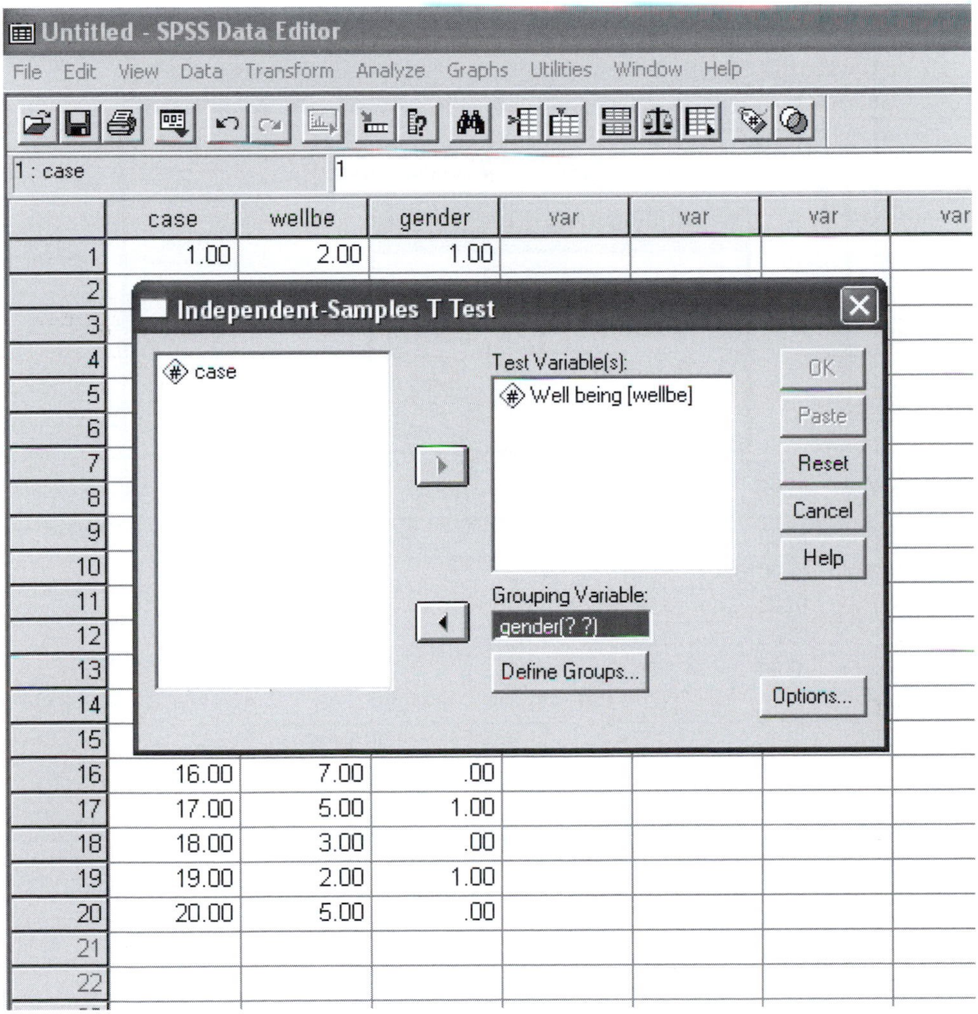

Figure 5.4 *Entering the test and grouping variables*

➤ Click on the **Define Groups** button.
➤ The dialog box shown in Figure 5.5 will open. Enter the two values of the independent variable in the white boxes. Because in our example males are coded 0 and females 1 (see Table 5.7), these are the two values shown in Figure 5.5.

125

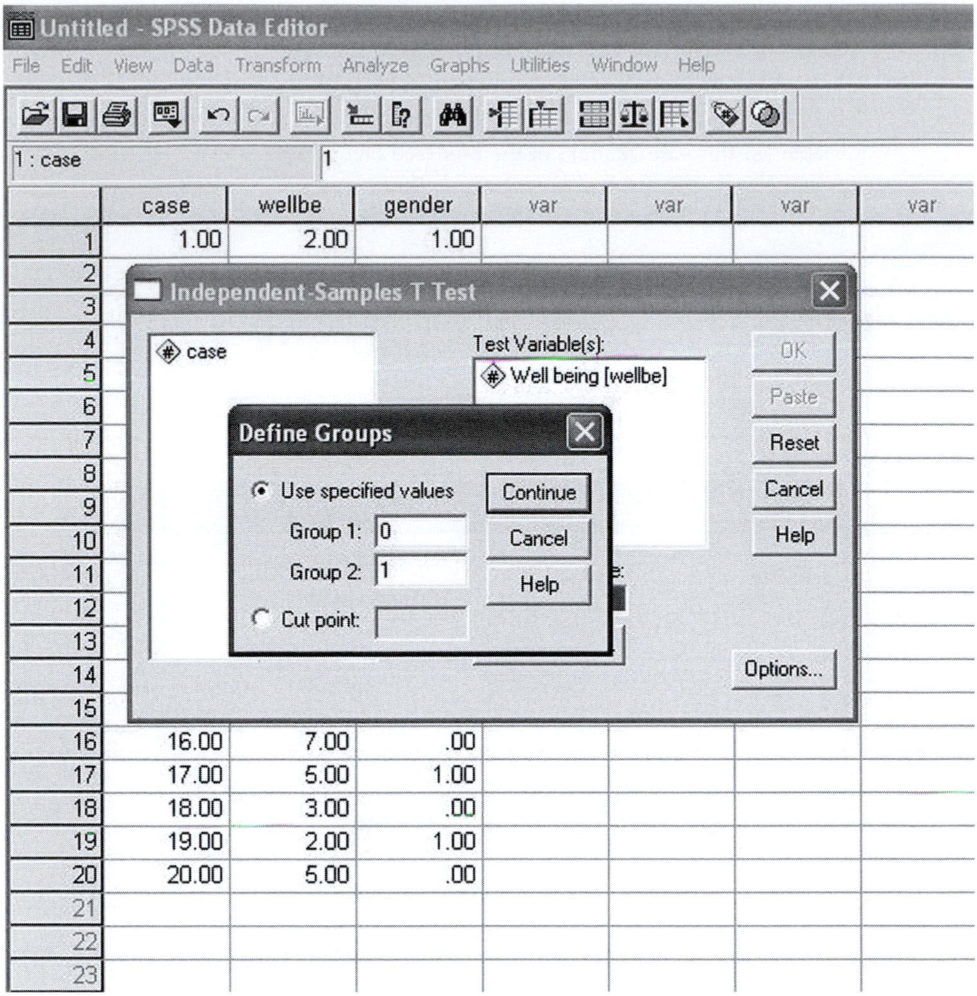

Figure 5.5 *Entering the levels of the independent variable*

➢ Click on **Continue**.
➢ Click on **OK**.

An output window will open with the results of the analysis as follows (see page 127).

In this example the *SPSS* results output indicated that there are 10 cases in each group, the means for men and women are 5.60 and 4.60 respectively, and the standard deviations are 1.96 and 2.12 respectively. In the *Independent Samples Test* table you will see that Levene's test of equality of variances is not significant in this example (because .87 is greater than the significance level of .05), and here we can therefore use, with confidence, the *t*-test results when equal variances are assumed. If Levene's test of equality of variances *had* been significant, it would be sensible to report the *t* value, degrees of freedom and probability value shown for *Equal variances not assumed* in the *Independent Samples Test* table.

Group statistics

Number of cases in each group.

The mean of each group (in this example males and females).

The standard deviation of each group.

	Gender	N	Mean	Std deviation	Std error mean
Well-being	Male	10	5.6000	1.9551	.6182
	Female	10	4.6000	2.1187	.6700

Independent samples test

		Levene's test for equality of variances		t-test for equality of means					95% confidence interval of the difference	
		F	Sig.	t	df	Sig. (2-tailed)	Mean difference	Std error difference	Lower	Upper
Well-being	Equal variances assumed	.027	.870	1.097	18	.287	1.0000	.9117	-.9153	2.9153
	Equal variances not assumed			1.097	17.885	.287	1.0000	.9117	-.9162	2.9162

Significance of Levene's test for equality of variances. If this figure is less than .05, use the t value, df, and significance level given for *Equal variances not assumed.*

t value.

Degrees of freedom.

Significance level: the probability of a difference in the means as great as the one here if the null hypothesis is true. This figure needs to be below .05 for statistical significance.

Referring to the *Independent Samples Test* table again we can see the results of the *t*-test. The *t* value is 1.10, there are 18 degrees of freedom and the (two-tailed) significance level is .287. The difference between the two groups' means is not significant in this case because .287 is greater than .05.

How to report the results of an independent samples *t*-test

The *SPSS* output would be reported as follows:

> The mean well-being scores were 5.60 (SD = 1.96) for males and 4.60 (SD = 2.12) for females. The 95 per cent confidence intervals for the means are 4.20 to 7.00 for males and 3.08 to 6.12 for females. The well-being scores of males and females were compared using an independent samples *t*-test. There was no significant difference between the well-being of males and females t (18) = 1.10, $p = 0.29$.

Comments

- SD refers to standard deviation.
- The figure in brackets after the *t* value refers to the degrees of freedom.
- The 95 per cent confidence intervals have been taken from the output of the *Explore* procedure carried out before the *t*-test.
- Sometimes the *t* value given in the *SPSS* output is a minus number. This will happen when the mean of the group coded 0 is greater than the group coded 1. However, in these circumstances it is not necessary to include the minus sign when reporting *t* as long as you provide the mean scores on the dependent variable for levels of the independent variable (i.e. males and females in the example used here).
- If the *t* value had been significant (say 2.86 instead of only 1.10, yielding a *p* value of 0.01), we would have said that there was a significant difference between males and females $t(18) = 2.86$, $p = 0.01$.
- If the *t* value is significant, it is very helpful to draw attention to the effect size when discussing the findings. For a difference in means the appropriate measure of effect size is *d*. This can be obtained by working out the difference between the two means and dividing this by the pooled standard deviation. An easy to use calculator which performs this function is available at www.dewberry-statistics.com. To use the calculator you simply need to enter the relevant means, standard deviations and sample sizes shown in the *Group Statistics* table on page 127. In this example the mean and standard deviation for males are 5.60 and 1.96 respectively. The mean and standard deviation for females are 4.60 and 2.12. Entering the figures for this example into the calculator we obtain a *d* of 0.49. However, in circumstances such as the one here in which statistical significance is not obtained, this effect size would not normally be reported.

Interpretation

A significant *t*-test result indicates that the population mean of one group is unlikely to be the same as the population mean for the other group. In the above example, if the mean for females was found to be statistically greater than the mean for males, you could conclude with 95 per cent confidence that, on average, women in the organization have greater well-being than the men who work there. A non-significant *t*-test result implies that we should accept the null hypothesis that there is no difference between the well-being of the two groups.

Of course, this conclusion depends on the extent to which you have representative samples of men and women. If your samples are not representative of men and women in general (if, for example, they are all middle managers) you need to be very cautious about generalizing your findings beyond people of this type. So, you could claim from your finding that, among middle managers in the organization, well-being is higher for women, but considerable caution is required in generalizing your findings beyond the type of people used in this sample. See the discussion of generalization on pages 50–1.

Whether the difference between the levels of the independent variable can be said to *cause* variations in the means on the dependent variable, depends on the nature of the research. If a significant difference in the means is found with a *t*-test, we can only infer that this is caused by the independent variable *if this is the only viable explanation*. In the example used here, even if the gender difference were significant, it would not be appropriate to claim that being male or being female causes a difference in well-being because there are many differences between men and women, not just one. In these circumstances, we may claim that males of the particular type sampled have greater well-being than females (or vice versa), but we cannot comment on why this is.

PAIRED SAMPLES *t*-TEST

When to use

Use the paired samples *t*-test when you have one independent variable and one dependent variable. Scores on the dependent variable are in pairs either because you have measured each person twice (you are using a repeated measures design) or because you have matched people on critical variables (e.g. age and gender) before collecting data from them (i.e. you have a matched subjects design). One score from each pair of scores will relate to one level of the independent variable, and the other score will relate to the other level of the independent variable. You wish to know if there is a difference between the population means for the two levels of the independent variable.

Examples

■   You want to compare the sales achieved by a group of salespeople: (a) when they are working in the office; and (b) when they are working from home. Half of the salespeople work from January to June in the office, and then July to December at home. The other half work from January to June at home and from July to December

129

in the office. Whether they are working at home or at the office is the independent variable, and the number of units they sell in a six-month period is the dependent variable. You wish to know whether the mean sales performance achieved by working in the office is significantly different from the sales performance when working from home.

■ You are interested in whether job commitment during the first year of employment is significantly greater or less than job commitment in the second year of employment. A group of newly employed people is identified, and their job commitment is measured half-way through the first year of employment and then again half-way through the second year. Here, the independent variable is first versus second year of employment, and the dependent variable is job commitment.

Assumptions and requirements

The paired samples measure t-test works by examining the distribution of scores produced when the difference between every pair of raw scores is calculated. The idea is a simple one: if the two samples are drawn from the same population (i.e. the null hypothesis is true), sometimes a score for level A of the independent variable will be greater than the score for level B, and sometimes the score for level B will be greater than the score for level A, but on average they will balance out, and the means will be the same. In other words, if the null hypothesis is true, the distribution of difference scores should have a mean of zero.

The main assumption of the paired samples t-test is that the population of scores from which the sample of difference scores has been drawn is normally distributed. However, the paired samples t-test is a robust technique and it can be used with difference scores drawn from populations which deviate markedly from a normal distribution.

The required sample size

Table 5.8 shows the sample sizes needed for a paired samples t-test for small, medium and large effect sizes with a power of 80 per cent assuming that the .05 significance level has been adopted. To increase the power to 90 per cent, increase the sample sizes shown by one third.

For the paired samples t-test, the necessary sample size depends not only on the usual parameters (i.e. the significance level, power and effect size) but also on the correlation between the two sets of scores. In Table 5.8 the sample sizes required for three different amounts of correlation are shown ($r = .4$, $r = .6$ and $r = .8$).

Table 5.8 shows that if you wish to be 80 per cent certain of detecting a statistical difference between the means of populations, if it exists, you are adopting the .05 significance level, you expect a correlation of about .6 between the two sets of scores, and you expect a medium effect size, you will require a sample size of 30. For information on how to decide on the effect size you can expect in your study see pages 49–50.

If you are unable to predict the effect size you will obtain in your study, assume a medium effect size and a correlation between the scores of .6 or a little less and use 30 to 40 people in your study.

Table 5.8 *The approximate sample sizes required for a paired samples t-test, assuming a power of 80% and a .05 significance level*

Effect size		Total sample size required for three levels of correlation		
	d	$r = .8$	$r = .6$	$r = .4$
Small	.2	80	160	250
Medium	.5	15	30	40
Large	.8	8	15	18

A worked example

In this example, a researcher is interested in whether a training course increases the job commitment of the employees who attend it. She randomly selects 20 employees and measures their job commitment on a 10-point scale before and after they attend the training course. The data are shown in Table 5.9.

How to carry out a paired samples t-test using SPSS

Begin by entering your data in the *SPSS* Data Editor. In this example, the variable name chosen for the measure of job commitment before attending the course is 'comitmt1', and the one for after they had attended the course is 'comitmt2'. Figure 5.6 shows what the data in Table 5.9 look like when they have been entered. The *Variable View* in the data editor is used to enter a full variable name of 'Commitment before training' for 'comitmt1' and 'Commitment after Training' for 'comitmt2'.

Table 5.9 *The job commitment of 20 people before and after a training programme*

Case	Commitment before training	Commitment after training
1	2	3
2	3	4
3	4	5
4	5	4
5	3	2
6	2	4
7	4	6
8	2	4
9	4	6
10	5	6
11	4	7
12	3	3
13	4	6
14	3	4
15	6	8
16	5	5
17	3	6
18	2	3
19	4	3
20	3	5

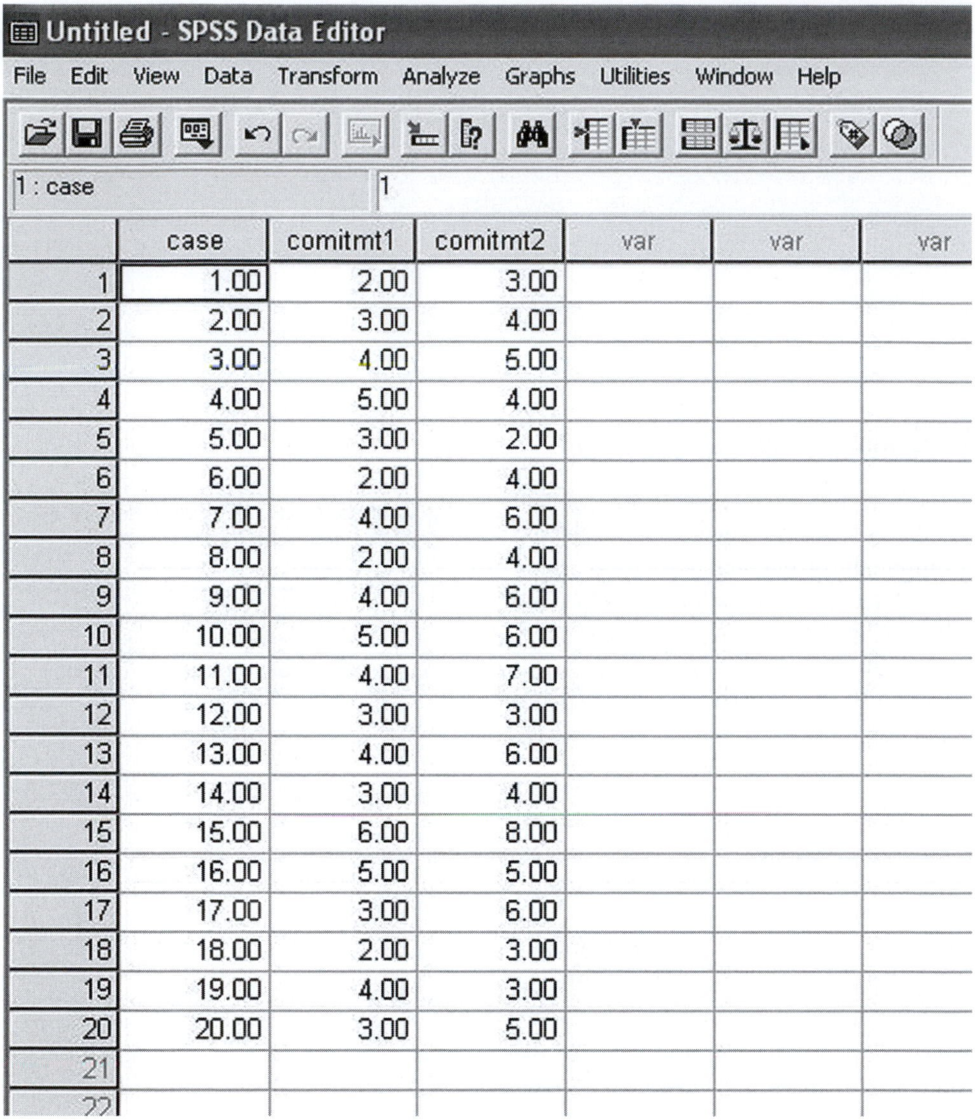

Untitled - SPSS Data Editor

File   Edit   View   Data   Transform   Analyze   Graphs   Utilities   Window   Help

1 : case   1

	case	comitmt1	comitmt2	var	var	var
1	1.00	2.00	3.00			
2	2.00	3.00	4.00			
3	3.00	4.00	5.00			
4	4.00	5.00	4.00			
5	5.00	3.00	2.00			
6	6.00	2.00	4.00			
7	7.00	4.00	6.00			
8	8.00	2.00	4.00			
9	9.00	4.00	6.00			
10	10.00	5.00	6.00			
11	11.00	4.00	7.00			
12	12.00	3.00	3.00			
13	13.00	4.00	6.00			
14	14.00	3.00	4.00			
15	15.00	6.00	8.00			
16	16.00	5.00	5.00			
17	17.00	3.00	6.00			
18	18.00	2.00	3.00			
19	19.00	4.00	3.00			
20	20.00	3.00	5.00			
21						
22						

Figure 5.6 *Paired samples t-test data entered in* SPSS

Next, run *Explore* in *SPSS*. To do this:

- ➤ Click on **Analyze**.
- ➤ Click on **Descriptive Statistics**.
- ➤ Click on **Explore** . . . .
- ➤ A dialog box will appear with the two levels of the independent variable in a white box on the left hand side. Click on each of these two variables and then on the black triangle to the left of the white box headed **Dependent List**. The two variables will be moved across to the **Dependent List** box. This is shown in Figure 5.7.
- ➤ Click on **OK**.

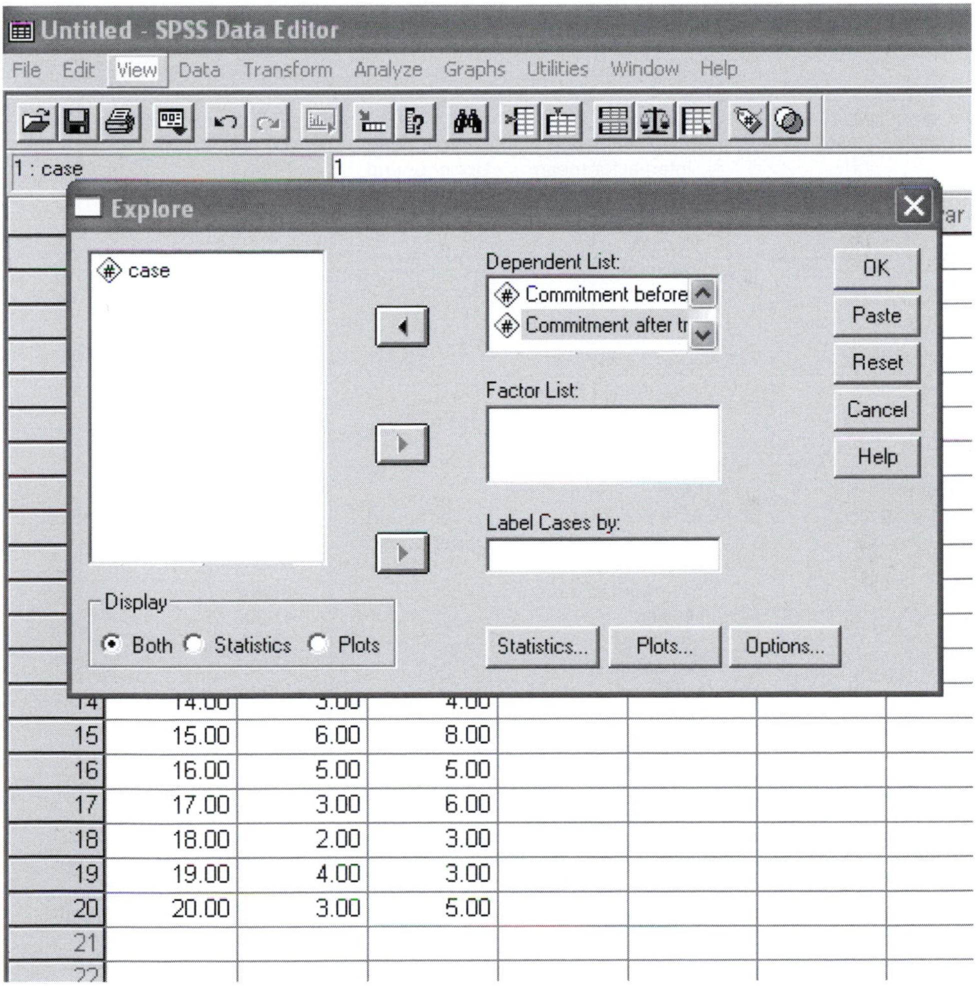

Figure 5.7 *Entering variables for* Explore *when carrying out a paired samples* t-test

Output in the following form will appear.

Explore

Case processing summary

	Cases					
	Valid		Missing		Total	
	N	Per cent	*N*	Per cent	*N*	Per cent
Commitment before training	20	100.0%	0	.0%	20	100.0%
Commitment after training	20	100.0%	0	.0%	20	100.0%

Descriptives

			Statistic	Std error
Commitment before training	Mean		3.5500	.25624
	95% confidence interval for mean	Lower bound	3.0137	
		Upper bound	4.0863	
	5% trimmed mean		3.5000	
	Median		3.5000	
	Variance		1.313	
	Std deviation		1.14593	
	Minimum		2.00	
	Maximum		6.00	
	Range		4.00	
	Interquartile range		1.0000	
	Skewness		.331	.512
	Kurtosis		−.474	.992
Commitment after training	Mean		4.7000	.34868
	95% confidence interval for mean	Lower bound	3.9702	
		Upper bound	5.4298	
	5% trimmed mean		4.6667	
	Median		4.5000	
	Variance		2.432	
	Std deviation		1.55935	
	Minimum		2.00	
	Maximum		8.00	
	Range		6.00	
	Interquartile range		2.7500	
	Skewness		.279	.512
	Kurtosis		−.501	.992

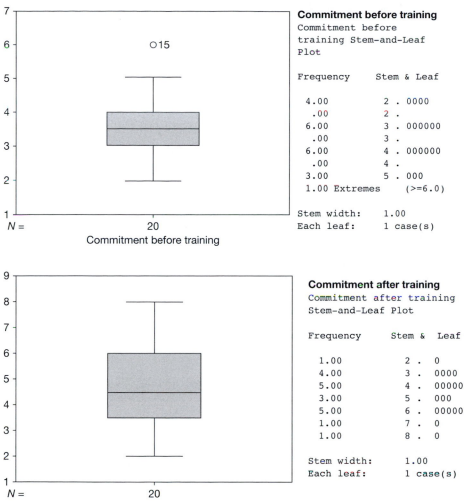

Commitment before training

```
Commitment before
training Stem-and-Leaf
Plot

Frequency        Stem & Leaf

    4.00         2 . 0000
     .00         2 .
    6.00         3 . 000000
     .00         3 .
    6.00         4 . 000000
     .00         4 .
    3.00         5 . 000
    1.00 Extremes    (>=6.0)

Stem width:    1.00
Each leaf:     1 case(s)
```

Commitment after training

```
Commitment after training
Stem-and-Leaf Plot

Frequency        Stem &  Leaf

    1.00         2 .  0
    4.00         3 .  0000
    5.00         4 .  00000
    3.00         5 .  000
    5.00         6 .  00000
    1.00         7 .  0
    1.00         8 .  0

Stem width:    1.00
Each leaf:     1 case(s)
```

In the table headed *Descriptives*, check that the minimum and maximum values given for your two variables seem correct, and in the box and whiskers plots look for any extreme scores. Details on how to do this are given on pages 90–1. If the minimum and maximum values are reasonable, and there are no outliers shown in the box and whiskers plot, follow the instructions below to perform the *t*-test.

If the minimum and maximum values don't look right, and/or there are outliers shown in the box and whiskers plot, check your data to make sure that the extreme values are not mistakes, and that from a research point of view it makes sense to include them in the analysis. If necessary, take steps to modify the data, and then run *Explore* again, repeating the process until you are confident that your data are sound. When you are confident that the data are acceptable, follow the instructions below to carry out the *t*-test.

In this example, one case with a score of 6 for *commitment before training* is highlighted as an extreme score in the box and whiskers plot. This data point was checked and found

135

to be acceptable. Therefore, no modification was made to the data file before running the *t*-test.

To run the paired samples *t*-test:

> ➤ Click on **Analyze**.
> ➤ Click on **Compare Means**.
> ➤ Click on **Paired-Samples T Test**.
> ➤ A dialog box will appear. Click on both of the variables you want to include in the analysis, and then click on the small back arrow to the left of the white box headed **Paired Variables**. The variables will move into the white box as in Figure 5.8.
> ➤ Click on **OK**.

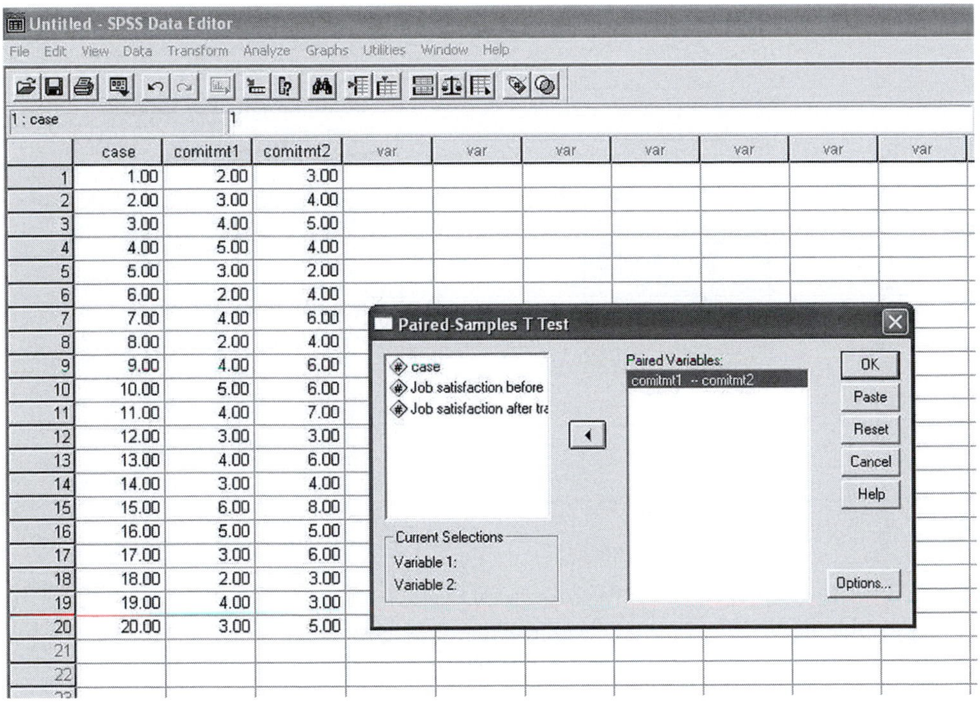

Figure 5.8 *Entering variables in a paired samples t-test*

The output will be as follows.

T-test

Paired samples statistics

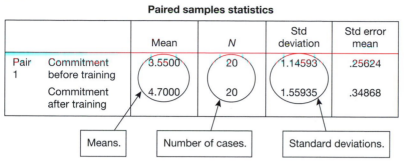

		Mean	N	Std deviation	Std error mean
Pair 1	Commitment before training	3.5500	20	1.14593	.25624
	Commitment after training	4.7000	20	1.55935	.34868

Means.	Number of cases.	Standard deviations.

Paired samples correlations

		N	Correlation	Sig.
Pair 1	Commitment before training and commitment after training	20	.627	.003

This table shows the correlation between the two sets of scores. You would expect the two sets of scores to be correlated because each pair of scores is either obtained from the same person or from pairs of people who have been matched on one or more critical variables. Here the correlation coefficient is .63.

Significance level: the probability of a difference in the means as great as the one here if the null hypothesis is true. This figure needs to be below .05 for statistical significance.

Paired samples test

		Paired differences							
					95% confidence interval of the difference				
		Mean	Std deviation	Std error mean	Lower	Upper	t	df	Sig. (2-tailed)
Pair 1	Commitment before training – commitment after training	−1.1500	1.22582	.27410	−1.7237	−.5763	−4.196	19	.000

t value.	Degrees of freedom.

How to report the results of a paired samples *t*-test

These results could be reported as follows:

> The mean job commitment was 3.55 (SD = 1.15) before the training course and 4.70 (SD 1.56) after the training course. The difference between the mean level of job commitment before and after the training course was examined with a paired samples *t*-test. Job commitment was significantly higher after the training course than before it *t* (19) = 4.20, *p* < .001.

Comments

- When the *t* statistic is reported, the letter *t* is followed by the degrees of freedom in brackets, then the *t* value, and finally the probability. Here, the *t* value actually given in the *SPSS* output is −4.20 rather than 4.20. The *t*-test statistic can be either positive or negative because it is sensitive to the difference in the means of two samples (see page 73). As long as you provide the mean scores for the two sets of scores (in this case the commitment scores before and after the training), it is not necessary to specify whether the *t* value is positive or negative. For this reason, the minus sign has been omitted here.
- Whereas in the independent samples *t*-test we gave the exact probability value, here it is reported as simply less than .001. The reason that we have not given the exact probability this time is that we do not know it. *SPSS* only gives the probability value to three decimal places. It is reported here as being .000, which means that, in fact, it might be .0002 or .00003, or *any* value less than .000. In this case the appropriate thing to say is simply that the probability is less than .001.
- If the *t* value had not been significant (say 0.02 instead of 4.26, yielding a *p* of 0.11), it would be appropriate to report that there was not a significant difference between the mean job commitment of employees before and after the training course *t*(19) = 0.02, *p* = 0.11.
- If the *t* value is significant, it is a good idea to draw attention to the effect size when discussing the findings. For a difference in means the appropriate measure of effect size is *d*. This can be obtained by working out the difference between the two means and dividing this by the pooled standard deviation. An easy to use calculator which performs this function is available at www.dewberry-statistics.com. To use the calculator you simply need to enter the relevant means, standard deviations and sample sizes shown in the *Paired Sample Statistics* table on page 137. In this example the mean and standard deviation for commitment before training are 3.55 and 1.15 respectively. The mean and standard deviation for commitment after training are 4.70 and 1.56. Entering the figures for this example into the calculator we obtain a *d* of 0.84. We can therefore say that not only is the difference between mean job commitment statistically significant, but also the effect size is large (*d* = 0.84).

Interpretation

A significant paired samples *t*-test result indicates that the population mean of one level of the independent variable is unlikely to be the same as the population mean for the other level. In the above case, the interpretation would be that job commitment tends to be higher midway through the second year of employment than midway through the first year.

As to whether we can say that the manipulation of the independent variable caused this effect, this depends on the nature of the research design rather than the nature of the statistical test. If a significant difference is found with a paired samples *t*-test, you can infer that this is caused by the independent variable *as long as this is the only viable explanation*.

In this example there are many factors other than the training programme that could have caused a difference between two sets of job commitment scores. All sorts of events could have taken place over the year within the organization, and outside it, that could lead the job commitment to change over time. Therefore, even if the difference between the means is significant, we cannot claim that the training programme was responsible for this.

INDEPENDENT SAMPLES ONE-WAY ANOVA

When to use

Use the independent samples one-way ANOVA when you have one independent variable and one continuous dependent variable, and the independent variable specifies which of three or more groups people belong to (for example, employees in HR, production and finance). You wish to know if there is a significant difference between the means of these three or more groups on the dependent variable. You may also wish to know whether there is a significant difference between the means of one or more pair of groups.

Example

■ An organization is based on three different sites. Turnover levels differ across the three sites, and management wish to know whether this may be because the extent to which employees are satisfied with their working environments differs across the sites. Fifty employees are randomly selected at each of the sites and given a questionnaire measuring how satisfied they currently are with the working environment. Therefore, the independent variable is which site the employees work at, and the dependent variable is how satisfied they are with the working environment.

Assumptions and requirements

In ideal circumstances the independent samples one-way ANOVA is used when three or more samples are drawn from normally distributed populations with the same variance. However, the ANOVA is a robust statistical technique, and stands up well to violations of these assumptions most of the time. Nevertheless, problems do arise when combinations of violations of assumptions occur, such as situations in which the populations have different variances, and the distributions are not normal, and the sample sizes used are not the same in each condition (Howell 1997). For these reasons it is sensible to check the assumption that the variances are equal with a test such as Levene's. If this indicates that the variances are likely to be unequal, use a test of the null hypothesis which will usually hold up even if there is evidence that variances are unequal. Welch (1951) has proposed such a test, and instructions on how to use the results of this test are given on page 150.

The required sample size

Cohen (1988) suggests the effect size measure f for determining the sample sizes required for an independent samples one-way ANOVA. This is obtained by finding the 'standard deviation' of sample means and dividing by the pooled sample standard deviation. If you are in a position to use a pilot study, or the results of previous research, you can use the effect size calculator for f at www.dewberry-statistics.com. This calculator requires information about the mean and standard deviation of the dependent variable obtained at each level of the independent variable, and the sample sizes these are based on. If you have run a pilot study to obtain this information, you can run *Explore* in *SPSS* to get the information you need. After using the calculator to obtain f, you can use Table 5.10 to find the approximate sample size you will require in your study. If you require a power of 90 per cent, increase the relevant sample size shown in Table 5.10 by 35 per cent.

If you have no way of estimating the expected effect size, f, before you carry out your study, use the sample sizes for a medium effect sizes shown in Table 5.10 if it is possible to do so.

Table 5.10 *The approximate sample sizes required for an independent samples one-way ANOVA, assuming a power of 80% and a .05 significance level*

Effect size		Total sample size required		
	Cohen's f	Number of independent variables		
		3	4	5
Small	0.10	1,000	1,100	1,200
Medium	0.25	150	180	200
Large	0.40	60	70	80

A worked example

In this example a researcher is interested in whether employees in the finance, production and sales departments of an organization differ in relation to job satisfaction. To investigate this she randomly selects 12 people in each department and measures their job satisfaction on a 12-point scale. The data are shown in Table 5.11. People are coded 1 if they are in finance, 2 if they are in production and 3 if they are in sales.

How to carry out an independent samples one-way ANOVA using SPSS

Begin by entering your data in the *SPSS* Data Editor. Figure 5.9 shows what the data in Table 5.11 look like when they have been entered. Use the *Variable View* in the data editor to enter full variable names, and to enter the value labels for the independent variable. In this example the variable names used were 'Job satisfaction' and 'Department', and because department is coded 1 for finance, 2 for production and 3 for sales, these were the values entered for 'Department' in the *SPSS Variable View*.

Next, run *Explore* in *SPSS*. To do this:

➤ Click on **Analyze**.
➤ Click on **Descriptive Statistics**.
➤ Click on **Explore** . . . .
➤ A dialog box will appear with the independent variable and the dependent variable in a white box on the left hand side. Click on the dependent variable and then on the black triangle to the left of the white box headed **Dependent List**. The dependent variable will be moved across to the **Dependent List** box.
➤ Next click on the independent variable and then on the black triangle to the left of the white box headed **Factor List**. The independent variable will be moved across to the **Factor List** box (see Figure 5.10).
➤ Click on **OK**.

Output in the following form will appear (see foot page 143).

Table 5.11 *The job satisfaction of 36 employees in three departments*

Case	Job satis-faction	Depart-ment
1	1	1
2	8	3
3	4	2
4	0	2
5	6	2
6	3	1
7	8	3
8	0	1
9	7	3
10	3	3
11	5	2
12	8	3
13	2	1
14	5	1
15	1	1
16	0	2
17	8	3
18	9	3
19	6	3
20	9	3
21	6	2
22	4	2
23	2	1
24	5	2
25	3	1
26	5	2
27	7	2
28	9	3
29	9	3
30	0	1
31	6	2
32	4	2
33	5	1
34	1	1
35	2	1
36	8	3

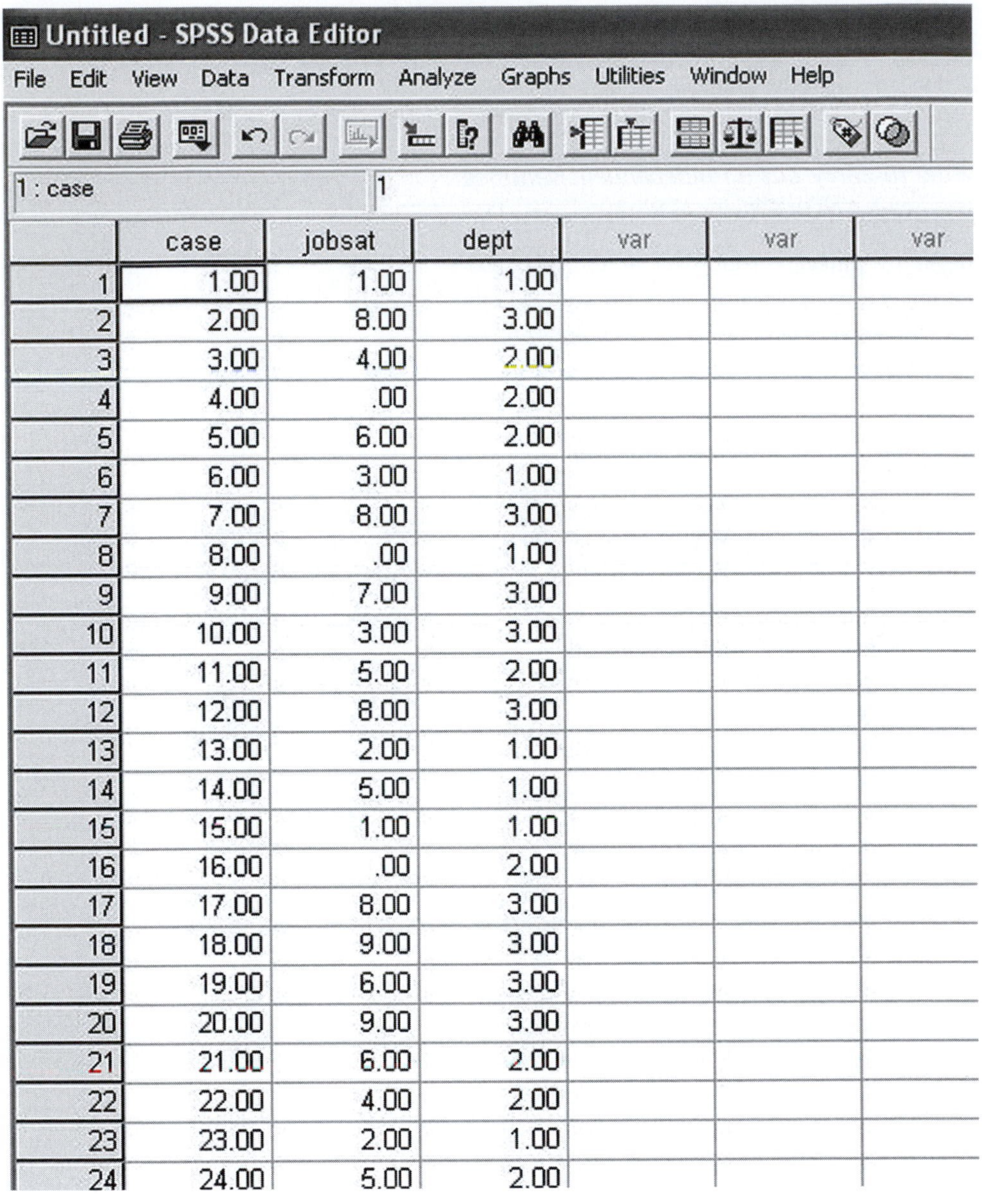

Untitled - SPSS Data Editor

File   Edit   View   Data   Transform   Analyze   Graphs   Utilities   Window   Help

1 : case   1

	case	jobsat	dept	var	var	var
1	1.00	1.00	1.00			
2	2.00	8.00	3.00			
3	3.00	4.00	2.00			
4	4.00	.00	2.00			
5	5.00	6.00	2.00			
6	6.00	3.00	1.00			
7	7.00	8.00	3.00			
8	8.00	.00	1.00			
9	9.00	7.00	3.00			
10	10.00	3.00	3.00			
11	11.00	5.00	2.00			
12	12.00	8.00	3.00			
13	13.00	2.00	1.00			
14	14.00	5.00	1.00			
15	15.00	1.00	1.00			
16	16.00	.00	2.00			
17	17.00	8.00	3.00			
18	18.00	9.00	3.00			
19	19.00	6.00	3.00			
20	20.00	9.00	3.00			
21	21.00	6.00	2.00			
22	22.00	4.00	2.00			
23	23.00	2.00	1.00			
24	24.00	5.00	2.00			

Figure 5.9 *Independent samples ANOVA data entered in* SPSS

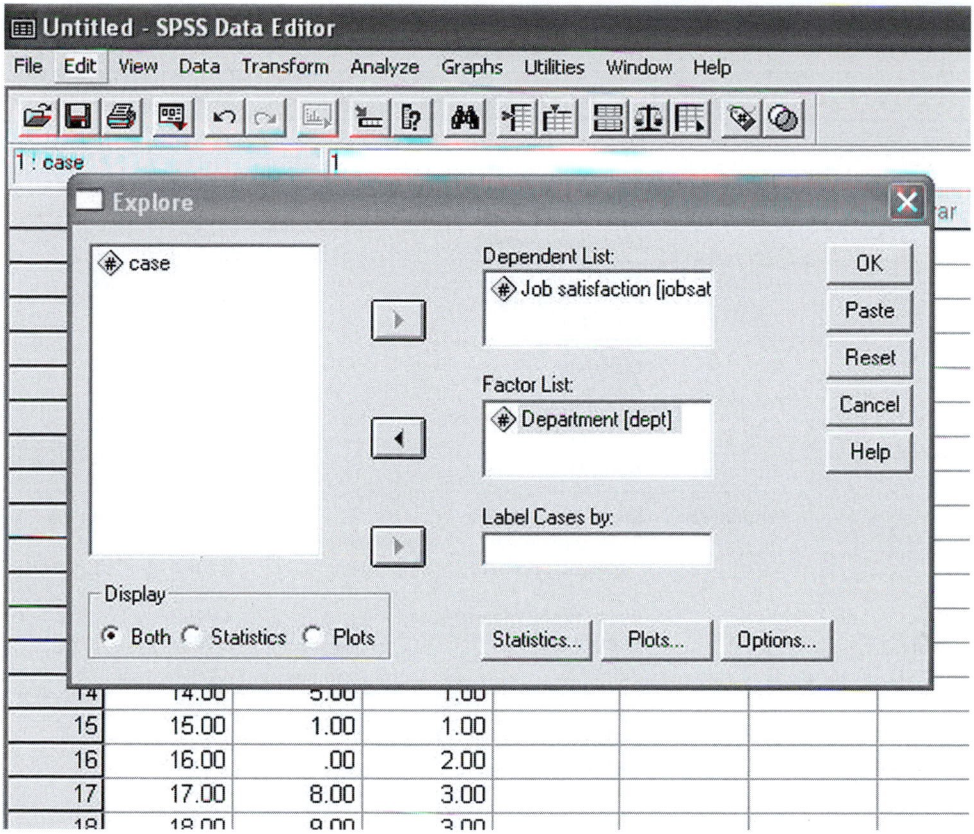

Figure 5.10 *Entering the independent and dependent variables for* Explore *when carrying out an independent samples one-way ANOVA*

Explore

Department

Case processing summary

		Cases					
		Valid		Missing		Total	
	Department	N	Per cent	N	Per cent	N	Per cent
Job satisfaction	Finance	12	100.0%	0	.0%	12	100.0%
	Production	12	100.0%	0	.0%	12	100.0%
	Sales	12	100.0%	0	.0%	12	100.0%

Descriptives

Department				Statistic	Std error
Job satisfaction	Finance	Mean		2.0833	.48396
		95% confidence	Lower bound	1.0181	
		interval for mean	Upper bound	3.1485	
		5% trimmed mean		2.0370	
		Median		2.0000	
		Variance		2.811	
		Std deviation		1.67649	
		Minimum		.00	
		Maximum		5.00	
		Range		5.00	
		Interquartile range		2.0000	
		Skewness		.678	.637
		Kurtosis		−.284	1.232
	Production	Mean		4.3333	.64354
		95% confidence	Lower bound	2.9169	
		interval for mean	Upper bound	5.7498	
		5% trimmed mean		4.4259	
		Median		5.0000	
		Variance		4.970	
		Std deviation		2.22928	
		Minimum		.00	
		Maximum		7.00	
		Range		7.00	
		Interquartile range		2.0000	
		Skewness		−1.271	.637
		Kurtosis		.940	1.232
	Sales	Mean		7.6667	.49747
		95% confidence	Lower bound	6.5717	
		interval for mean	Upper bound	8.7616	
		5% trimmed mean		7.8519	
		Median		8.0000	
		Variance		2.970	
		Std deviation		1.72328	
		Minimum		3.00	
		Maximum		9.00	
		Range		6.00	
		Interquartile range		1.7500	
		Skewness		−2.065	.637
		Kurtosis		4.809	1.232

Job satisfaction

Stem-and-Leaf Plots

```
Job satisfaction Stem-        Job satisfaction Stem-        Job satisfaction Stem-
and-Leaf Plot for             and-Leaf Plot for             and-Leaf Plot for
DEPT= Finance                 DEPT= Production              DEPT= Sales

Frequency  Stem & Leaf        Frequency  Stem &  Leaf       Frequency  Stem &  Leaf

   2.00     0 .  00            2.00 Extremes    (=<.0)       1.00 Extremes    (=<3.0)
   3.00     1 .  000           3.00       4 .  000           1.00       6 .  0
   3.00     2 .  000           3.00       5 .  000           1.00       7 .  0
   2.00     3 .  00            3.00       6 .  000           5.00       8 .  00000
    .00     4 .                1.00       7 .  0             4.00       9 .  0000
   2.00     5 .  00

Stem width:  1.00            Stem width:    1.00            Stem width:    1.00
Each leaf:   1 case(s)       Each leaf:     1 case(s)       Each leaf:     1 case(s)
```

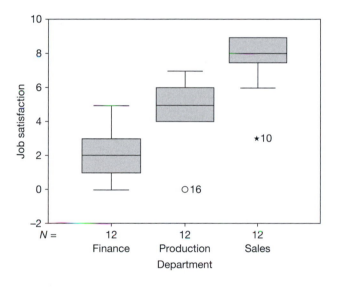

In the table headed *Descriptives*, check that the minimum and maximum values given for your three or more variables seem correct, and in the box and whiskers plots look for any extreme scores. Details on how to do this are given on pages 90–1. If the minimum and maximum values are reasonable, and there are no outliers shown in the box and whiskers plot, follow the instructions below to perform the ANOVA.

If the minimum and maximum values don't look right, and/or there are outliers shown in the box and whiskers plot, check your data to make sure that the extreme values are not mistakes, and that from a research point of view it makes sense to include them in the analysis. If necessary, take steps to modify the data, and then run *Explore* again, repeating the process until you are confident that your data are sound. When you are confident that the data are acceptable, follow the instructions below to carry out the ANOVA.

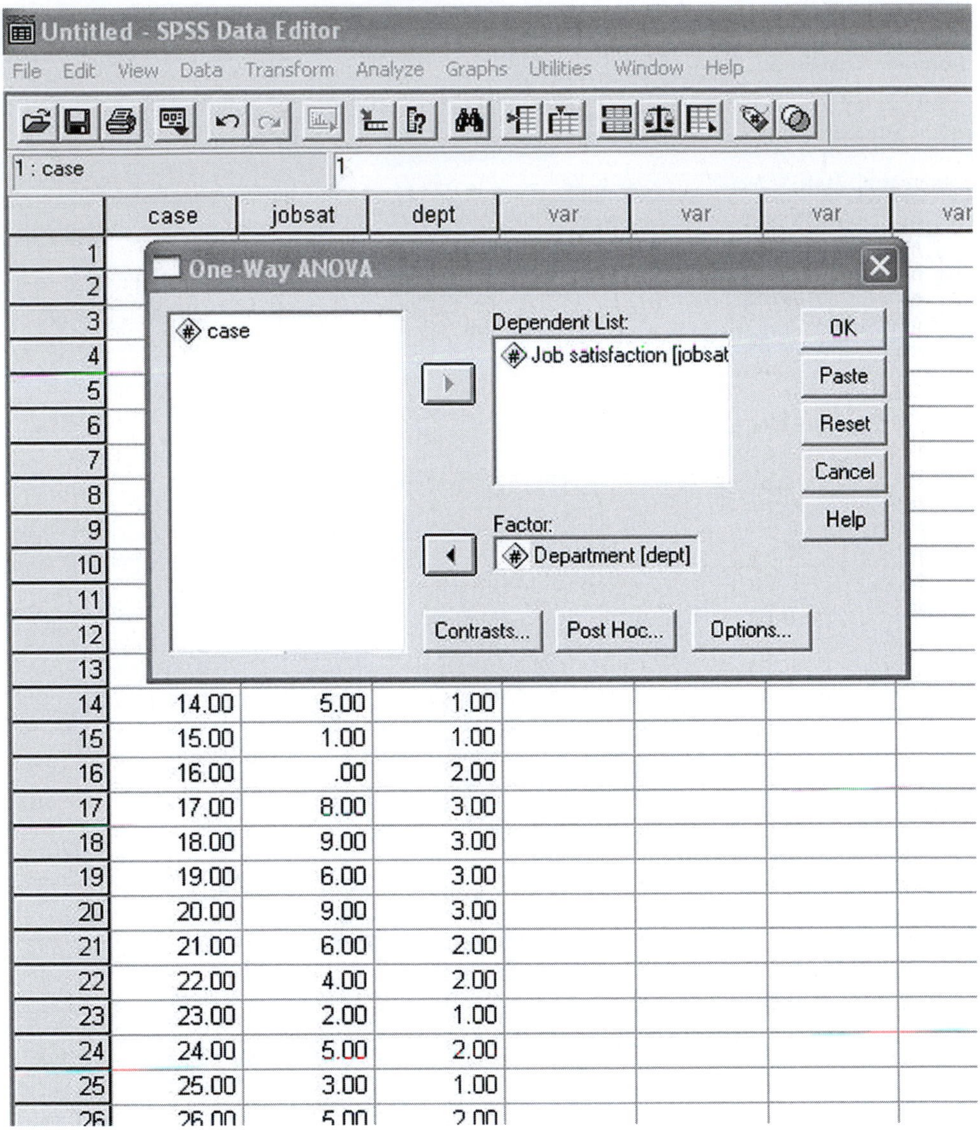

Figure 5.11 *Entering the independent and dependent variables when carrying out an independent samples one-way ANOVA*

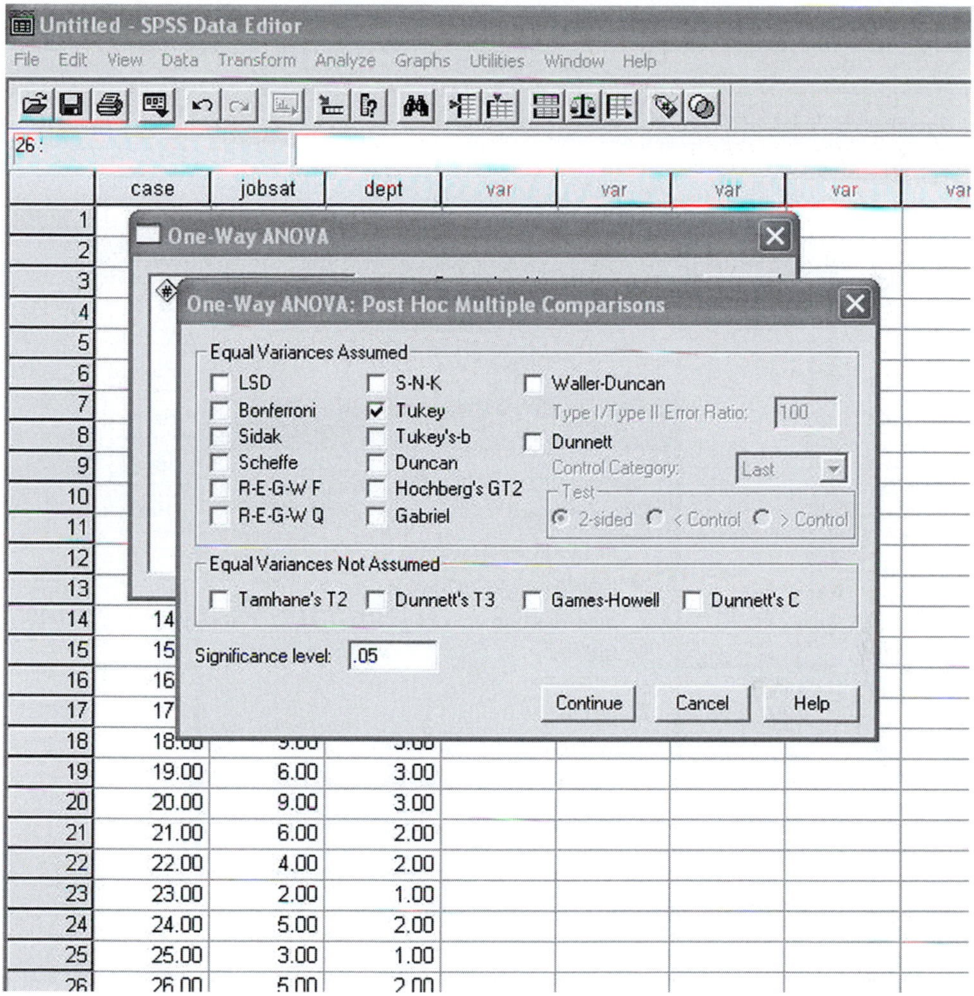

Figure 5.12 *Specifying Post Hoc Multiple Comparisons when carrying out an independent samples one-way ANOVA*

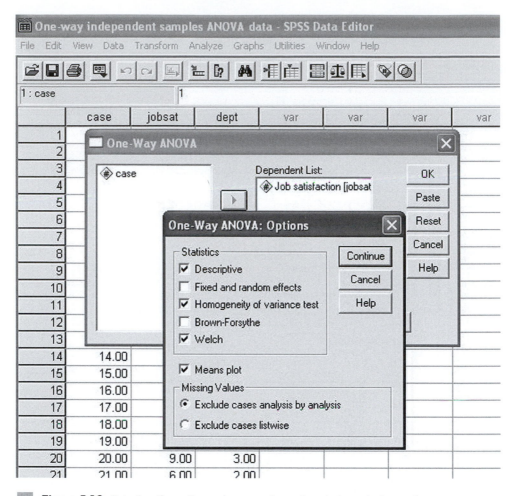

Figure 5.13 *Entering the options when carrying out an independent samples one-way ANOVA*

(Note that the dialog box is slightly different in *SPSS* version 10)

In this example, two extreme values appear to have been identified on the box and whiskers plot. Case number 46, from production, is identified as getting a particularly low score of 0; and case number 10, from sales, gets a relatively low score of 3. In fact, the case number 46 does not actually exist. Because *SPSS* found several outlying values of zero for production (i.e. cases 4, 8, 16 and 30) it has attempted to print them all on the box and whiskers plot, and has ended up just printing case 16 on top of case 4. This illustrates the importance of checking data carefully for outlying values rather than just relying on the *SPSS* output to identify all of them. In this example these four data points were checked and found to be acceptable. Therefore, no modification was made to the data file before running the ANOVA.

To run an independent samples one-way ANOVA in *SPSS*:

> ➤ Click on **Analyze**.
> ➤ Click on **Compare Means**.
> ➤ Click on **One-Way ANOVA . . . .**
> ➤ A dialog box will appear. Click on the dependent variable. It will be highlighted in blue. Click on the black triangle to the left of the box headed **Dependent List**. The dependent variable will be moved across to this box.
> ➤ Click on the independent variable. It will be highlighted in blue. Click on the black triangle to the left of the box headed **Factor**. The dependent variable will be moved across to this box (see Figure 5.11).
> ➤ Click on **Post Hoc . . . .** A dialog box will appear.
> ➤ Click on the white box next to **Tukey**. A tick will appear in the box (see Figure 5.12).
> ➤ Click on **Continue**.
> ➤ Click on **Options . . . .**
> ➤ Click in the white boxes next to **Descriptive, Homogeneity-of-variance test, Welch,**[1] and **Means plot** (see Figure 5.13).
> ➤ Click on **Continue**.
> ➤ Click on **OK**.

The results will appear in the output file as follows.

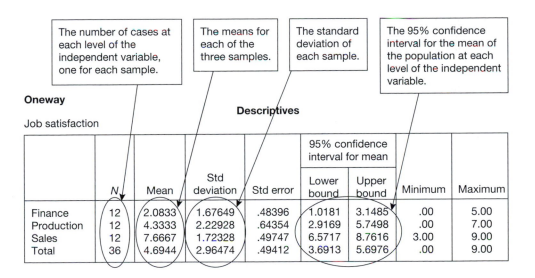

| The number of cases at each level of the independent variable, one for each sample. | The means for each of the three samples. | The standard deviation of each sample. | The 95% confidence interval for the mean of the population at each level of the independent variable. |

Oneway

Descriptives

Job satisfaction

	N	Mean	Std deviation	Std error	95% confidence interval for mean		Minimum	Maximum
					Lower bound	Upper bound		
Finance	12	2.0833	1.67649	.48396	1.0181	3.1485	.00	5.00
Production	12	4.3333	2.22928	.64354	2.9169	5.7498	.00	7.00
Sales	12	7.6667	1.72328	.49747	6.5717	8.7616	3.00	9.00
Total	36	4.6944	2.96474	.49412	3.6913	5.6976	.00	9.00

....

1 Not available in *SPSS* version 10.

Test of homogeneity of variances

Job satisfaction

Levene statistic	df1	df2	Sig.
.414	2	33	.664

Significance of a test that the samples are drawn from populations with the same variance. If this test is significant (i.e. less than .05) you should use the robust test of equality of means.

ANOVA

Job satisfaction

	Sum of squares	df	Mean square	F	Sig.
Between groups	189.389	2	94.694	26.426	.000
Within groups	118.250	33	3.583		
Total	307.639	35			

The probability that the null hypothesis is true, given the differences between the means of the groups examined. The value needs to be less than .05 for statistical significance.

Degrees of freedom.

The test statistic, F.

Robust tests of equality of means

Job satisfaction

	Statistic[a]	df1	df2	Sig.
Welch	31.591	2	21.710	.000

[a] Asymptotically F distributed.

The test statistic, F, that should be used if the test for homogeneity of variances is significant. This is not available in *SPSS* version 10.

The probability that the null hypothesis is true, given the differences between the means of the groups examined. This figure must be below .05 for statistical significance.

Degrees of freedom.

Post hoc tests

Multiple comparisons

Dependent variable: Job satisfaction
Tukey HSD

(I) Department	(J) Department	Mean difference (I–J)	Std error	Sig.	95% confidence interval	
					Lower bound	Upper bound
Finance	Production	−2.2500*	.77280	.017	−4.1463	−.3537
	Sales	−5.5833*	.77280	.000	−7.4796	−3.6870
Production	Finance	2.2500*	.77280	.017	.3537	4.1463
	Sales	−3.3333*	.77280	.000	−5.2296	−1.4370
Sales	Finance	5.5833*	.77280	.000	3.6870	7.4796
	Production	3.3333*	.77280	.000	1.4370	5.2296

* The mean difference is significant at the .05 level

Homogeneous subsets

Job satisfaction

Tukey HSD[a]

Department	N	Subset for alpha = .05		
		1	2	3
Finance	12	2.0833		
Production	12		4.3333	
Sales	12			7.6667
Sig.		1.000	1.000	1.000

Means for groups in homgeneous subsets are displayed.
[a] Uses harmonic mean sample size = 12.000.

> These values give the probability, based on Tukey's honestly significant difference test (HSD), that there is a difference between a given pair of independent variable levels. In this example the first value is concerned with the difference between Finance and Production (p = .017), the second between Finance and Sales (p = .000), and so on.

Means plots

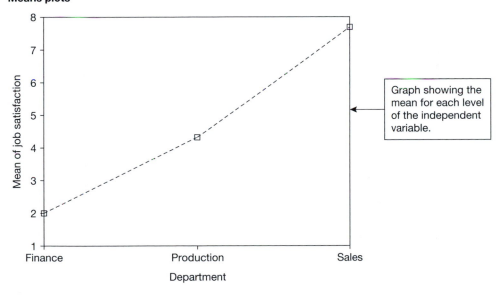

> Graph showing the mean for each level of the independent variable.

How to report the results of an independent samples one-way ANOVA

These results can be reported as follows:

> The mean levels of job satisfaction were compared between people in the finance, production and sales departments. The mean levels of job satisfaction were 2.08 (SD = 1.68) for finance, 4.33 (SD = 2.23) for production and 7.67 (SD = 1.72) in sales. The 95 per cent confidence intervals for the means are 1.02 to 3.15 for finance, 2.92 to 5.75 for production and 6.57 to 8.76 for sales. An independent samples one-way analysis of variance showed that there is a significant difference between the level of satisfaction across the three departments $F(2, 33) = 26.43$, $p < .001$.

151

Tukey HSD tests were used to examine the differences between the mean job satisfaction in specific pairs of departments, and significant differences in mean job satisfaction were found between the departments of finance and production, $p = .017$, and between the departments of production and sales, $p < .001$.

Comments

- The means, standard deviations and 95 per cent confidence intervals are taken from the first table in the output: *Descriptives*.
- For ANOVA it is necessary to provide both the degrees of freedom between groups and the degrees of freedom within groups. That is why when the results of the ANOVA are reported there are two numbers in the brackets after the F value: two for the between groups degrees of freedom, and 33 for the within groups degrees of freedom.
- SD refers to the standard deviation.
- In this example, Levene's test of homogeneity of variances has a value of .664. To be statistically significant, this figure must be below .05. In this example, Levene's statistic is not significant and, consequently, the F value, degrees of freedom and significance value reported, are taken from the main ANOVA results table.
- If Levene's test is significant (i.e. less than .05), the ANOVA F value, degrees of freedom and significance value should be taken from the *Robust Test of Equality of Means* table. Unfortunately this is not possible in *SPSS* version 10.
- The results for the Tukey test have been taken from the *Multiple Comparisons* table. Which of the various pairs of the levels of the independent variable are presented in this table depends on what is of interest to you in the context of the research. For example, here, no Tukey significance level is given for the comparison between the job satisfaction in the finance and sales departments, but this information is available in the *Multiple Comparisons* table if required.
- If the F value is significant, it is very helpful to draw attention to the effect size when discussing the findings. For a difference in means the appropriate measure of effect size is d. For a particular pair of means this can be obtained by working out the difference between the two and dividing this by the pooled standard deviation. An easy to use calculator which performs this function is available at www.dewberry-statistics.com. To use the calculator you simply need to enter the relevant means, standard deviations and sample sizes shown in the *Descriptive Statistics* table on page 149. In this example, if we wished to report the effect size of the difference between finance and production we would need the mean and standard deviation of each of these. Consulting the descriptive statistics table, the mean and standard deviation for finance are 2.08 and 1.68 respectively. The mean and standard deviation for production are 4.33 and 2.23. Entering the figures for this example into the calculator we obtain a d of 1.14. We can therefore say that not only is the difference between mean finance and production statistically significant according to

Tukey's honestly significant difference (HSD) test, but also the effect size is large ($d = 1.14$). Which of the effect sizes you choose to mention will depend on the particular focus of your research, and what you consider relevant in the light of this.

Interpretation

If the results of a one-way ANOVA are found to be significant, the interpretation is that the population means are different across the three or more groups. In the above case, if a significant difference had been found between the three sites, you could conclude that the mean level of satisfaction with the working environment probably differs across the three sites.

If a statistical difference is found across the three or more groups this does not imply that there is a difference in the population means of any *pair* of groups. It simply indicates that the groups entered into the ANOVA are unlikely to be drawn from populations with the same mean. A non-significant one-way ANOVA indicates that we cannot be at least 95 per cent certain that the groups have the same population mean on the dependent variable.

If comparisons are required between particular pairs of levels of the independent variable it is possible to examine this with a series of independent samples t-tests. However, the Tukey test requested in this analysis is better because it controls for the inflated risk of a Type I error which occurs when several pairs of means are compared.

Whether the difference between the levels of the independent variable can be said to *cause* variations in the means on the dependent variable, depends on the nature of the research. If a significant difference in the means is found with an ANOVA, we can only infer that this is caused by the independent variable *if this is the only viable explanation*. In the example used here, even if there is a significant difference between the three levels of the independent variable, it would not be appropriate to claim that whether people work in finance, production or sales causes a difference in mean job satisfaction, because there are many potential differences between the people who work in these three departments. In these circumstances, we may claim that mean job satisfaction varies across the departments, but we cannot comment on why this is.

REPEATED MEASURES ONE-WAY ANOVA

When to use

Use the repeated measures one-way ANOVA when you have one independent variable and one dependent variable, and the independent variable has three or more levels. Each level of the independent variable specifies a particular time or situation in which the same people have been measured. Therefore, you have three or more sets of scores, all obtained from the same sample of people, but each one collected at a different time or situation. You wish to know if there is a significant difference between the means of the three or more variables. You may also wish to know whether there is a significant difference between the means of one or more pairs of levels of the independent variable.

153

Examples

■ An organization decides to modify its organizational structure. One of the goals of this is to increase the performance of sales staff. A decision is taken to compare the performance of the sales staff before the restructuring takes place and then again six months and one year later. This will produce three performance scores for each salesperson, the score before the restructuring, a score six months after restructuring, and a score one year after restructuring. One hundred sales people are randomly selected from the organization and their three-monthly sales figures are recorded at each of the three time points. A repeated measures one-way ANOVA is used to examine whether there is a significant difference in sales across the three periods.

■ A company is aware that staff are unhappy at the very long hours they have to work. This seems particularly problematic for men and women with children as they find it difficult to maintain the working hours that are expected of them and to spend enough time with their families. A consultancy is brought in to help with this problem, and they recommend several changes to existing organizational practices. The organization decides to look for evidence that these new practices are effective, and decides to measure the extent to which staff with children are satisfied with the amount of time they have for their families before the new practices are implemented, and at three points of time afterwards. A repeated measures one-way ANOVA is used to compare the mean level of satisfaction of the staff at these four time points.

Assumptions and requirements

The main assumption of a repeated measures ANOVA is equality of covariance. This is best explained with an example. Imagine that we measure the well-being of 50 employees on three occasions: (a) before; (b) immediately after; and (c) three years after an organizational change programme. We have three sets of 50 well-being scores, and this makes it possible to correlate each of the three possible combinations of scores (that is, a with b, a with c, and b with c). By doing this we obtain three correlation coefficients. The assumption of equality of covariance states that the degree of correlation will not vary across these three combinations. Often, there is reason to believe that this assumption may be violated. In the example used here it is quite possible that the degree of well-being immediately before and after the change programme may be more similar than the degree of well-being three years later. If this is the case, the assumption of equality of covariance is violated. Fortunately there are a number of steps that can be taken to deal with this potential problem, and a good discussion of the issues can be found in Tabachnick and Fidell (2001). Here, we will adopt the approach of using the Huynh-Feldt correction. This corrects for any violation of the equality of covariance assumption without the loss of much statistical power.

The required sample size

Providing recommended sample sizes for a repeated measures one-way ANOVA is a little tricky. Cohen (1988) does not provide sample size tables for repeated measures designs, and while Bausell and Li (2002) do so, they don't adopt any conventions for small, medium and large effect sizes. Furthermore, Bausell and Li compute effect sizes for ANOVAs differently from Cohen. Cohen's approach is described in the section on determining sample sizes for the independent samples one-way ANOVA. Bausell and Li measure effect size by deciding on the groups expected to have the smallest and largest means in a one-way ANOVA design, in each case dividing the mean expected by the standard deviation expected, and then subtracting one from the other. They then adjust this by taking into account the pattern of means across the levels of the independent variable (e.g. are they expected to be equally dispersed, or are some expected to be bunched together?). Another complication is that, as for the paired samples t-test, the sample size required for a repeated measures one-way ANOVA depends not only on the required power, the adopted significance level and the estimated effect size, but also on the correlation between the scores at each level of the dependent variable.

Despite these difficulties, it is still worthwhile providing a table showing the required samples for small, medium and large effects for the repeated measures one-way ANOVA, even if the effect sizes (and correlations) on which these are based are inevitably a little arbitrary. It is better for the researcher to have some indication of required sample size than none at all. Table 5.12 shows the approximate sample sizes required for Bausell and Li effect sizes of .20, .60 and 1.00 for a power of 80 per cent, a significance level of .05 and an average correlation between the scores at the various levels of the independent variables of .4. These effect sizes have been chosen because they provide a reasonable spread of the values that typically occur in research involving the repeated measures one-way ANOVA and they, therefore, provide a useful guide to the sample sizes required.

To increase the power to 90 per cent, increase the sample sizes by 35 per cent. It is worth noting that for all but very small effect sizes (of about .3 or less), sample sizes of less than 100 are satisfactory if 80 per cent power is required and the .05 significance level is adopted. If you are unable to use the results of previous research or a pilot study to establish the expected effect size before you carry out your own study, use the sample size for a medium effect size if it is possible to obtain enough people.

Table 5.12 The approximate sample sizes required for a repeated measures one-way ANOVA, assuming a power of 80% and a .05 significance level

Effect size	Bausell and Li ES	Total sample size required		
		Number of independent variables		
		3	4	5
Small	0.2	300	325	360
Medium	0.6	36	40	40
Large	1.0	15	16	16

Table 5.13 The job commitment of 30 employees before, six months after, and one year after an organizational change programme

Case	Commitment before change programme	Commitment 6 months after change programme	Commitment 1 year after change programme
1	4	7	6
2	6	7	5
3	3	4	2
4	2	5	4
5	4	6	6
6	3	5	7
7	1	4	3
8	2	3	3
9	3	5	6
10	5	5	4
11	4	6	6
12	2	4	4
13	4	5	8
14	3	4	6
15	2	4	3
16	4	6	2
17	3	5	3
18	2	5	4
19	4	5	5
20	2	4	5
21	5	4	6
22	1	5	4
23	2	4	2
24	5	4	4
25	2	3	3
26	4	6	6
27	5	3	4
28	3	4	2
29	4	3	4
30	3	5	4

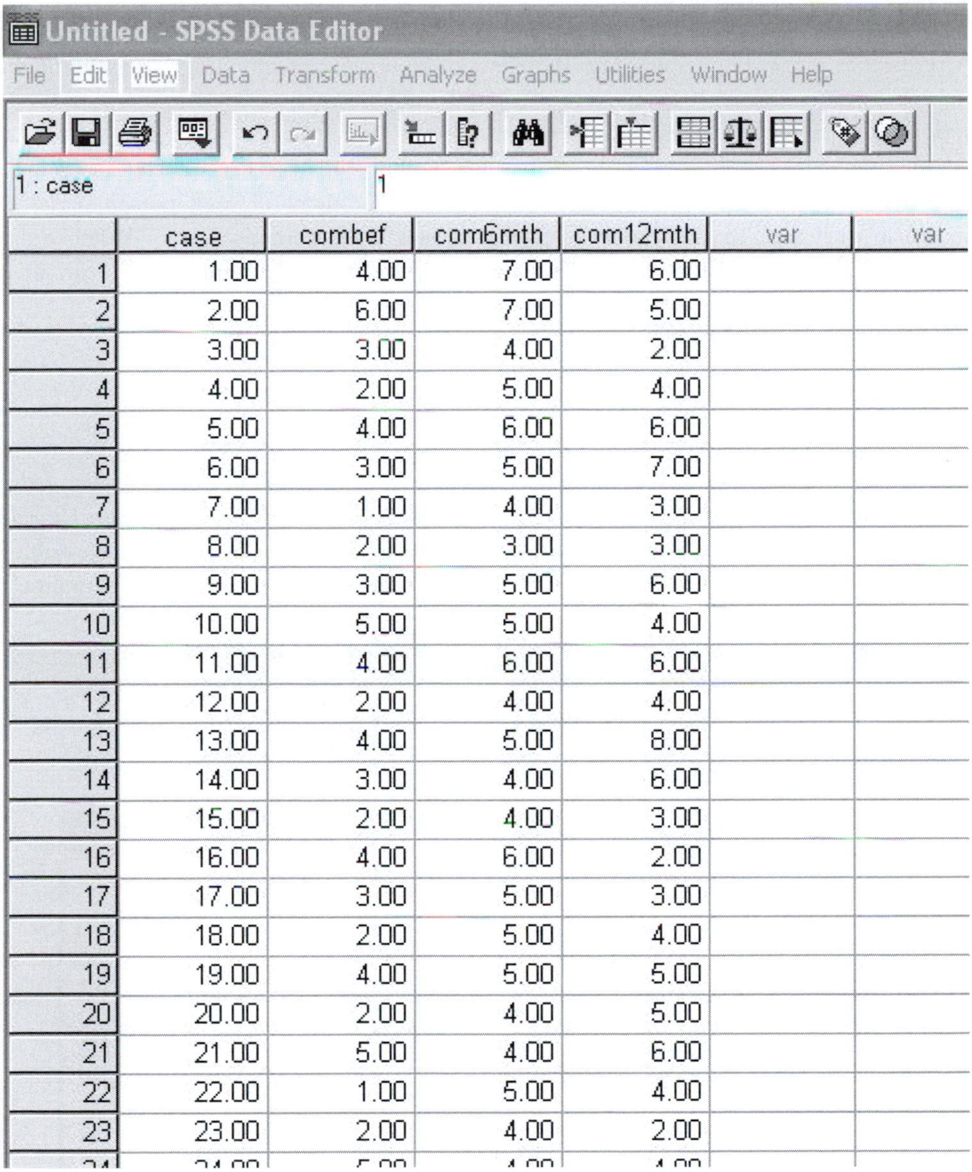

	case	combef	com6mth	com12mth	var	var
1	1.00	4.00	7.00	6.00		
2	2.00	6.00	7.00	5.00		
3	3.00	3.00	4.00	2.00		
4	4.00	2.00	5.00	4.00		
5	5.00	4.00	6.00	6.00		
6	6.00	3.00	5.00	7.00		
7	7.00	1.00	4.00	3.00		
8	8.00	2.00	3.00	3.00		
9	9.00	3.00	5.00	6.00		
10	10.00	5.00	5.00	4.00		
11	11.00	4.00	6.00	6.00		
12	12.00	2.00	4.00	4.00		
13	13.00	4.00	5.00	8.00		
14	14.00	3.00	4.00	6.00		
15	15.00	2.00	4.00	3.00		
16	16.00	4.00	6.00	2.00		
17	17.00	3.00	5.00	3.00		
18	18.00	2.00	5.00	4.00		
19	19.00	4.00	5.00	5.00		
20	20.00	2.00	4.00	5.00		
21	21.00	5.00	4.00	6.00		
22	22.00	1.00	5.00	4.00		
23	23.00	2.00	4.00	2.00		
24	24.00	5.00	4.00	4.00		

Figure 5.14 SPSS *Data Editor after repeated measures one-way ANOVA data are entered*

A worked example

A researcher carries out a study into the effect of an organizational change programme on the job commitment of 30 employees. Their job commitment is measured on a 10-point scale before the change programme, six months after the change programme has been completed, and 12 months after the change programme has been completed. The results of the study are shown in Table 5.13. The job commitment of each person (case) is shown in each row, so case number 1 had a measured job commitment of 4 before the change programme, 7 six months after the change programme, and 6 one year after the change programme.

How to carry out a repeated measures one-way ANOVA using SPSS

Begin by entering your data in the *SPSS* Data Editor. Figure 5.14 shows what the above data look like when they have been entered. The names used for the three levels of the commitment variable here are 'combef', 'com6mth', and 'com12mth'. Use the *Variable View* in the data editor to enter full variable names. In this example, the variable names entered in the *SPSS Variable View* were 'Commitment before change programme',

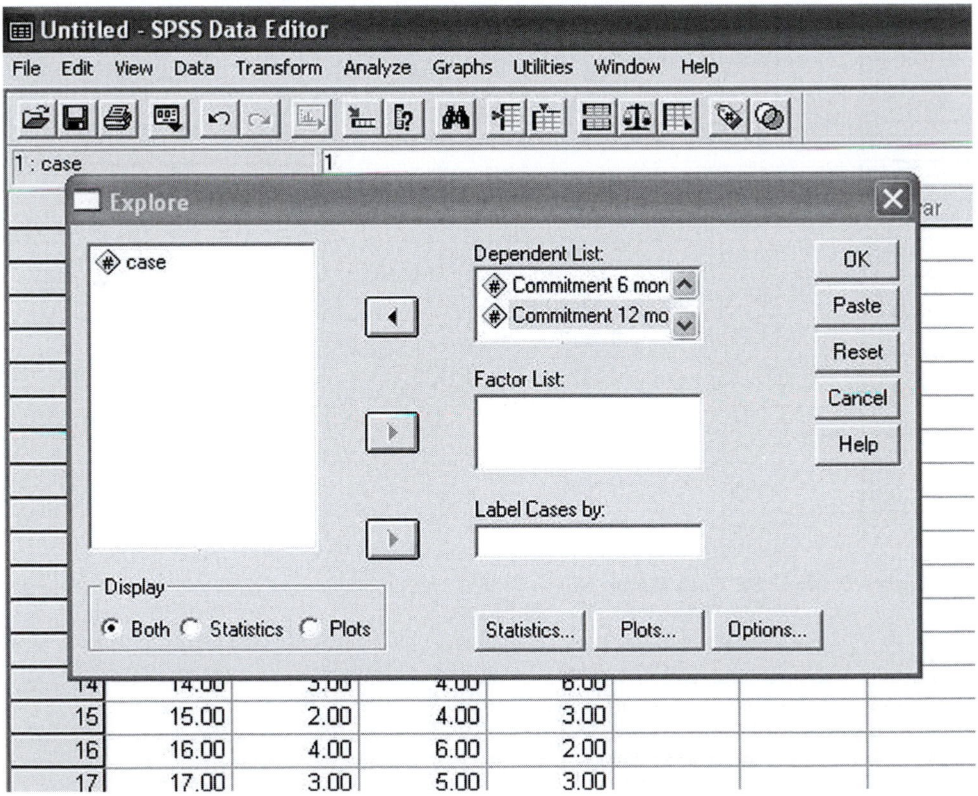

Figure 5.15 *Entering the variables in* Explore *when carrying out a repeated measures one-way ANOVA*

'Commitment 6 months after change programme', and 'Commitment 12 months after change programme'.

Next, run *Explore* in *SPSS*. To do this:

> Click on **Analyze**.
> Click on **Descriptive Statistics**.
> Click on **Explore** . . . .
> A dialog box will appear with the names of the scores at each level of the independent variable. Click on sets of scores you wish to include in the ANOVA and then on the black triangle to the left of the white box headed **Dependent List**. The sets of scores will be moved across to the **Dependent List** box (see Figure 5.15).
> Click on **OK**.

Output in the following form will appear.

Explore

Case processing summary

	Cases					
	Valid		Missing		Total	
	N	Per cent	N	Per cent	N	Per cent
Commitment before	30	100.0%	0	.0%	30	100.0%
Commitment 6 months after	30	100.0%	0	.0%	30	100.0%
Commitment 12 months after	30	100.0%	0	.0%	30	100.0%

Descriptives

			Statistic	Std error
Commitment before	Mean		3.2333	.23333
	95% confidence interval for mean	Lower bound	2.7561	
		Upper bound	3.7106	
	5% trimmed mean		3.2222	
	Median		3.0000	
	Variance		1.633	
	Std deviation		1.27802	
	Minimum		1.00	
	Maximum		6.00	
	Range		5.00	
	Interquartile range		2.0000	
	Skewness		.167	.427
	Kurtosis		−.656	.833
Commitment 6 months after	Mean		4.6667	.19962
	95% confidence interval for mean	Lower bound	4.2584	
		Upper bound	5.0749	
	5% trimmed mean		4.6296	
	Median		5.0000	

	Variance		1.195	
	Std deviation		1.09334	
	Minimum		3.00	
	Maximum		7.00	
	Range		4.00	
	Interquartile range		1.0000	
	Skewness		.389	.427
	Kurtosis		−.224	.833
Commitment 12 months after	Mean		4.3667	.28960
	95% confidence interval for mean	Lower bound	3.7744	
		Upper bound	4.9590	
	5% trimmed mean		4.3148	
	Median		4.0000	
	Variance		2.516	
	Std deviation		1.58622	
	Minimum		2.00	
	Maximum		8.00	
	Range		6.00	
	Interquartile range		3.0000	
	Skewness		.289	.427
	Kurtosis		−.552	.833

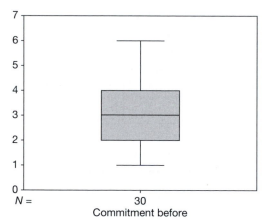

Commitment before
```
Commitment before
Stem-and-Leaf Plot

Frequency    Stem & Leaf

   2.00      1 .  00
   8.00      2 .  00000000
   7.00      3 .  0000000
   8.00      4 .  00000000
   4.00      5 .  0000
   1.00      6 .  0

Stem width: 1.00
Each leaf:  1 case(s)
```

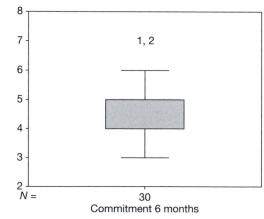

Commitment 6 months after
```
Commitment 6 months after
Stem-and-Leaf Plot

Frequency      Stem & Leaf

   4.00        3 .  0000
    .00        3 .
  10.00        4 .  0000000000
    .00        4 .
  10.00        5 .  0000000000
    .00        5 .
   4.00        6 .  0000
   2.00 Extremes    (>=7.0)

Stem width:    1.00
Each leaf:     1 case(s)
```

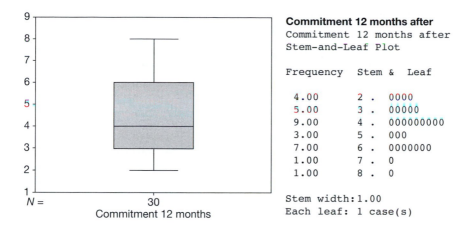

Commitment 12 months after
```
Commitment 12 months after
Stem-and-Leaf Plot

Frequency   Stem &   Leaf

   4.00      2 .   0000
   5.00      3 .   00000
   9.00      4 .   000000000
   3.00      5 .   000
   7.00      6 .   0000000
   1.00      7 .   0
   1.00      8 .   0

Stem width:1.00
Each leaf: 1 case(s)
```

In the table headed *Descriptives*, check that the minimum and maximum values given for your three or more variables seem correct, and in the box and whiskers plots look for any extreme scores. Details on how to do this are given on pages 90–1. If the minimum and maximum values are reasonable, and there are no outliers shown in the box and whiskers plot, follow the instructions below to perform the ANOVA.

If the minimum and maximum values don't look right, and/or there are outliers shown in the box and whiskers plot, check your data to make sure that the extreme values are not mistakes, and that from a research point of view it makes sense to include them in the analysis. If necessary, take steps to modify the data, and then run *Explore* again, repeating the process until you are confident that your data are sound. When you are confident that the data are acceptable, follow the instructions below to carry out the ANOVA.

In this example, a relatively extreme value of 7 has been identified in the boxplot for job commitment six months after the change programme. It turns out that two cases, 1 and 2, had an outlying or extreme value of 7 for commitment six months after the change programme. These data points were checked and found to be acceptable. Therefore, no modification was made to the data file before running the ANOVA.

To run a repeated measures one-way ANOVA in *SPSS*:

- ➤ Click on **Analyze**.
- ➤ Click on **General Linear Model**.
- ➤ Click on **Repeated Measures** . . . .
- ➤ A dialog box will appear. Click in the white box to the right of **Within-Subject Factor Name** and delete the phrase **factor 1**. Write in a suitable name for your independent variable. This name must not be longer than eight characters, must begin with a letter rather than a number, and must not contain any spaces. For example, if, as in this example, you measured the job commitment of people before some training, immediately after the training, and again one year later,

you might call the independent variable **time**, because the difference between these three levels of the independent variable is the time at which they were measured. If you are following this example, write in the word *time*.

➤ In the white box to the right of **Number of Levels** enter the number of levels of the independent variable. If you were to measure job satisfaction before an organization was involved in a merger, during the merger, immediately after the merger, and one year later, you would enter the figure 4, as the independent variable would have four levels. In the example of job commitment in relation to a change programme being used here, the independent variable has three levels, so the value of 3 is entered.

➤ Click on **Add**. The name of the independent variable, and the number of levels of the independent variable in brackets, will appear in the white box below (see Figure 5.16).

➤ Click on **Define**. A dialog box will appear. A list of your variables will appear in the rectangular white box to the left. Click on the first variable you wish to enter into your analysis. It will be highlighted in blue. Click on the single black triangle half-way down the left side of the white box headed **Within-Subjects**

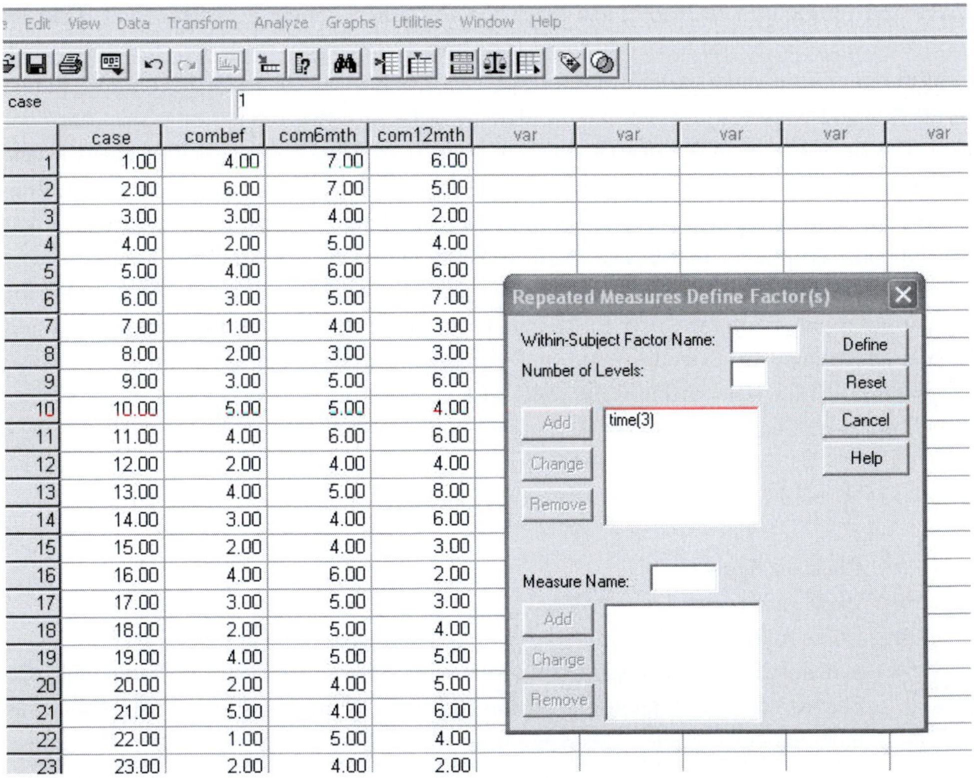

Figure 5.16 *Entering the repeated measures factor when carrying out a repeated measures one-way ANOVA*

Variables. The name of the first level of the independent variable will be entered in this box together with a number indicating which level it is. Repeat this until all the variables are entered (see Figure 5.17).

➤ Click on **Plots** . . . .

➤ A dialog box will appear. Click on the name of your independent variable which will be shown in the white box under **Factors** (see Figure 5.18).

➤ Then click on the black triangle to the left of the white box headed **Horizontal Axis**.

➤ Click on **Add**.

➤ Click on **Continue**.

➤ Click on **Options** . . . .

➤ A dialog box will appear. Click on the white box next to **Descriptive Statistics**. A tick will appear in the box.

➤ In the white box beneath the heading **Factor(s) and Factor Interactions** you will see the names of your repeated measures factor. Click on this and then click on the black triangle to the left of the white box headed **Display Means for**.

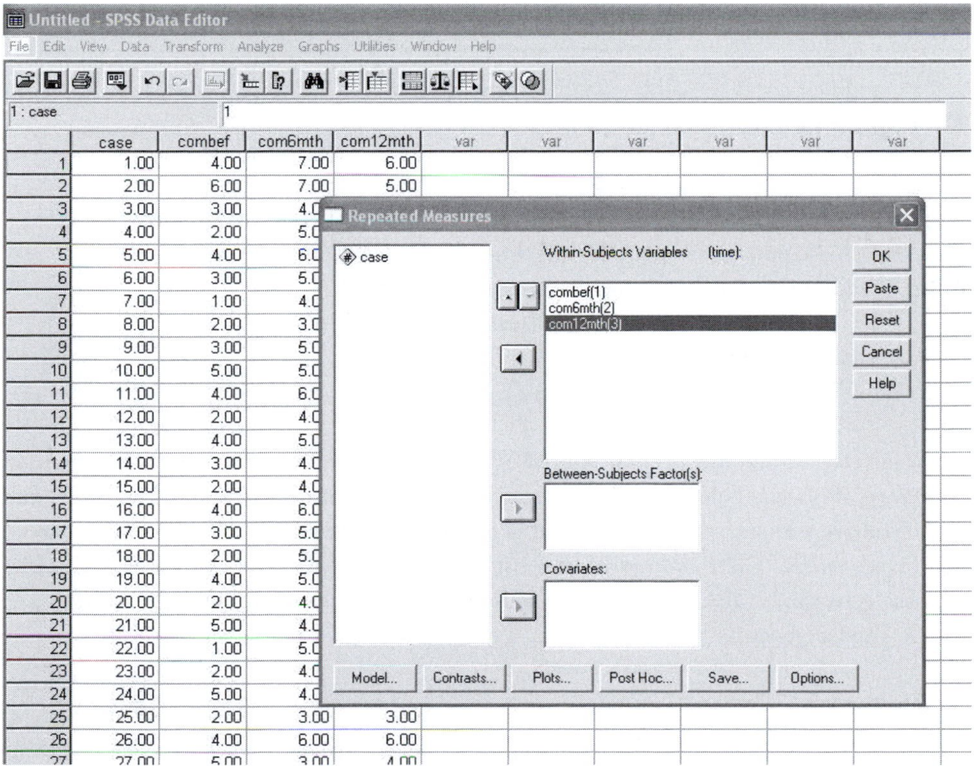

Figure 5.17 *Entering the within-subject variables when carrying out a repeated measures one-way ANOVA*

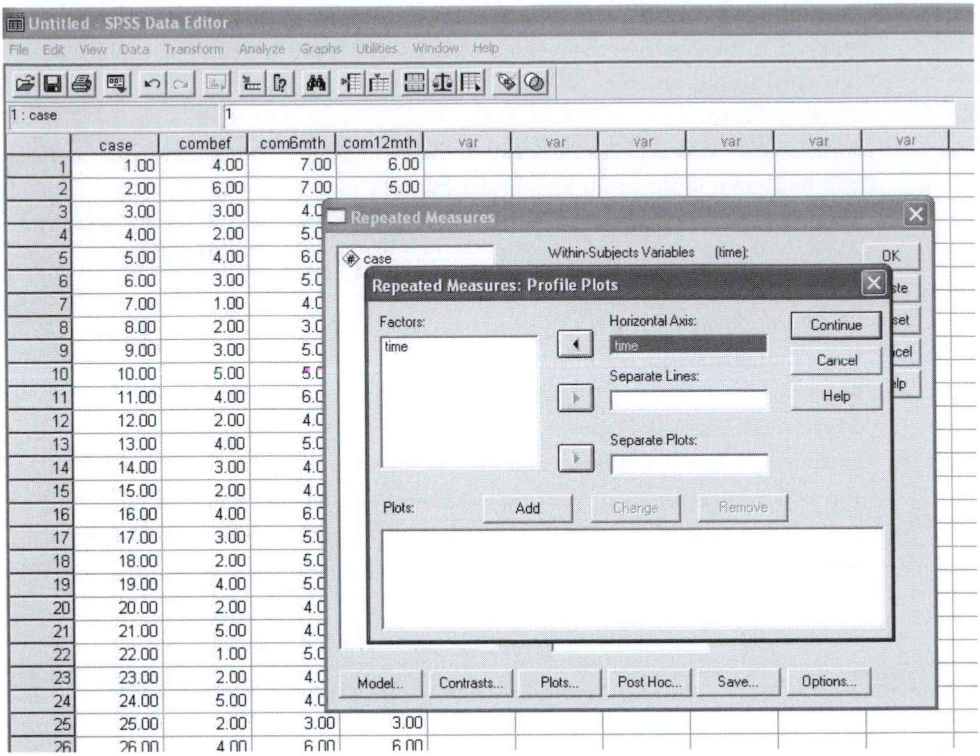

Figure 5.18 *Entering the plotted factor when carrying out a repeated measures one-way ANOVA*

➤ Click on the white box next to **Compare main effects**.
➤ In the pull-down menu for the white box headed **Confidence interval adjustment** select Bonferroni (see Figure 5.19).
➤ Click inthe white box next to **Descriptive statistics**.
➤ Click on **Continue**.
➤ Click on **OK**.

When the output has been produced it will contain some superfluous information. Therefore, it is a good idea to delete the material you don't need before viewing the results. To do so have a look at the large white area on the left hand side of the *SPSS* output screen (see Figure 5.20). There, you will see a list of the titles of the various results tables that *SPSS* has generated. Click on each of the following to highlight it, and then press the delete key on your keyboard.

– Multivariate Tests;
– Mauchly's Test of Sphericity;
– Tests of Within-Subjects Contrasts;
– Tests of Between-Subjects Effects;
– Multivariate Tests (which is within Estimated Marginal Means).

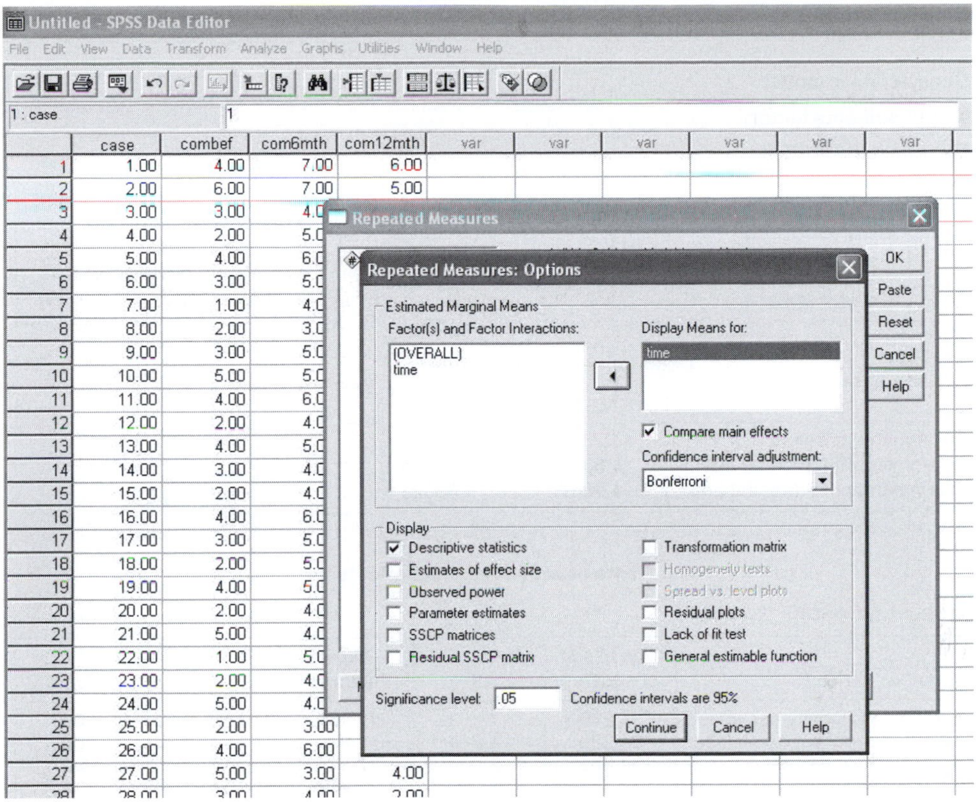

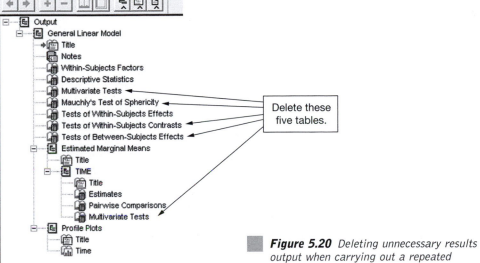

Figure 5.19 (above) *Entering the options when carrying out a repeated measures one-way ANOVA*

Figure 5.20 *Deleting unnecessary results output when carrying out a repeated measures one-way ANOVA*

The following *SPSS* results output will remain.

General linear model

Within-subjects factors

Measure: MEASURE_1

TIME	Dependent variable
1	COMBEF
2	COM6MTH
3	COM18MTH

This table shows the mean and standard deviation for commitment at each level of the independent variable. It also shows the sample size (*N*).

Descriptive statistics

	Mean	Std deviation	*N*
Commitment before	3.2333	1.27802	30
Commitment 6 months after	4.6667	1.09334	30
Commitment 12 months after	4.3667	1.58622	30

Tests of within-subjects effects

Measure: MEASURE_1

Source		Type III sum of squares	df	Mean square	*F*	Sig.
TIME	Sphericity assumed	34.289	2	17.144	15.133	.000
	Greenhouse-Geisser	34.289	1.914	17.915	15.133	.000
	Huynh-Feldt	34.289	2.000	17.144	15.133	.000
	Lower-bound	34.289	1.000	34.289	15.133	.001
TIME	Sphericity assumed	65.711	58	1.133		
	Greenhouse-Geisser	65.711	55.507	1.184		
	Huynh-Feldt	65.711	58.000	1.133		
	Lower-bound	65.711	29.000	2.266		

Degrees of freedom for error.

Use Huynh-Feldt as a test of the null hypothesis that the means are the same across all levels of the independent variable. The value for *Sig.* needs to be less than .05 for the result to be statistically significant. In this case the *F* value of 15.13 is reported as .000, indicating that the difference between the three means is statistically significant.

Estimated marginal means
TIME

Estimates

Measure: MEASURE_1

TIME	Mean	Std error	95% confidence interval	
			Lower bound	Upper bound
1	3.233	.233	2.756	3.711
2	4.667	.200	4.258	5.075
3	4.367	.290	3.774	4.959

This table shows the 95% confidence interval for the mean of each level of the independent variable.

Pairwise comparisons

Measure: MEASURE_1

(I) TIME	(J) TIME	Mean difference (I–J)	Std error	Sig.[a]	95% confidence interval for difference[a]	
					Lower bound	Upper bound
1	2	−1.433*	.248	.000	−2.063	−.804
	3	−1.133*	.298	.002	−1.892	−.375
2	1	1.433*	.248	.000	.804	2.063
	3	.300	.276	.858	−.401	1.001
3	1	1.133*	.298	.002	.375	1.892
	2	−.300	.276	.858	−1.001	.401

Based on estimated marginal means
 * The mean difference is significant at the .05 level.
 [a] Adjustment for multiple comparisons: Bonferroni.

This table indicates whether the difference between each pair of levels of the independent variable is significant after making the Bonferroni adjustment. For an explanation see below.

Profile plots

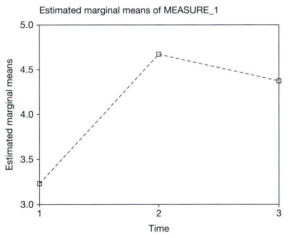

Estimated marginal means of MEASURE_1

How to report the results of a repeated measures one-way ANOVA

The results of the example used in this case could be reported as follows:

> The mean levels of job commitment were compared before the organizational change programme, six months after it was completed and 12 months after it was completed. The means, standard deviations and 95 per cent confidence intervals for the means are shown in Table 5.14.
>
> A repeated measures one-way analysis of variance showed that there was a significant difference between the level of commitment across the three times it was measured $F(2, 58) = 15.13$, $p < .001$.
>
> Bonferroni tests were used to examine the differences between the mean job commitment before the change programme and at the two subsequent points in time. The difference between mean commitment before the change programme and six months after it was significant, $p < .001$, as was the difference between mean commitment before the change programme and twelve months after it, $p = .002$.

Table 5.14 *Means, standard deviations and 95 per cent confidence intervals for job commitment before the change programme and 6 and 12 months afterwards*

	Mean	Standard deviation	Number	95% confidence intervals	
				Lower	Upper
Before the change programme	3.23	1.28	30	2.76	3.71
Six months after the change programme	4.67	1.09	30	4.26	5.08
Twelve months after the change programme	4.37	1.59	30	3.77	4.96

Comments

- The means, standard deviations and 95 per cent confidence intervals are taken from the *Descriptive Statistics* and *Estimated Marginal Means* tables.
- For repeated measures ANOVA it is necessary to provide both the between groups degrees of freedom and the degrees of freedom for error. The necessary figures appear in the *Tests of within-subjects effects* table. For the Huynh-Feldt tests used here you will see that the degrees of freedom for the independent variable, Time, is reported as 2.000, and degrees of freedom for error is reported as 58.000. Accordingly, after the *F* value, there are two numbers in the brackets: 2 for the between groups degrees of freedom, and 58 for the error degrees of freedom.

■ The reason that the Huynh-Feldt test has been used for the overall difference between the means is that it works whether or not the sphericity assumption is met. The sphericity assumption is that the standard errors of all possible pairs of levels of the independent variable are the same. Because this assumption is difficult to test in practice, we have adopted Howell's (1997) suggestion, and used the Huynh-Feldt test because this is effective whether or not the sphericity assumption is met.

■ The *Pairwise Comparisons* table is very helpful because it allows you to see whether a comparison between each pair of levels of the independent variable is significant. So, in this example, we can see whether or not there is a significant difference between commitment: (a) before the organizational training programme and six months after it; (b) before the programme and 12 months after it; and (c) six and 12 months after the programme. Unfortunately, the table does not provide the names of each level of the independent variable, but this is quite easy to work out. In the left hand column of the table under *I* is a different number for each level of your independent variables. Number 1 refers to the variable you entered on the left hand side when you inputted your variables under Data Entry, number 2 refers to the variable immediately to the right of it, number 3 to the variable to the right of that, and so on. So in this example, commitment before the training programme is number 1, commitment six months after it is number 2, and commitment 12 months after it is number 3. You can see whether each pair of levels of the independent variable have significantly different means by looking at the significance level under *Sig.*, the fourth column in the table. For example, if you wished to see whether there is a significant difference between the means for commitment six months after the change programme (Number 2), and commitment 12 months after the change programme (Number 3), you would look up 2 under *(I)* and 3 under *(J)* and read off the significance level. In this case the result is .858. This figure needs to be below .05 for statistical significance and, as .858 is greater than .05 we cannot claim significance in this case. However, as you can see, the other two paired comparisons here are significant.

■ The test that has been used to examine the difference between each pair of levels of the independent variable is Bonferroni, which is actually a modified form of the *t*-test. The Bonferroni *t*-test has been used because it does a good job of controlling for the tendency to make Type I errors when several means are compared simultaneously. Therefore, it is better to use this than to compare each pair of levels of the independent variable with paired samples *t*-tests.

■ The .05 significance level for the Bonferroni *t*-test results presented in the *SPSS* results output should only be used if you are looking at specific comparisons between means that you had planned to make before you carried out the research. If you want to use post-hoc comparisons, that is you want to examine whether a pair of levels of the independent variable are significantly different when you hadn't planned to do so before you looked at the results, you need to adjust the required significance level so that the increased likelihood of Type I errors are controlled. In these circumstances, the recommended significance level you should use depends on the number of levels of your independent variable: 3 levels .017, 4 levels .013, 5 levels .010, 6 levels

169

.008, 7 levels .007, 8 levels .062, 9 levels .006, or 10 levels .005. So, if your repeated measures ANOVA has an independent variable with four levels, and you want to examine the statistical significance of the difference between one or more pairs of means that you had not planned to compare before you looked at the results of the analysis, you should examine whether or not the Bonferroni t-test significance level is below .013, not whether it is below .05.

■ If the F value is significant, it is very helpful to draw attention to the effect size when discussing the findings. For a difference in means, the appropriate measure of effect size is d. For a particular pair of means this can be obtained by working out the difference between the two and dividing this by the pooled standard deviation. An easy to use calculator which performs this function is available at www.dewberry-statistics.com. To use the calculator you simply need to enter the relevant means and standard deviations shown in the *Descriptive Statistics* table on page 166. For example, if we wished to report the effect size of the difference between commitment before the change programme and commitment six months after the change programme we would need the mean and standard deviation of each of these. Consulting the descriptive statistics table, the mean and standard deviation for before the change programme are 3.23 and 1.28 respectively. The mean and standard deviation for production are 4.67 and 1.09. Entering the figures for this example into the calculator we obtain a d of 1.21. We can therefore say that not only is the difference between mean commitment before the change programme and mean commitment six months after the change programme statistically significant after making the Bonferroni adjustment, but also that the effect size is large ($d = 1.21$). Which of the effect sizes you choose to mention will depend on the particular focus of your research, and what you consider relevant in the light of this.

Interpretation

If the results of a repeated measures one-way ANOVA are found to be significant, the interpretation is that the population means are different across the three or more levels of the independent variable. In the above case, where a significant difference was found between levels of commitment before the change programme, six months after it and 12 months after it, we can conclude that the mean level of commitment was different across the three times it was measured.

If a statistical difference is found across the three or more groups this does not imply that there is a difference in the population means for any two of these groups. It simply indicates that the groups are not all drawn from populations with the same mean. A non-significant repeated measures one-way ANOVA indicates that there is insufficient evidence to reject the null hypothesis that all levels of the independent variable have the same populations mean.

If the ANOVA is statistically significant, whether or not you can conclude that the independent variable had a causal influence on the dependent variable depends on the design of the study. Only in circumstances in which there is only one possible factor that could have led to the change in the means can we conclude that this factor caused this change in the means. In the example used here, we should certainly not conclude that the change programme caused job commitment to increase, because there are factors other than the change programme that could cause job commitment to rise over time. As well as the change programme, all sorts of other historical events might have occurred to the people involved in the study between the three times their job commitment was measured. Therefore, it would be very unwise to claim that the change programme caused the change in commitment levels.

INDEPENDENT SAMPLES FACTORIAL ANOVA

When to use

Use an independent samples factorial ANOVA when you have two or more independent variables and one dependent variable, and the independent variables specify which of two or more groups people belong to (for example, one independent variable might be men versus women and, another, people working in sales versus those working in finance). You wish to know if there is a significant difference between the means of the groups across each independent variable. So, if the independent variables were gender and whether people work in production or sales, and the dependent variable was well-being, you might want to know whether there is a significant difference in the well-being of: (a) men and women; and (b) those who work in production and those who work in sales. You may also wish to know whether there is one or more interaction between the independent variables and the dependent variable. The nature of these interaction effects is explained below.

Example

- Research has suggested that some managers adopt a task-based approach to management, focusing on the tasks that need to be achieved, whereas others are more focused on building good relationships with employees. A researcher wishes to examine if there is a relation between whether or not male and female managers are task- or people-focused and the job satisfaction of the employees who work under them. To do so, she examines the job satisfaction of 100 employees. Fifty of them are men and, of this 50, 25 work for task-oriented managers and 25 for people-oriented managers. Another 50 are female, and 22 of them work for task-oriented managers with the remaining 28 working for people-oriented managers. An independent samples factorial ANOVA is used to examine whether the mean level of job satisfaction is different for people managed by: (a) males versus females; and (b) those with a task-focused manager versus those with a person-focused manager.

Background

With *t*-tests, and the one-way ANOVA, you are examining whether there is a difference in the means of a dependent variable across two or more levels of a single independent

Table 5.15 *Job commitment by gender and education level*

	Degree-educated	Not degree-educated
Male	3	3
	1	4
	2	5
	1	5
	2	2
Female	3	3
	4	1
	2	2
	3	3
	4	1

variable. For example, with an independent samples *t*-test you might examine whether there is a significant difference in mean job commitment across two levels of gender (males and females). However, sometimes you may wish to design research so that you can simultaneously examine whether two or more independent variables affect the dependent variable. Perhaps you wish to know not just whether there is a difference in mean job commitment as a function of gender (males versus females), but also as a function of education (degree-educated versus not degree-educated). Data of this type are set out in Table 5.15.

The figures in Table 5.15 indicate the mean job commitment of 20 people measured on a 5-point scale, where the higher the score, the higher the job commitment. So, five degree-educated males have job-commitment scores of 3, 1, 2, 1 and 2 respectively. Obviously, you would be unlikely to have such a small sample of cases in practice, but this is sufficient to illustrate the nature of the data.

How might you analyse these data? Well, one possibility would be to carry out two independent measures *t*-tests. First, you could carry out a *t*-test to examine whether there is a significant difference in the mean job commitment of the 10 males and the 10 females. Then, you could carry out a second *t*-test to see if there is a significant difference between the mean job commitment of people who have, and have not, been educated to degree level. Carrying out these *t*-tests would not be wrong, but there is a danger that something very interesting about the data might be lost if you took this approach.

If you compute the means for the four combinations of job-commitment scores here (i.e. males degree-educated, males not degree-educated, females degree-educated, females not degree-educated), you obtain the results shown in Table 5.16.

Table 5.16 shows that the mean job-commitment score for males (i.e. 2.8), and the mean for females (2.6), are very similar. Therefore, it is quite possible that you would find no significant difference between the mean job commitment of men and women. Similarly, the mean job-commitment scores of degree-educated employees (2.5) and non degree-educated employees (2.9) are also similar and, again, it is quite possible that you would not find a significant difference between the job commitment of degree-educated and non degree-educated employees. So, carrying out two *t*-tests, one on level of education, and one on gender, may well tell you that there are no significant differences here, and so you might conclude that gender and level of education are unimportant in relation to job commitment.

However, if this were your conclusion you would probably be making a major oversight. To understand why, have a look at the graph shown in Figure 5.21. In this graph the

Table 5.16 *The mean job commitment of employees by whether or not they are degree-educated*

Gender	Education	Mean	N
Males	Degree-educated	1.8	5
	Not degree-educated	3.8	5
	Males overall	2.8	10
Females	Degree-educated	3.2	5
	Not degree-educated	2.0	5
	Females overall	2.6	10
Males and females overall	Degree-educated	2.5	10
	Not degree-educated	2.9	10
	For all employees	2.7	20

mean of each possible combination of the independent variables has been plotted. Furthermore, the two means for degree-educated people have been joined with a line as have the two means for non degree-educated people.

Figure 5.21 shows the mean for degree-educated males, degree-educated females, non degree-educated males and non degree-educated females. This graph clearly shows you something that you would not have known by just carrying out the *t*-tests. That is, the effect of gender on job commitment depends on whether employees are degree-educated

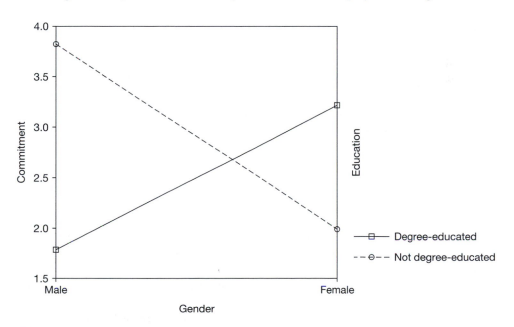

Figure 5.21 *Job commitment: a crossover interaction between gender and education*

173

or not. For degree-educated employees, females show substantially more job commitment than males, whereas for non degree-educated employees, males show markedly more job commitment than females.

What we are actually saying here is that the effect of one independent variable on the dependent variable depends on the other independent variable (in this case, the effect of education on job commitment depends on gender). When the effect of one independent variable on the dependent variable depends on one or more other independent variables, we say that we have an **interaction effect**.

You can always tell whether you may have an interaction effect by plotting out the means of the various combinations of independent variables on a graph like the one shown in Figure 5.21. In this graph, the two lines connecting the means for males and females cross over each other. For this reason this is referred to as a 'crossover interaction'. However, not all interactions are crossover interactions. In the graph shown in Figure 5.22 the two lines do not cross each other so there is not a crossover interaction. There is still an interaction though *because the lines are not parallel*. Whenever you plot the combinations of means in your factorial design and find that a pair of them are not parallel, this indicates an interaction in your sample data. Of course, this does not necessarily mean that there is an interaction for the statistical *populations* you are interested in. Just as a difference in the means of two statistical samples may occur even if there is no difference in the mean of the populations from which they have been drawn (in other words, the null hypothesis is true), so you may find an interaction effect in your sample data even if there is no interaction in the statistical populations from which you have sampled. As a consequence, you need to examine whether any apparent interaction effects are statistically significant.

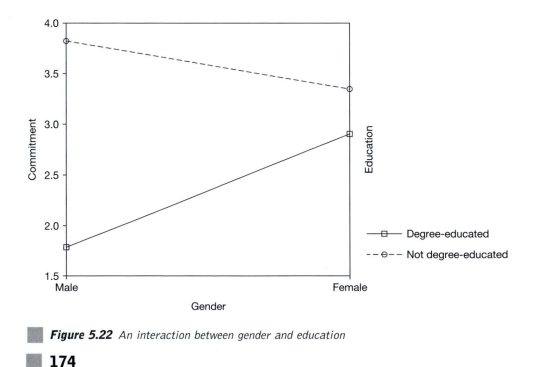

Figure 5.22 An interaction between gender and education

Factorial analysis of variance is used because, unlike t-tests or the one-way analysis of variance, it allows you to examine interaction effects. In addition, it is also possible to examine **main effects** which are the effects of one independent variable on the dependent variable when the other independent variable (or variables) is ignored, and **simple effects**, the effect of an independent variable on the dependent variable at a particular level of another independent variable. There is a possible main effect for every independent variable in your research design. So, in the case of the data considered above there is a possible main effect for gender and another possible main effect for education level. To this you add the interaction effects for every possible combination of independent variables, which in this case is simply the combination of gender and education level. If instead of the two independent variables of gender and education level you added a third, ethnicity (white versus black), you would have three possible main effects (for gender, education level and ethnicity) and four possible interactions (gender with education level, gender with ethnicity, education level with ethnicity, and gender with education level with ethnicity). The interaction between two independent variables is known as a two-way interaction. In the same way, the interaction between three independent variables is a three-way interaction, four independent variables is a four-way interaction and so on.

Factorial ANOVAs are normally referred to by the number of independent variables, and the number of levels of each independent variable. A 2×2 ANOVA means that there are two independent variables, each with two levels. A $2 \times 3 \times 3 \times 5$ ANOVA has four independent variables, with the first variable having two levels, the second and third having three levels and the fourth having five levels.

Assumptions and requirements

In ideal circumstances the independent samples factorial ANOVA is used when the samples being compared are drawn from normally distributed populations with the same variance. However, as explained earlier, ANOVA is a robust statistical technique, and it stands up well to violations of these assumptions most of the time.

The required sample size

The sample size required for an independent samples factorial ANOVA depends primarily on the power required, the significance level adopted and the weakest effect size (i.e. the effect size for the independent variable expected to have the weakest effect size in terms of differences between the two or more means). As for one-way independent measures designs, Cohen (1988) suggests the effect size measure f. If you are in a position to use the results of previous research or a pilot study to estimate the effect size, f, for each independent variable in your factorial ANOVA, you can do so by using the calculator at www.dewberry-statistics.com (see page 140). When you have established f for each independent variable, take the smallest one and use it in Table 5.17 to look up the sample size you will require in your study.

Table 5.17 *The approximate sample sizes required for an independent samples factorial ANOVA, assuming a power of 80% and a .05 significance level*

Effect size		Total sample size required		
		Number of independent variables		
	Cohen's f	2	3	4
Small	0.10	800	1,000	1,100
Medium	0.25	130	160	180
Large	0.40	54	64	72

For example, if you plan to use a 2 × 3 independent samples ANOVA, and find that the independent variable with the smallest effect size (which has, say, three levels) has an f of 0.4, you would need a sample size of about 64 (i.e. approximately 21 in each group) if you wanted to be 80 per cent confident of finding a difference between the means, if one exists, and you are using the .05 significance level.

If you have no way of estimating f before your study, use the estimate for a medium effect size. If you wish to increase power to 90 per cent, increase the relevant sample sizes by 35 per cent.

A worked example

In this example, a researcher is interested in whether the job performance of employees in an organization varies as a function of their gender and whether they work in the finance department or the production department. She randomly selects ten males and ten females from each of these two departments and obtains measures of their job performance on a 7-point rating scale. The data are shown in Table 5.18.

Table 5.18 shows data for the dependent variable, performance, and two independent variables. The first independent variable, gender, has been coded 1 for males and 2 for females. The other one, department, has been coded 1 for people who work in the production department of the organization, and 2 for people who work in the finances department. Setting out the data this way enables us to specify the combination of gender and department for each case (e.g. case 1, who has a job-performance score of 4, is a male working in production).

How to carry out an independent samples factorial ANOVA using SPSS

Begin by entering your data in the *SPSS* Data Editor. Figure 5.23 shows what the above data look like when they have been entered. The variable names used in this case are 'perform' (for job performance), 'dept' (for department) and gender. Use the *Variable View* in the data editor to enter full variable names, and to enter the value labels for the

Table 5.18 *The job performance of 20 employees by gender and department*

Case	Job performance	Gender	Department
1	4	1	1
2	3	1	2
3	4	1	1
4	2	1	2
5	1	1	1
6	4	1	2
7	3	1	1
8	6	1	2
9	4	1	1
10	5	1	2
11	4	2	1
12	5	2	2
13	7	2	1
14	7	2	2
15	6	2	1
16	5	2	2
17	6	2	1
18	5	2	2
19	4	2	1
20	3	2	2

independent variables. In this example, the variable names used were 'Performance', 'Gender' and 'Department'. The values entered were 1 for males and 2 for females, and 1 for production and 2 for finance.

Next, run *Explore* in *SPSS*. To do this:

- ➤ Click on **Analyze**.
- ➤ Click on **Descriptive Statistics**.
- ➤ Click on **Explore** . . . .
- ➤ A dialog box will appear with the independent variables and the dependent variable in a white box on the left hand side. Click on the dependent variable and then on the black triangle to the left of the white box headed **Dependent List**. The dependent variable will be moved across to the **Dependent List** box.

177

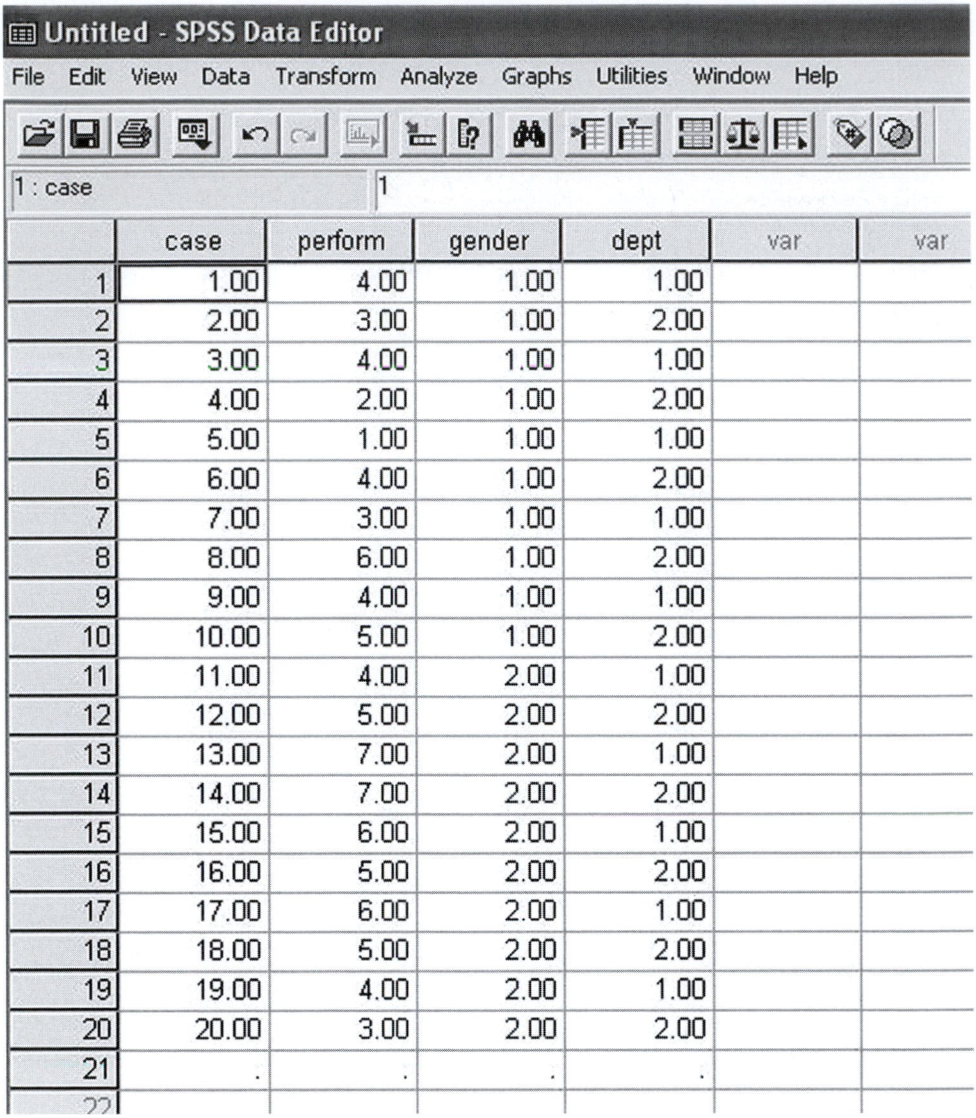

	case	perform	gender	dept	var	var
Untitled - SPSS Data Editor						
File Edit View Data Transform Analyze Graphs Utilities Window Help						
1 : case			1			

	case	perform	gender	dept	var	var
1	1.00	4.00	1.00	1.00		
2	2.00	3.00	1.00	2.00		
3	3.00	4.00	1.00	1.00		
4	4.00	2.00	1.00	2.00		
5	5.00	1.00	1.00	1.00		
6	6.00	4.00	1.00	2.00		
7	7.00	3.00	1.00	1.00		
8	8.00	6.00	1.00	2.00		
9	9.00	4.00	1.00	1.00		
10	10.00	5.00	1.00	2.00		
11	11.00	4.00	2.00	1.00		
12	12.00	5.00	2.00	2.00		
13	13.00	7.00	2.00	1.00		
14	14.00	7.00	2.00	2.00		
15	15.00	6.00	2.00	1.00		
16	16.00	5.00	2.00	2.00		
17	17.00	6.00	2.00	1.00		
18	18.00	5.00	2.00	2.00		
19	19.00	4.00	2.00	1.00		
20	20.00	3.00	2.00	2.00		
21	.	.	.	.		
22						

Figure 5.23 SPSS *Data Editor after independent samples factorial ANOVA data are entered*

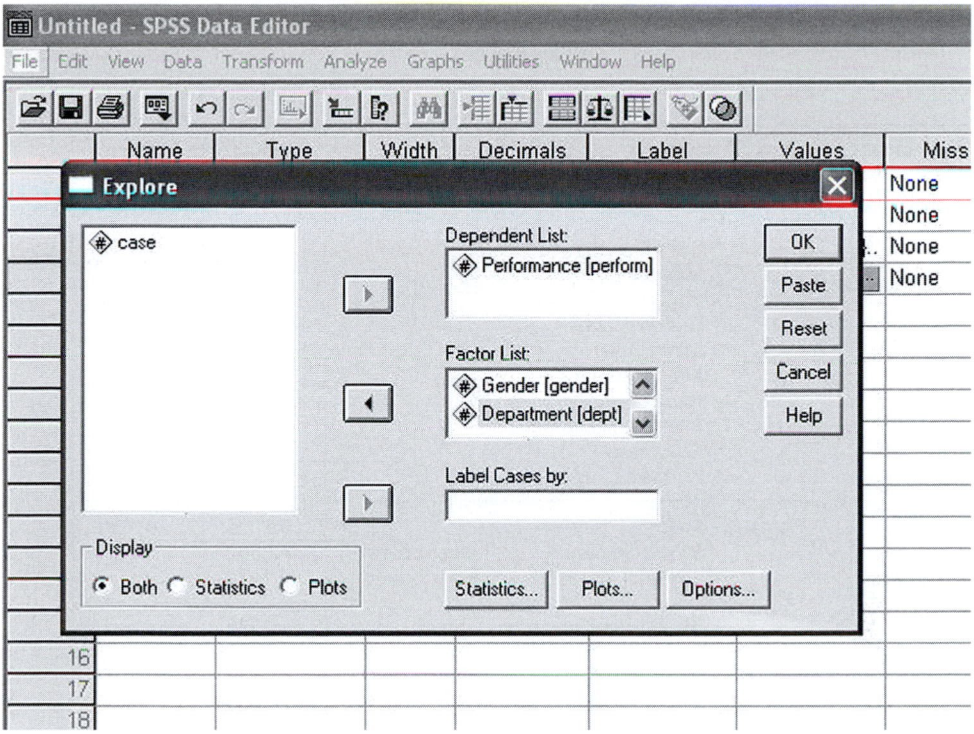

Figure 5.24 *Entering the dependent variable and the independent variables for* Explore *when carrying out an independent samples factorial ANOVA*

➤ Next click on the first independent variable and then on the black triangle to the left of the white box headed **Factor List**. The independent variable will be moved across to the **Factor List** box. Then click on each of the other independent variables in turn and move these across to the box headed **Factor List** (see Figure 5.24).

➤ Click on **OK**.

Output in the following form will appear.

Explore

Gender

Case processing summary

		Cases					
		Valid		Missing		Total	
	Gender	N	Per cent	N	Per cent	N	Per cent
Performance	Male	10	100.0%	0	.0%	10	100.0%
	Female	10	100.0%	0	.0%	10	100.0%

Descriptives

Gender				Statistic	Std error
Performance	Male	Mean		3.6000	.45216
		95% confidence interval for mean	Lower bound	2.5772	
			Upper bound	4.6228	
		5% trimmed mean		3.6111	
		Median		4.0000	
		Variance		2.044	
		Std deviation		1.42984	
		Minimum		1.00	
		Maximum		6.00	
		Range		5.00	
		Interquartile range		1.5000	
		Skewness		−.251	.687
		Kurtosis		.341	1.334
	Females	Mean		5.2000	.41633
		95% confidence interval for mean	Lower bound	4.2582	
			Upper bound	6.1418	
		5% trimmed mean		5.2222	
		Median		5.0000	
		Variance		1.733	
		Std deviation		1.31656	
		Minimum		3.00	
		Maximum		7.00	
		Range		4.00	
		Interquartile range		2.2500	
		Skewness		−.088	.687
		Kurtosis		−.751	1.334

Performance

Stem-and-Leaf Plots

```
Performance Stem-and-Leaf Plot        Performance Stem-and-Leaf Plot
for GENDER= Males                     for GENDER= Females

Frequency      Stem &  Leaf           Frequency    Stem &  Leaf

 1.00 Extremes      (=<1.0)            1.00          3 .  0
 1.00          2 .  0                  2.00          4 .  00
 2.00          3 .  00                 3.00          5 .  000
 4.00          4 .  0000               2.00          6 .  00
 1.00          5 .  0                  2.00          7 .  00
 1.00 Extremes      (>=6.0)
                                       Stem width:  1.00
                                       Each leaf:   1 case(s)
Stem width:    1.00
Each leaf:     1 case(s)
```

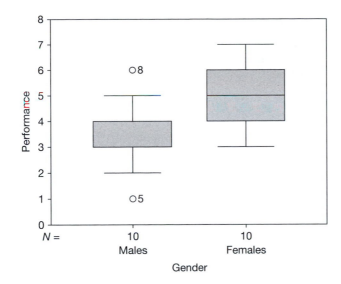

Department

Case processing summary

		Cases					
		Valid		Missing		Total	
	Department	N	Per cent	N	Per cent	N	Per cent
Performance	Production	10	100.0%	0	.0%	10	100.0%
	Finance	10	100.0%	0	.0%	10	100.0%

Descriptives

	Department			Statistic	Std error
Performance	Production	Mean		4.3000	.53852
		95% confidence interval for mean	Lower bound	3.0818	
			Upper bound	5.5182	
		5% trimmed mean		4.3333	
		Median		4.0000	
		Variance		2.900	
		Std deviation		1.70294	
		Minimum		1.00	
		Maximum		7.00	
		Range		6.00	
		Interquartile range		2.2500	
		Skewness		–.246	.687
		Kurtosis		.626	1.334
	Finance	Mean		4.5000	.47726
		95% confidence interval for mean	Lower bound	3.4204	
			Upper bound	5.5796	

181

5% trimmed mean	4.5000	
Median	5.0000	
Variance	2.278	
Std deviation	1.50923	
Minimum	2.00	
Maximum	7.00	
Range	5.00	
Interquartile range	2.2500	
Skewness	−.121	.687
Kurtosis	−.401	1.334

Performance

Stem-and-Leaf Plots

```
Performance Stem-and-Leaf Plot      Performance Stem-and-Leaf Plot
for DEPT= Production                for DEPT= Finance

Frequency     Stem &  Leaf          Frequency    Stem &  Leaf

 1.00 Extremes      (=<1.0)          1.00         2 .  0
 1.00         3 .  0                 2.00         3 .  00
 5.00         4 .  00000            1.00         4 .  0
  .00         5 .                   4.00         5 .  0000
 2.00         6 .  00               1.00         6 .  0
 1.00         7 .  0                1.00         7 .  0

Stem width:    1.00                 Stem width:  1.00
Each leaf:     1 case(s)            Each leaf:   1 case(s)
```

Boxplots

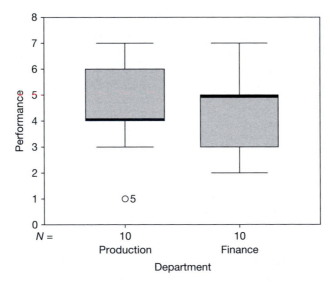

A separate set of information will be produced for each independent variable. In this example such information has been produced first for Gender and then for Department. Take each of these sets of information in turn. In the table headed *Descriptives*, check that the minimum and maximum values given for the two or more levels of the independent variable seem correct, and in the box and whiskers plots look for any extreme scores. Details on how to do this are given on pages 90–1. If the minimum and maximum values are reasonable, and there are no outliers shown in the box and whiskers plot, follow the instructions below to perform the ANOVA.

If the minimum and maximum values don't look right, and/or there are outliers shown in the box and whiskers plot, check your data to make sure that the extreme values are not mistakes, and that from a research point of view it makes sense to include them in the analysis. If necessary, take steps to modify the data and then run *Explore* again, repeating the process until you are confident that your data are sound. When you are confident that the data are acceptable, follow the instructions below to carry out the ANOVA.

In this example, two extreme values have been identified. Case number 8, a male, is identified as getting a particularly high score of 6; and case number 5, another male, gets a relatively low score of 1. These two data points were checked and found to be acceptable. Therefore, no modification was made to the data file before running the ANOVA.

To run the independent samples factorial ANOVA:

- ➢ Click on **Analyze**.
- ➢ Click on **General Linear Model**.
- ➢ Click on **Univariate** . . . .
- ➢ Click on the dependent variable. It will be highlighted in blue. Click the black triangle to the left of the box headed **Dependent Variable**. The dependent variable will be moved across to this box.
- ➢ Click on the first independent variable. It will be highlighted in blue. Click on the black triangle to the left of the box headed **Fixed Factor(s)**. The dependent variable will be moved across to this box.
- ➢ Move all other independent variables across to the **Fixed Factor(s)** box in this way (see Figure 5.25).
- ➢ Click on **Plots** . . . . A dialog box will open. This allows you to request line graphs showing the means for each independent variable plotted against another independent variable. Decide on the two independent variables you wish to see in each graph (if you are carrying out a two-way ANOVA, as in this example, there will of course only be two independent variables available anyway). For a particular graph, click on one independent variable and then on the black triangle to the left of the box headed **Horizontal Axis**. Then click on the other independent variable followed by the box headed **Separate Lines**.
- ➢ Click on **Add**. The two independent variables will appear, separated by an asterisk, in the white box at the bottom of the dialog box (see Figure 5.26). Repeat this process for any other pairs of independent variables you wish to see plotted. Note that if you have more than two independent variables you can

183

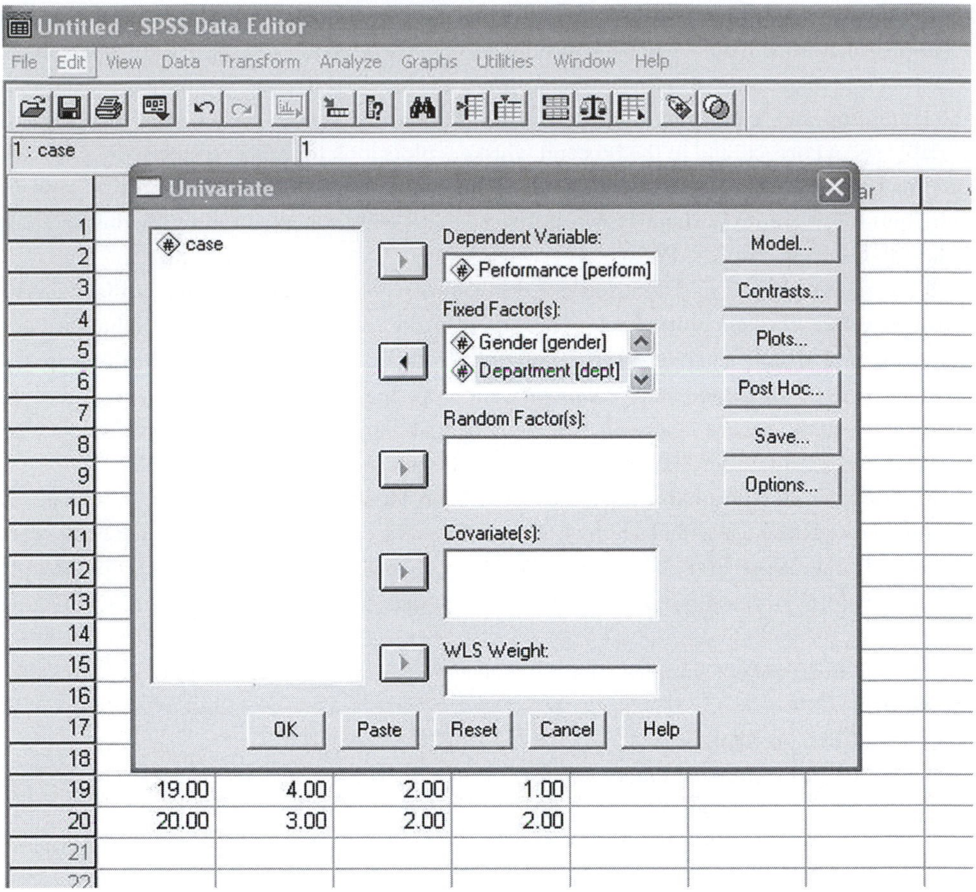

Figure 5.25 *Entering the independent and dependent variables when carrying out an independent samples factorial ANOVA*

request a plot for any two of these broken down by a third by entering this third one in **Separate Plots** before clicking on **Add**.

➢ Click on **Continue**.

➢ Click on **Options**. A dialog box will appear.

➢ Click in the small box next to **Descriptive Statistics** and also the one next to **Homogeneity Tests**. Ticks will appear in these boxes.

➢ Click on **Continue**.

➢ If any of your independent variables have three or more levels, and you wish to examine whether the means are different across each pair of levels (e.g. you are comparing the job satisfaction of people in sales, finance and production departments, and you wish to compare job satisfaction for sales versus finance, finance versus production, and sales versus production), click on **Post Hoc** .... A dialog box will appear. In the white box on the left you will see your independent variables. Click on one of these variables with three or more levels to highlight it, and then on the black triangle to the right. The variable will

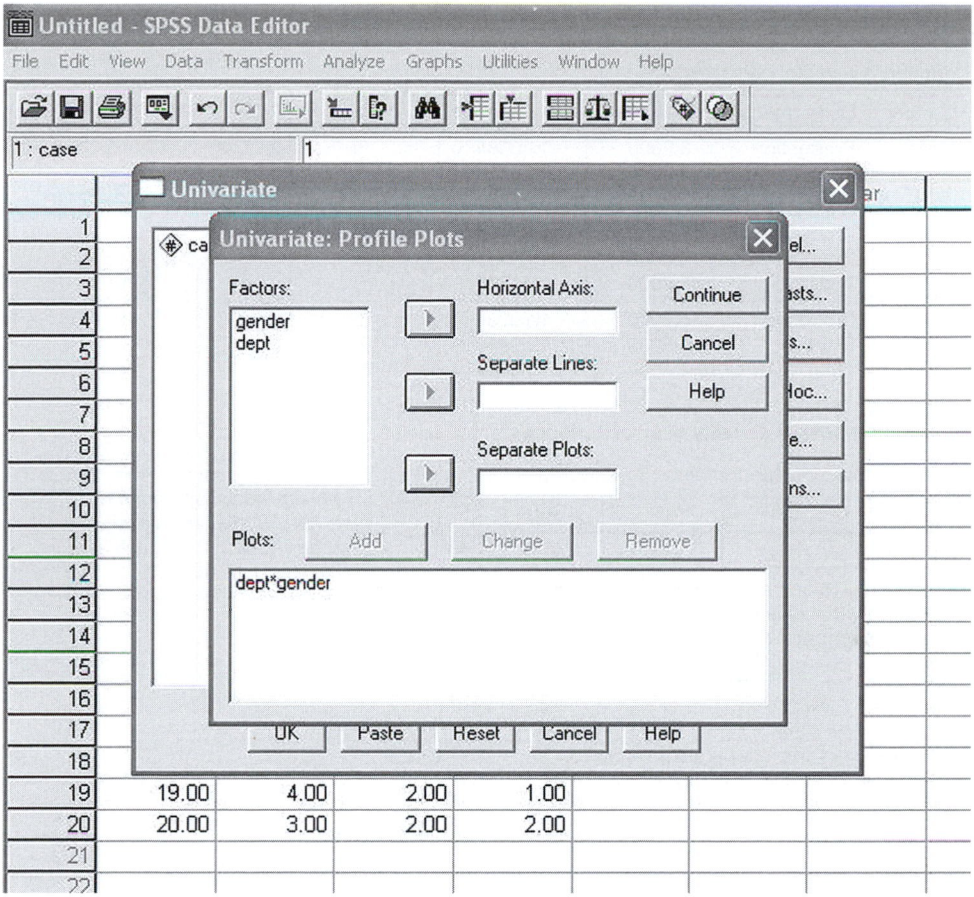

Figure 5.26 *Entering the variables to be plotted when carrying out an independent samples factorial ANOVA*

be moved to the box headed **Post Hoc Tests for** .... Repeat for all of the independent variables with three or more levels that you want to examine. Then click the white box next to Bonferroni, followed by **Continue**. This does not apply here as the independent variables only have two levels.

➤ Click on **OK**.

The results will appear in the output file as follows.

Univariate analysis of variance

Between-subjects factors

		Value label	N
Gender	1.00	Males	10
	2.00	Females	10
Performance	1.00	Production	10
	2.00	Finance	10

Descriptive statistics

Dependent variable: performance

Gender	Department	Mean	Std deviation	N
Males	Production	3.2000	1.30384	5
	Finance	4.0000	1.58114	5
	Total	3.6000	1.42984	10
Females	Production	5.4000	1.34164	5
	Finance	5.0000	1.41421	5
	Total	5.2000	1.31656	10
Total	Production	4.3000	1.70294	10
	Finance	4.5000	1.50923	10
	Total	4.4000	1.56945	20

> Mean and standard deviation for each combination of independent variables.

Levene's test of equality of error variances[a]

Dependent variable: performance

F	df1	df2	Sig.
.235	3	16	.871

> To meet the assumptions of the ANOVA this value should not be significant. That is, it should be less than .05.

Tests the null hypothesis that the error variance of the dependent variable is equal across groups.
[a] Design: Intercept+GENDER+DEPT+GENDER * DEPT

> The names of the independent variables, each one representing a main effect.

Tests of between-subjects effects

Dependent variable: performance

Source	Type III sum of squares	df	Mean square	F	Sig.
Corrected model	14.800[a]	3	4.933	2.467	.100
Intercept	387.200	1	387.200	193.600	.000
GENDER	12.800	1	12.800	6.400	.022
DEPT	.200	1	.200	.100	.756
GENDER * DEPT	1.800	1	1.800	.900	.357
Error	32.000	16	2.000		
Total	434.000	20			
Corrrected total	46.800	19			

[a] R Squared = .316 (Adjusted R squared = .188)

Interaction effect.

Degrees of freedom.

F values.

> Significance levels, showing the probability of the difference in the sample means being as large as you have found them to be if the null hypothesis is true, for each main effect and each interaction. Each of these values needs to be below .05 for statistical significance.

Profile plots

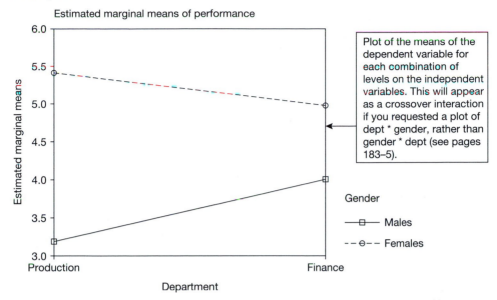

Estimated marginal means of performance

Plot of the means of the dependent variable for each combination of levels on the independent variables. This will appear as a crossover interaction if you requested a plot of dept * gender, rather than gender * dept (see pages 183–5).

How to report the results of an independent samples factorial ANOVA

The results can be reported as follows:

A 2 × 2 independent measures ANOVA was carried out using gender and type of department (production versus finance) as the independent variables, and performance as the dependent variable. Means and standard deviations are shown in Table 5.19, and a line graph of the results is shown in Figure 5.27. There was a

Table 5.19 *Means and standard deviations of job performance by gender and type of department*

Gender	Department	Mean	Standard deviation	Number
Male	Production	3.20	1.30	5
	Finance	4.00	1.58	5
	Total	3.60	1.43	10
Female	Production	5.40	1.34	5
	Finance	5.00	1.41	5
	Total	5.20	1.32	10
Total	Production	4.30	1.70	10
	Finance	4.50	1.51	10
	Total	4.40	1.57	20

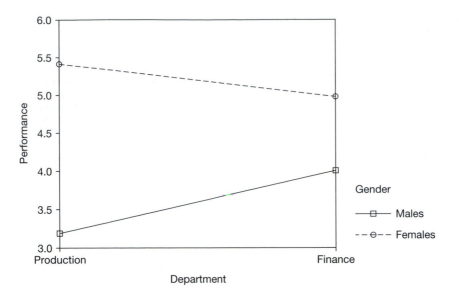

Figure 5.27 *Line graph of performance by gender and department*

main effect for gender, with women performing significantly better than men, $F(1, 16) = 6.40$, $p = .02$. However, the main effect for type of department was not significant, $F(1, 16) = 0.10$, $p = .76$, and nor was the interaction between department and gender, $F(1, 16) = 0.90$, $p = .36$.

Comments

- In the case of a factorial analysis of variance, two sets of degrees of freedom are given in the brackets after the *F* value. The first one is the degree of freedom for the independent variable or interaction in question. So, for example, the analysis of variance summary table indicates that there is one degree of freedom for department (i.e. dept). The second degree of freedom is for error, which the summary table shows in this case to be 16. This is why the degrees of freedom for department are shown as (1, 16) when the results are reported.
- The means and standard deviation are taken from the first table in the results output: *Descriptive Statistics*.
- If the *F* value is significant, it is very helpful to draw attention to the effect size when discussing the findings. For a difference in means, the appropriate measure of effect size is *d*. For a particular pair of means this can be obtained by working out the difference between the two and dividing this by the pooled standard deviation. An easy to use calculator which performs this function is available at www.dewberry-statistics.com. To use the calculator you simply need to enter the relevant means, standard deviations and sample sizes shown in the *Descriptives Statistics* table on page 186. For example, if we wished to report the effect size of the difference

between males and females we would need the mean and standard deviation of each of these. Consulting the *Descriptive Statistics* table, the mean and standard deviation for males are 3.60 and 1.43 respectively. The mean and standard deviation for females are 5.20 and 1.32. Entering the figures for this example into the calculator we obtain a d of 1.16. We can therefore say that the effect size is large ($d = 1.16$). Which of the effect sizes you choose to mention will depend on the particular focus of your research, and what you consider relevant in the light of this.

■ If any of the independent variables have three or more levels, and you have compared the differences between pairs of means with Bonferroni tests, the output of these tests should be interpreted as for an independent samples one-way ANOVA (see pages 169–70).

Interpretation

In interpreting the results of a factorial analysis of variance, it is important to consider each of the main effects and the interactions, since all are likely to be relevant to the research hypotheses. If you find significant interaction effects it may well be that these are more important than the main effects; indeed, some people recommend ignoring the main effects and just focusing on the interaction effects in this situation. The important thing is to look closely at the 'Profile Plots' graph produced by *SPSS*, and to consider what this means in relation to the question you are trying to answer with your research.

As always, it is also good practice to be aware of the effect sizes, and to remember that with very large samples even small main effects and interactions are likely to reach statistical significance.

As for causality, the principles applying to the statistical methods already discussed apply here also. Causality can only be inferred if the research is designed in such a way that there is only one viable explanation for a significant main effect or interaction. So, if the dependent variable is job performance and gender is a significant independent variable, you cannot infer that gender is having a causal influence on job performance because there are all sorts of variables associated with gender which might be responsible for this.

REPEATED MEASURES FACTORIAL ANOVA

When to use

Use a repeated measures factorial ANOVA when you have two or more independent variables and one dependent variable, and on all independent variables the same people have been measured on more than one occasion. You wish to know if there is a significant difference between the means across the two or more levels (i.e. the two or more repeated measurements) on each independent variable. You may also wish to know whether there is one or more interactions between the independent variables and the dependent variable. The material below on the repeated measures ANOVA assumes knowledge of what is meant by main effects and interactions. For a discussion of this see pages 171–5.

189

Example

■ A new software system is introduced into an organization. Managers wish to know how positive employees feel about both the old system and the new system. A measure of employees' attitude towards the old and the new system is developed. This is scored out of 10, where 1 indicates that employees are highly negative about the system and 10 indicates that they are highly positive. The managers suspect that employees will be relatively negative about the new system shortly after it has been introduced, but that they will become more positive after they have used it for about a year. Therefore, they decide to distribute the attitude measure immediately after the introduction of the new system and again 12 months later. A repeated measures factorial ANOVA is used to examine whether there is a difference in: (a) mean attitude towards the two software systems; and (b) mean attitude immediately after the introduction of the new software system, and 12 months later. The repeated measures factorial ANOVA will also be used to examine whether or not there is an interaction between the software system (old versus new) and the time that attitudes are measured (immediately after the introduction of the new system and 12 months later).

Assumptions and requirements

The main assumption of a repeated measures factorial ANOVA is equality of covariance. This is briefly explained on page 154. As in the case of the repeated measures one-way ANOVA we will deal with this potential problem by adopting the Huynh-Feldt correction. This corrects for a violation of the equality of covariance assumption without the loss of much statistical power.

The required sample size

The sample size required for a repeated measures factorial ANOVA depends on the power required, the adopted significance level, the effect size of the independent variable with the weakest effect size among those used, and the degree of correlation between the scores across the levels of that independent variable. For a brief discussion of these issues see the section on required sample sizes for the repeated measures one-way ANOVA (pages 154–5).

If you are in a position to use the results of a pilot study or relevant previous research to estimate the effect size expected in the research you expect to analyse with a repeated measures factorial ANOVA, for each independent variable on which you have data:

1 Take the levels of the independent variable expected to have the smallest and largest means, and in each case divide the mean (found in the pilot study or previous research) by the standard deviation (found in the pilot study or previous research).
2 Obtain the effect size by subtracting the result for the smallest mean from the result for the largest mean.
3 Use the independent variable with the weakest effect size as your guide to the effect size you will expect in your study.

Table 5.20 *The approximate sample sizes required for a repeated measures factorial ANOVA, assuming a power of 80% and a .05 significance level*

Effect size		Total sample size required		
		Number of levels of the independent variable		
	Bausell and Li ES	3	4	5
Small	0.2	300	325	360
Medium	0.6	36	40	40
Large	1.0	15	16	16

Table 5.20 shows the approximate sample sizes required for Bausell and Li effect sizes of .20, .60 and 1.00 for a power of 80 per cent, a significance level of .05, and an average correlation between the scores of the various levels of the independent variables of .4. As for the repeated measures one-way ANOVA, these effect sizes have been chosen because they provide a reasonable spread of the values that typically occur in research, and they therefore provide a useful guide to the sample sizes required.

If you are not able to estimate the effect size you expect to find in your research, use Table 5.20 to find the sample size required for a medium effect size. For the number of levels of the independent variable, choose the independent variable you are using which has the highest number of levels. For example, if you are using a 2 × 3 × 2 design, use the table to look up the sample size required with a medium effect size and an independent variable with three levels.

A worked example

A new software system is to be introduced in an organization, and managers are concerned that people may have a very negative attitude to it. A researcher is asked to investigate these attitudes. She decides to measure employees' attitudes to both the old software system and the new one, and to do so: (a) before the old system is replaced by the new one (here employees' attitudes towards the new system will be speculative); (b) immediately after the introduction of the new system; and (c) again two years later. Table 5.21 shows the attitude scores, measured out of 10, with the most positive attitudes being 10 and the least positive 1.

How to carry out a repeated measures factorial ANOVA using SPSS

Begin by entering your data in the *SPSS* Data Editor. Figure 5.28 shows what the above data look like when they have been entered. Use the *Variable View* in the data editor to enter full variable names. In this example the variable names used were as follows:

- before new system installed/old system: 'beforold';
- before new system installed/new system: 'befornew';

Table 5.21 *The attitudes of 20 employees to old and new software systems measured before and at two points after the new system was introduced*

Case	Attitude before new software system installed		Attitude immediately after new software system installed		Attitude two years after new software system installed	
	Old system	New system	Old system	New system	Old system	New system
1	6	7	9	3	2	7
2	7	8	5	2	3	8
3	4	5	6	5	4	6
4	5	6	8	3	2	9
5	6	8	5	6	5	7
6	7	5	8	2	3	9
7	5	9	9	1	4	9
8	6	7	6	3	2	7
9	4	8	7	4	3	8
10	7	7	5	2	4	9
11	5	9	7	5	5	10
12	6	7	9	3	2	10
13	7	6	7	5	3	8
14	5	8	5	3	4	8
15	4	7	7	2	2	7
16	7	8	10	6	3	9
17	5	5	7	4	4	10
18	7	8	8	2	4	7
19	4	7	6	5	2	9
20	4	7	7	3	3	7

- immediately after the new system was installed/old system: 'afterold';
- immediately after the new system was installed/new system: 'afternew';
- two years after the new system was installed/old system: 'laterold';
- two years after the new system was installed/new system: 'laternew'.

And the following labels were used for each of the six variables:

- 'Attitude to old software before';
- 'Attitude to new software before';
- 'Attitude to old software just after';

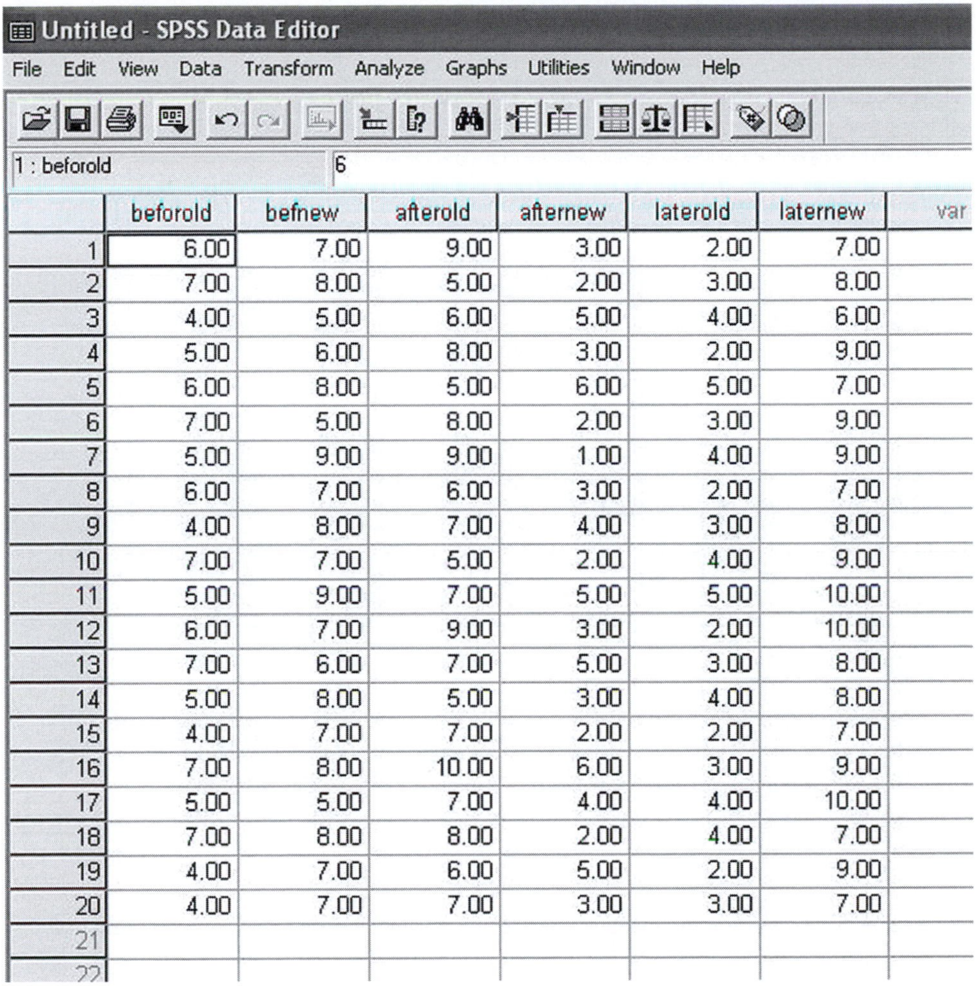

	beforold	befnew	afterold	afternew	laterold	laternew	var
1	6.00	7.00	9.00	3.00	2.00	7.00	
2	7.00	8.00	5.00	2.00	3.00	8.00	
3	4.00	5.00	6.00	5.00	4.00	6.00	
4	5.00	6.00	8.00	3.00	2.00	9.00	
5	6.00	8.00	5.00	6.00	5.00	7.00	
6	7.00	5.00	8.00	2.00	3.00	9.00	
7	5.00	9.00	9.00	1.00	4.00	9.00	
8	6.00	7.00	6.00	3.00	2.00	7.00	
9	4.00	8.00	7.00	4.00	3.00	8.00	
10	7.00	7.00	5.00	2.00	4.00	9.00	
11	5.00	9.00	7.00	5.00	5.00	10.00	
12	6.00	7.00	9.00	3.00	2.00	10.00	
13	7.00	6.00	7.00	5.00	3.00	8.00	
14	5.00	8.00	5.00	3.00	4.00	8.00	
15	4.00	7.00	7.00	2.00	2.00	7.00	
16	7.00	8.00	10.00	6.00	3.00	9.00	
17	5.00	5.00	7.00	4.00	4.00	10.00	
18	7.00	8.00	8.00	2.00	4.00	7.00	
19	4.00	7.00	6.00	5.00	2.00	9.00	
20	4.00	7.00	7.00	3.00	3.00	7.00	
21							
22							

Figure 5.28 SPSS *Data Editor after repeated measures factorial ANOVA data are entered*

- 'Attitude to new software just after';
- 'Attitude to old software later';
- 'Attitude to old software later'.

Note that unlike the previous examples in this book, a separate variable for case number has not been used here. Whether or not you choose to include it is up to you.

Next, run *Explore* in *SPSS*. To do this:

➢ Click on **Analyze**.
➢ Click on **Descriptive Statistics**.
➢ Click on **Explore** . . . .

193

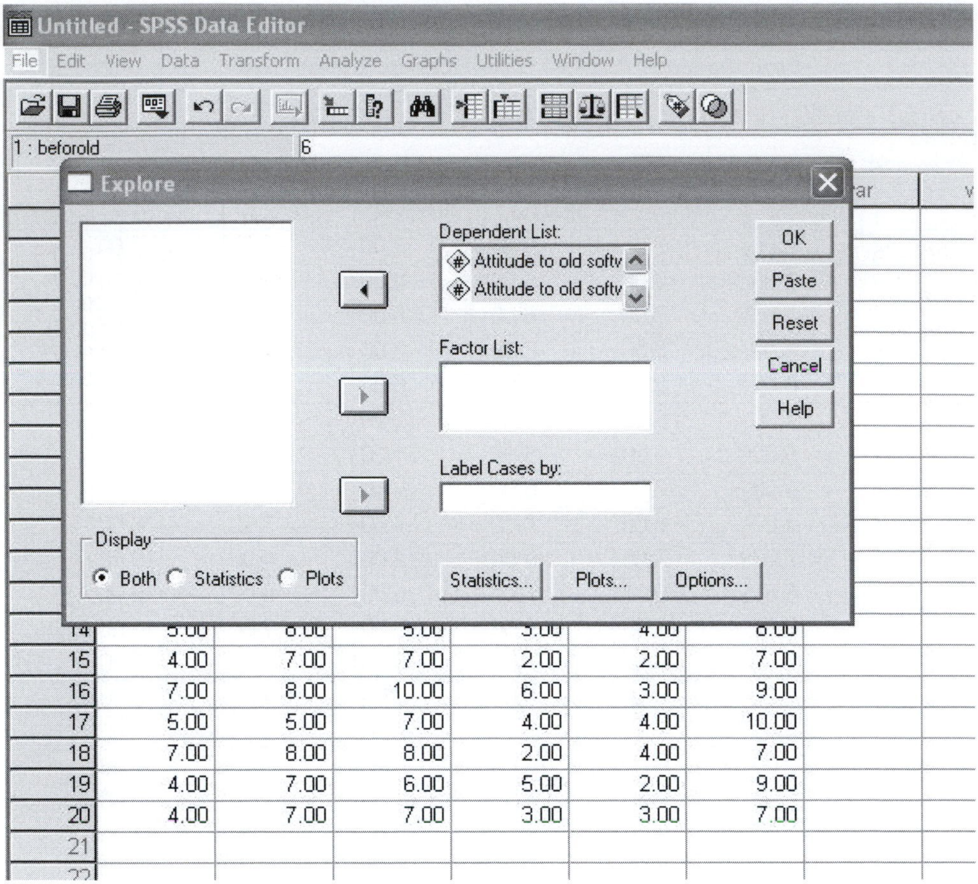

Figure 5.29 *Entering the repeated measures variables in a repeated measures factorial ANOVA*

➢ A dialog box will appear with the repeated measures variables in a white box on the left hand side. Click on the first of these and then on the black triangle to the left of the white box headed **Dependent List**. The first repeated measures variable will be moved across to the **Dependent List** box. Repeat this procedure until all the repeated measures variables have been moved across to the **Dependent List** box (see Figure 5.29).

➢ Click on **OK**.

Output in the following form will appear.

Explore

Case processing summary

	Cases					
	Valid		Missing		Total	
	N	Per cent	N	Per cent	N	Per cent
Attitude to old software before	20	100.0%	0	.0%	20	100.0%
Attitude to new software before	20	100.0%	0	.0%	20	100.0%
Attitude to old software just after	20	100.0%	0	.0%	20	100.0%
Attitude to new software just after	20	100.0%	0	.0%	20	100.0%
Attitude to old software later	20	100.0%	0	.0%	20	100.0%
Attitude to new software later	20	100.0%	0	.0%	20	100.0%

Descriptives

			Statistic	Std error
Attitude to old software before	Mean		5.5500	.26631
	95% confidence interval for mean	Lower bound	4.9926	
		Upper bound	6.1074	
	5% trimmed mean		5.5556	
	Median		5.5000	
	Variance		1.418	
	Std deviation		1.19097	
	Minimum		4.00	
	Maximum		7.00	
	Range		3.00	
	Interquartile range		2.7500	
	Skewness		−.028	.512
	Kurtosis		−1.528	.992
Attitude to new software before	Mean		7.1000	.27048
	95% confidence interval for mean	Lower bound	6.5339	
		Upper bound	7.6661	
	5% trimmed mean		7.1111	
	Median		7.0000	
	Variance		1.463	
	Std deviation		1.20961	
	Minimum		5.00	
	Maximum		9.00	
	Range		4.00	
	Interquartile range		1.7500	
	Skewness		−.408	.512
	Kurtosis		−.459	.992
Attitude to old software just after	Mean		7.0500	.33619
	95% confidence interval for mean	Lower bound	6.3463	
		Upper bound	7.7537	
	5% trimmed mean		7.0000	
	Median		7.0000	
	Variance		2.261	

	Std deviation		1.50350	
	Minimum		5.00	
	Maximum		10.00	
	Range		5.00	
	Interquartile range		2.0000	
	Skewness		.216	.512
	Kurtosis		−.771	.992
Attitude to new software just after	Mean		3.4500	.32827
	95% confidence interval for mean	Lower bound	2.7629	
		Upper bound	4.1371	
	5% trimmed mean		3.4444	
	Median		3.0000	
	Variance		2.155	
	Std deviation		1.46808	
	Minimum		1.00	
	Maximum		6.00	
	Range		5.00	
	Interquartile range		3.0000	
	Skewness		.331	.512
	Kurtosis		−.954	.992
Attitude to old software later	Mean		3.2000	.22478
	95% confidence interval for mean	Lower bound	2.7295	
		Upper bound	3.6705	
	5% trimmed mean		3.1667	
	Median		3.0000	
	Variance		1.011	
	Std deviation		1.00525	
	Minimum		2.00	
	Maximum		5.00	
	Range		3.00	
	Interquartile range		2.0000	
	Skewness		.249	.512
	Kurtosis		−.999	.992
Attitude to new software later	Mean		8.2000	.26754
	95% confidence interval for mean	Lower bound	7.6400	
		Upper bound	8.7600	
	5% trimmed mean		8.2222	
	Median		8.0000	
	Variance		1.432	
	Std deviation		1.19649	
	Minimum		6.00	
	Maximum		10.00	
	Range		4.00	
	Interquartile range		2.0000	
	Skewness		−.016	.512
	Kurtosis		−1.078	.992

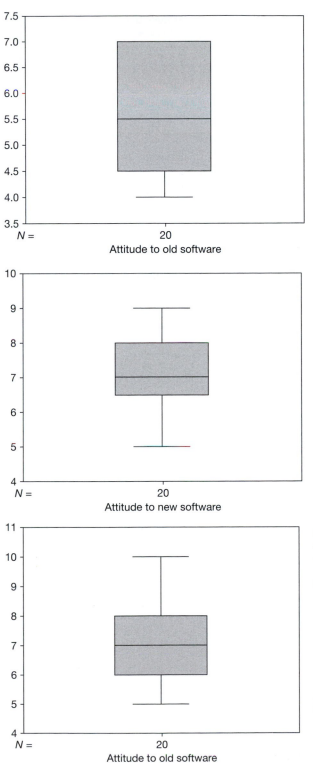

Attitude to old software before

Attitude to old software
before Stem-and-Leaf Plot

```
Frequency     Stem &  Leaf

    5.00       4 .  00000
     .00       4 .
    5.00       5 .  00000
     .00       5 .
    4.00       6 .  0000
     .00       6 .
    6.00       7 .  000000

Stem width:  1.00
Each leaf:   1 case(s)
```

Attitude to new software before

Attitude to new software
before Stem-and-Leaf Plot

```
Frequency     Stem &  Leaf

    3.00       5 .  000
    2.00       6 .  00
    7.00       7 .  0000000
    6.00       8 .  000000
    2.00       9 .  00

Stem width:  1.00
Each leaf:   1 case(s)
```

Attitude to old software just after

Attitude to old software just
after Stem-and-Leaf Plot

```
Frequency     Stem &  Leaf

    4.00       5 .  0000
    3.00       6 .  000
    6.00       7 .  000000
    3.00       8 .  000
    3.00       9 .  000
    1.00      10 .  0

Stem width:   1.00
Each leaf:    1 case(s)
```

197

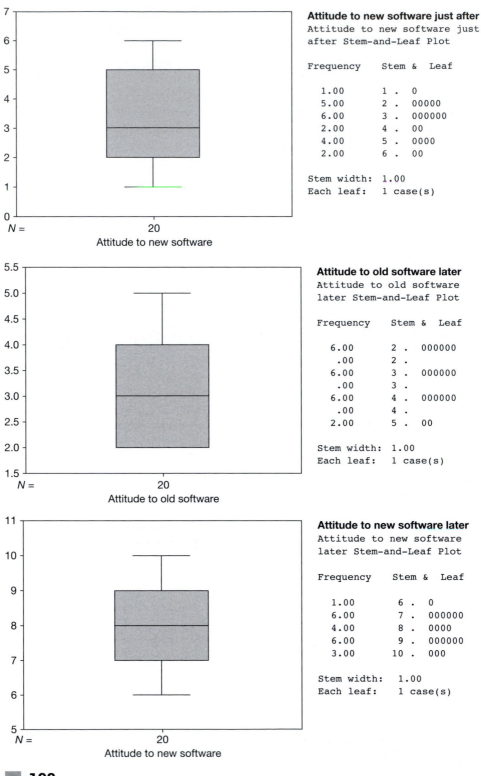

Attitude to new software just after
```
Attitude to new software just
after Stem-and-Leaf Plot

Frequency     Stem &   Leaf

   1.00        1 .  0
   5.00        2 .  00000
   6.00        3 .  000000
   2.00        4 .  00
   4.00        5 .  0000
   2.00        6 .  00

Stem width:  1.00
Each leaf:   1 case(s)
```

Attitude to old software later
```
Attitude to old software
later Stem-and-Leaf Plot

Frequency     Stem &   Leaf

   6.00        2 .  000000
    .00        2 .
   6.00        3 .  000000
    .00        3 .
   6.00        4 .  000000
    .00        4 .
   2.00        5 .  00

Stem width:  1.00
Each leaf:   1 case(s)
```

Attitude to new software later
```
Attitude to new software
later Stem-and-Leaf Plot

Frequency     Stem &   Leaf

   1.00        6 .  0
   6.00        7 .  000000
   4.00        8 .  0000
   6.00        9 .  000000
   3.00       10 .  000

Stem width:  1.00
Each leaf:   1 case(s)
```

A separate set of information is produced for each repeated measure. In this example, such information has been produced for the two sets of three repeatedly measured attitude scores. Take each of these sets of information in turn. In the table headed *Descriptives*, check that the minimum and maximum values given for the values of each of your repeated measures seem correct, and in the box and whiskers plots look for any extreme scores. Details on how to do this are given on pages 90–1. If the minimum and maximum values are reasonable, and there are no outliers shown in the box and whiskers plot, follow the instructions below to perform the repeated measures factorial ANOVA.

If the minimum and maximum values don't look right, and/or there are outliers shown in the box and whiskers plot, check your data to make sure that the extreme values are not mistakes, and that from a research point of view it makes sense to include them in the analysis. If necessary, take steps to modify the data, and then run *Explore* again, repeating the process until you are confident that your data are sound. When you are confident that the data are acceptable, follow the instructions below to carry out the ANOVA.

In this example, the minimum and maximum values were correct and no extreme values are identified in the box and whiskers plots. Therefore, it was possible to proceed straight to the ANOVA.

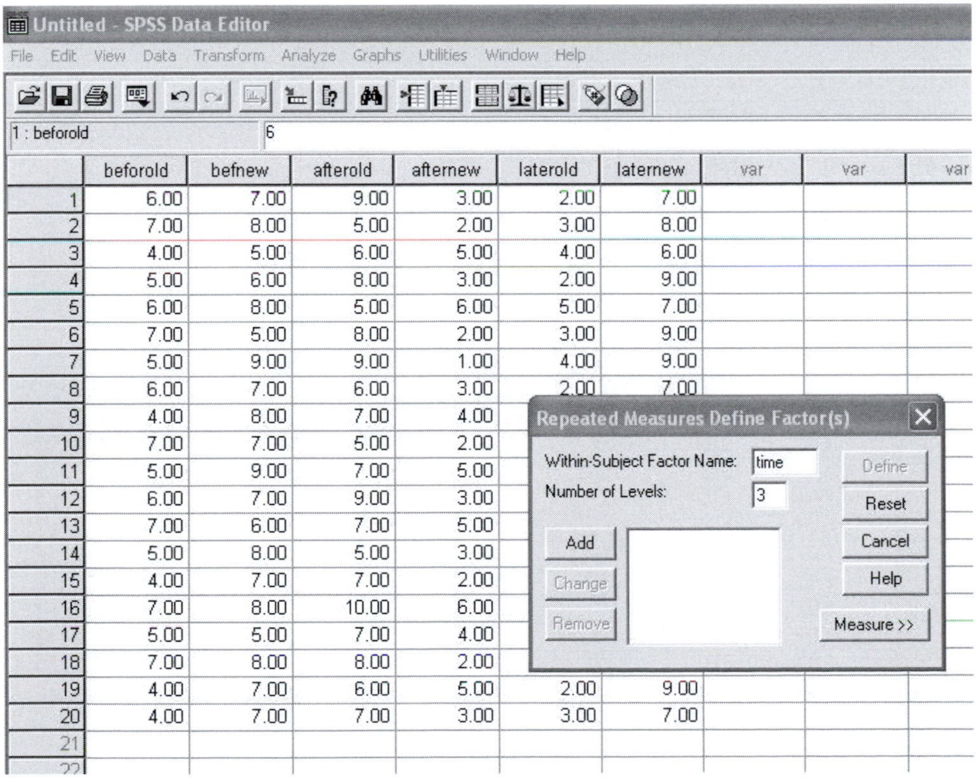

Figure 5.30 *Entering the first repeated measures (or within-subject) factor in a repeated measures factorial ANOVA*

199

To run the repeated measures factorial ANOVA:

> ➤ Click on **Analyze**.
> ➤ Click on **General Linear Model**.
> ➤ Click on **Repeated Measures** ....
> ➤ A dialog box will appear. Click in the white box to the right of **Within-Subject Factor Name** and delete the phrase **factor 1**. Write in a suitable name for your first repeated measures variable. This name must not be longer than eight characters, must begin with a letter rather than a number, and must not contain any spaces. In this example, well-being has been measured at three times, so the first repeated measures variable is called **time**.
> ➤ In the white box to the right of **Number of Levels** enter the number of levels of the repeated measures variable. In this example, time had three levels (before the new software was introduced, immediately after its introduction and two years later) so the number of levels entered is 3 (see Figure 5.30).
> ➤ Click on **Add**. The name of the repeated measures variable, and the number of levels of the independent variable in brackets, will appear in the white box below.

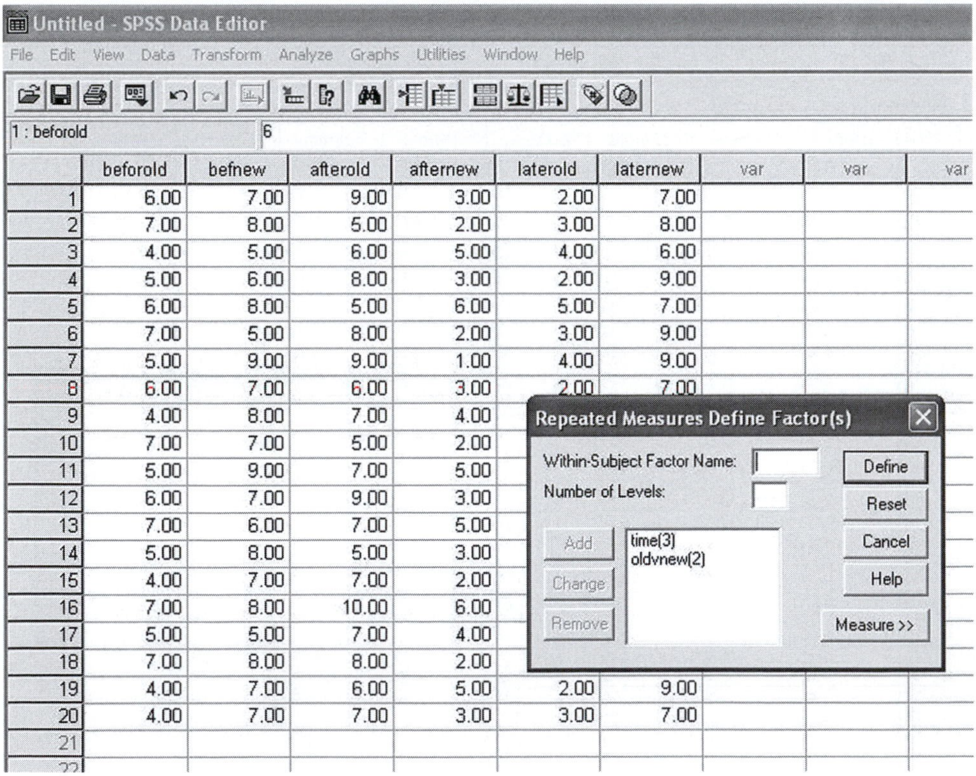

Figure 5.31 *Defining the factors in a repeated measures factorial ANOVA*

> Repeat the previous two steps for additional repeated measures variables. In this example, the second repeated variable was whether the attitude was measured towards the old or the new software system. So this variable, which has two levels (old versus new) was called **oldvnew** (see Figure 5.31).

> Click on **Define**. A dialog box will appear (see Figure 5.32). In the rectangular white box to the left you will see a list of your repeated measures variables. To the right you will see a white box headed **Within-Subjects Variables** followed by the names you have given your independent variables (in the case of this example, 'time' and 'old versus new' ('time', 'oldvnew'). If you look in the white box headed **Within-Subjects Variables** you will see a series of dashes separated by one or more question marks, and after this two or more figures separated by commas, in brackets. The figures refer to the levels of the independent variable, so in this example the first figure refers to each of the three levels of the first independent variable, 'time', and the second one refers to each of the two levels of the second independent variable, 'oldvnew'. You need to be careful here, because your task is to match up the name of each repeated measures variable with the corresponding levels. In this example, the first variable **beforold** is at the first level of time (i.e. before the new software was introduced) and at the first level of old versus new (i.e. it refers to

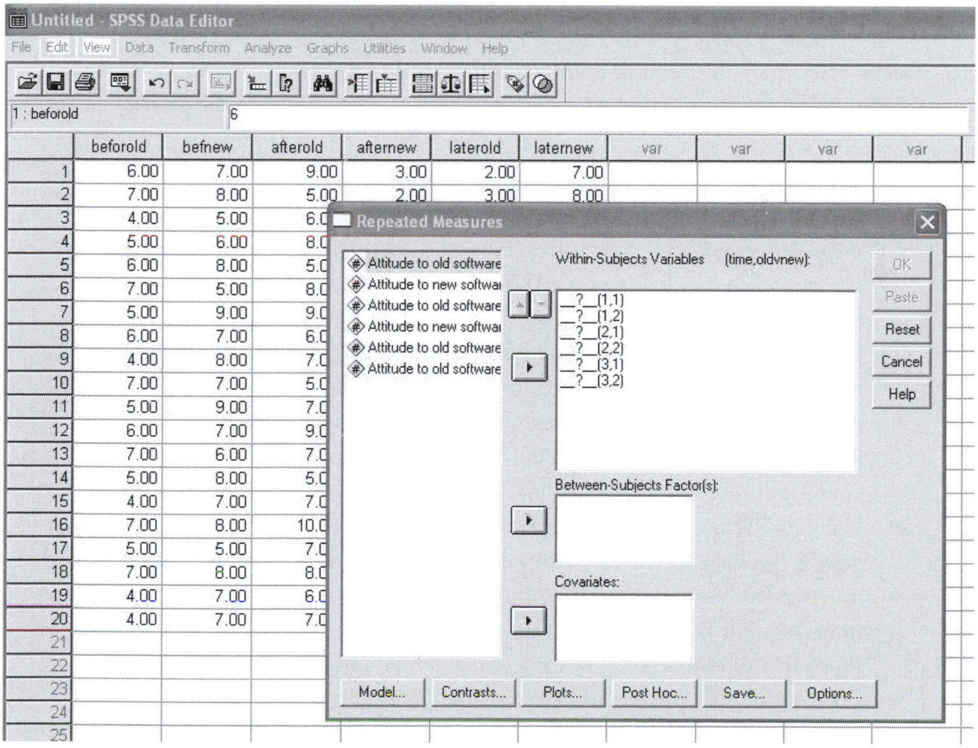

Figure 5.32 *The Within-Subject dialog box in a repeated measures factorial ANOVA*

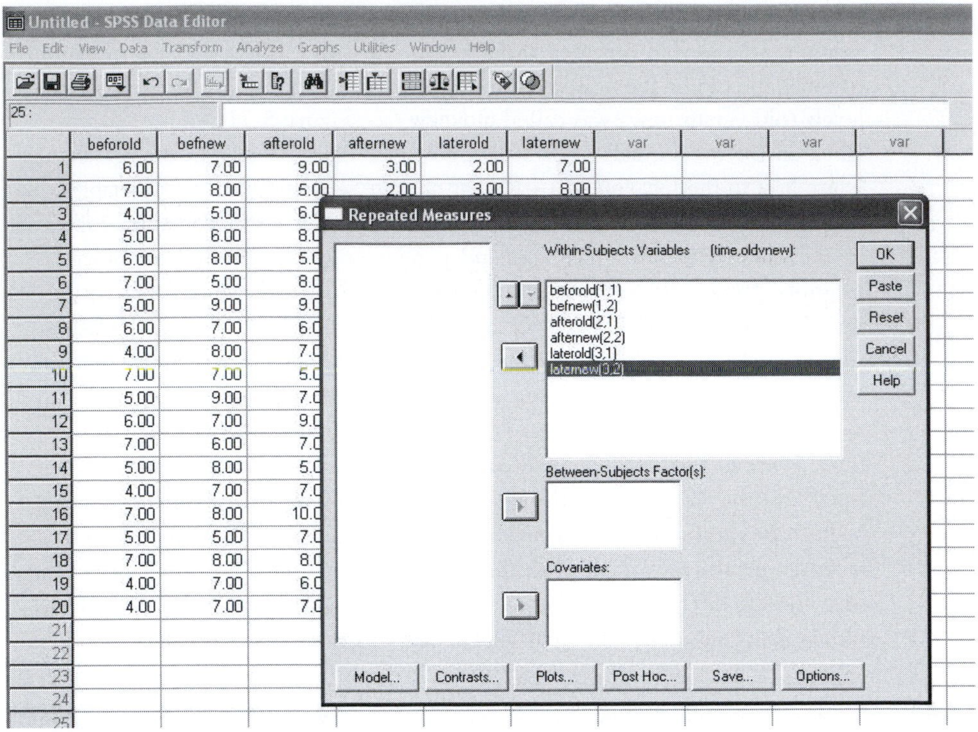

Figure 5.33 *After the levels of each factor have been specified in a repeated measures factorial ANOVA*

attitudes towards the old software system rather than the new one). Since the first set of levels in the box under **Within-Subjects Variables** is 1,1 (i.e. level 1 for time, and level 1 for old versus new) this is the correct set in this case, so we can begin by clicking on **Attitude to new software before [beforold]**. It will be highlighted in blue. Then click on the single black triangle half-way down the left side of the white box headed **Within-Subjects Variables**. The name of the first repeated measures variable (in this case, 'beforold') will be entered in this box next to the figures indicating which level it is on each independent variable. Repeat this until all of the repeated measures variables are correctly entered (see Figure 5.33).

➢ Click on **Plots** .... A dialog box will open. This allows you to request line graphs showing the means for each independent variable plotted against another independent variable. Decide on the two independent variables you wish to see in each graph (if you are carrying out a two-way ANOVA, as in this example, there will of course only be two independent variables available anyway). For a particular graph, click on one independent variable and then on the black triangle to the left of the box headed **Horizontal Axis**. Then click on the other independent variable followed by the box headed **Separate Lines** (see Figure 5.34).

202

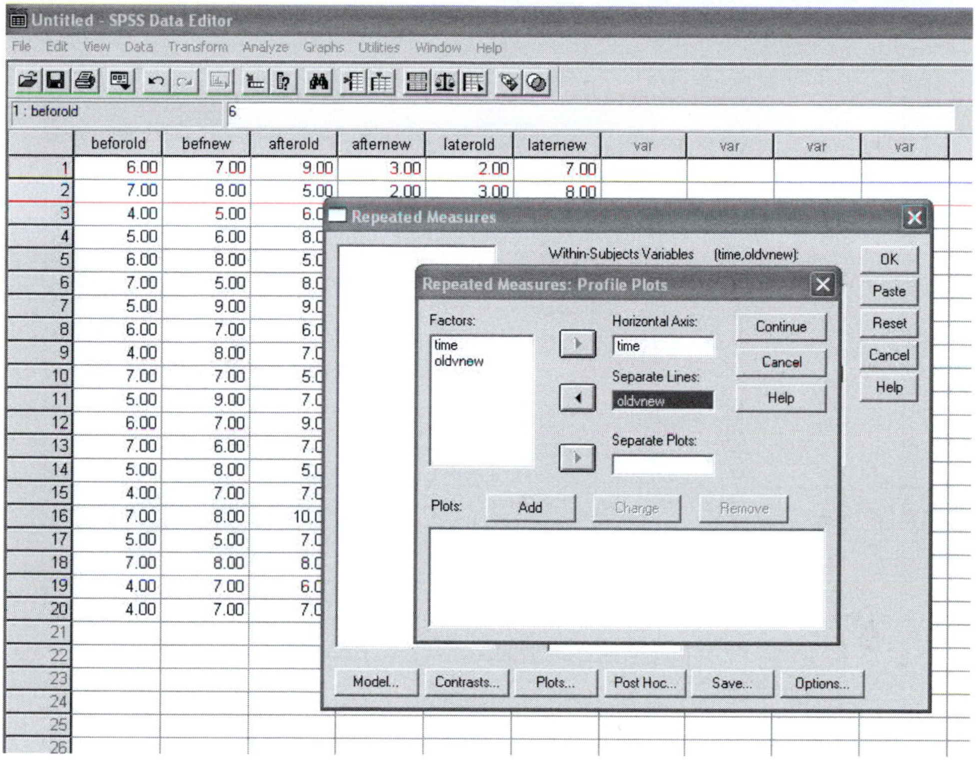

	beforold	befnew	afterold	afternew	laterold	laternew	var	var	var	var
1	6.00	7.00	9.00	3.00	2.00	7.00				
2	7.00	8.00	5.00	2.00	3.00	8.00				
3	4.00	5.00	6.0							
4	5.00	6.00	8.0							
5	6.00	8.00	5.0							
6	7.00	5.00	8.0							
7	5.00	9.00	9.0							
8	6.00	7.00	6.0							
9	4.00	8.00	7.0							
10	7.00	7.00	5.0							
11	5.00	9.00	7.0							
12	6.00	7.00	9.0							
13	7.00	6.00	7.0							
14	5.00	8.00	5.0							
15	4.00	7.00	7.0							
16	7.00	8.00	10.0							
17	5.00	5.00	7.0							
18	7.00	8.00	8.0							
19	4.00	7.00	6.0							
20	4.00	7.00	7.0							
21										
22										
23										
24										
25										
26										

Figure 5.34 *Specifying the graph required in a repeated measures factorial ANOVA*

➢ Click on **Add**. The two independent variables will appear, separated by an asterisk, in the white box at the bottom of the dialog box. Repeat this process for any other pairs of independent variables you wish to see plotted. Note that if you have more than two independent variables you can request a plot for any two of these broken down by a third by entering the third variable in **Separate Plots** before clicking on **Add**.
➢ Click on **Continue**.
➢ Click on **Options**. A dialog box will appear.
➢ Click in the small box next to **Descriptive Statistics** (see Figure 5.35).
➢ Click on **Continue**.
➢ Click on **OK**.

When the output has been produced it will contain a lot of detailed information that is not necessary. Therefore, it is a good idea to delete the material you don't need before viewing the results. To do this, have a look at the large white area on the left hand side of the screen (see Figure 5.36). There, you will see a list of the titles of the various results tables that *SPSS* has generated. Delete the four tests shown at the top of page 205 by first clicking on each one to highlight it, and then pressing the delete key on your keyboard.

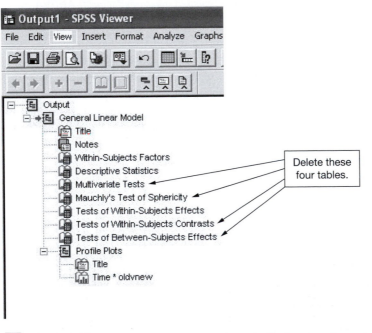

	beforold	befnew	afterold	afternew	laterold	laternew	var	var	var	var
1	6.00	7.00	9.00	3.00	2.00	7.00				
2	7.00	8.00	5.00	2.00	3.00	8.00				
3	4.00	5.00	6.0							
4	5.00	6.00	8.0							
5	6.00	8.00	5.0							
6	7.00	5.00	8.0							
7	5.00	9.00	9.0							
8	6.00	7.00	6.0							
9	4.00	8.00	7.0							
10	7.00	7.00	5.0							
11	5.00	9.00	7.0							
12	6.00	7.00	9.0							
13	7.00	6.00	7.0							
14	5.00	8.00	5.0							
15	4.00	7.00	7.0							
16	7.00	8.00	10.0							
17	5.00	5.00	7.0							
18	7.00	8.00	8.0							
19	4.00	7.00	6.0							
20	4.00	7.00	7.0							

Figure 5.35 Specifying the options in a repeated measures factorial ANOVA

Figure 5.36 Deleting unnecessary results output when carrying out a repeated measures factorial ANOVA

- Multivariate Tests;
- Mauchly's Test of Sphericity;
- Tests of Within-Subjects Contrasts;
- Tests of Between-Subjects Effects.

The results will appear in the output file as follows.

General linear model

Within-subjects factors

Measure: MEASURE_1

TIME	OLDVNEW	Dependent variable
1	1 2	BEFOROLD BEFNEW
2	1 2	AFTEROLD AFTERNEW
3	1 2	LATEROLD LATERNEW

> Mean and standard deviation for each repeated measures variable.

Descriptive statistics

	Mean	Std deviation	N
Attitude to old software before	5.5500	1.19097	20
Attitude to new software before	7.1000	1.20961	20
Attitude to old software just after	7.0500	1.50350	20
Attitude to new software just after	3.4500	1.46808	20
Attitude to old software later	3.2000	1.00525	20
Attitude to new software later	8.2000	1.19649	20

Tests of within-subjects effects

> The relevant Huynh-Feldt F values.

Measure: MEASURE_1

Source		Type III sum of squares	df	Mean square	F	Sig.
TIME	Sphericity assumed	23.317	2	11.658	8.201	.001
	Greenhouse-Geisser	23.317	1.829	12.747	8.201	.002
	Huynh-Feldt	23.317	2.000	11.658	8.201	.001
	Lower-bound	23.317	1.000	23.317	8.201	.010
Error (TIME)	Sphericity assumed	54.017	38	1.421		
	Greenhouse-Geisser	54.017	34.755	1.554		
	Huynh-Feldt	54.017	38.000	1.421		
	Lower-bound	54.017	19.000	2.843		
OLDVNEW	Sphericity assumed	29.008	1	29.008	24.505	.000
	Greenhouse-Geisser	29.008	1.000	29.008	24.505	.000
	Huynh-Feldt	29.008	1.000	29.008	24.505	.000
	Lower-bound	29.008	1.000	29.008	24.505	.000

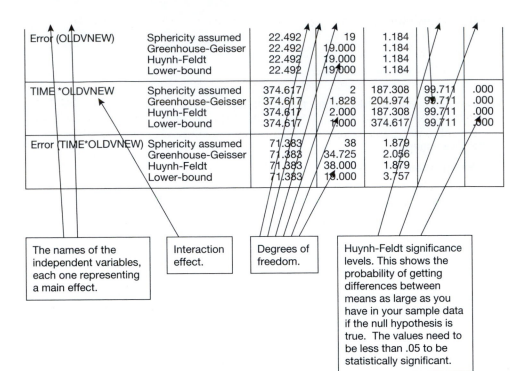

Error (OLDVNEW)	Sphericity assumed	22.492	19	1.184		
	Greenhouse-Geisser	22.492	19.000	1.184		
	Huynh-Feldt	22.492	19.000	1.184		
	Lower-bound	22.492	19.000	1.184		
TIME *OLDVNEW	Sphericity assumed	374.617	2	187.308	99.711	.000
	Greenhouse-Geisser	374.617	1.828	204.974	99.711	.000
	Huynh-Feldt	374.617	2.000	187.308	99.711	.000
	Lower-bound	374.617	1.000	374.617	99.711	.000
Error (TIME*OLDVNEW)	Sphericity assumed	71.383	38	1.879		
	Greenhouse-Geisser	71.383	34.725	2.056		
	Huynh-Feldt	71.383	38.000	1.879		
	Lower-bound	71.383	19.000	3.757		

The names of the independent variables, each one representing a main effect.

Interaction effect.

Degrees of freedom.

Huynh-Feldt significance levels. This shows the probability of getting differences between means as large as you have in your sample data if the null hypothesis is true. The values need to be less than .05 to be statistically significant.

Profile plots

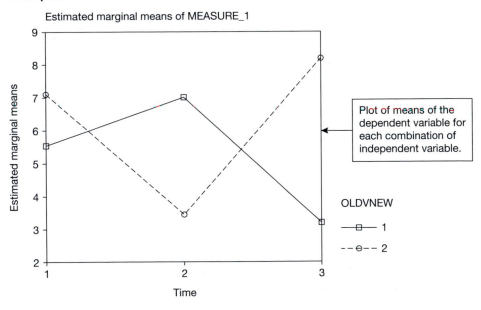

Estimated marginal means of MEASURE_1

Plot of means of the dependent variable for each combination of independent variable.

OLDVNEW

—□— 1

--○-- 2

How to report the results of a repeated measures factorial ANOVA

These results can be reported as follows:

A 3 × 2 repeated measures factorial ANOVA was carried out using time of measurement (before the new software was introduced, immediately after the new software was introduced and two years after the new software was introduced) and type of software (old system versus new system) as the independent variables and attitude towards the software as the dependent variable. Means and standard deviations are shown in Table 5.22, and a line graph of the results is shown in Figure 5.37. There was a main effect for time of measurement $F(2, 38) = 8.20$, $p = .001$, and a main effect for old versus new software system $F(1, 19) = 24.51$, $p < .001$. There was also a significant interaction between time and old versus new software system $F(2, 38) = 99.71$, $p < .001$, and an examination of Figure 5.37 indicates that attitudes to the old and new software systems were similar before the new system was introduced, that the new system was viewed considerably more negatively than the old system immediately after the new system had been introduced, but that two years later the new system was viewed considerably more positively than the old one.

Table 5.22 *Means and standard deviations of attitudes towards two software systems at three points in time*

Time of measurement	Software concerned	Mean	Standard deviation	Number
Before new software introduced	Old	5.55	1.19	20
	New	7.10	1.21	20
Immediately after new software introduced	Old	7.05	1.50	20
	New	3.45	1.47	20
Two years after new software introduced	Old	3.20	1.01	20
	New	8.20	1.20	20

Comments

- The means and standard deviations are taken from the first table in the results output.
- In the case of a factorial analysis of variance, two sets of degrees of freedom are given in the brackets after the F value. The first one is the degree of freedom for the independent variable or interaction in question. So, for example, the analysis of variance summary table indicates that there are two degrees of freedom for time. The second of these degrees of freedom is for error. There is a separate value for the degrees of freedom for error after each main effect and each interaction. So, in this example, the degrees of freedom for error are labelled Error(Time) for the error degrees of freedom for time, Error(OLDVNEW) for the degrees of

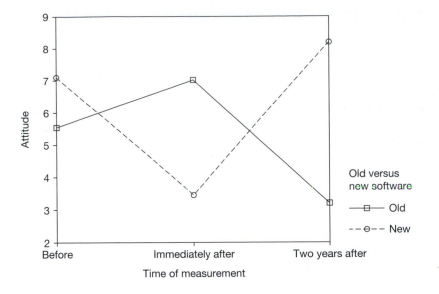

Figure 5.37 *Line graph of attitude by time and new versus old software system*

freedom for old versus new software system, and Error(TIME*OLDVNEW) for the degrees of freedom for the interaction between time and old versus new software system. Therefore, the degrees of freedom for old versus new software system is reported as (1, 19) as there is one degree of freedom for the old versus new independent variable, and 19 degrees of freedom for the error of this independent variable.

■ If the *F* value is significant for a particular independent variable, it is very helpful to draw attention to the effect size when discussing the findings. For a difference in means, the appropriate measure of effect size is *d*. For a particular pair of means this can be obtained by working out the difference between the two and dividing this by the pooled standard deviation. An easy to use calculator which performs this function is available at www.dewberry-statistics.com. To use the calculator you simply need to enter the relevant means, standard deviations and samples sizes shown in the *Descriptive Statistics* table on page 205. For example, if we wished to report the effect size of the difference between attitudes to the old software before and just after the new system was introduced we would need the mean and standard deviation of each of these. Consulting the *Descriptive Statistics* table, the mean and standard deviation for attitude to the old software before the new system was introduced are 5.55 and 1.19 respectively. The mean and standard deviation for attitude to the old software just after the new system was introduced are 7.05 and 1.50. Entering the figures for this example into the calculator we obtain a *d* of 1.11. We can therefore say that the effect size is large (*d* = 1.11). Which of the effect sizes you choose to mention will depend on the particular focus of your research, and what you consider relevant in the light of this.

Interpretation

In interpreting the results of a factorial analysis of variance, it is important to consider each of the main effects and the interactions, since all are likely to be relevant to the research hypotheses. If you find significant interaction effects it may well be that these are more important than the main effects; indeed, some people recommend ignoring the main effects and just focusing on the interaction effects in this situation. The important thing is to look closely at the graph produced by *SPSS*, and to consider what this means in relation to the question you are trying to answer with your research.

As always, it is also good practice to be aware of the effect sizes, and to remember that with very large samples even small main effects and interactions are likely to reach statistical significance.

As for causality, the principles applying to the statistical methods already discussed apply here also. Causality can only be inferred if the research is designed in such a way that there is only one viable explanation for a significant main effect or interaction. So, in this example, where there is an interaction between whether the software system was old or new, and the time of measuring attitudes, it is only possible to infer that these two variables caused changes in attitudes if this is the only viable explanation for the findings.

MIXED MEASURES FACTORIAL ANOVA

When to use

Use a mixed measures factorial ANOVA when you have two or more independent variables and one dependent variable, and one or more independent variables concern different groups of people while for one or more other independent variables the same people have been measured on more than one occasion. You wish to know if there is a significant difference between the means across the two or more levels (i.e. the two or more groups, or the two or more repeated measurements) on each independent variable. You may also wish to know whether there is one or more interactions between the independent variables and the dependent variable. The material below on the mixed measures factorial ANOVA assumes a knowledge of main effects and interactions. For a discussion of these see pages 171–5.

Example

■ An organization wishes to investigate whether a training programme improves the annual appraisal ratings of employees. The appraisal ratings of 200 employees are recorded on two occasions, with a one-year interval between the two appraisals. Half of these people attend a two-week training programme between the two appraisals whereas the other half does not. A mixed measures factorial ANOVA is used to investigate if there is an interaction between time of measurement and whether or not the employees attended the training programme.

Assumptions and requirements

A mixed measures factorial ANOVA makes different assumptions for the repeated measures independent variable(s) and the independent samples independent variable(s). The assumption of the repeated measures variable(s) is equality of covariance. This is briefly explained on page 154. This potential problem is dealt with here by adopting the Huynh-Feldt correction. This corrects for a violation of the equality of covariance assumption without the loss of much statistical power. In ideal circumstances the independent variables with independent samples should be used when the samples being compared are drawn from normally distributed populations with the same variance. However, the ANOVA is a robust statistical technique, and stands up well to violations of these assumptions most of the time.

The required sample size

In most cases the sample size required for a mixed measures factorial ANOVA will be dictated by whichever independent variables, using independent samples, have the weakest effect size. For this reason, the required sample size can be found by using the instructions for the independent samples factorial ANOVA. However, if you suspect that one or more of the repeated variables will have a small effect size, use the instructions for finding the sample size for a repeated measures factorial ANOVA as well, and then select the sample size that this indicates to be necessary only if it turns out to be greater than the sample size for the weakest independent variable with independent samples.

If you have no idea of the effect sizes you expect to find in your research, assume that you will obtain a medium effect size and look up the sample size required in Table 5.17 for your independent variable (with independent samples) with the largest number of levels.

A worked example

A researcher is interested in the possible effect of a training programme on the job performance of those who attend it. The training takes place in January, and annual appraisals are carried out in July. She decides to use the appraisal ratings as a measure of job performance, and collects the ratings of 20 employees in the July of the year before the training takes place and in the July of the year of the training. Because factors other than the training may influence appraisal scores she also decides to compare the appraisal performance of employees who attend the training with those who do not. Of the 20 employees used in the study, 10 are randomly selected to attend the training and the other 10 do not attend it. If the training affects appraisal scores, there should be an interaction between whether or not employees attended training and the time of their appraisal (i.e. before and after the training programme). For a discussion of interaction effects see pages 171–5.

The study involves one independent samples factor (whether or not the employees attended the training programme) and one repeated factor (the first appraisal versus the second appraisal). Therefore, this is a 2 × 2 mixed measures ANOVA design. The data obtained by the researcher are shown in Table 5.23.

How to carry out a mixed measures factorial ANOVA using SPSS

Begin by entering your data in the *SPSS* Data Editor. Figure 5.38 shows what the above data look like when they have been entered.

In this example, the variable names used were as follows:

— first time that the appraisal scores were collected: 'astime1';
— second time that the appraisal scores were collected: 'astime2'.

To indicate whether a given person was trained or not a third variable, 'tranotra' (which stands for training/no training) was used. For this variable people are coded 1 if they did not receive the training, and 2 if they did receive the training.

Use the *Variable View* in the data editor to enter full variable names for the three variables and value labels for 'tranotrain'. In this example the full variable names chosen are as follows: for astime1 *Appraisal score at time 1*, for astime2

Table 5.23 *Appraisal scores of 20 employees by whether or not they attended a training programme and time of appraisal*

Training	Case	Appraisal scores	
		Time 1	Time 2
No	1	6	5
	2	3	2
	3	4	3
	4	5	5
	5	3	4
	6	4	2
	7	4	3
	8	3	5
	9	6	3
	10	5	5
Yes	11	4	6
	12	3	8
	13	5	7
	14	3	6
	15	6	8
	16	3	7
	17	4	6
	18	4	8
	19	5	6
	20	3	7

Appraisal score at time 2, and for tranotra *Training or not*. The value labels entered for whether people were trained or not were 2 if they had been trained and 1 if they had not been trained.

Next, run *Explore* in *SPSS*. To do this:

➢ Click on **Analyze**.
➢ Click on **Descriptive Statistics**.
➢ Click on **Explore** . . . .
➢ A dialog box will appear with the repeatedly measured variables in a white box on the left hand side. Click on the first of these and then on the black triangle

211

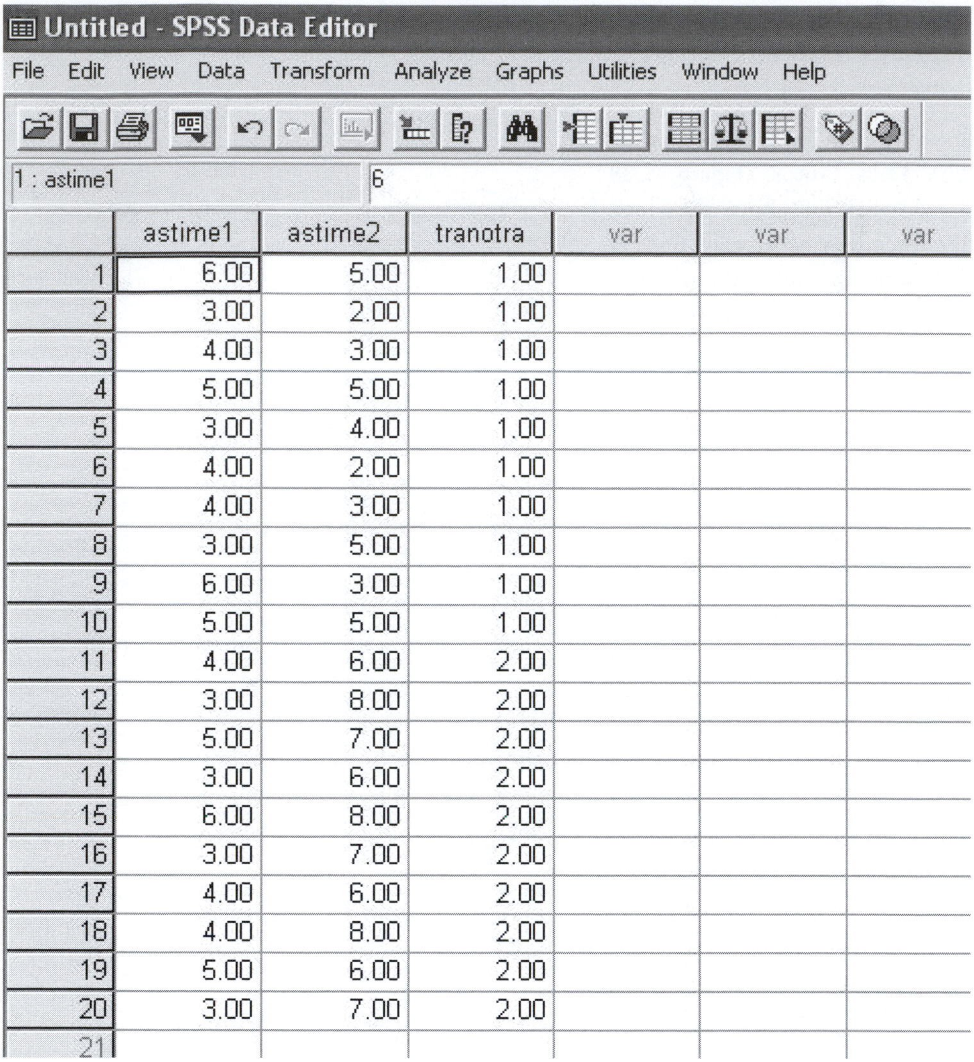

	astime1	astime2	tranotra	var	var	var
1	6.00	5.00	1.00			
2	3.00	2.00	1.00			
3	4.00	3.00	1.00			
4	5.00	5.00	1.00			
5	3.00	4.00	1.00			
6	4.00	2.00	1.00			
7	4.00	3.00	1.00			
8	3.00	5.00	1.00			
9	6.00	3.00	1.00			
10	5.00	5.00	1.00			
11	4.00	6.00	2.00			
12	3.00	8.00	2.00			
13	5.00	7.00	2.00			
14	3.00	6.00	2.00			
15	6.00	8.00	2.00			
16	3.00	7.00	2.00			
17	4.00	6.00	2.00			
18	4.00	8.00	2.00			
19	5.00	6.00	2.00			
20	3.00	7.00	2.00			
21						

Figure 5.38 SPSS *Data Editor after mixed measures ANOVA data are entered*

to the left of the white box headed **Dependent List**. The first repeated measures variable will be moved across to the **Dependent List** box. Repeat this procedure until all the repeated measures variables have been moved across to the **Dependent List** box.

➤ Click on the independent variable (or the first of them if you have more than one) and then on the black triangle to the left of the white box headed **Factor List**. The independent variable will be moved across to the **Factor List** box. Then click on any other independent variables in turn and move these across to the box headed **Factor List** in the same way (see Figure 5.39).

➤ Click on **OK**.

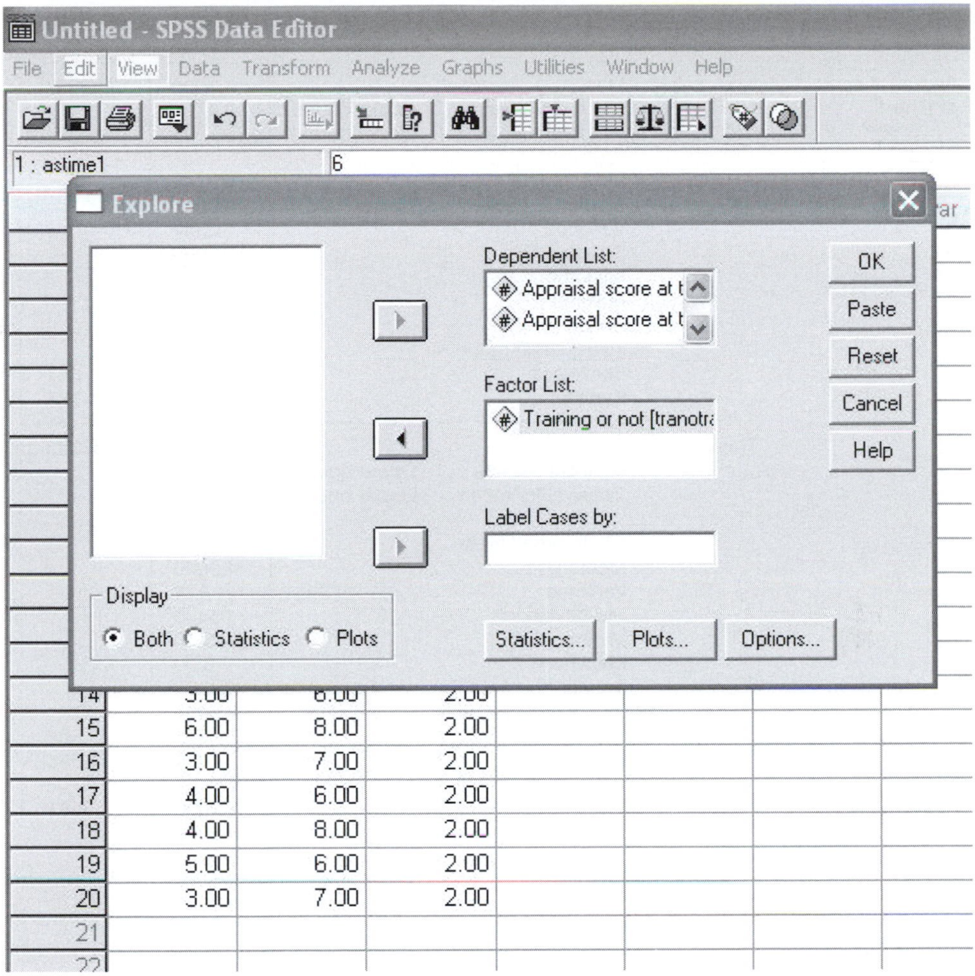

Figure 5.39 *Entering variables for* Explore *when carrying out a mixed measures factorial ANOVA*

Output in the following form will appear.

Explore
Training or not

Case processing summary

| | | \multicolumn{6}{c}{Cases} | | | | | |
| | | Valid | | Missing | | Total | |
	Training or not	N	Per cent	N	Per cent	N	Per cent
Appraisal score at time 1	No training	10	100.0%	0	.0%	10	100.0%
	Training	10	100.0%	0	.0%	10	100.0%
Appraisal score at time 2	No training	10	100.0%	0	.0%	10	100.0%
	Training	10	100.0%	0	.0%	10	100.0%

Descriptives

	Training or not			Statistic	Std error
Appraisal score at time 1	No training	Mean		4.3000	.36667
		95% confidence interval for mean	Lower bound	3.4705	
			Upper bound	5.1295	
		5% trimmed mean		4.2778	
		Median		4.0000	
		Variance		1.344	
		Std deviation		1.15950	
		Minimum		3.00	
		Maximum		6.00	
		Range		3.00	
		Interquartile range		2.2500	
		Skewness		.342	.687
		Kurtosis		−1.227	1.334
	Training	Mean		4.0000	.33333
		95% confidence interval for mean	Lower bound	3.2459	
			Upper bound	4.7541	
		5% trimmed mean		3.9444	
		Median		4.0000	
		Variance		1.111	
		Std deviation		1.05409	
		Minimum		3.00	
		Maximum		6.00	
		Range		3.00	
		Interquartile range		2.0000	
		Skewness		.712	.687
		Kurtosis		−.450	1.334
Appraisal score at time 2	No training	Mean		3.7000	.39581
		95% confidence interval for mean	Lower bound	2.8046	
			Upper bound	4.5954	
		5% trimmed mean		3.7222	
		Median		3.5000	
		Variance		1.567	
		Std deviation		1.25167	
		Minimum		2.00	
		Maximum		5.00	
		Range		3.00	
		Interquartile range		2.2500	
		Skewness		−.144	.687
		Kurtosis		−1.773	1.334
	Training	Mean		6.9000	.27689
		95% confidence interval for mean	Lower bound	6.2736	
			Upper bound	7.5264	
		5% trimmed mean		6.8889	
		Median		7.0000	
		Variance		.767	
		Std Deviation		.87560	
		Minimum		6.00	
		Maximum		8.00	
		Range		2.00	
		Interquartile range		2.0000	
		Skewness		.223	.687
		Kurtosis		−1.734	1.334

Appraisal score at time 1

Stem-and-Leaf Plots

```
Appraisal score at time 1          Appraisal score at time 1
Stem-and-Leaf Plot for             Stem-and-Leaf Plot for
TRANOTRA= No training              TRANOTRA= Training

Frequency    Stem &  Leaf          Frequency    Stem &  Leaf

    3.00      3 .  000                 4.00       3 .  0000
    3.00      4 .  000                 3.00       4 .  000
    2.00      5 .  00                  2.00       5 .  00
    2.00      6 .  00                  1.00       6 .  0

Stem width:   1.00                  Stem width:   1.00
Each leaf:    1 case(s)             Each leaf:    1 case(s)
```

Appraisal score at time 2
Stem-and-Leaf Plots

```
Appraisal score at time 2          Appraisal score at time 2
Stem-and-Leaf Plot for             Stem-and-Leaf Plot for
TRANOTRA= No training              TRANOTRA= Training

Frequency    Stem &  Leaf          Frequency    Stem &  Leaf

    2.00      2 .  00                 4.00       6 .  0000
    3.00      3 .  000                 .00       6 .
    1.00      4 .  0                  3.00       7 .  000
    4.00      5 .  0000               .00       7 .
                                     3.00       8 .  000
Stem width:   1.00
Each leaf:    1 case(s)             Stem width:   1.00
                                    Each leaf:    1 case(s)
```

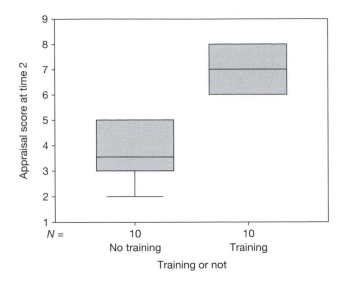

A separate set of information is produced for each repeated measure. In this example, such information has been produced first for Appraisal at time 1 and then for Appraisal at time 2. Take each of these sets of information in turn. In the table headed *Descriptives*, check that the minimum and maximum values given for the values of each of your repeated measures seem correct, and in the box and whiskers plots look for any extreme scores. Details on how to do this are given on pages 90–1. If the minimum and maximum values are reasonable, and there are no outliers shown in the box and whiskers plot, follow the instructions below to perform the repeated measures factorial ANOVA.

If the minimum and maximum values don't look right, and/or there are outliers shown in the box and whiskers plot, check your data to make sure that the extreme values are not mistakes, and that from a research point of view it makes sense to include them in the analysis. If necessary, take steps to modify the data, and then run *Explore* again, repeating the process until you are confident that your data are sound. When you are confident that the data are acceptable, follow the instructions below to carry out the ANOVA.

In this example, the minimum and maximum values were correct and no extreme values are identified in the box and whiskers plots. Therefore, it was possible to proceed straight to the ANOVA.

To run the mixed measures factorial ANOVA:

> ➢ Click on **Analyze**.
> ➢ Click on *General Linear Model*.
> ➢ Click on **Repeated Measures** . . . .
> ➢ A dialog box will appear. Click in the white box to the right of **Within-Subject Factor Name** and delete the phrase **factor 1**. Write in a suitable name for your first repeated measures variable. This name must not be longer than eight characters, must begin with a letter rather than a number, and must not contain

Untitled - SPSS Data Editor

File   Edit   View   Data   Transform   Analyze   Graphs   Utilities   Window   Help

1 : astime1   6

	astime1	astime2	tranotra	var	var	var	var	var	var
1	6.00	5.00	1.00						
2	3.00	2.00	1.00						
3	4.00	3.00	1.00						
4	5.00	5.00	1.00						
5	3.00	4.00	1.00						
6	4.00	2.00	1.00						
7	4.00	3.00	1.00						
8	3.00	5.00	1.00						
9	6.00	3.00	1.00						
10	5.00	5.00	1.00						
11	4.00	6.00	2.00						
12	3.00	8.00	2.00						
13	5.00	7.00	2.00						
14	3.00	6.00	2.00						
15	6.00	8.00	2.00						
16	3.00	7.00	2.00						
17	4.00	6.00	2.00						
18	4.00	8.00	2.00						
19	5.00	6.00	2.00						
20	3.00	7.00	2.00						
21									
22									

Repeated Measures Define Factor(s)   ⊠

Within-Subject Factor Name: Define

Number of Levels: Reset

Add   time(2)   Cancel

Change   Help

Remove   Measure >>

Figure 5.40 *Defining factors when carrying out a mixed measures factorial ANOVA*

any spaces. In this example, appraisal scores have been measured at two times, so the first repeated measures variable is called **time**.

➤ In the white box to the right of **Number of Levels** enter the number of levels of the repeated measures variable. In this example, time had two levels (the first appraisal scores and then the appraisal scores a year later) so the number of levels entered is two.

➤ Click on **Add**. The name of the repeated measures variable, and the number of levels of the independent variable in brackets, will appear in the white box below (see Figure 5.40).

➤ Repeat the previous two steps for any additional repeated measures variables.

➤ Click on **Define**. A dialog box will appear. In the rectangular white box to the left you will see a list of your repeated measures variables, and independent variables. To the right you will see a white box headed **Within-Subjects Variables,** and to the right of this heading the names you have given your repeated measures variables (in this case there is just one independent variable which we have called **time**). If you look in the white box headed **Within-Subjects Variables** you will see a series of dashes separated by one or more

217

question marks, and after this another figure in brackets. The figures refer to the levels of the independent variable so, in this example, the first figure refers to each of the two levels of the repeated measures independent variable, time. Your task is to match up the name of each repeated measures variable with the corresponding levels. In this example, the first variable **Appraisal score at time 1 [astime1]** is at the first level of time (i.e. the first time that appraisal scores are used). Since the first set of levels in the box under **Within-Subjects Variables** is 1 (i.e. level 1 for time), this is the correct one in this case. So, we can begin by clicking on **Appraisal score at time astime1**. It will be highlighted in blue. Then click on the single black triangle half-way down the left side of the white box headed **Within-Subjects Variables**. The name of the first repeated measures variable (in this case 'astime1') will be entered in this box next to the figure indicating which level it is on each independent variable (in this case, level 1). Repeat this until all of the repeated measures variables are correctly entered.

➤ Click on the name of each of the independent samples independent variables and then on the black triangle to the left of the white box headed **Between-Subjects Factor(s)**. In this example there is just one independent samples

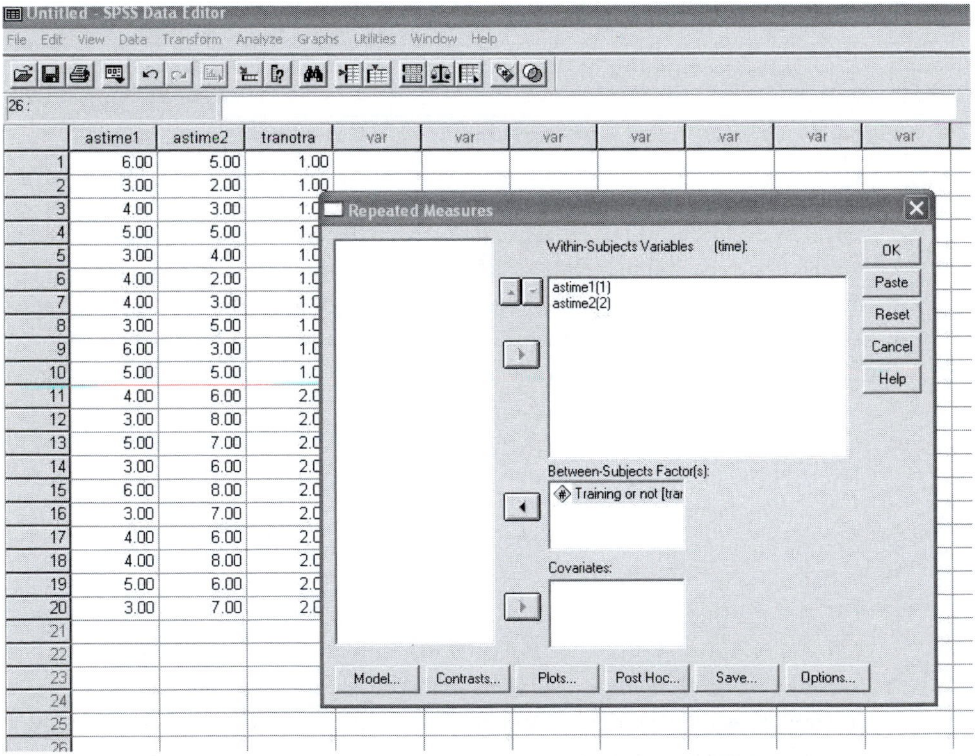

Figure 5.41 *Specifying repeated (within-subjects) factors and independent (between-subjects) factors when carrying out a mixed measures factorial ANOVA*

218

independent variable, **tranotra** and, consequently, this is the variable added to the **Between-Subjects Factor(s)** box (see Figure 5.41).

➤ Click on **Plots** .... A dialog box will open. This allows you to request line graphs showing the means for each independent variable plotted against another independent variable. Decide on the two independent variables you wish to see in each graph (if you are carrying out a two-way ANOVA, as in this example, there will of course only be two independent variables available anyway). For a particular graph, click on one independent variable and then on the black triangle to the left of the box headed **Horizontal Axis**. Then click on the other independent variable followed by the box headed **Separate Lines** (see Figure 5.42).

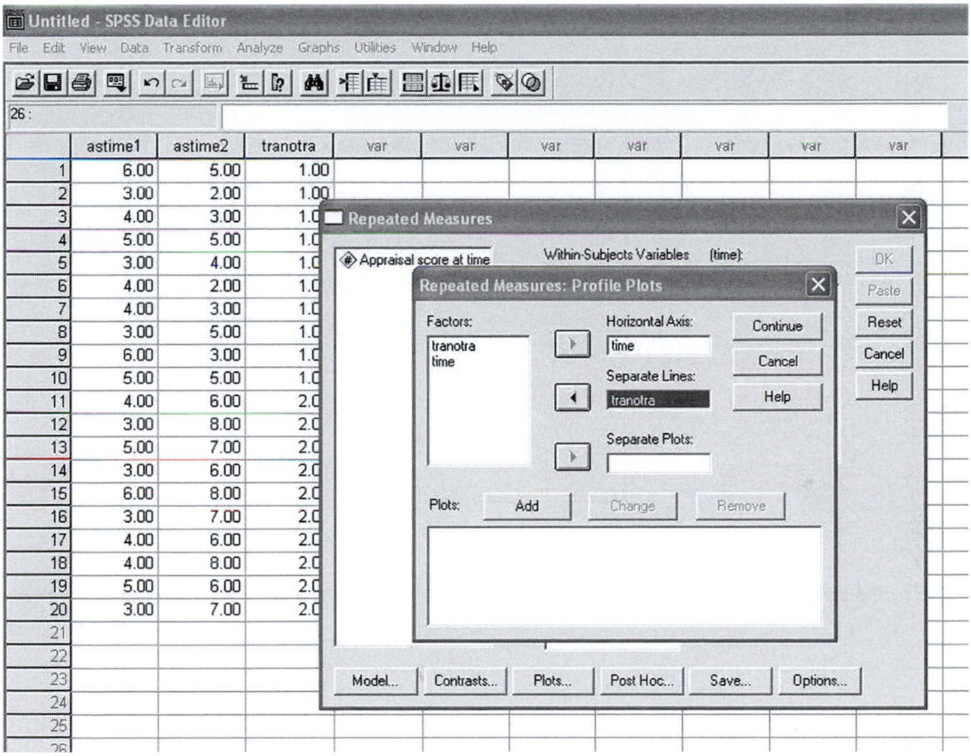

Figure 5.42 *Specifying the required graph when carrying out a mixed measures factorial ANOVA*

➤ Click on **Add**. The two independent variables will appear, separated by an asterisk, in the white box at the bottom of the dialog box. Repeat this process for any other pairs of independent variables you wish to see plotted. Note that if you have more than two independent variables you can request a plot for any two of these broken down by a third by entering the third variable in **Separate Plots** before clicking on **Add**.

219

➤ Click on **Continue**.
➤ Click on **Options**. A dialog box will appear.
➤ Click in the small box next to **Descriptive Statistics**. A tick will be added to the box (see Figure 5.43).

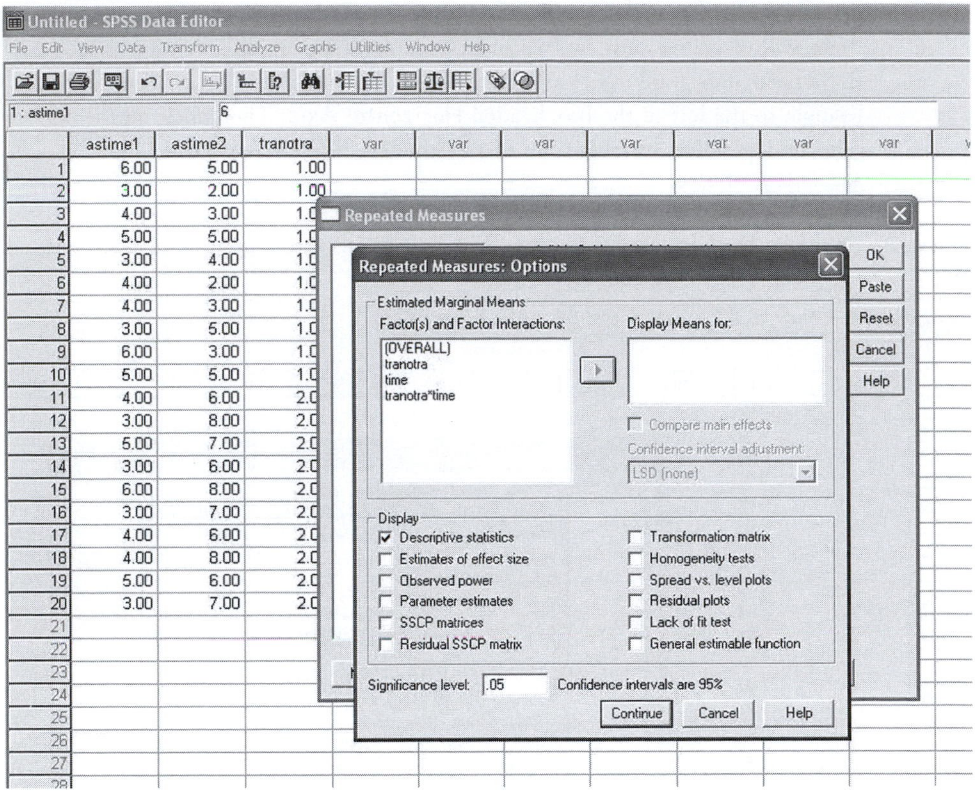

Figure 5.43 *Specifying the required options when carrying out a mixed measures factorial ANOVA*

➤ Click on **Continue**.
➤ If any of your independent samples independent variables have three or more levels (which in this example they do not, of course), and you wish to examine whether the means are different across each pair of levels (e.g. you are comparing the job satisfaction of people in sales, finance and production departments, and you wish to compare job satisfaction for sales versus finance, finance versus production, and sales versus production), click on **Post Hoc** . . . . A dialog box will appear. In the white box on the left you will see your independent variables. Click on one of these variables with three or more levels to highlight it, and then on the black triangle to the right. The variable will be moved to the box headed **Post Hoc Tests for** . . . . Repeat for all the

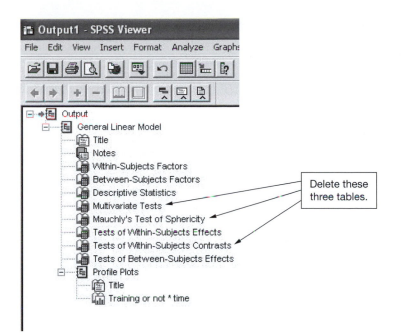

Figure 5.44 *The results output after deleting unnecessary information when carrying out a mixed measures factorial ANOVA*

independent variables with three or more levels that you want to examine. Then click the white box next to **Bonferroni**, followed by **Continue**.

➤ Click on **OK**.

When the output has been produced it will contain a lot of detailed information that is not necessary. Therefore, it is a good idea to delete the material you don't need before viewing the results. To do this have a look at the large white area on the left hand side of the screen (see Figure 5.44). There you will see a list of the titles of the various results tables that *SPSS* has generated. Click on each of the following to highlight it, and then press the delete key on your keyboard:

— Multivariate Tests;
— Mauchly's Test of Sphericity;
— Tests of Within-Subjects Contrasts.

The results will appear in the output file as follows.

General linear model

Within-subjects factors

Measure: MEASURE_1

TIME	Dependent variable
1	ASTIME1
2	ASTIME2

Mean and standard deviation of the appraisal scores for each level of the two independent variables.

Between-subjects factors

		Value label	N
Training	1.00	No training	10
or not	2.00	Training	10

Descriptive statistics

	Training or not	Mean	Std deviation	N
Appraisal score at time 1	No training	4.3000	1.15950	10
	Training	4.0000	1.05409	10
	Total	4.1500	1.08942	20
Appraisal score at time 2	No training	3.7000	1.25167	10
	Training	6.9000	.87560	10
	Total	5.3000	1.94936	20

Tests of within-subjects effects

Measure: MEASURE_1

F value of the interaction effect.

Source		Type III sum of squares	df	Mean square	F	Sig.
TIME	Sphericity assumed	13.225	1	13.225	14.297	.001
	Greenhouse-Geisser	13.225	1.000	13.225	14.297	.001
	Huynh-Feldt	13.225	1.000	13.225	14.297	.001
	Lower-bound	13.225	1.000	13.225	14.297	.001
TIME * TRANOTRA	Sphericity assumed	30.625	1	30.625	33.108	.000
	Greenhouse-Geisser	30.625	1.000	30.625	33.108	.000
	Huynh-Feldt	30.625	1.000	30.625	33.108	.000
	Lower-bound	30.625	1.000	30.625	33.108	.000
Error(TIME)	Sphericity assumed	16.650	18	.925		
	Greenhouse-Geisser	16.650	18.000	.925		
	Huynh-Feldt	16.650	18.000	.925		
	Lower-bound	16.650	18.000	.925		

Degrees of freedom for error.

Degrees of freedom for the repeated measures independent variable (TIME) and then for the interaction effect (TIME * TRANOTRA).

F value of the repeated measures independent variable.

Huynh-Feldt significance levels. For each repeated measure main effect, and for the repeated measure by independent sample interaction, this shows the probability of obtaining differences in means as large as you have in your sample data if the null hypothesis (of no main effect in the population, or no interaction in the population) is true. The values need to be less than .05 to be statistically significant.

Tests of between-subjects effects

Measure: MEASURE_1
Transformed variable: average

Source	Type III sum of squares	df	Mean square	F	Sig.
Intercept	893.025	1	893.025	607.730	.000
TRANOTRA	21.025	1	21.025	14.308	.001
Error	26.450	18	1.469		

Degree of freedom for the independent samples independent variable.

F value of the independent samples independent variable.

Significance level for the independent samples independent variable. This shows the probability that the null hypothesis is true, given the data. The value needs to be less than .05 for statistical significance.

Profile plots

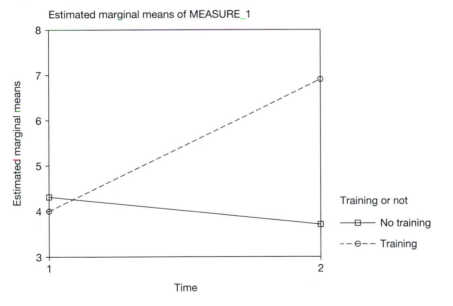

Estimated marginal means of MEASURE_1

Training or not

No training

Training

How to report the results of a mixed measures factorial ANOVA

These results could be reported as follows:

A 2 × 2 mixed measures factorial ANOVA was carried out using time of appraisal (three months before and nine months after the training programme took place), and whether or not employees were trained, as the independent variables, and appraisal scores as the dependent variable. Means and standard deviations are shown

223

Table 5.24 *Means and standard deviations of appraisal scores by whether or not employees attended a training programme and time of appraisal*

Time of appraisal	Appraisal scores			
	Training given?	Mean	Standard deviation	Number
Before training	No	4.30	1.16	10
	Yes	4.00	1.05	10
After training	No	3.70	1.25	10
	Yes	6.90	0.88	10

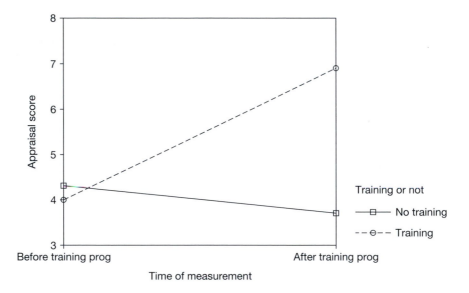

Figure 5.45 *Line graph of appraisal scores by time of measurement and whether employees were trained or not*

in Table 5.24, and a line graph of the results is shown in Figure 5.45. There was a main effect for time of measurement, $F(1, 18) = 14.30$, $p = .001$, a main effect for whether or not employees were trained or not, $F(1, 18)$ 14.31, $p = .001$, and also a significant interaction between time of measurement and whether or not employees were trained, $F(1, 88) = 30.63$, $p < .001$. An examination of Figure 5.45 indicates that appraisal scores of both the trained and non-trained groups are very similar before the training programme took place. However, after the training programme appraisal scores are considerably higher for employees who attended the training programme. This suggests that the training programme may have had a marked positive effect on job performance.

Comments

- The means and standard deviation are taken from the *Descriptives Statistics* table in the results output.
- In the case of a mixed measures factorial ANOVA, two sets of *F* values and degrees of freedom are given. Those for the repeated measures variable and the interaction are given in the table labelled *Tests of within-subjects effects*. Here, the interaction effect is the one in which the variables listed in the left hand column are separated with an asterisk. The degrees of freedom for the repeated measures factor, for the interaction, and for error, are highlighted. When reporting each of these, the degrees of freedom for the relevant factor is followed by a comma and then the degrees of freedom for error. The relevant values for the independent samples factor is given in the table labelled *Tests of between-subjects effects*. Again, the degrees of freedom for the factor in question should be reported in brackets followed by the associated degrees of freedom for error.
- If the *F* value is significant for a particular independent variable, or for the interaction between two or more independent variables, it is very helpful to draw attention to the effect size when discussing the findings. For a difference in means, the appropriate measure of effect size is *d*. For a particular pair of means this can be obtained by working out the difference between the two and dividing this by the pooled standard deviation. An easy to use calculator which performs this function is available at www.dewberry-statistics.com. To use the calculator you simply need to enter the relevant means, standard deviations and sample sizes shown in the *Descriptive Statistics* table on page 222. For example, if we wished to report the effect size of the difference in appraisal scores at the second time of measurement between those people who had been trained, and those who had not, we would need the mean and standard deviation of each of these. Consulting the *Descriptive Statistics* table, the mean and standard deviation for appraisal scores at the second time of measurement for those without training are 3.70 and 1.25 respectively. The mean and standard deviation for the second time of measurement for those who were trained are 6.90 and 0.88. Entering the figures for this example into the calculator we obtain a *d* of 2.96. We can therefore say that the effect size is large ($d = 2.96$). Which of the effect sizes you choose to mention will depend on the particular focus of your research, and what you consider relevant in the light of this.

Interpretation

In interpreting the results of a factorial analysis of variance, it is important to consider each of the main effects and the interactions, since all are likely to be relevant to the research hypotheses. If you find significant interaction effects it may well be that these are more important than the main effects; indeed, some people recommend ignoring the main effects and just focusing on the interaction effects in this situation. The important thing is to look closely at the graph produced by *SPSS*, and to consider what this means in relation to the question you are trying to answer with your research.

As for causality, the principles applying to the statistical methods already discussed apply here also. Causality can only be inferred if the research is designed in such a way that there is only one viable explanation for a significant main effect or interaction. In this example we could only claim that training people has a causal influence of their appraisal scores if we are satisfied that this training is the only possible explanation for the statistically significant interaction effect observed here.

FURTHER READING

If you wish to learn more about statistical methods for examining differences, the text by Howell (2002) provides a good general overview, and for the advanced techniques of multivariate analysis of variance and covariance, which have not been covered in this chapter, Tabachnich and Fidell, (2001) is also recommended.

Chapter 6

Statistical methods for examining associations

This chapter covers many of the commonly used techniques for examining associations: correlations, simple regression, multiple regression, logistic regression, factor analysis and Cronbach's alpha coefficient. As well as providing an introduction to these techniques, the way in which they can be carried out using *SPSS* will be explained, and information about how to interpret the results of the *SPSS* output produced by the analyses, and how to write up the results of the analyses is provided. In addition, two other increasingly popular techniques, structural equation modelling and meta-analysis, are briefly discussed.

WHEN TO USE PARTICULAR METHODS FOR EXAMINING ASSOCIATIONS

If you wish to examine the relationship between two continuous variables, or between a continuous variable and a categorical variable, the correlation coefficient is usually used. If you need to examine the relation between several predictor variables and a continuous dependent variable, such as job satisfaction measured on a 10-point scale, use multiple regression. If the intention is to examine the relation between several predictor variables and a dichotomous dependent variable, such as whether or not people are made redundant, use logistic regression. If you want to see if a large number of variables can be reduced to a smaller number of variables, or whether the items in a questionnaire measure the set of dimensions they are expected to, factor analysis is the appropriate technique. Finally, if the intention is to examine how reliable a set of questionnaire items are in measuring a dimension, use Cronbach's alpha coefficient.

CORRELATION AND SIMPLE REGRESSION

The background to correlation

Often, we wish to examine the extent to which two variables are associated with each other. For example, is it the case that people who obtain high scores on one variable also obtain high scores on another (i.e. a positive association), is it the case that people who have high scores on one variable tend to get low scores on another (i.e. a negative association), or is there no relationship at all between the size of the scores people get on two variables (i.e. no association). Associations can be weak (there is only a slight tendency for people getting high scores on variable *a* to get high scores on variable *b*, and for those who get low scores on variable *a* to get low scores on variable *b*) or strong (people who get high scores on variable *a* almost always get high scores on variable *b*, and people who get low scores on variable *a* almost always get low scores on variable *b*). If there is any association at all between two variables, this association will have a direction, meaning that it will either be positive or negative.

The direction and strength of an association between two variables is usually expressed as a **correlation coefficient**. A correlation coefficient is a figure between 1 and −1. If the correlation coefficient is 0, this means that there is no association at all between the two variables, if it is 1 there is a perfect positive association between the two variables, and if it is −1 there is a perfect negative correlation between the variables. Examples of data that would produce a perfect positive correlation of 1, a perfect negative correlation of −1, and a less than perfect positive correlation of 0.4 are shown in Tables 6.1, 6.2 and 6.3. Some types of correlation involve more than two variables, but here we just focus on the two-variable type (sometimes called zero order correlations).

Table 6.1 *A perfect positive association between well-being and job commitment (correlation coefficient = 1.0)*

Case	Well-being	Job commitment
1	5	7
2	4	6
3	3	5
4	2	4
5	1	3

Table 6.2 *A perfect negative association between well-being and job commitment (correlation coefficient = −1.0)*

Case	Well-being	Job commitment
1	5	3
2	4	4
3	3	5
4	2	6
5	1	7

Table 6.3 *A less than perfect positive association between well-being and job commitment (correlation coefficient = 0.4)*

Case	Well-being	Job commitment
1	5	5
2	4	1
3	3	4
4	2	3
5	1	2

As you can see, for the perfect positive correlation there is a very simple positive relationship between well-being and job commitment: relatively high well-being scores are always paired with relatively high job-commitment scores, and relatively low well-being scores are always paired with relatively low job-commitment scores. In fact, in this example, for every case the job-commitment score is exactly equal to the well-being score plus two points. There is no variation from this at all. A similar relationship exists between the two variables in the perfect negative correlation, except here relatively high well-being scores are paired with relatively low job-commitment scores, and vice versa.

In the real world, it is virtually unheard of to obtain a perfect positive or negative correlation or, indeed, a correlation of exactly zero. If you carry out some research you are very unlikely to obtain a correlation of 1, 0 or −1 in practice, nor are you likely to see these values reported in journal articles. The situation is much more likely to be like that in Table 6.3. Here, there is a positive association between the two variables, but it is less than perfect. Higher well-being scores *tend* to be associated with higher job-commitment scores, but this is not always the case (as in Case 2 in Table 6.3). In the same way, less than perfect negative correlations are also very common in real-world research.

A helpful way to think about what a correlation actually means is to plot the values of one variable against another in a graph called a scatterplot. An example of a scatterplot is shown in Figure 6.1. Here, the age of several cases has been plotted against their salary because we are interested in whether there is a relationship between how much people earn in an organization and how old they are. Each point on the graph corresponds to a particular case. So, for example, the case highlighted with the arrow is about 53 years old and earns about $45,000.

The correlation coefficient effectively expresses an answer to the following question:

> If you were to draw a straight line through the points on the graph, placing it in such a position that it minimized the difference between the points and the line, how good would the line be at predicting where the points are?

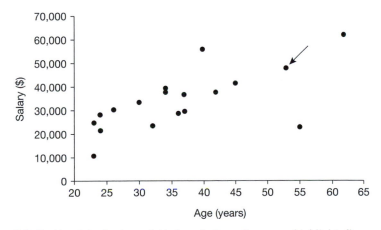

Figure 6.1 *Scatterplot of salary plotted against age (one case highlighted)*

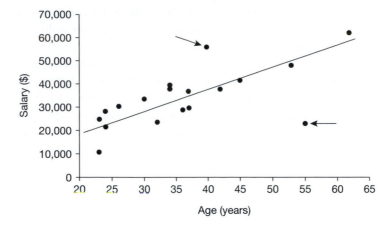

Figure 6.2 Scatterplot of salary plotted against age (two outlier cases highlighted)

Figure 6.2 shows a line drawn through the scatterplot points that were displayed in Figure 6.1. If the points on the graph are all very close to the line this means that you have a high positive correlation, whereas if the points are a long way from the line, the correlation is weaker (closer to zero). In the case of the data plotted in Figures 6.1 and 6.2 above, the correlation turns out to be 0.68, indicating a strong positive correlation between age and salary. This strong positive relationship can be seen on the scatterplot – the line is reasonably good at predicting where each point on the graph will be. Only the positions of the two cases highlighted by arrows in Figure 6.2 are poorly predicted by the straight line. Therefore, you can say that there is a reasonably good straight-line (or 'linear' to use the technical term) positive relationship here between age and salary, and this is why a strong and positive correlation coefficient of .68 is obtained.

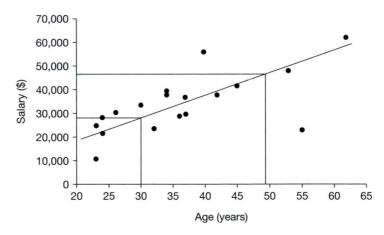

Figure 6.3 Scatterplot of salary plotted against age: predicting salaries at ages 30 and 49

The straight line drawn in Figures 6.2 and 6.3 is technically known as a regression line. In statistical analysis, regression can be interpreted as meaning the same thing as prediction. So, the regression line is a prediction line: you can use it to predict the score on one variable from the score on another variable. You can predict from the regression line that if someone is 49 years old, they are likely to be earning about $48,000 a year, and if they are 30 years old they are likely to be earning just under $30,000 a year. This is shown in Figure 6.3. To get the estimated salary you draw a vertical line up from age to the prediction line, and then a horizontal one across to the salary levels. The difference between the salary that someone of a particular age is predicted to earn by the regression line, and the salary they actually earn is technically known as the **residual**. So in Figure 6.3 we can see that according to the regression line someone 55 years old is expected to earn $52,000, but the one person who is actually 55 years old here only earns $23,000; consequently in the case of this person the residual, or error of prediction, is $29,000.

Regression lines are not always straight, they can in fact be any shape. However, in statistics it is relatively simple, and very common, to use straight regression lines. A straight regression line can be defined with the simple formula:

$$\hat{Y} = A + BX$$

where A and B are both constants, $\hat{Y}$ (which is pronounced y-hat) is the predicted value of dependent variable Y, X is a specific value of the independent variable, and BX means multiply B by X.

If you wish, you can see how this works yourself by taking a piece of graph paper, deciding on whatever value you want values A and B to have (it is better to keep B no greater than 2), working out $\hat{Y}$ for various values of X, and plotting the results on a graph with $\hat{Y}$ on the y (i.e. vertical) axis and X on the x (horizontal) axis. You will find that a straight line is produced, that the point at which $\hat{Y}$ intersects with the y axis when X is 0 is the value of A, and that the steepness of the slope of the line depends on B.

The correlation coefficient: a measure of the effect size of an association

As mentioned earlier, the correlation coefficient is, in fact, a measure of the effect size of the association between two continuous variables. If you find a strong correlation of .82 between two variables you could also say that the estimated effect size of the association between the two variables is a correlation of .82. You say that this is an *estimated* effect size because the correlation you have found with your data is, of course, only an estimate of the actual correlation between the variables. Once again, you need to be aware that a sample statistic, such as the correlation between two variables in 100 people, is only an estimate of the population parameter which, in this case, is the correlation you would find if you measured everyone to whom you wish to generalize your results on the two variables.

231

The percentage of variance accounted for

The effect size of an association between two variables is also often expressed in a slightly different way as the percentage of variance accounted for. So, you might say that the correlation between cognitive ability scores and job performance is 0.5, and that cognitive ability accounts for 25 per cent of the variation in job performance. It is very easy to obtain the percentage of variance that one variable accounts for in another if you know the size of the Pearson correlation coefficient between them. All that you have to do to get the percentage of variance accounted for from the correlation coefficient is to square it and then multiply by 100. So, a correlation between interview scores and job performance of .50 means that 25 per cent of the variation in job performance is accounted for by cognitive ability (because .50 squared, and then multiplied by 100 is 25). Similarly, if the correlation between cognitive ability and job performance is .70, you can say that cognitive ability accounts for 49 per cent of the variation in job performance.

You can represent the degree to which one variable accounts for variance in another not only with a percentage score, but also with a Venn diagram. So, if there is a correlation of .70 between cognitive ability and job performance, this means that 49 per cent of the variance in job performance is accounted for by cognitive ability, and this can be represented graphically as shown in Figure 6.4.

In Figure 6.4, the circle on the left represents the variance in cognitive ability, the one on the right represents the variance in job performance, and the area of overlap between them represents the proportion of the variance in one variable accounted for by the other. So, as we obtained data which indicated that 49 per cent of the variance in job performance is accounted for by cognitive ability, 49 per cent of the circle representing the variance in job performance is covered by the circle representing cognitive ability. If the correlation between these two variables had been lower, there would have been less area of overlap between the circles, and if it had been higher the area of overlap would be larger too. Understanding how the percentage of variance can be represented in a Venn diagram like this will make the topic of multiple regression, to be discussed later, easier to understand.

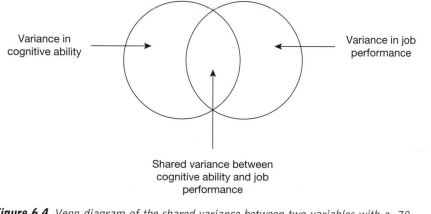

Figure 6.4 *Venn diagram of the shared variance between two variables with a .70 correlation*

When to use the Pearson product-moment correlation coefficient

Although there is more than one way of correlating variables, the Pearson product-moment correlation coefficient is the most widely used, and the one we shall deal with here. Use the Pearson correlation coefficient if you have measured people on two or more continuous variables and you wish to know the strength and direction of the association between their scores on any pair of variables. You can also use the Pearson correlation if you wish to know the association between a continuous variable and a categorical-dichotomous variable. A categorical-dichotomous variable is a categorical variable which only has two categories, and a widely used example is gender. The Pearson correlation coefficient will tell you the strength of the positive or negative correlation between the variables. You can also obtain the statistical significance of the correlation.

However, it is important to view the statistical significance of correlations in organizational research with some caution. This is because it is hard to imagine any two variables that you might measure in organizational research which really do have absolutely no association at all with each other. Therefore, in a sense, a significant correlation is telling you what you already know – that the variables are associated, at least to a small degree. Certainly, being aware of the *size* of the correlation coefficient (i.e. the effect size of the association between the two variables) is at least as important as whether the correlation is statistically significant or not. It is also often helpful to compare the sizes of different, but related, correlation coefficients. For example, a human resource manager involved in personnel selection might measure the performance of candidates at an interview, and on measures of verbal and numerical reasoning ability. If she is interested in the extent to which these various selection methods are valid predictors of job performance, she might collect data about the job performance of those selected with these measures, and then compare the sizes of the correlations between job performance and each of the three selection methods.

Examples

- A researcher is interested in how strong the relationship is between job commitment and job performance. The commitment and performance of 50 managers are measured, and the Pearson correlation coefficient is used to examine the strength of this relationship.
- A researcher is interested in the strength of the association between gender and salary levels. The gender of 100 employees is correlated with how much they earn using the Pearson correlation coefficient.

Assumptions and requirements

The main assumption behind the use of the Pearson correlation coefficient is that the two variables to be correlated have a linear (or straight-line) relationship. This can easily be checked by producing a scatterplot of the pair of variables you wish to correlate, and checking that the points do not form a clearly defined curve. If the variables do lie on a curved line, the correlation coefficient will underestimate the degree of association between them. Instructions for producing a scatterplot are shown below.

The required sample size

If you are interested in examining whether or not there is a statistically significant correlation between two variables, it is possible to identify the sample size you will require from an estimate of the effect size you expect to find. For correlations, the correlation coefficient itself is a good measure of effect size. Therefore, if it is possible to use the results of previous research, or a pilot study, to establish the correlation coefficient, r, between the variables you expect to find in your own study, you can take this estimate of r and use it in Table 6.4 to provide a guide to the sample size you will require.

If you wish to increase power to 90 per cent, increase the sample sizes to 850, 90 and 30 for predicted r values of .1, .3 and .5 respectively. If you have no idea what effect size to expect in your study, use the sample size required for a medium effect size (i.e. 70 for 80 per cent power) if this is possible.

A worked example

A researcher is interested in the correlation between the job commitment of people in an organization, their ages and how much they earn. She collects data on the age and salary of 20 employees and then measures their job commitment on a 7-point scale. The resulting data are shown in Table 6.5.

Table 6.4 The approximate sample sizes required to examine the statistical significance of a correlation coefficient, assuming a power of 80% and a .05 significance level

Effect size		Sample
	r	size
Small	.10	620
Medium	.30	70
Large	.50	22

Table 6.5 The age, salary and job commitment of 20 employees

Case	Age	Salary ($)	Job commitment
1	23	25,000	5
2	25	27,000	6
3	26	32,000	3
4	36	37,000	6
5	45	42,000	8
6	23	19,000	5
7	42	38,000	6
8	41	56,000	4
9	55	25,000	7
10	32	25,000	6
11	54	47,000	5
12	62	61,000	4
13	34	38,000	3
14	25	23,000	5
15	34	37,000	6
16	36	31,000	4
17	34	40,000	7
18	35	29,000	5
19	30	34,000	7
20	34	38,000	5

How to carry out correlations using SPSS

To carry out a correlation, the first step is to enter the data in the *SPSS* Data Editor. Figure 6.5 shows what the above data look like when they have been entered. The variable name used for job commitment is 'jobcom'. The *Variable View* in the *SPSS* Data Editor has been used to enter variable labels for age, salary and jobcom as follows: 'Age', 'Salary', and 'Job commitment'.

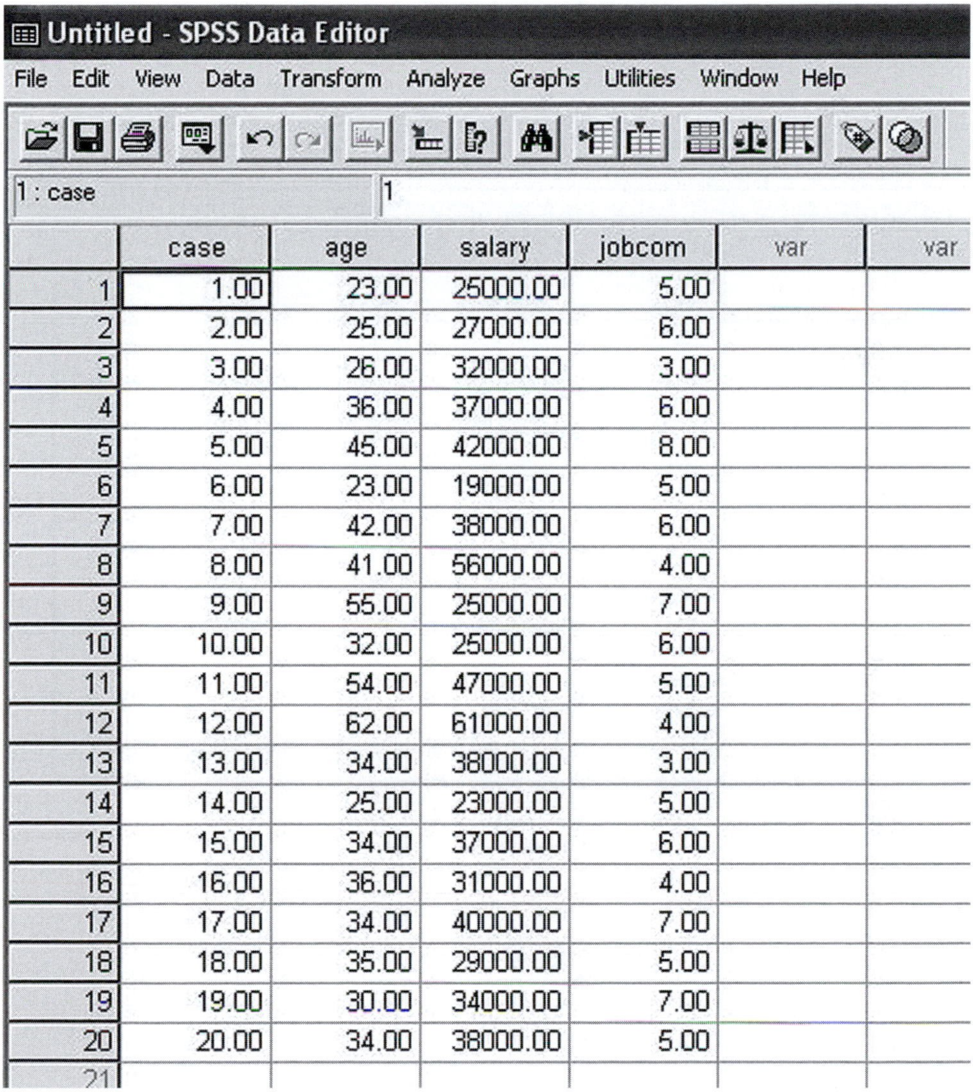

☷ Untitled - SPSS Data Editor

File   Edit   View   Data   Transform   Analyze   Graphs   Utilities   Window   Help

1 : case   1

	case	age	salary	jobcom	var	var
1	1.00	23.00	25000.00	5.00		
2	2.00	25.00	27000.00	6.00		
3	3.00	26.00	32000.00	3.00		
4	4.00	36.00	37000.00	6.00		
5	5.00	45.00	42000.00	8.00		
6	6.00	23.00	19000.00	5.00		
7	7.00	42.00	38000.00	6.00		
8	8.00	41.00	56000.00	4.00		
9	9.00	55.00	25000.00	7.00		
10	10.00	32.00	25000.00	6.00		
11	11.00	54.00	47000.00	5.00		
12	12.00	62.00	61000.00	4.00		
13	13.00	34.00	38000.00	3.00		
14	14.00	25.00	23000.00	5.00		
15	15.00	34.00	37000.00	6.00		
16	16.00	36.00	31000.00	4.00		
17	17.00	34.00	40000.00	7.00		
18	18.00	35.00	29000.00	5.00		
19	19.00	30.00	34000.00	7.00		
20	20.00	34.00	38000.00	5.00		
21						

Figure 6.5 SPSS *Data Editor after correlation data are entered*

Next, run *Explore* in *SPSS*. To do this:

> ➤ Click on **Analyze**.
> ➤ Click on **Descriptive Statistics**.
> ➤ Click on **Explore** . . . .
> ➤ A dialog box will appear with your variables in a white box on the left hand side. Click on each of the variables you wish to correlate and then on the black triangle to the left of the white box headed **Dependent List**. The variables will be moved across to the **Dependent List** box (see Figure 6.6).
> ➤ Click on **OK**.

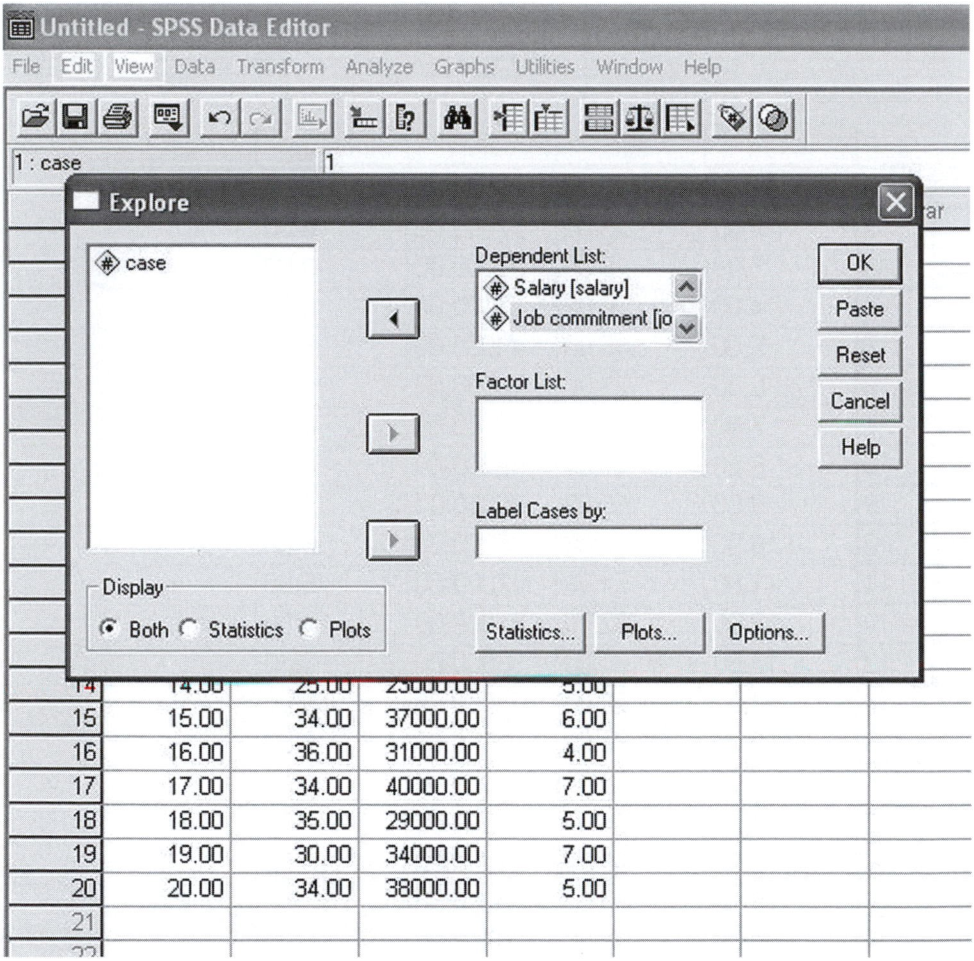

Figure 6.6 *Entering the variables when using* Explore

The following output will appear.

Explore

Case processing summary

	Cases					
	Valid		Missing		Total	
	N	Per cent	N	Per cent	N	Per cent
Age	20	100.0%	0	.0%	20	100.0%
Salary	20	100.0%	0	.0%	20	100.0%
Job commitment	20	100.0%	0	.0%	20	100.0%

Descriptives

			Statistic	Std error
Age	Mean		36.3000	2.43343
	95% confidence interval for mean	Lower bound	31.2068	
		Upper bound	41.3932	
	5% trimmed mean		35.6111	
	Median		34.0000	
	Variance		118.432	
	Std deviation		10.88263	
	Minimum		23.00	
	Maximum		62.00	
	Range		39.00	
	Interquartile range		14.7500	
	Skewness		.950	.512
	Kurtosis		.439	.992
Salary	Mean		35200.00	2403.506
	95% confidence interval for mean	Lower bound	30169.40	
		Upper bound	40230.60	
	5% trimmed mean		34666.67	
	Median		35500.00	
	Variance		1.2E+08	
	Std deviation		10748.81	
	Minimum		19000.00	
	Maximum		61000.00	
	Range		42000.00	
	Interquartile range		14000.00	
	Skewness		.856	.512
	Kurtosis		.695	.992
Job commitment	Mean		5.3500	.30153
	95% confidence interval for mean	Lower bound	4.7189	
		Upper bound	5.9811	
	5% trimmed mean		5.3333	
	Median		5.0000	
	Variance		1.818	
	Std deviation		1.34849	
	Minimum		3.00	
	Maximum		8.00	
	Range		5.00	
	Interquartile range		1.7500	
	Skewness		−.003	.512
	Kurtosis		−.404	.992

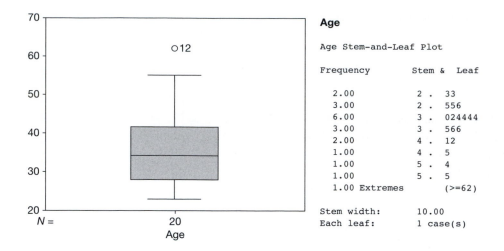

Age

```
Age Stem-and-Leaf Plot

Frequency          Stem &  Leaf

   2.00              2 .  33
   3.00              2 .  556
   6.00              3 .  024444
   3.00              3 .  566
   2.00              4 .  12
   1.00              4 .  5
   1.00              5 .  4
   1.00              5 .  5
   1.00 Extremes        (>=62)

Stem width:        10.00
Each leaf:         1 case(s)
```

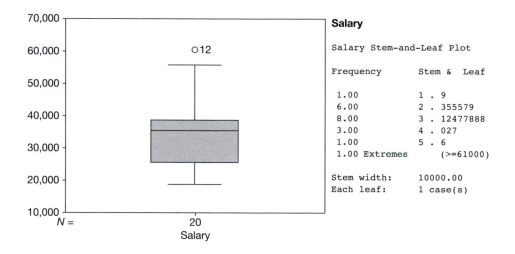

Salary

```
Salary Stem-and-Leaf Plot

Frequency          Stem &  Leaf

   1.00              1 . 9
   6.00              2 . 355579
   8.00              3 . 12477888
   3.00              4 . 027
   1.00              5 . 6
   1.00 Extremes        (>=61000)

Stem width:        10000.00
Each leaf:         1 case(s)
```

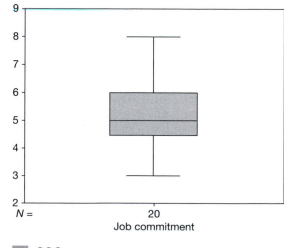

Job commitment

```
Job commitment
Stem-and-Leaf Plot

Frequency          Stem &  Leaf

   2.00              3 . 00
   3.00              4 . 000
   6.00              5 . 000000
   5.00              6 . 00000
   3.00              7 . 000
   1.00              8 . 0

Stem width:        1.00
Each leaf:         1 case(s)
```

As you can see, a separate set of descriptive information is produced for each of the variables you wish to correlate. For each variable, in the table headed *Descriptives*, check that the minimum and maximum values seem correct, and in the box and whiskers plots look for any outliers or extreme scores. Details on how to do this are given on pages 90–1. If the minimum and maximum values are reasonable, and there are no outliers shown in the box and whiskers plot, follow the instructions below to perform the correlations.

If the minimum and maximum values don't look right, and/or there are outliers shown in the box and whiskers plot, check your data to make sure that the outlying or extreme values are not mistakes, and that from a research point of view it makes sense to include them in the analysis. If necessary, take steps to modify the data, and then run *Explore* again, repeating the process until you are confident that your data are sound. When you are confident that the data are acceptable, follow the instructions below to carry out the correlation or correlations.

In this example, one case (number 12) is highlighted as having an outlying score in two box and whiskers plots: salary and age. This data point was checked and found to be acceptable. Therefore, no modification was made to the data file before running the correlations.

As a key assumption of the Pearson correlation coefficient is that the variables you wish to correlate do not have a curvilinear relationship, the next step is to check that such a curvilinear relationship is not present. It is necessary to do this for each pair of variables you wish to correlate. This is achieved as follows.

➢ Click on **Graphs**.
➢ Click on **Scatter**.
➢ A dialog box will appear. Click on **Define**.
➢ Another dialog box will appear. In the white box to the left you will see the names of the variables you wish to correlate. Place the cursor over the first of these and left-click your mouse. The variable will be highlighted. Next, click the small black triangle to the left of the box headed **Y Axis**. The variable will be moved across to this box.
➢ Now, go back to the large white box on the left and place your cursor over the name of one of the variables you wish to correlate with the one you have just placed in the **Y Axis** box. Normally, you will choose the next one in the list. Left-click and then click the small black triangle to the left of the box headed **X Axis**. The variable will be moved across to this **X Axis** box (See Figure 6.7).
➢ Click on **OK**.

A scatterplot will appear on the *SPSS* output page. In this example the graph shown in Figure 6.8 appears.

➢ Repeat this process until you have produced a scatterplot of each pair of variables you wish to correlate.

Examine each of the graphs to ensure that the points on the scatterplots do not seem to form a curved shape. Instead, they can either be scattered in an apparently random fashion

239

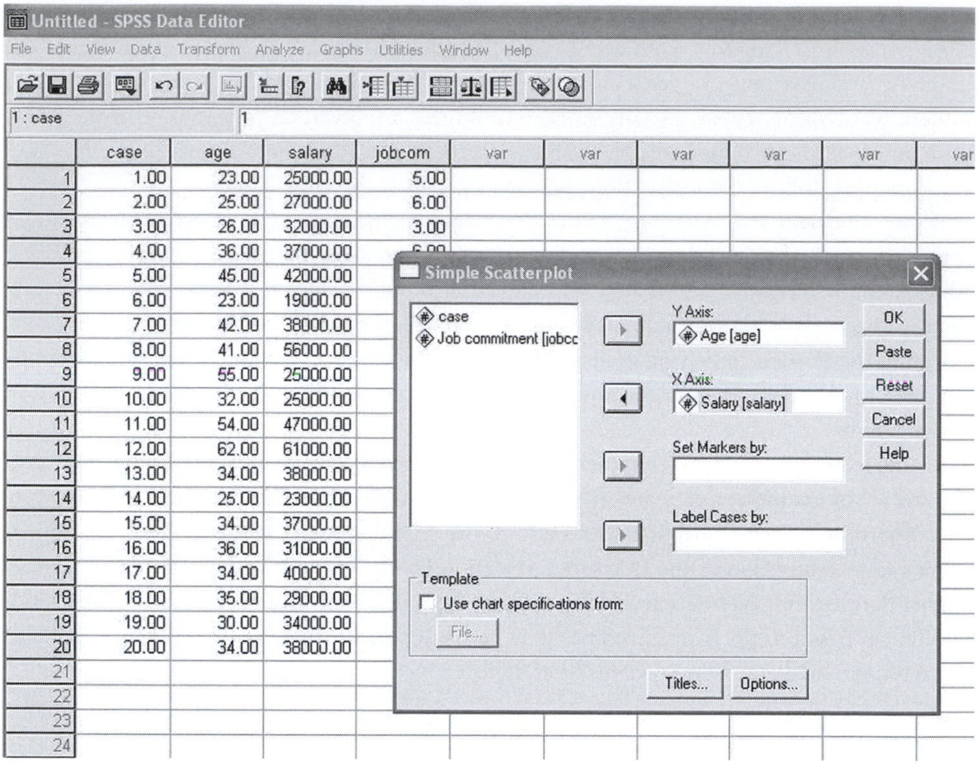

Figure 6.7 *Entering the variables for a scatterplot*

(which will indicate to you that the correlation between the variables will be very low) or they will form a roughly straight line (as they do in Figure 6.8).

Figure 6.9 shows an example of a scatterplot in which the points form a curved line. If such a curved line appears, a correlation coefficient, which assumes that there is a linear (i.e. straight-line) relationship between the variables, will give a misleading indication of the extent to which they are related. That is, it will indicate that the relationship between the variables is less strong than it actually is because a straight line won't capture this relationship as well as a curved line would.

Assuming that you do not find a curvilinear relationship between the variables you want to correlate, you can proceed to correlate them as follows:

➢ Click on **Analyze**.
➢ Click on **Correlate**.
➢ Click on **Bivariate**.
➢ A dialog box will open and within this your variables will appear in a white box on the left hand side.
➢ Click on a variable you wish to correlate to highlight it, and then click on the small black triangle to the left of the white box headed **Variables**. Your variable will be moved across to the **Variables** box.

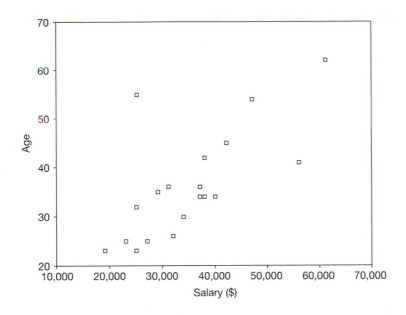

Figure 6.8 *Scatterplot produced by* SPSS *in which age is plotted against salary*

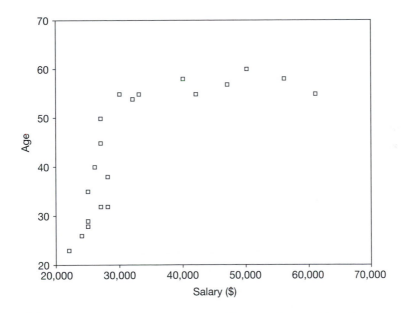

Figure 6.9 *An example of a scatterplot suggesting that there might* not *be a linear relationship between the variables of age and salary*

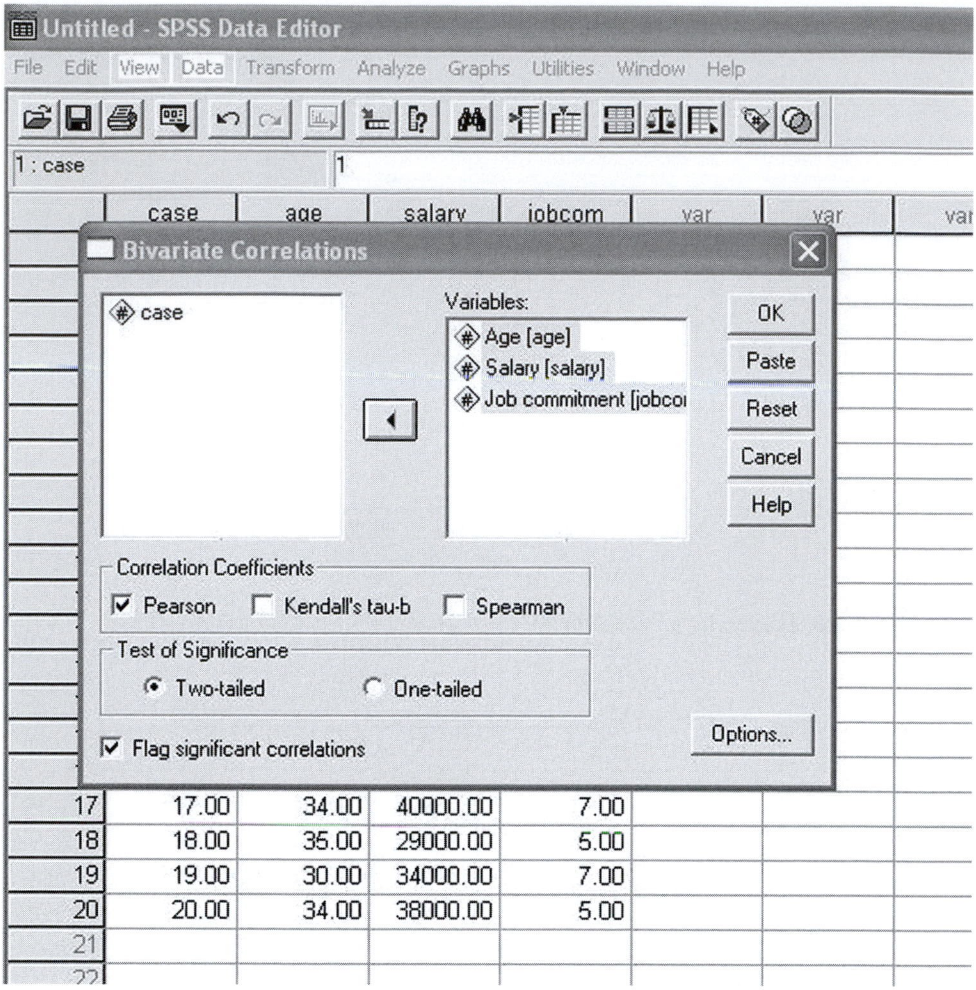

Figure 6.10 *Entering the variables to be correlated*

➤ Repeat this for every other variable you wish to correlate. If you wish to correlate all of the variables, you can drag your cursor over them while holding down the left button on your mouse. This will highlight them all and clicking on the black triangle will transfer them to the **Variables** box. If you wish to correlate just some of the variables you can click on each one while holding down the control key on your keyboard, and when you have highlighted all those you are interested in click on the black triangle (see Figure 6.10).
➤ Click on **OK**.

Output in the following form will appear.

Correlations

Correlations

		Age	Salary	Job commitment
Age	Pearson correlation	1	.675**	.104
	Sig. (2-tailed)	.	.001	.664
	N	20	20	20
Salary	Pearson correlation	.675**	1	−.168
	Sig. (2-tailed)	.001	.	.478
	N	20	20	20
Job commitment	Pearson correlation	.104	−.168	1
	Sig. (2-tailed)	.664	.478	.
	N	20	20	20

** Correlation is significant at the 0.01 level (2-tailed).

The correlation coefficient between age and salary.	Statistical significance. This figure needs to be below .05 for statistical significance to be claimed. The figure indicates the probability of getting a correlation as great as this if there is no linear relationship at all between age and salary.	The number of cases on which the correlation coefficient between age and salary is based.

For each pair of variables you entered, the *SPSS* output shows the correlation between the two, the statistical significance of this correlation, and the size of the sample on which the correlation is based. So, in the example here, the correlation between age and salary is .68, the correlation between age and job commitment is .10, and the correlation between salary and job commitment is −.17. This indicates the correlations between age and salary and age and job commitment are positive (e.g. the older the people are the more they earn), and the minus sign before the correlation between salary and job commitment indicates that this is a negative relationship (i.e. the higher the salary the lower the job commitment). The note at the bottom of the table explains that any correlation marked with a double asterisk is statistically significant at the .01 level. In this case, the table shows that the probability of getting a correlation as large as .68 between age and salary if there is no relationship at all between these variables in the population is .001. Because .001 is equal to or less than .01 this is marked with the two asterisks. The asterisks produced by *SPSS* can be useful when you have correlated several variables, and you wish to get a quick indication of how many are statistically significant.

Reporting correlations

If there are only one or two correlations to report this can be done in text. For example, to report just the correlation between age and salary from this example you could say that:

> A significant positive correlation was found between age and salary
> $r = .68$, $p = .001$.

Note that it is the convention to refer to the Pearson correlation coefficient with the letter r in italics.

Sometimes you may wish to report the correlation between several variables. This is best done with a correlation matrix, a table which shows the correlation between every possible combination of the variables you have correlated. For example, to report the correlations between the three variables in this example you could state the following:

> The Pearson correlation coefficients between age, salary and job commitment are shown in Table 6.6.

Table 6.6 *Correlations between age, salary and job commitment*

	Age	Salary	Job commitment
Age	–	.68*	.10
Salary		–	–.17
Job commitment			–

*$p < .01$

Note that a dash is inserted in cells where the correlation is between a variable and itself (which will always be perfect of course, giving a meaningless correlation coefficient of 1). Also, where entering correlation coefficients in the table would duplicate correlation coefficients already entered, these are left blank (i.e. the correlation coefficients that could be placed in the bottom left of the table would duplicate those already there). Statistically significant correlations are usually marked with an asterisk, and the significance level that the asterisk denotes is shown at the bottom of the table. In this case, a single asterisk is used to indicate that the significance level of .01 has been reached. However, if some of the correlations reached the .05 significance level whereas others reached .01, you could use * to indicate those correlations reaching the .05 level, and ** for those reaching .01.

Interpretation

Because the correlation coefficient is a direct measure of effect size, it is always a good idea to consider how large it is and, perhaps, to compare it to the convention for the effect sizes of small correlations (around 0.1), medium-sized ones (around 0.3) and large ones (0.5 and over). So, if you found that the correlation between age and salary was 0.68, this would indicate a large effect size: there is clearly quite a strong association between these two variables. Another way to express the degree of association between two continuous variables is with the percentage of variance accounted for. As explained earlier, the percentage of variance in Variable A accounted for by Variable B (or vice versa) can be worked out simply by squaring the correlation coefficient between them and multiplying by 100. Sometimes it is easier to meaningfully convey to someone the strength of the relationship between two variables with the percentage of variance accounted for than with the correlation coefficient. For example, someone might find it more helpful to know that variations in personnel interview scores account for 9 per cent of the variance in job performance than to know that the correlation between interview scores and job performance is .30. Finally, the scatterplot can also be used to communicate the degree of association between variables. Actually seeing the way that the points are scattered around the graph can provide a good feel for the data. Remember that the correlation coefficient you have computed is only an *estimate*, based on the data you have collected, of the true correlation between the variables. To obtain the range of values within which the true correlation between the variables is likely to fall (i.e. the confidence interval of the correlation), see www.dewberry-statistics.com.

It is often said that correlations tell you nothing at all about causal relationships. The argument is that if two variables, A and B, are found to be correlated, it may be that variations in A are causing variations in B, that variations in B are causing variations in A, or that some other variable (or variables) is causing variations in both A and B. In short, the correlation coefficient can suggest that two variables are associated, but it cannot tell you *why* they are associated. While this is usually the case, there are, nevertheless, circumstances in which correlations can give us evidence of causality. Imagine that you randomly select 100 people and administer to them, in controlled conditions, a drug known to produce flu-like symptoms. Each person is given a different quantity of the drug. You then correlate the amount of the drug given with the degree of flu-like symptoms shown. If you find a correlation between the amount of drug administered, and the degree of flu-like symptoms, you can reasonably conclude that the drug is causing the symptoms. Whether or not it is possible to conclude from a correlation coefficient that one variable is causing changes in the other depends on the research design. If the design is such that the only viable explanation for a correlation between variable A and variable B is variations in variable A (or variable B), we can conclude that there is a causal relationship between the variables. However, in organizational research, it is very rare to find correlations for which there is only one viable explanation, and it is almost always the case that causal relationship cannot be inferred from correlations.

Correlation coefficients tell you the extent that two variables are linearly related. That is, they tell you how well a *straight line* drawn on a scatterplot is a good fit in that the points on the scatterplot tend to be close to the line rather than spread all around it. It might be possible to capture the relationship between the two variables better by drawing a curved line on the scatterplot, and if this is the case (the variables here are said to have a curvilinear relationship rather than a linear one) the correlation coefficient should not be used. However, linear relationships are surprisingly common and, generally, the use of the correlation coefficient is perfectly satisfactory. To be safe though, it is good practice to produce a scatterplot before computing the correlation coefficient so that you can check visually that the variables don't have a curvilinear relationship before going ahead with the correlation.

MULTIPLE REGRESSION

Background to multiple regression

As explained in the previous section, in statistical analysis the word regression can be interpreted as meaning the same thing as prediction. Often we are interested in how well we can predict one variable from one or more other variables. For example, in the context of personnel selection you might be interested in how well you can predict job performance from cognitive ability and from interview scores. If the job performance of employees can be predicted accurately from how well they do on a cognitive ability test and/or how well they perform at a structured interview, this suggests that these techniques may be very useful in selecting future employees, because if you select applicants who score highly for cognitive ability and interview performance, you can be confident that their job performance will be better than if you select applicants at random.

As explained in the previous section on correlation, simple regression enables you to predict the scores of one variable from scores on one other variable, and it is closely related to correlation. The correlation coefficient can be conceived as a measure of the extent to which attempts to use a straight line to predict scores on one variable from scores on another variable are accurate (producing a large correlation coefficient), or result in considerable error (producing a small correlation coefficient). Consider again the scatterplot which was used in Figure 6.1 when the meaning of the correlation coefficient was discussed (this is shown again in Figure 6.11).

Here, we can see that a straight line drawn through the points on the graph would be reasonably good at capturing the relationship between these points. However, it would be by no means perfect because it is not possible to draw any straight line through the points which predicts very closely where every one of the points lies.

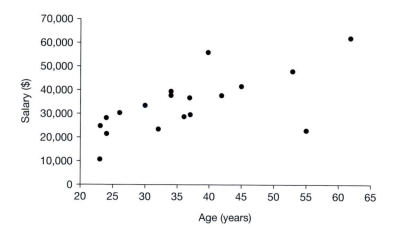

Figure 6.11 *Scatterplot of salary plotted against age*

Multiple predictor variables

In the case of multiple regression, rather than using one variable (such as cognitive ability) to predict one other variable (such as job performance), you use two or more variables (for example, cognitive ability, interview performance and biodata scores) to predict one other variable (such as job performance). It is called multiple regression because instead of using one predictor variable you are simultaneously using multiple predictor variables.

In the case of simple regression we saw that the regression line can be defined with the simple formula $\hat{Y} = A + BX$. With multiple regression, the formula is an extension of this: $\hat{Y} = A + B_1 X_1 + B_2 X_2 + B_3 X_3 \ldots B_k X_k$. Here $\hat{Y} =$ is the predicted value of Y (the dependent variable), A is a constant, B_1 to B_k are regression coefficients, and X_1 to X_k are each of the independent variables.

Multiple regression is a powerful and flexible technique which often proves very useful in organizational research.

When to use multiple regression

Common uses include the following:

- Establishing the correlation between multiple predictor variables and the dependent variable.

  Example: A researcher wishes to examine the correlation between the predictor variables of age, education level and gender on the one hand, and the dependent variable of training performance on the other.

- Examining the extent to which each predictor variable uniquely predicts the dependent variable. That is, the multiple regression model enables you to consider the unique importance of each independent variable in predicting the dependent variable.

  Example: After taking into account age and gender, a researcher wishes to know the extent to which education level, taken on its own, predicts training performance.

- Investigating whether one or more predictor variables explain variation in the dependent variable over and above one or more other predictor variables.

  Example: A researcher wants to find out whether training-related variables (training performance, time taken to train, etc.) can predict sales performance after taking into account the relationship between sales performance and demographic variables (gender, age, nationality, etc.).

Each of these uses will be examined in turn.

Establishing the correlation between multiple predictor variables and the dependent variable

In the earlier section on correlation, it was explained that the size of a correlation coefficient between two variables can be used to work out the percentage of variance in one variable that is accounted for by the other. So, if you find a correlation of .30 between annual salary and well-being, you can say that 9 per cent of the variance in well-being is accounted for by salary (because .30 squared and multiplied by 100 = 9).

You also saw how the degree of variance accounted for by another variable can be expressed in a Venn diagram such as Figure 6.12.

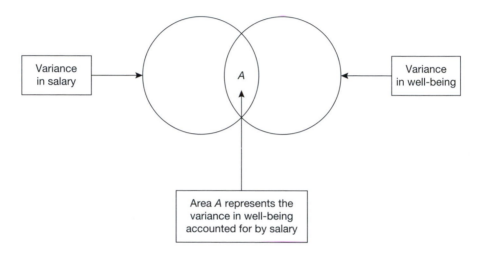

Figure 6.12 *Venn diagram showing the shared variance between two variables: salary and well-being*

Understanding how multiple predictor variables can be correlated with the dependent variable is quite straightforward once you have an understanding of the relationship between the correlation coefficient, the percentage of variance in one variable accounted for by the other, and how this can be represented in a Venn diagram. This simply involves a slight extension of the Venn diagram so that you are dealing not just with one predictor variable, but with several. To keep things as simple and straightforward as possible here, consider the case in which there are just two predictor variables. However, once you have understood the logic of this, you should be able to appreciate how it would apply if you had more than two.

Imagine that you collected data on the cognitive ability, structured interview performance and job performance of 100 employees. What you want to know is: how well does a combination of cognitive ability and structured interview performance allow you to predict the job performance of employees? If they enable you to predict job performance well, you may decide to use these two techniques in your selection process, and if they don't you may just use one, or possibly neither of them. The question of how well two or more predictor variables (here, cognitive ability scores and structured interview scores) predict

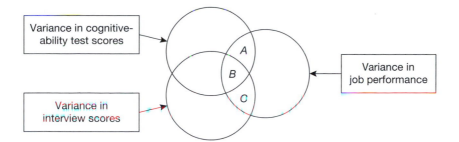

Figure 6.13 *Venn diagram showing the shared variance between two predictor variables and a dependent variable*

a dependent variable (here, job performance) is one of the questions to which you can find an answer with multiple regression.

In the Venn diagram shown in Figure 6.13 there are two predictor variables (cognitive-ability scores and structured interview scores) and one dependent variable (job perform-ance). The variances in cognitive ability scores and interview scores are shown in the two circles on the left, and the variance in job performance is shown in the circle on the right. Where there is an overlap between the circle for cognitive ability scores and the circle for job-performance scores (areas *A* and *B*), the area represents the degree of variance in job performance accounted for by cognitive ability scores. In the same way, where there is an overlap between the circle for interview scores and the circle for job performance (areas *B* and *C*), the area represents the degree of variance in job performance accounted for by the interview scores. The implication of this is that the amount of variance in job performance accounted for by cognitive ability and interviews is the sum of the areas *A*, *B* and *C*.

One of the things you can get multiple regression to do is to tell you the multiple correl-ation between all of the predictor variables on the one hand, and the dependent variable on the other. This is known as the multiple correlation coefficient, and it is the equivalent of the ordinary Pearson correlation coefficient discussed in the previous section on corre-lations. Whereas the ordinary Pearson correlation coefficient tells you the correlation between just two variables, the multiple correlation coefficient tells you the correlation between two or more predictor variables and the dependent variable.

The square of the multiple correlation coefficient multiplied by 100, just like the square of the simple correlation coefficient multiplied by 100, tells you the percentage of variance accounted for. In the case of multiple regression, the square of the multiple correlation coefficient multiplied by 100 tells you the percentage of variance in the dependent variable that is accounted for by all of the predictor variables together (in this case the sum of areas *A*, *B* and *C* in Figure 6.13).

Examining the extent to which each predictor variable uniquely predicts the dependent variable

You have seen that in the Venn diagram presented as Figure 6.13, areas *A*, *B* and *C* add up to the amount of variance in the dependent variable collectively accounted for by the two predictor variables. If you have a look at the diagram again, you will see that area *B* is the part of the variance in job performance that is predicted by both cognitive ability and interview scores. However, area *A* is the variance in job performance that is predicted by cognitive ability only. Area *A* is a part of the variance in job performance that is not overlapped at all by the circle representing the variance in interview scores. By the same token, area *C* is the variance in job performance predicted uniquely by interview scores since, here, there is no overlap with cognitive ability.

Multiple regression is able to identify this unique contribution that each predictor variable makes to the dependent variable. This can be very useful in research. For example, imagine that you wish to know whether it makes sense to use assessment centres to select people for jobs in a particular organization. If you correlate assessment centre scores with job performance, and find that the correlation coefficient is .24, this may constitute a strong enough relationship for you to go ahead and use this selection technique. But what if someone says that there is evidence that assessment centre scores are highly correlated with school examination results? If this is the case then going to all the expense of running an assessment centre might be unnecessary – you could simply find an overall measure of how well people did in their school examinations instead.

Multiple regression can be used to investigate this. You obtain the assessment centre scores, and scores indicating overall school performance from, say, 400 people. You can then also obtain job-performance ratings on them. Finally, with multiple regression, you can identify the *unique* correlation of assessment centres with job performance. This will tell you the amount of variance in job performance predicted by assessment centre scores, but not by school examination result scores. If this unique correlation is substantial, it adds weight to the case to continue to use assessment centres in addition to information about school examination results.

On the other hand, if, after controlling for school examination performance, assessment centres add little or nothing extra to the prediction of job performance, there would be little or no justification for using them if you can easily obtain the school examination scores of job applicants.

Examining how well the dependent variable can be predicted with two different sets of predictor variables

Another thing you can do with multiple regression is to examine the correlation of one or more predictor variables with the dependent variable, and then examine the change in the size of the multiple correlation when one or more variables are added. For example, you could look at the multiple correlation of cognitive ability and interview scores with job performance, and then introduce scores for biodata and conscientiousness to examine how much the multiple correlation is increased when these additional variables are added.

Types of multiple regression

There are three main types of multiple regression: standard, hierarchical (sometimes also called sequential) and stepwise. Each of these is briefly discussed below.

Table 6.7 *Correlations between verbal ability, numerical ability and job performance*

	Verbal ability	Numerical ability	Job performance
Verbal ability	–	.91	.45
Numerical ability		–	.37
Job performance			–

Standard multiple regression

This is the default type in *SPSS*. All independent variables are entered into the regression model at once. The unique contribution of each independent variable to the model is then assessed by examining what it adds to the ability of the model to predict over and above all of the other independent variables.

It is possible for an independent variable to have a high level of correlation with the dependent variable but a low level of *unique* correlation with it. This will happen if the independent variable is strongly correlated with other independent variables. For example, imagine that verbal ability and numerical ability are both used to predict job performance, and that the correlation between the three is as shown in Table 6.7.

In Table 6.7, verbal ability predicts job performance quite well ($r = .45$). However, verbal ability is also highly correlated with numerical ability ($r = .91$). So it follows that relatively little variance in job performance is predicted *uniquely* by verbal ability, because verbal ability shares so much of its variance with numerical ability. In fact, if you recall the section on correlations, you will know that the proportion of variance shared between verbal and numerical ability is, in fact, over 80 per cent (because .91 squared and multiplied by 100 = 83).

One of the reasons why standard multiple regression is so helpful is that it allows us to estimate the extent to which a variable is not only associated with a dependent variable, but how much it is uniquely associated with that dependent variable.

Hierarchical (or sequential) multiple regression

Here, the researcher specifies the order in which the independent variables enter into the regression model. Each variable is assessed according to the contribution it makes to the model at the point at which it is entered. Normally, the researcher decides the order in which to enter the independent variables on logical or theoretical grounds. One basis for deciding this is temporal order. For example, in the prediction of sales performance the educational records of sales staff might be entered before the amount of sales training they are given. Alternatively, variables that are considered irrelevant to the question being asked might be entered first so that their effect is controlled. So, to examine the extent of which school performance and bio data scores predict sales performance, *after* controlling for age and gender, you could run one regression model based on age and gender, then a second one in which school performance and bio data scores are added, and then examine how much more predictive the second model is.

Stepwise regression

With stepwise regression the order in which the variables are entered into the regression model depends on certain statistical features of the sample. The problem is that small fluctuations in the characteristics of the sample can lead to major differences in the outcome of the regression analysis, and this technique is not recommended here.

Assumptions and requirements

Multiple regression is quite a complex statistical technique which makes several assumptions about the data and the underlying populations. The first and simplest of the assumptions is that the predictor variables are either continuous (e.g. age) or dichotomous (e.g. gender), and that the dependent variable is continuous. In fact, it is possible to use non-dichotomous predictor variables in multiple regression (e.g. whether or not salespeople operate in the North, South, East or West of a country), but in order to do so it is necessary to recode such a variable into what are called dummy variables. The procedure for doing so is explained later. If you have a dichotomous dependent variable (e.g. whether or not people are made redundant or not) you should use **logistic regression** or **discriminant function analysis** instead of multiple regression.

Another three important assumptions of multiple regression are as follows:

1   The predictor variables are normally distributed.
2   The variables have a linear relationship with each other (i.e. if we plot each pair of variables on a scatterplot, the points would lie roughly on a straight line rather than on a curved line). As explained in the previous section on correlation, this is the same assumption as that made when computing the Pearson correlation coefficient between just two variables.
3   The variability of scores in the dependent variable at one value of a predictor variable is roughly the same as the variability at other levels of the predictor variable. This is known as homoscedasticity.

Fortunately, the assumptions of normality, linearity and homoscedasticity can be checked quite easily by examining a scatterplot of the values of the dependent variable predicted by the regression model against the residuals. The residuals are the errors which occur when the regression model is used to predict the actual values of the dependent variable (see page 231). In the case of multiple regression, when these critical three assumptions are met, a scatterplot in which the values of the dependent variable predicted by the regression model are plotted against the residuals will have a roughly rectangular shape. The instructions on how to use *SPSS* to carry out a multiple regression will explain how to produce the necessary scatterplot, and what to look for.

A potential problem when running a multiple regression is that two or more predictor variables are very highly intercorrelated with each other. This is referred to as **multicollinearity** (or sometimes just **collinearity**). The problem with multicollinearity is that it is likely to prevent any of the individual predictors from being significant. This is a potentially serious problem, and *SPSS* provides *collinearity diagnostics* which can be used to detect this problem if it exists in your data.

In certain cases, an extreme form of multicollinearity called **singularity** occurs. In the case of singularity the values of one predictor variable can be predicted perfectly from knowledge of one or more other predictor variables. This is more likely to occur than you might expect, especially to the inexperienced researcher. For example, if one predictor variable is used to specify whether or not cases are males, and another one specifies whether or not they are females, singularity will exist between the two because whether or not cases are males can obviously be exactly predicted from whether or not they are females.

The required sample size

The sample size required to examine whether a multiple correlation coefficient (R^2) is statistically significant depends on the power required, the significance level adopted and the number of predictor variables involved. Cohen (1988) suggests f^2 as a measure of effect size, and when you are just interested in whether the predictor variables are collectively associated with the dependent variable, f^2 has a simple relationship with the multiple correlation coefficient R^2. If you are able to use the results of previous research, or a pilot study, to estimate the size of the multiple correlation coefficient you expect to find in your own study, use this estimate together with information about the number of predictor variables you will be using to look up the sample size you will require in Table 6.8.

For example, with five predictor variables and a predicted R^2 of .13, you would require a sample size of 90. If you require a power of 90 per cent, increase the relevant sample size by 30 per cent. If you have no idea of what multiple correlation to expect before carrying out the study, use the sample size required for a medium effect size.

Table 6.8 *The approximate sample sizes required for multiple regression, assuming a power of 80% and a .05 significance level*

	Effect size		Number of predictor variables	Sample size required
	f^2	R^2		
Small	0.02	.02	2	480
			5	640
			10	840
Medium	0.15	.13	2	70
			5	90
			10	120
Large	0.35	.26	2	32
			5	40
			10	55

A worked example

A researcher is interested in whether the training performance of employees in an organization can be predicted from their age, the department they work in and how well they performed at the selection interview carried out before they were appointed. She collects data on 25 people, and this is shown in Table 6.9.

Table 6.9 *The training performance, age, department and selection interview performance of 25 employees*

Case	Predictor variables			Dependent variable
	Age	Department	Selection interview performance	Training performance
1	32	1	3	2
2	35	2	9	8
3	36	3	5	3
4	36	1	3	4
5	28	2	2	5
6	37	2	6	2
7	33	1	4	4
8	36	3	7	6
9	29	1	4	4
10	41	3	3	3
11	35	3	7	5
12	32	2	7	3
13	55	1	4	6
14	46	2	8	6
15	27	3	6	5
16	36	3	5	7
17	38	1	8	9
18	27	2	3	4
19	42	3	5	3
20	38	2	9	8
21	33	1	7	8
22	39	2	7	6
23	47	1	5	4
24	20	1	4	6
25	48	3	3	5

	case	age	deptment	intperfm	trnperfm	var
Untitled - SPSS Data Editor						
File Edit View Data Transform Analyze Graphs Utilities Window Help						
1 : case			1			
1	1.00	32.00	1.00	3.00	2.00	
2	2.00	35.00	2.00	9.00	8.00	
3	3.00	36.00	3.00	5.00	3.00	
4	4.00	36.00	1.00	3.00	4.00	
5	5.00	28.00	2.00	2.00	5.00	
6	6.00	37.00	2.00	6.00	2.00	
7	7.00	33.00	1.00	4.00	4.00	
8	8.00	36.00	3.00	7.00	6.00	
9	9.00	29.00	1.00	4.00	4.00	
10	10.00	41.00	3.00	3.00	3.00	
11	11.00	35.00	3.00	7.00	5.00	
12	12.00	32.00	2.00	7.00	3.00	
13	13.00	55.00	1.00	4.00	6.00	
14	14.00	46.00	2.00	8.00	6.00	
15	15.00	27.00	3.00	6.00	5.00	
16	16.00	36.00	3.00	5.00	7.00	
17	17.00	38.00	1.00	8.00	9.00	
18	18.00	27.00	2.00	3.00	4.00	
19	19.00	42.00	3.00	5.00	3.00	
20	20.00	38.00	2.00	9.00	8.00	
21	21.00	33.00	1.00	7.00	8.00	
22	22.00	39.00	2.00	7.00	6.00	
23	23.00	47.00	1.00	5.00	4.00	
24	24.00	20.00	1.00	4.00	6.00	
25	25.00	48.00	3.00	3.00	5.00	
26						
27						

Figure 6.14 SPSS *Data Editor after multiple regression data are entered*

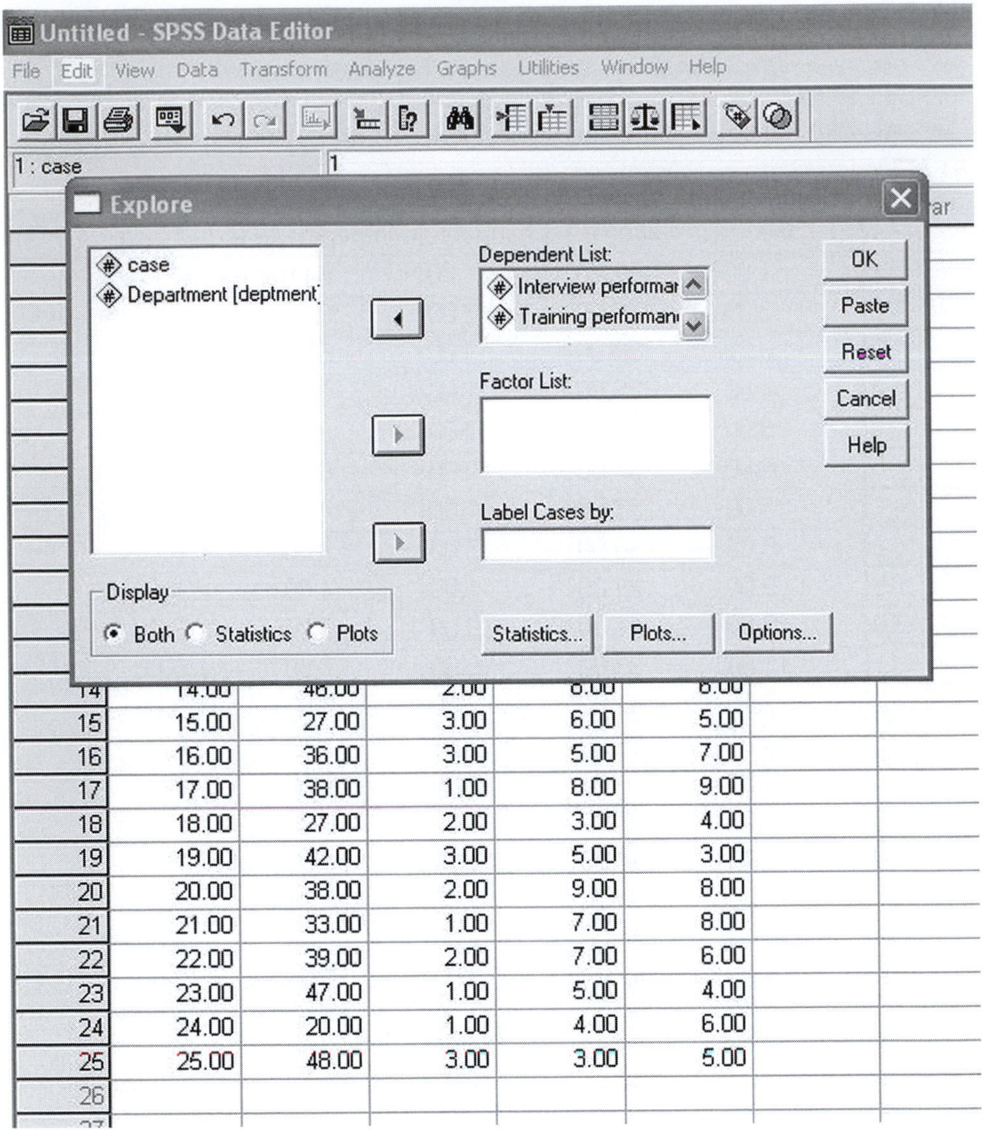

Untitled - SPSS Data Editor

File   Edit   View   Data   Transform   Analyze   Graphs   Utilities   Window   Help

1 : case   1

Explore

case
Department [deptment]

Dependent List:
Interview performar
Training performan

Factor List:

Label Cases by:

Display
Both   Statistics   Plots

Statistics...   Plots...   Options...

OK
Paste
Reset
Cancel
Help

14	14.00	46.00	2.00	8.00	8.00
15	15.00	27.00	3.00	6.00	5.00
16	16.00	36.00	3.00	5.00	7.00
17	17.00	38.00	1.00	8.00	9.00
18	18.00	27.00	2.00	3.00	4.00
19	19.00	42.00	3.00	5.00	3.00
20	20.00	38.00	2.00	9.00	8.00
21	21.00	33.00	1.00	7.00	8.00
22	22.00	39.00	2.00	7.00	6.00
23	23.00	47.00	1.00	5.00	4.00
24	24.00	20.00	1.00	4.00	6.00
25	25.00	48.00	3.00	3.00	5.00
26					

Figure 6.15 *Entering the variables for* Explore *when carrying out a multiple regression*

How to carry out a standard multiple regression using SPSS

Begin by entering your data in the *SPSS* Data Editor. Figure 6.14 shows what the above data look like when they have been entered. The variable names used for department, selection interview performance and training performance are 'deptment', 'intperfm', and 'trnperfm' respectively. The *Variable View* in the *SPSS* Data Editor has been used to enter variable labels for the variables 'age', 'deptment', 'intperfm' and 'trnperfm' as 'Age', 'Department', 'Interview performance' and 'Training performance' respectively. As 'Department' was coded 1 for people working in finance, 2 for people working in marketing and 3 for production staff, these were the values entered under 'deptment' in the *Variable View* under *Values*.

The first step is to run *Explore* in *SPSS* to examine the continuous variables. To do this:

- ➤ Click on **Analyze**.
- ➤ Click on **Descriptive Statistics**.
- ➤ Click on **Explore**.
- ➤ A dialog box will appear with the variables to be correlated in a white box on the left hand side. Click on each of the continuous variables (in this example these are 'Age', 'Interview performance' and 'Training performance', but not 'Department' as this is a categorical variable), and then on the black triangle to the left of the white box headed **Dependent List**. The variables will be moved across to the **Dependent List** box (see Figure 6.15).
- ➤ Click on **OK**.

The following output will appear.

Explore

Case processing summary

	Cases					
	Valid		Missing		Total	
	N	Per cent	N	Per cent	N	Per cent
Age	25	100.0%	0	.0%	25	100.0%
Interview performance	25	100.0%	0	.0%	25	100.0%
Training performance	25	100.0%	0	.0%	25	100.0%

Descriptives

			Statistic	Std error
Age	Mean		36.2400	1.52018
	95% confidence interval for mean	Lower bound	33.1025	
		Upper bound	39.3775	
	5% trimmed mean		36.1000	
	Median		36.0000	
	Variance		57.773	

	Std deviation		7.60088	
	Minimum		20.00	
	Maximum		55.00	
	Range		35.00	
	Interquartile range		8.0000	
	Skewness		.383	.464
	Kurtosis		.747	.902
Interview performance	Mean		5.3600	.41183
	95% confidence	Lower bound	4.5100	
	interval for mean	Upper bound	6.2100	
	5% trimmed mean		5.3333	
	Median		5.0000	
	Variance		4.240	
	Std deviation		2.05913	
	Minimum		2.00	
	Maximum		9.00	
	Range		7.00	
	Interquartile range		3.5000	
	Skewness		.218	.464
	Kurtosis		−1.090	.902
Training performance	Mean		5.0400	.38936
	95% confidence	Lower bound	4.2364	
	interval for mean	Upper bound	5.8436	
	5% trimmed mean		5.0000	
	Median		5.0000	
	Variance		3.790	
	Std deviation		1.94679	
	Minimum		2.00	
	Maximum		9.00	
	Range		7.00	
	Interquartile range		2.5000	
	Skewness		.344	.464
	Kurtosis		−.653	.902

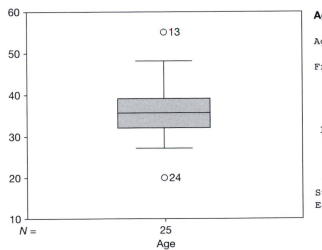

```
Age

Age Stem-and-Leaf Plot

Frequency          Stem & Leaf

   1.00 Extremes     (=<20)
   4.00          2 . 7789
   4.00          3 . 2233
  10.00          3 . 5566667889
   2.00          4 . 12
   3.00          4 . 678
   1.00 Extremes     (>=55)

Stem width:      10.00
Each leaf:       1 case(s)
```

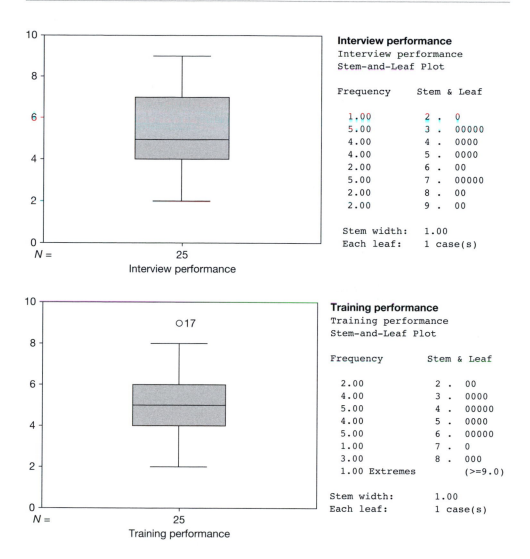

Interview performance

Interview performance
Stem-and-Leaf Plot

Frequency		Stem & Leaf
1.00	2 .	0
5.00	3 .	00000
4.00	4 .	0000
4.00	5 .	0000
2.00	6 .	00
5.00	7 .	00000
2.00	8 .	00
2.00	9 .	00

Stem width: 1.00
Each leaf: 1 case(s)

Training performance

Training performance
Stem-and-Leaf Plot

Frequency		Stem & Leaf
2.00	2 .	00
4.00	3 .	0000
5.00	4 .	00000
4.00	5 .	0000
5.00	6 .	00000
1.00	7 .	0
3.00	8 .	000
1.00 Extremes		(>=9.0)

Stem width: 1.00
Each leaf: 1 case(s)

As you can see, a separate set of descriptive information is produced for each of the variables you wish to correlate. For each variable, in the table headed *Descriptives*, check that the minimum and maximum values seem correct, and in the box and whiskers plots look for any outlying or extreme scores. Details on how to do this are given on pages 90–1. If the minimum and maximum values are reasonable, and there are no outliers shown in the box and whiskers plot, follow the instructions below to perform the correlations.

If the minimum and maximum values don't look right, and/or there are outliers shown in the box and whiskers plot, check your data to make sure that the outlying or extreme values are not mistakes, and that from a research point of view it makes sense to include them in the analysis. If necessary, take steps to modify the data, and then run *Explore* again, repeating the process until you are confident that your data are sound. When you are confident that the data are acceptable, follow the instructions to move on to the next stage of the multiple regression analysis.

259

In this example, cases 13 and 24 are identified as outliers in the box and whiskers plot for age, and case 17 is highlighted as an outlier in the box and whiskers plot for training performance. These data points were checked and found to be entered correctly. Therefore, no modification was made to the data file before proceeding to the next stage of the analysis.

Because there is a categorical variable in this example, 'Department', it is also necessary to examine this. As explained in Chapter 4, the way to examine a categorical variable is as follows:

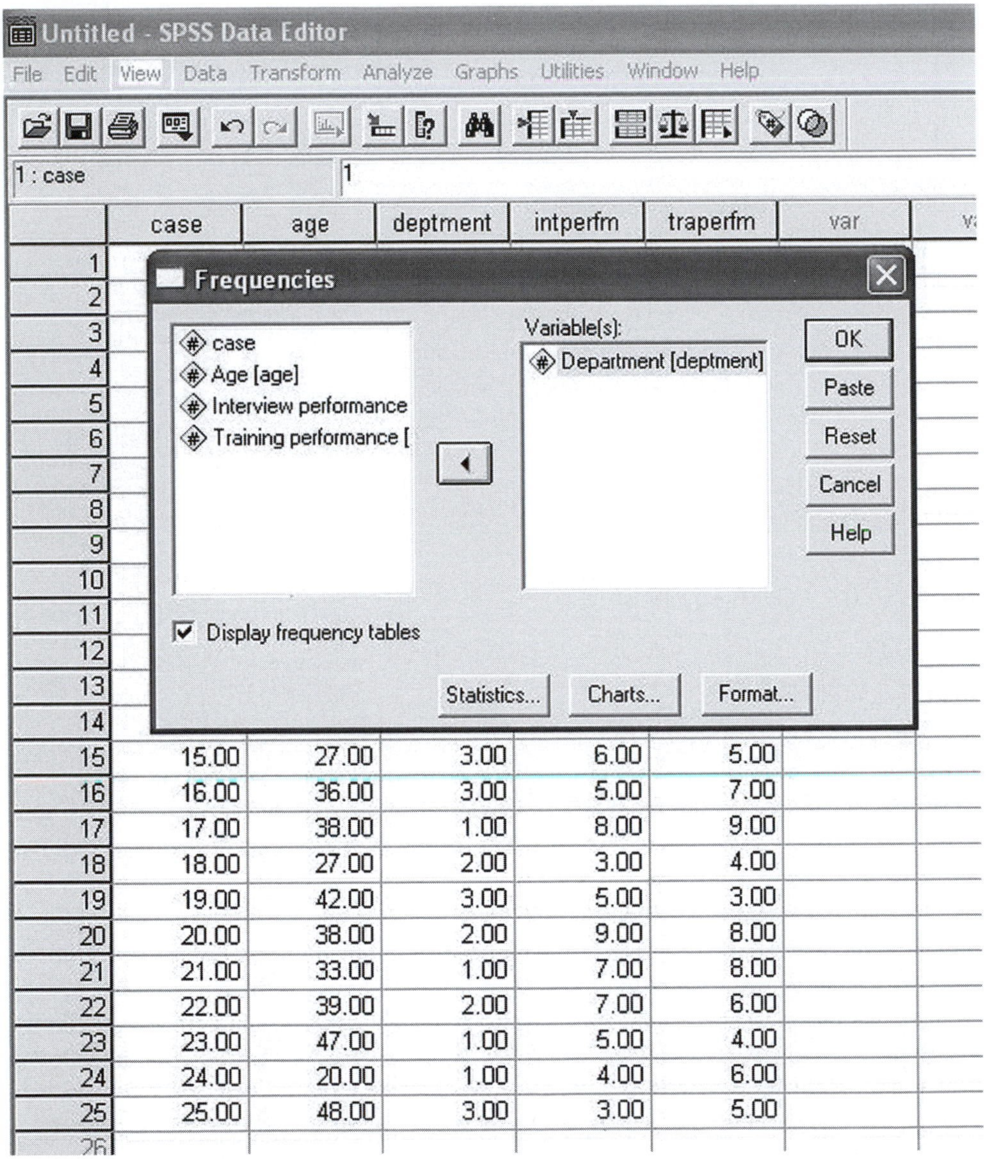

Figure 6.16 *Entering categorical variable for a frequency analysis when carrying out a multiple regression*

➢ Click on **Analyze**.
➢ Click on **Descriptive Statistics**.
➢ Click on **Frequencies**.
➢ A dialog box will open. In the white box on the right hand side of the dialog box is a list of the variables. Click on a categorical variable and then on the small black triangle to the left of the white box headed **Variable(s)**. The categorical variable will be moved across to the **Variables** box. Repeat this procedure for any other categorical variables you wish to examine prior to running the multiple regression analysis (see Figure 6.16).
➢ Click on **OK**.

Output like the following will appear.

Frequencies

Statistics

Department

N	Valid	25
	Missing	0

Department

		Frequency	Per cent	Valid per cent	Cumulative per cent
Valid	Finance	9	36.0	36.0	36.0
	Marketing	8	32.0	32.0	68.0
	Production	8	32.0	32.0	100.0
	Total	25	100.0	100.0	

This table shows that there are nine people in finance, eight in marketing and eight in production. This is the correct number in this case, indicating that there are no mistakes in the data entry process and, therefore, no corrections were made.

If there are non-dichotomous categorical variables in the analysis it is now necessary to create appropriate dummy variables. If you do not have any such variables you can skip the following step and proceed to page 269.

Dummy variables

As stated under Assumptions and requirements, it is necessary to recode categorical predictor variables which have more than two levels. This is achieved by using the non-dichotomous predictor variable to create several 'dummy' variables. In the context of multiple regression, a **dummy variable** is a dichotomous variable which is used to present part of the information captured by a categorical variable which has three or more levels. The number of dummy variables created is always one less than the number of levels of the categorical variable. For example, if people are from finance, marketing and production,

Table 6.10 *Example of dummy variable coding for a non-dichotomous predictor variable*

Non-dichotomous predictor variable	Dummy variable 1 Name: 'finornot'	Dummy variable 2 Name: 'mkornot'
The department in which someone works. Coded 1 for finance, 2 for marketing and 3 for production	Indicates whether or not someone works in finance	Indicates whether or not someone works in marketing
Finance	1	0
Marketing	0	1
Production	0	0

the variable 'Department' has three levels and this means that it will be necessary to create two (i.e. 3 − 1 = 2) dummy variables. If finance, marketing and production are coded as:

— finance: 1;
— marketing: 2;
— production: 3

then we could create two dummy *SPSS* variables called, say, 'mkornot' (indicating whether or not people work in marketing) and 'finornot' (indicating whether or not they work in finance). The values given to people on these new dummy variables will depend on the values they had on the original categorical variable, and the way they are coded in this example is shown in Table 6.10.

So, if a case is someone who works in finance they will receive a score of 1 for a dummy variable called 'finornot', and 0 for a dummy variable called 'mkornot'. If a case is someone who works in marketing they will receive a score of 0 for the dummy variable called 'finornot', and 1 for the dummy variable 'mkornot'. Finally, if they work in production they will receive score of 0 for both 'finornot' and 'mkornot'. Because the newly created dummy variables of 'finornot' and 'mkornot' are dichotomous, they can be used in the multiple regression.

Before explaining how to create these dummy variables, it is important to consider what we have done here and what the implications are. The reason it has been necessary to create dummy variables is that if we had used the original coding for the variable 'Department' (i.e. 1, 2 and 3), *SPSS* would have treated this as a continuous variable. As a consequence, someone working in production (coded 3 for the variable 'Department') would be interpreted as receiving a higher score than someone in marketing (coded 2). This is clearly absurd. However, you might quite reasonably ask why we did not create three variables to get around this problem: the first might indicate whether or not people work in finance, the second whether or not they work in marketing and the third whether or not they work in production.

The reason for this is that if we create such dichotomous variables we will breach the singularity assumption. As explained above, singularity occurs when the values of one predictor variable can be predicted perfectly from knowledge of one or more other predictor variables. If we create a variable which indicates whether or not people work in finance, a variable which indicates whether or not they work in marketing, and a variable which indicates whether or not they work in production, we can perfectly predict the value that someone will receive on any one of these three variables from a knowledge of the values they have on the other two. For example, if the values that someone has for the finance (or not) and marketing (or not) variables indicate that they do not work in these two departments, it follows that the value for production *must* indicate that they work there. That is, if we have classified people as to whether they work in finance, marketing or production, and a particular person doesn't work in finance or marketing, it necessarily follows that they must work in production. In the same way, we can ascertain whether or not someone works in finance from a knowledge of whether or not they work in marketing or production, and we can decide whether or not someone works in marketing from a knowledge of whether or not they work in finance or production. Because the value of one variable, here, can be perfectly predicted from information about the other two variables, we have singularity and, consequently, we have breached one of the assumptions of multiple regression.

Having clarified why dummy variables are necessary, it is now important to be clear about the information that is captured in each dummy variable. In the example above, the coding for the dummy variable 'mkornot' shown in Table 6.10 indicates whether someone works in marketing (coded 1) versus whether they work *in any other department* (coded 0). This is true for all dummy variables: each one tells us whether someone is in one category or *any* of the other categories. An awareness of this is very important when we interpret the results of a multiple regression analysis involving dummy variables. If the dependent variable is well-being, and we find that when we use 'mkornot' in a multiple regression model this variable is found to have some (shared or unique) correlation with well-being scores, this simply means that whether or not people are in marketing is to some extent predictive of their well-being. Similarly, the scores people receive for 'finornot' indicate whether working in the finance department is associated with well-being.

However, you may be aware that in our example there is another department, production, which is not represented with a dummy variable (see Table 6.10). In these circumstances how do we know whether there is a relationship between whether people work in production and their well-being? The short answer is that we don't know. When dummy variables are created, there will always be one level of the categorical variable on which they are based that is left out. This level will be the one that is coded zero on all of the newly created dummy variables. This draws our attention to the important point that the process of deciding which level of the categorical variables to 'leave out' is critical. How we decide which one to leave out is not a statistical issue: it should be considered in light of what you are trying to find out with your data. If, for theoretical or practical reasons, you are particularly interested in whether there is an association between whether or not people work in marketing and their well-being, this level of the categorical variable 'Department' should certainly be coded as a dummy variable. If whether or not people work in marketing is seen to be of little interest in relation to well-being, then perhaps this level of the 'Department' variable should not be given a dummy variable. It is up to you to decide.

263

There are circumstances, however, when you are actually interested in whether all levels of the categorical variable are important. That is, to use the example here, you might be interested in whether working in all three of the departments is associated with well-being. The only way to deal with this situation satisfactorily is to run two multiple regressions. In the first you might choose to create a dummy variable for whether or not people work in finance and another one for whether or not they work in marketing. Then you might carry out another regression which is identical to the first except that this time the dummy variables are whether or not people work in marketing and whether or not they work in production. By looking at the results of both regressions you can ascertain the association between the dependent variable of all levels of the categorical variable on which the dummy variables are based.

In Table 6.9 there is one non-dichotomous categorical variable: 'Department'. As 'Department' has three levels, two dummy variables are required in order to represent it. Let us say that in this example we are particularly interested in: (a) whether the fact that people work in marketing is associated with training performance; and (b) whether the fact that they work in production is associated with training performance. In this case, therefore, we will create two new dummy variables, one indicating whether people work in marketing or the remaining two departments (to be called 'mkornot'), and one indicating whether they work in production or the remaining two departments (to be called 'prornot').

To create the first dummy variable, in this case 'mkornot':

➤ Click on **Transform**.
➤ Click on **Recode**.
➤ Click on **Into Different Variables**.
➤ A dialog box will appear with the list of your variables in a white box to the left. Click on the categorical variable out of which you wish to create a dummy variable (in this case 'Department') and then on the small black triangle to the left of the white box headed **Numeric Variable -> Output Variable**. The categorical variable will be moved across to the **Numeric Variable -> Output Variable** box, and to the left of it will be two dashes, a greater than sign and a question mark see Figure 6.17.
➤ You next need to give the dummy variable a name. Since the first dummy variable in this example is to be called **mkornot** (i.e. marketing or not) we need to type 'mkornot' under **Name** and, so that we know what this means when we see the analysis of the results of the multiple regression, we should also give it a full label. To do so type 'mkornot' in the white box headed **Name** and 'Marketing or not' in the white box under **Label**. Click on **Change**. You will see that the name of the new dummy variable, in this case 'mkornot', replaces the question mark in the box headed **Numeric Variable -> Output Variable** (see Figure 6.18).
➤ The next step is to indicate what values you wish to give the dummy variable. Normally, the dummy variable is coded 1 if a case is a member of the particular level of the categorical variable you are interested in here (in this example this

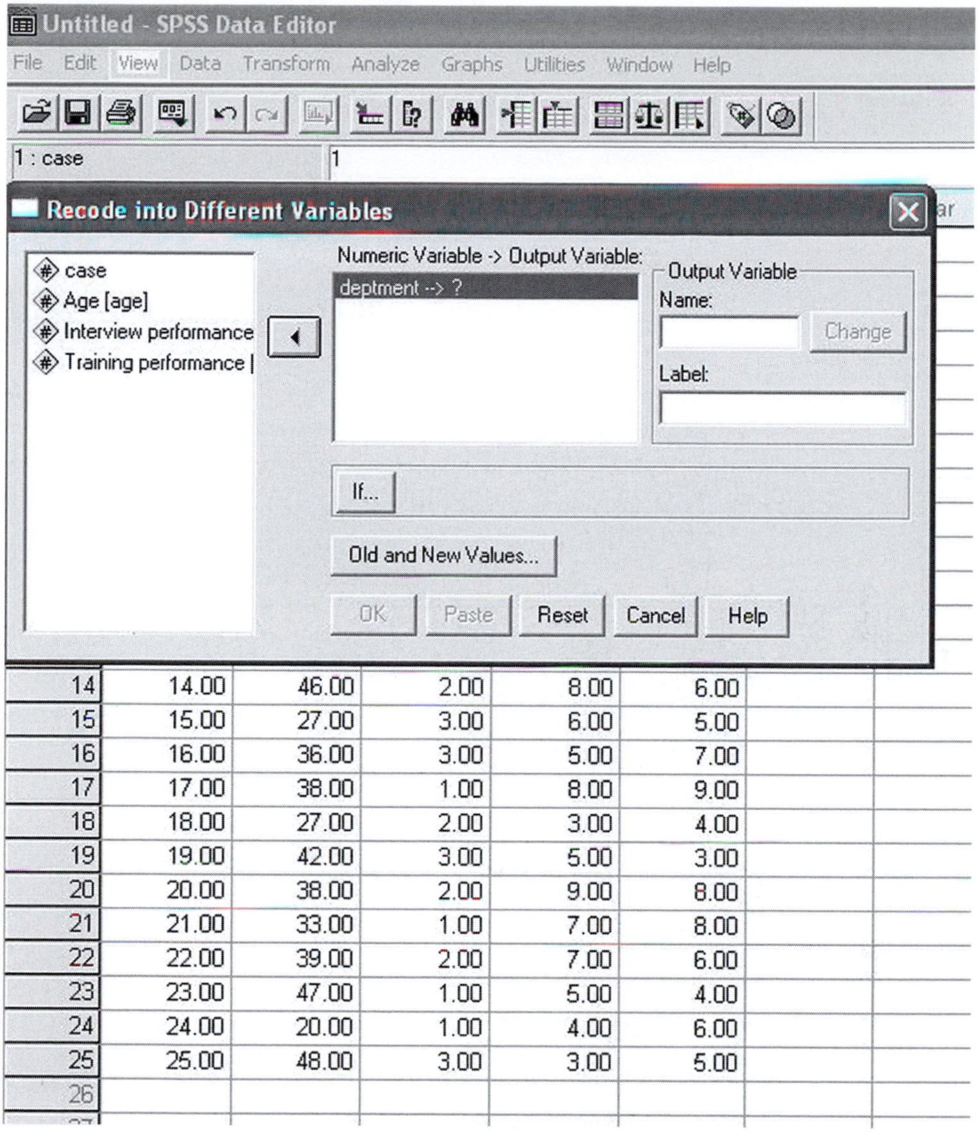

Figure 6.17 *Entering the numeric variable to be recoded*

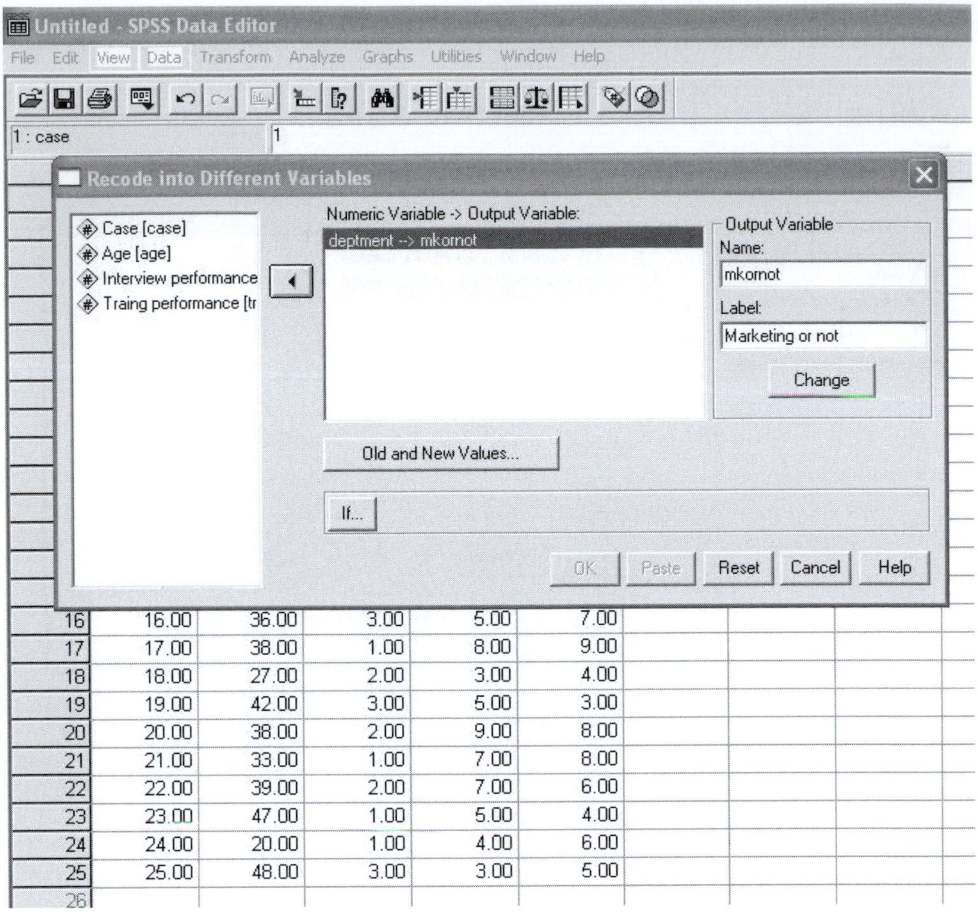

Figure 6.18 *Entering the output variable when recoding*

means that they are a member of the marketing department), and 0 otherwise. To do this, click on **Old and New Values**. A dialog box will appear. Since people in marketing are coded 2 under the original categorical variable of **Deptment**, we need to get a 2 for 'Department' coded as 1 on the new variable, **mkornot**. To do so, click on the white circle to the left of **Value** under **Old Value** to highlight this, and then enter a 2 in the white rectangle to the right of **Value**.

➤ We now need to give the value of the new dummy variable when the categorical variable is coded in the way indicated under **Old Value**, **Value** (i.e. in this case, 2). In this example, we have agreed that when 'Department' is coded 2, indicating that a person belongs to the marketing department, the new variable, **mkornot**, should be coded 1. So we enter a 1 in the rectangular box to the right of **New Value**, **Value**.

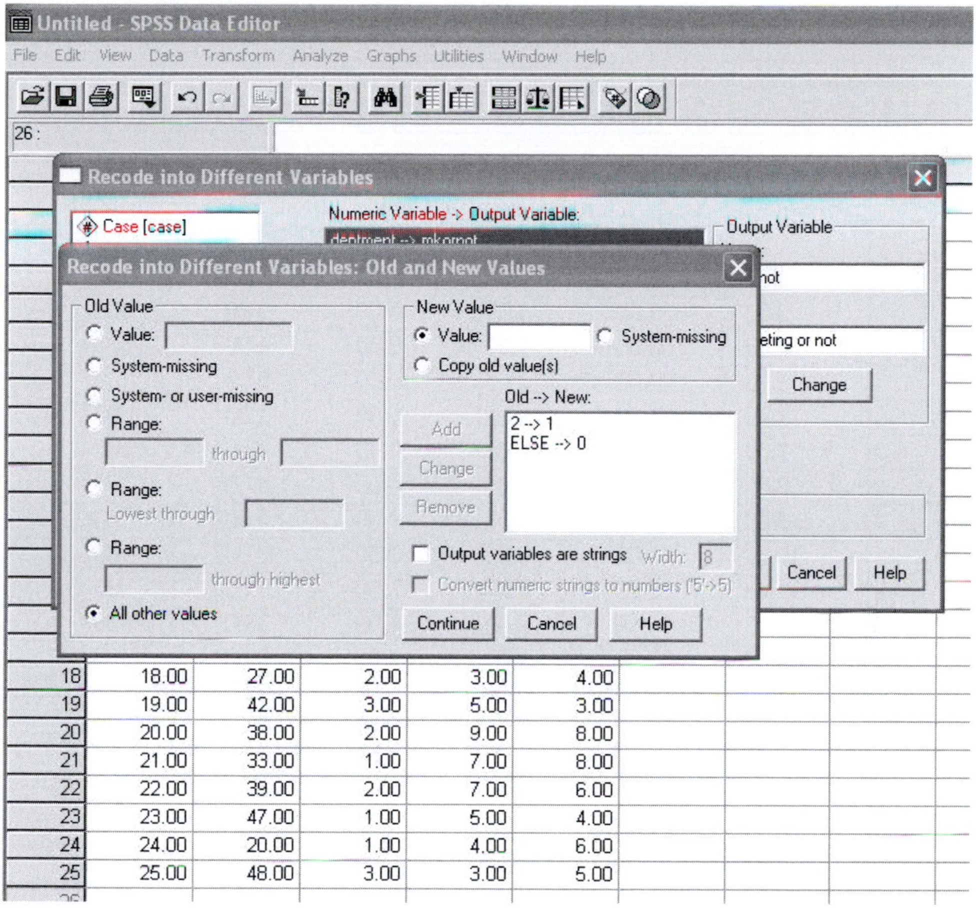

Figure 6.19 *Entering the old and new values when recoding*

➤ Now click on **Add**. The coding of the value of the original categorical variable (in this example, 2 for 'Deptment') is now linked to a code for the new variable (in this example, 1 for 'mkornot') in the white box headed **Old -> New**.

➤ If, for the variable 'Department', someone is coded with anything other than 2, this means that they are not in marketing and, consequently, need to be coded 0 on the new dummy variable. To do this, click on the white circle to the left of **All other values** and then enter the value 0 in the rectangular box next to **New Value, Value**. Next, click on **Add**. You will find that **Else -> 0** appears in the white box headed **Old -> New**. What the figures in this white box signify is that if someone is coded 2 for **Department** they should be coded 1 for the new dummy variable **mkornot**, and if they are coded anything else for 'Department' they should be coded 0 for **mkornot**. This is what we wanted in this case (see Figure 6.19).

Untitled - SPSS Data Editor

File Edit View Data Transform Analyze Graphs Utilities Window Help

1 : case 1

	case	age	deptment	intperfm	traperfm	mkornot	var
1	1.00	32.00	1.00	3.00	2.00	.00	
2	2.00	35.00	2.00	9.00	8.00	1.00	
3	3.00	36.00	3.00	5.00	3.00	.00	
4	4.00	36.00	1.00	3.00	4.00	.00	
5	5.00	28.00	2.00	2.00	5.00	1.00	
6	6.00	37.00	2.00	6.00	2.00	1.00	
7	7.00	33.00	1.00	4.00	4.00	.00	
8	8.00	36.00	3.00	7.00	6.00	.00	
9	9.00	29.00	1.00	4.00	4.00	.00	
10	10.00	41.00	3.00	3.00	3.00	.00	
11	11.00	35.00	3.00	7.00	5.00	.00	
12	12.00	32.00	2.00	7.00	3.00	1.00	
13	13.00	55.00	1.00	4.00	6.00	.00	
14	14.00	46.00	2.00	8.00	6.00	1.00	
15	15.00	27.00	3.00	6.00	5.00	.00	
16	16.00	36.00	3.00	5.00	7.00	.00	
17	17.00	38.00	1.00	8.00	9.00	.00	
18	18.00	27.00	2.00	3.00	4.00	1.00	
19	19.00	42.00	3.00	5.00	3.00	.00	
20	20.00	38.00	2.00	9.00	8.00	1.00	
21	21.00	33.00	1.00	7.00	8.00	.00	
22	22.00	39.00	2.00	7.00	6.00	1.00	
23	23.00	47.00	1.00	5.00	4.00	.00	
24	24.00	20.00	1.00	4.00	6.00	.00	
25	25.00	48.00	3.00	3.00	5.00	.00	
26							
27							

Figure 6.20 *A newly created dummy variable shown in the* SPSS *Data Editor*

- ➢ Click on **Continue**.
- ➢ Click on **OK**.
- ➢ The new dummy variable **mkornot** will be created. You can view this by looking at the variable under **Dataview** (see Figure 6.20).

You now need to repeat this for each of the other values of the categorical variable that are to be dummy variable coded. In this example, the dummy variable of 'prornot' is created to indicate whether or not people work in production. To do this in this example we can

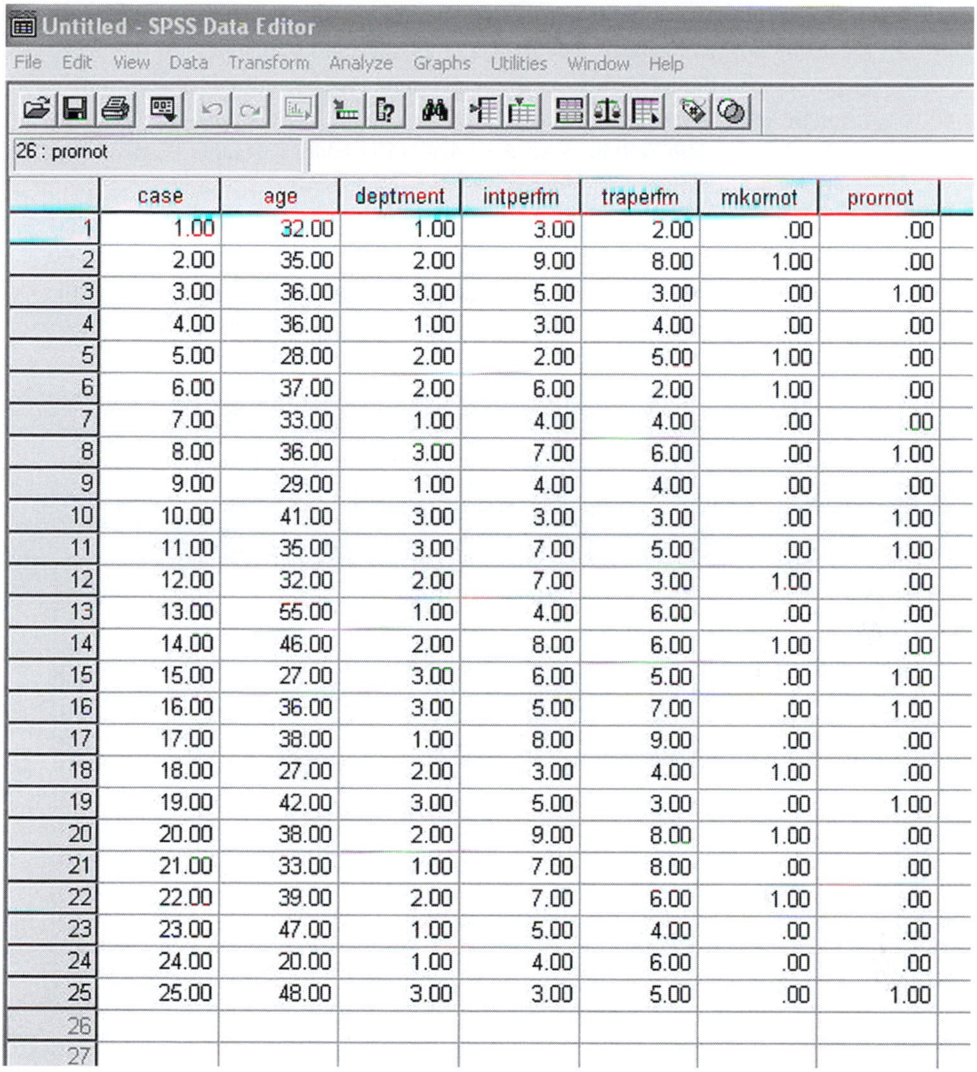

	case	age	deptment	intperfm	traperfm	mkornot	prornot
1	1.00	32.00	1.00	3.00	2.00	.00	.00
2	2.00	35.00	2.00	9.00	8.00	1.00	.00
3	3.00	36.00	3.00	5.00	3.00	.00	1.00
4	4.00	36.00	1.00	3.00	4.00	.00	.00
5	5.00	28.00	2.00	2.00	5.00	1.00	.00
6	6.00	37.00	2.00	6.00	2.00	1.00	.00
7	7.00	33.00	1.00	4.00	4.00	.00	.00
8	8.00	36.00	3.00	7.00	6.00	.00	1.00
9	9.00	29.00	1.00	4.00	4.00	.00	.00
10	10.00	41.00	3.00	3.00	3.00	.00	1.00
11	11.00	35.00	3.00	7.00	5.00	.00	1.00
12	12.00	32.00	2.00	7.00	3.00	1.00	.00
13	13.00	55.00	1.00	4.00	6.00	.00	.00
14	14.00	46.00	2.00	8.00	6.00	1.00	.00
15	15.00	27.00	3.00	6.00	5.00	.00	1.00
16	16.00	36.00	3.00	5.00	7.00	.00	1.00
17	17.00	38.00	1.00	8.00	9.00	.00	.00
18	18.00	27.00	2.00	3.00	4.00	1.00	.00
19	19.00	42.00	3.00	5.00	3.00	.00	1.00
20	20.00	38.00	2.00	9.00	8.00	1.00	.00
21	21.00	33.00	1.00	7.00	8.00	.00	.00
22	22.00	39.00	2.00	7.00	6.00	1.00	.00
23	23.00	47.00	1.00	5.00	4.00	.00	.00
24	24.00	20.00	1.00	4.00	6.00	.00	.00
25	25.00	48.00	3.00	3.00	5.00	.00	1.00
26							
27							

Figure 6.21 SPSS *Data Editor after all dummy variables have been created*

repeat the above process, this time entering ‘prornot’ as the name of the dummy variable (with the label ‘Production or not’), and indicate that this should be set to 1 if ‘Department’ is coded 3, and 0 otherwise.

This entire process should be repeated for each non-dichotomous categorical variable to be entered into the regression analysis (see Figure 6.21).

To run a standard multiple regression:

- ➢ Click on Analyze.
- ➢ Click on Regression.

➤ Click on **Linear** ....
➤ A dialog box will appear. The names of all variables will appear in the large white box to the left. Click on the dependent variable to highlight it, and then on the black triangle to the left of the box headed **Dependent**. The dependent variable will be moved across to the white rectangle headed **Dependent**.
➤ Click on the first predictor variable and then on the black triangle to the left of the box headed **Independent(s)**. The first dependent variable will be moved across to the box. Repeat this for each of the other predictor variables until they are all shown in the **Independent(s)** box. In this example, the predictor

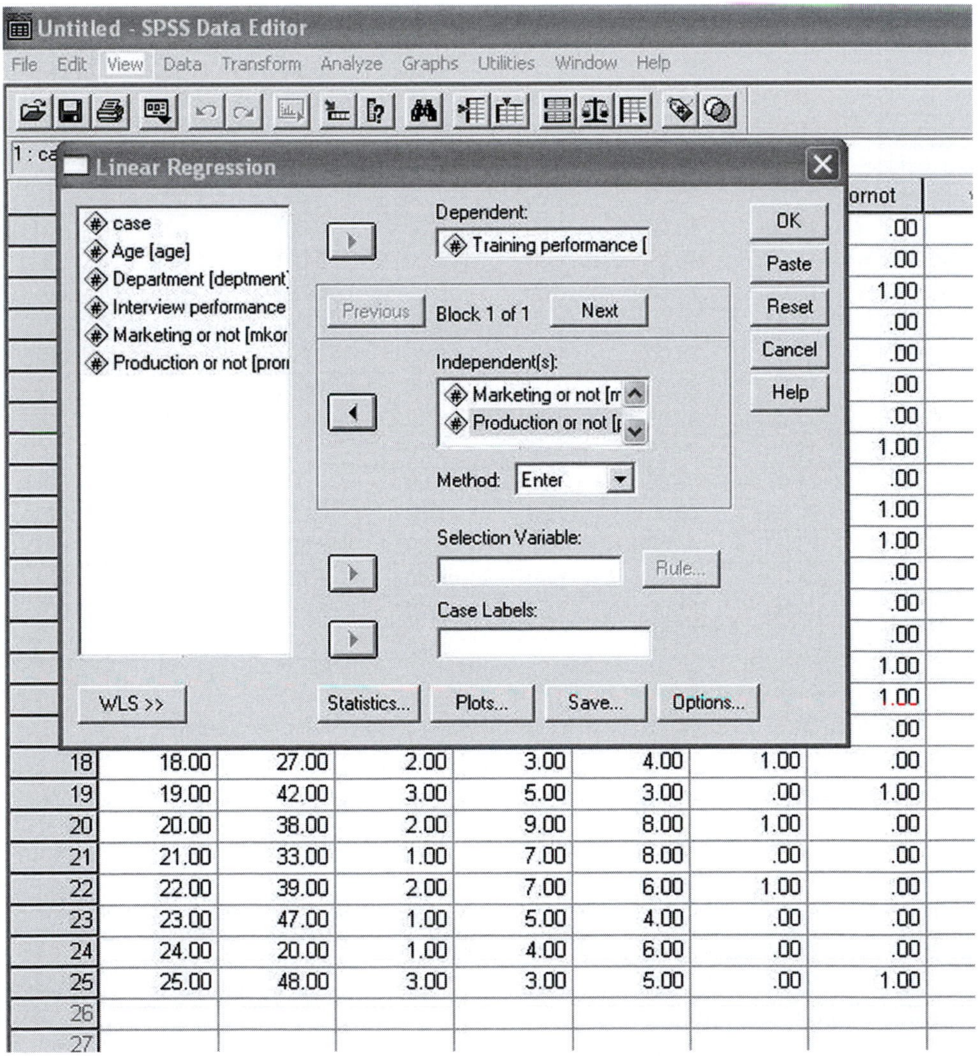

Figure 6.22 *Entering the dependent and independent (predictor) variables when carrying out a multiple regression*

270

variables **Age**, **Interview performance**, and the two dummy variables of **mkornot** and **prornot** are moved across to the **Independent(s)** box. The variable **Department** is not moved across because we have extracted the two dummy variables from it, and because, as a non-dichotomous categorical variable, it cannot be included in the regression analysis (see Figure 6.22).

➢ Click on **Statistics** .... A dialog box will open. Click in the white boxes next to **Confidence Intervals**, **Descriptives** and **Collinearity Diagnostics**. Ticks will appear in these boxes as you do this.

➢ Click on **Continue**.

➢ Click on **Plots** .... A dialog box will open. Click on ***ZRESID** and then on the black triangle to the left of the white box labelled **Y**.

➢ Click on ***ZPRED** and then on the black triangle to the left of the white box labelled **X**.

➢ Click on **Continue**.

➢ Click on **OK**.

Output in the following form will appear.

Regression

Descriptive statistics

	Mean	Std deviation	N
Training performance	5.0400	1.94679	25
Age	36.2400	7.60088	25
Interview performance	5.3600	2.05913	25
Marketing or not	.3200	.47610	25
Production or not	.3200	.47610	25

Means and standard deviations of each variable.

Correlations

		Training performance	Age	Interview performance	Marketing or not	Production or not
Pearson correlation	Training performance	1.000	.058	.578	.076	−.149
	Age	.058	1.000	.114	−.091	.128
	Interview performance	.578	.114	1.000	.345	−.080
	Marketing or not	.076	−.091	.345	1.000	−.471
	Production or not	−.149	.128	−.080	−.471	1.000
Sig. (1-tailed)	Training performance	.	.391	.001	.360	.238
	Age	.391	.	.294	.332	.272
	Interview performance	.001	.294	.	.046	.352
	Marketing or not	.360	.332	.046	.	.009
	Production or not	.238	.272	.352	.009	.
N	Training performance	25	25	25	25	25
	Age	25	25	25	25	25
	Interview performance	25	25	25	25	25
	Marketing or not	25	25	25	25	25
	Production or not	25	25	25	25	25

Correlation matrix showing the zero-order correlation between each variable and every other variable, the statistical significance of each correlation, and the number of cases used in each correlation.

Variables entered/removed[b]

Model	Variables entered	Variables removed	Method
	Production or not, interview performance, age, marketing or not[a]		Enter

[a] All requested variables entered
[b] Dependent variable: training performance

Table indicating which predictor variables have been entered in the regression model.

Model summary[b]

Model	R	R square	Adjusted R square	Std error of the estimate
1	.623[a]	.388	.265	1.66895

[a] Predictors: (constant), production or not, interview performance, age, marketing or not.
[b] Dependent variable: training performance.

In this table R is the multiple correlation between the predictor variables and the dependent variable (in this case .62). It also shows R square which is simply the square of R (in this case .39). Multiplying R square by 100 gives the percentage of variance in the dependent variable that the predictor variables collectively account for (in this case 39%).

Degrees of freedom of the ANOVA.

F value of the ANOVA.

ANOVA[b]

Model		Sum of squares	df	Mean square	F	Sig.
1	Regression	35.252	4	8.813	3.164	.036[a]
	Residual	55.708	20	2.785		
	Total	90.960	24			

[a] Predictors: (constant), production or not, interview performance, age, marketing or not.
[b] Dependent variable: training performance.

Statistical significance of the ANOVA. If this value is less than .05, the null hypothesis that there is no association between the predictor variables and the dependent variable is rejected.

This table shows a test of the null hypothesis, using Analysis of Variance (ANOVA), that the regression model does not account for any variance in the dependent variable.

The tolerance and VIF (variance inflation factor) provide two ways of checking that you do not have multicollinearity. As these two indices are directly related to each other we will just use one, the VIF. As a rule of thumb, you can assume that you do *not* have a multicollinearity problem for a particular variable as long as the VIF is less than 10. In this example all of the VIFs are considerably less than 10, so there is no problem.

Note: A VIF greater than 10 would mean that over 90% of the variance in a given predictor variable can be collectively accounted for by the other predictor variables.

Coefficients[a]

Model	Unstandardized coefficients		Standardized coefficients	t	Sig.	95% confidence interval for B		Collinearity statistics	
	B	Std. error	Beta			Lower bound	Upper bound	Tolerance	VIF
1 (Constant)	2.462	1.815		1.356	.190	-1.325	6.248		
Age	-2.84E-03	.046	-.011	-.062	.951	-.098	.093	.961	1.040
Interview performance	.613	.179	.649	3.424	.003	.240	.987	.853	1.172
Marketing or not	-1.022	.869	-.250	-1.176	.253	-2.834	.790	.678	1.474
Production or not	-.873	.818	-.214	-1.068	.298	-2.579	.832	.766	1.306

[a] Dependent variable: Training performance

This table contains information about the amount of *unique* variance that each predictor variable accounts for in the dependent variable.

It also allows us to examine whether multicollinearity is a problem.

The standardized coefficients (or Beta values) give an indication of the relative importance of the predictor variables in uniquely accounting for variance in the dependent variable. The greater the Beta value (positive or negative) the more important the predictor variable is in accounting for unique variance in the dependent variable. So in this example the most important unique predictor of training performance (the dependent variable) is interview performance (Beta value = .649), and the least important is age (Beta value = -.011).

The *t*-test is used to examine whether the variance explained by each predictor variable is statistically significant. For statistical significance, the *Sig* figure needs to be less than .05. So in this example only interview performance is statistically significant in accounting for unique variance in the dependent variable, 'training performance'.

Charts

Scatterplot

Dependent variable: Training performance

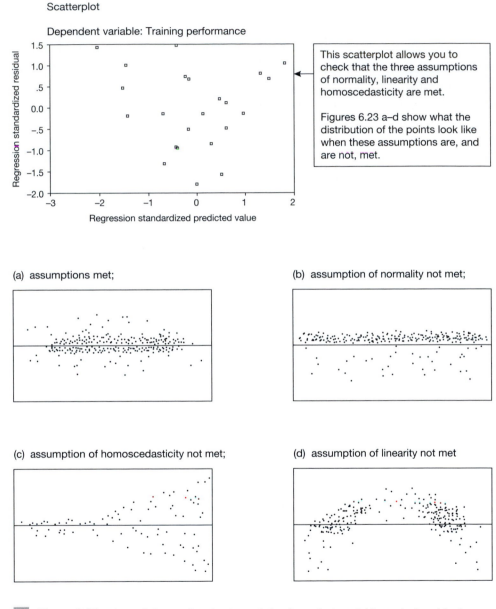

This scatterplot allows you to check that the three assumptions of normality, linearity and homoscedasticity are met.

Figures 6.23 a–d show what the distribution of the points look like when these assumptions are, and are not, met.

(a) assumptions met;

(b) assumption of normality not met;

(c) assumption of homoscedasticity not met;

(d) assumption of linearity not met

Figure 6.23 *Plots of the predicted values of the dependent variable against residuals (after Tabachnick and Fidell, 2001, p. 120): (a) assumptions met; (b) assumption of normality not met; (c) assumption of homoscedasticity not met; (d) assumption of linearity not met*

Reporting the results of a standard multiple regression

The results of a multiple regression analysis might be reported as follows:

A standard multiple regression analysis was carried out using training performance as the dependent variable and age in years, selection interview performance, whether or not the employee worked in marketing, and whether or not they worked in production, as the predictor variables.

Descriptive statistics and correlations between the variables entered into the model are presented in Table 6.11 below, and the results of the regression analysis are shown in Table 6.12. Table 6.11 shows that interview performance has a strong

Table 6.11 Correlations between training performance, age, interview performance, whether or not an employee works in the marketing department, and whether or not an employee works in the sales department

Variables		Mean	Standard deviation	1	2	3	4	5
1	Training performance	5.04	1.95	–	.06	.58**	.08	−.15
2	Age	36.24	7.60		–	.11	−.09	.13
3	Interview performance	5.36	2.06			–	.35*	−.08
4	Whether or not works in marketing	0.32	0.48				–	−.47**
5	Whether or not works in production	0.32	0.48					–

* $p < .05$
** $p < .01$

Codes: Worked in marketing: 1, didn't work in marketing: 0.
Worked in production: 1, didn't work in production: 0.

Table 6.12 Regression of training performance on predictor variables

Variables	B	Beta
(Constant)	2.46	
Age	0.00	−.01
Interview performance	0.61*	.65
Marketing or not	−1.02	−.25
Production or not	−0.87	−.21
R = .62		
R^2 = .39		
Adjusted R^2 = .27		

*$p < .05$

275

correlation with training performance, but that the correlations between training performance and other predictor variables is weak. The results of the multiple regression analysis show that over a third (39 per cent) of the variation in training performance can be explained with the predictor variables, and that the best unique predictor of training performance is interview performance.

Interpretation

The correlation matrix

In interpreting the results of multiple regression analysis, the first thing to look at is the correlation matrix. This not only shows the ordinary (i.e. zero-order) Pearson correlation coefficient between the dependent variable and every predictor variable, but also the correlation between all the predictor variables as well. This will give you a sense of how highly inter-correlated the variables are. If any predictor variables have a correlation greater than .7 they are clearly quite highly associated with each other. In these circumstances consider dropping one of the two highly correlated variables from the analysis, or creating a new variable by adding together each person's score on the two variables. The reason for taking one of these steps is that if the variables are highly correlated it will be difficult to disentangle the effect that each of them has independently in accounting for variation in the dependent variable. Incidentally, this is a conceptual problem rather than a statistical one: the regression will run satisfactorily from a technical point of view with correlations somewhat higher than .7. The problem is that the output will be difficult to interpret.

The multiple regression coefficient

The next thing to look at is the multiple regression coefficient R, and the square of the multiple regression coefficient R^2. R is the equivalent of the ordinary Pearson correlation coefficient, r, except that here it shows the correlation between: (a) the dependent variable; and (b) all the predictor variables together. So, the greater the multiple R, the more the predictor variables are jointly predictive of the dependent variable. As explained on page 232, the square of the ordinary Pearson correlation coefficient multiplied by 100 tells you the percentage of variance in one variable accounted for by the other. This is also the case for the multiple correlation coefficient. The R^2 value multiplied by 100 shows the percentage of variance in the dependent variable jointly accounted for by the predictor variables. In this case, the R^2 value is .39, so we can say that 39 per cent, or almost two-fifths of the variance in training performance is accounted for by the predictor variables used here.

You will also see the value given for Adjusted R^2. This is obtained from R^2 by adjusting for the number of cases and the number of predictor variables used in the analysis. Normally Adjusted R^2 is slightly lower than R^2. However, if the ratio of cases to predictor variables is high (i.e. a relatively large number of predictor variables and a small number of cases), Adjusted R^2 will be considerably lower than R^2. Unlike, R^2, Adjusted R^2 does not indicate the percentage of variance in the dependent variable accounted for by the predictor variables, and it is therefore less useful.

Beta values

The last thing to look at are the beta values. These tell you the relative extent to which each of the predictor variables *uniquely* predicts the dependent variable. In the above example, you can see that interview performance, with a beta value of .65, is the strongest unique predictor of training performance. In this case, the correlation matrix shows that interview performance also has a higher zero-order correlation with the dependent variable than any other predictor variable. This means that interview performance has both the highest correlation with training performance when the other predictor variables are ignored (i.e. the highest zero-order correlation) and the highest unique correlation with training performance when its shared variation with the other predictor variables is taken into account (i.e. the highest beta value). However, this is not always the case. Sometimes predictor variables with high zero-order correlations, because they are quite highly intercorrelated, do not account for the largest amount of unique variance in the predictor variable.

Causality

A final consideration in interpreting the results of a multiple regression is causality. It is possible to use multiple regression to examine causal relationships, but this is quite rare in organizational research. Causality can only be inferred if the research is designed in such a way that there is only one explanation for the significant contribution of a predictor variable to the regression model.

Moderating variables

Often research is carried out to examine evidence that given variables have certain relationships. In fact, as explained in Chapter 2 (pages 38–44), whenever a test of statistical significance is carried out implicitly or explicitly a null hypothesis that there is no association (or difference) between variables, and an alternative hypothesis that there is such an association (or difference) is being tested. Sometimes however, you may have a more sophisticated hypothesis about the relationship between the variables you are studying. In fact, in the section on interactions in the discussion of ANOVA (pages 171–5) we have already considered a relatively complex hypothesis. A two-way interaction examines the hypothesis that the effect of one independent variable on a dependent variable may depend on another independent variable. For example, the extent to which there is a difference between the salary levels of men and women may depend on the department they work in: there may be a large difference between the salaries of men and women working in production, but a smaller difference between the salaries of men and women working in finance. In this case the simple hypothesis that an independent variable affects a dependent variable is replaced by the more complex hypothesis that the extent to which an independent variable affects a dependent variable depends on another independent variable. Examining the statistical significance of more complex interaction effects (e.g. three-way, four-way etc.) enables us to test even more complex null hypotheses than those proposed for two-way interactions.

Another way of expressing the notion of an interaction is to say that one variable moderates the effect that another independent variable has on the dependent variable (Baron and Kenny 1986). In the example above we might say that department moderates the effect that gender has on salary levels. This can be expressed graphically as shown in Figure 6.24.

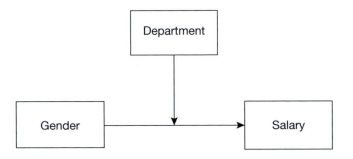

Figure 6.24 *A graphical representation of the moderating effect that department has on the relationship between gender and salary*

In the context of ANOVA, moderation takes place when there is one continuous dependent variable and two or more independent variables with a finite number of levels (usually between two and five). However, there are circumstances in which we may wish to examine whether a *continuous* variable moderates the effect of another *continuous* variable on a dependent variable. An example of this would be where we wish to know whether the relationship between employees' appraisal scores and their salary levels is moderated by their age. Perhaps it is the case that the better the appraisal scores that employees obtain, the more they tend to earn, but that this relationship is weaker for older employees than for younger ones. This relationship is presented graphically in Figure 6.25.

A hypothesis like this one, that the effect of one continuous variable on the dependent variable depends on the effect of a second continuous variable can be tested quite simply using standard multiple regression. Before explaining how this is done, a word about terminology is necessary. In the context of ANOVA, we usually refer to independent and dependent variables. So in the hypothesized moderation effect shown in Figure 6.24, the independent variables are department and gender, and the dependent variable is salary. Similarly, in the context of multiple regression, researchers also sometimes refer to independent and dependent variables. For example, in the relationships between variables hypothesized in Figure 6.25, age and appraisal scores would be the independent variables and salary the dependent variable. However, at other times researchers carrying out multiple

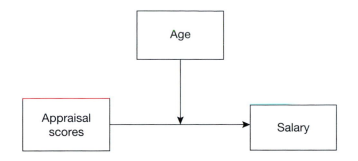

Figure 6.25 *A graphical representation of the moderating effect that appraisal scores have on the relationship between age and salary*

regression refer to predictor variables rather than to independent variables. In this case, age and appraisal scores in Figure 6.25 would be referred to as predictor variables rather than independent variables. The reason that people use the term independent variables in the context of ANOVA is that this statistical technique is much used by researchers to analyse the results of controlled experiments. In this experimental context, researchers can be said to be independently manipulating the situation with which the research participants are presented (an example from experimental psychology would be people trying to remember words under conditions in which these words are either common or uncommon and either abstract or non-abstract). However, multiple regression has generally been used in circumstances in which such controlled experiments are not possible, and this includes most of the research carried out in organizations. Here, where people cannot usually be independently assigned to pre-specified experimental conditions, it seems more appropriate to refer to predictor variables than to independent variables. When multiple regression is used for organizational research we are usually examining whether we can predict dependent variables with predictor variables rather than independently manipulating variables in an experimental design. For this reason in this chapter on multiple regression I have referred to predictor variables rather than to independent variables. However, it is worth bearing in mind that when multiple regression is used, people often use the terms predictor variables and independent variables interchangeably.

Having dealt with issues of terminology, we can now look at how multiple regression can be used to examine moderator effects such as that shown in Figure 6.25 in which the predictor and dependent variables are all continuous. The way to do this is to carry out a multiple regression in which the following are entered: the dependent variable, the two moderator variables, and the product of the predictor and moderator variable variables. The product of the predictor and moderator variables is simply obtained by multiplying the predictor variable by the hypothesized moderator variable. This newly created product variable captures the moderation effect. If, after controlling for the predictor and moderator variables, the product explains a statistically significant amount of variance in the dependent variable, we can conclude that the effect of the predictor variable on the dependent variable is, indeed, moderated by the moderator variable.

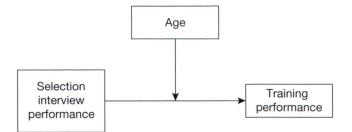

Figure 6.26 *A graphical representation of the moderating effect that age has on the relationship between selection interview performance and salary*

This is best explained with an example. Imagine that you collect the data shown in Table 6.9 on page 254, and age moderates the effect of selection interview performance on training performance. This relationship is depicted graphically in Figure 6.26.

To examine this you would begin by creating a new variable which is the product of the predictor and moderator variables. So here we will create a variable called 'proageint' (so named because it is the *product* of *age* and *int*erview performance).

Having entered the data in Table 6.9,

➤ Click on **Transform**.
➤ Click on **Compute**.
➤ A dialog box will open.
➤ In the white triangle at the top left headed **Target Variable** type in the name of the new variable to be created, in this case **proageint**.
➤ Click on **Type and Label** and enter a new suitable label for this variable. In this case this might be 'The product of age and interview performance'.
➤ Click on the predictor variable in the rectangle below, and then on the black triangle to the bottom left of the large white box headed **Numeric Expression**. The predictor variable will be moved into the **Numeric Expression** box.
➤ Beneath the numeric expression box you will see a series of arithmetic operators (e.g. +, − etc.). Click on the asterisk, the multiplication sign (the third one down on the left). The asterisk will appear to the right of age in the **Numeric Expression** box.
➤ Click on the moderator variable, which in the case of this example is **age** and then again on the black triangle to the bottom left of the large white box headed **Numeric Expression**. The variable **age** will be moved to the right of the asterisk.

We have now set up the instruction to compute a new variable called 'proageint' and to make this the product of the scores people obtain for the predictor variable of selection interview performance and the hypothesized moderator variable of age.

280

➤ Click on **OK**.

The new variable called 'proageint', the product of the predictor and hypothesized moderator variables, will be created. You can check this by Looking in the *Variable View* and *Data View*.

All you need to do now is to run a multiple regression using the instructions on pages 269–71. If, the hypothesized moderator variable is indeed moderating the effect of the predictor variable on the dependent variable, it will obtain a significance level of less than .05 in the sixth column from the left in the *Coefficients* table produced by the analysis (see page 273).

Hierarchical regression analysis

In a hierarchical (sometimes called sequential) regression analysis, the order in which the predictor variables are entered into the regression model is controlled. Typically, the intention is to examine whether one or more predictor variables can account for variance in the dependent variable over and above the variance already accounted for by others. For example, a researcher may be interested in whether salary, and the degree of congruence between an employee's personal values, and the perceived values of the organization, contribute to variance in job satisfaction after taking account of the relation that job satisfaction has with age and gender. To put this slightly differently the question is: after controlling for age and gender, does level of salary and degree of congruence between personal and organizational values, contribute to variance in job satisfaction, and if so by how much?

The way that this is done is to create a multiple regression model based on the first two hierarchical variables, then a second one based on all four predictor variables, and examine the extent to which the multiple correlation with the dependent variable is greater in the second model than in the first.

Since much of the logic, and many of the practical steps, involved in carrying out a hierarchical regression analysis are the same as for the standard method we will not repeat these here. Therefore, the reader who wishes to carry out a hierarchical regression analysis is strongly advised to read the preceding section on a standard multiple regression before proceeding any further with this section.

Assuming that you are familiar with standard regression we can focus on just those aspects of carrying out and interpreting a hierarchical regression which differ from this.

A worked example

As explained above, a researcher might be interested in whether salary and the degree of congruence between personal and organizational values, contribute to variance in job satisfaction after taking account of the relation that job satisfaction has with age and gender. Let's say the researcher notes the age, gender and salary of 20 employees in an organization and then measures the degree to which their personal values match with the values they perceive the organization to have (on a 7-point scale), and their job satisfaction

281

Table 6.13 *The age, gender, salary and person–organization value congruence of 20 employees*

Case	Age	Gender	Salary ($)	Person–organization value congruence	Job satisfaction
1	34	0	34,000	4	7
2	37	0	28,500	3	4
3	28	1	36,700	2	3
4	46	1	39,750	5	5
5	36	1	41,600	6	5
6	33	0	35,800	3	3
7	26	0	34,400	5	5
8	48	1	36,730	3	3
9	41	0	46,700	4	2
10	39	0	38,900	7	5
11	31	1	35,750	2	2
12	29	1	33,000	3	3
13	36	0	36,500	4	4
14	35	0	36,480	6	6
15	50	1	40,100	7	5
16	42	0	45,500	5	5
17	37	1	36,000	3	3
18	25	0	46,000	2	5
19	44	0	37,400	6	3
20	37	0	34,600	3	5

(again on a 7-point scale). She is interested in whether person–organization value congruence, and salary level, contribute to the variance in job satisfaction *over and above* age and gender. The data are shown in Table 6.13. Gender is coded 1 for females and 0 for males.

The first steps are to enter the data into the *SPSS* Data Editor and run the *Explore* command to check on the validity of the data. However, as these steps are the same in standard and hierarchical regression we will not repeat them here, and the reader who is unsure how to carry out these steps is referred to the previous section on standard multiple regression. Once the data is entered and *Explore* has been used to make sure they are acceptable, it is possible to carry out the hierarchical regression analysis as follows.

How to carry out a hierarchical multiple regression using SPSS

➤ Click on **Analyze**.
➤ Click on **Regression**.
➤ Click on **Linear** . . . .
➤ A dialog box will appear. The names of all variables will appear in the large white box to left. Click on the dependent variable (in this case 'job satisfaction') to highlight it, and then on the black triangle to the left of the box headed **Dependent**. The dependent variable will be moved across to the white rectangle headed **Dependent**.
➤ You now need to enter the predictor variables in two blocks. The first block consists of the variables you wish to enter first, and the second block of the variables you wish to enter second. In fact, it is possible to enter further variables in third, fourth or fifth blocks if you want to. In this example, the intention is to enter age and gender first to create the first regression model, and then to enter salary and value congruence second to see if these remaining two variables explain some variance in the dependent variable over and above the first two. So, the first step is to enter the first two variables.
➤ Click on a predictor variable to be entered in the first block and then on the black triangle to the left of the box headed **Independent(s)**. The predictor variable will be moved across to the **Independent(s)** box. Repeat this for each of the predictor variables to be entered in the first block until they are all shown in the predictor box. In this example the predictor variables in the first block, 'Age' and 'Gender', are moved across to the **Independent(s)** box.
➤ Click on **Next**. You will see that the block which was labelled **Block 1 of 1** has now changed to **Block 2 of 2**. You are now in a position to add the predictor variables to be entered in this second block. In this example, the variables are 'salary' and 'value congruence', so click on one of these predictor variables and then on the black triangle to the left of the box headed **Independent(s)**. The predictor variable will be moved across to the **Independent(s)** box. Repeat this for each of the other predictor variables to be entered in this block until they are all shown in the predictor box.
➤ Click on **Statistics** . . . . A dialog box will open. Click in the white boxes next to **Confidence Intervals**, **R Square Change**, **Descriptives** and **Collinearity diagnostics**. Ticks will appear in these boxes as you do this.
➤ Click on **Continue**.
➤ Click on **Plots** . . . . A dialog box will open. Click on ***ZRESID** and then on the black triangle to the left of the white box headed **Y**.
➤ Click on ***ZPRED** and then on the black triangle to the left of the white box headed **X**.
➤ Click on **Continue**.
➤ Click on **OK**.

Output in the following form will appear.

Regression

Descriptive statistics

	Mean	Std deviation	N
Job satisfaction	4.1500	1.34849	20
Age	36.7000	7.03450	20
Gender	.4000	.50262	20
Salary	37720.50	4550.97384	20
Value congruence	4.1500	1.63111	20

Means and standard deviations of each variable.

Correlations

		Job satisfaction	Age	Gender	Salary	Value congruence
Pearson correlation	Job satisfaction	1.000	−.001	−.326	.018	.468
	Age	−.001	1.000	.170	.210	.513
	Gender	−.326	.170	1.000	−.049	−.141
	Salary	.018	.210	−.049	1.000	.233
	Value congruence	.468	.513	−.141	.233	1.000
Sig. (1-tailed)	Job satisfaction	.	.499	.080	.470	.019
	Age	.499	.	.237	.187	.010
	Gender	.080	.237	.	.419	.276
	Salary	.470	.187	.419	.	.161
	Value congruence	.019	.010	.276	.161	.
N	Job satisfaction	20	20	20	20	20
	Age	20	20	20	20	20
	Gender	20	20	20	20	20
	Salary	20	20	20	20	20
	Value congruence	20	20	20	20	20

Correlation matrix showing the zero-order correlation between each variable and every other variable, the statistical significance of each correlation, and the number of cases used in each correlation.

Variables entered/removed[b]

Model	Variables entered	Variables removed	Method
1	Gender, age[a]	.	Enter
2	Salary, value congruence[a]	.	Enter

[a] All requested variables entered
[b] Dependent variable: job satisfaction

This table shows the variables entered for each regression model. So in this case gender and age were entered into the first model, and salary and value congruence were added for the second model.

Model summary[c]

Model	R	R square	Adjusted R square	Std. error of the estimate	Change statistics				
					R square change	F change	df1	df2	Sig. F change
1	.331[a]	.109	.005	1.34532	.109	1.045	2	17	.373
2	.582[b]	.339	.163	1.23371	.230	2.608	2	15	.107

[a] Predictors: (constant), gender, age.
[b] Predictors: (constant), gender, age, salary,
  value congruence.
[c] Dependent variable: job satisfaction.

In this table R is the multiple correlation between the predictor variables and the dependent variable and R *Square* is simply the square of R. Multiplying R *Square* by 100 gives the percentage of variance in the dependent variable that the predictor variables collectively account for. For an explanation of the *Adjusted R Square* see pages 276–7.

As this is a hierarchical regression analysis, R, R *Square* and *Adjusted R Square* are given for both the first regression model and the second one. So when the predictor variables are 'age' and 'gender' the R is .33, but when salary and value congruence are added this rises to .58.

Under *Change Statistics* we can see that the increase in the R *Square* when salary and value congruence were added is .23. The significance of this change is assessed with the F statistic. To indicate that the R *Square* of the second regression model is significantly greater than that of the first model (i.e. that the salary and value congruence variables have increased the amount of variance explained in job satisfaction over age and gender, and this increase is statistically significant) value of the *Sig of F. Change* would need to be less than .05. In this case, the observed value of .107 is greater than .05, so we can report that the increase in the R *Square* value of .23 when salary and value congruence are added to the regression model is not significant, $F (2,15) = .11$. Here the values in brackets are the relevant degrees of freedom for the F statistic in the second regression model, the one including all four predictor variables. These are shown as df1 and df2 in the model summary table. Note that the way this F value is reported is the same as for the ANOVAs in Chapter 5. Indeed, this significance test is, effectively, an analysis of variance.

ANOVA[c]

Model		Sum of squares	df	Mean square	F	Sig.
1	Regression	3.782	2	1.891	1.045	.373[a]
	Residual	30.768	17	1.810		
	Total	34.550	19			
2	Regression	11.719	4	2.930	1.925	.158[b]
	Residual	22.831	15	1.522		
	Total	34.550	19			

[a] Predictors: (constant), gender, age.
[b] Predictors: (constant), gender, age, salary, value congruence.
[c] Dependent variable: job satisfaction.

The rest of the output can be interpreted as for the standard multiple regression. Note however, that for a sequential regression analysis the ANOVA table reports the statistical significance of each regression model in turn. In this case neither model makes a statistically significant contribution to the variance in job satisfaction as the significance of each, .373 and .158 is above .05. Remember to check for multicollinearity by examining the Collinearity diagnostics and making sure that none of the VIFs are greater than 10.

Coefficients[a]

Model		Unstandardized coefficients B	Unstandardized coefficients Std. error	Standardized coefficients Beta	t	Sig.	Collinearity statistics Tolerance	Collinearity statistics VIF
1	(Constant)	4.113	1.638		2.511	.022		
	Age	1.081E–02	.045	.056	.243	.811	.971	1.030
	Gender	–.901	.623	–.336	–1.446	.166	.971	1.030
2	(Constant)	4.970	2.593		1.917	.075		
	Age	–4.79E–02	.049	–.250	–.973	.346	.667	1.499
	Gender	–5.49	.594	–.205	–.925	.370	.898	1.113
	Salary	–2.25E–05	.000	–0.76	–.349	.732	.932	1.073
	Value congruence	.484	.212	.585	2.283	.037	.671	1.490

[a] Dependent variable: job satisfaction.

Excluded variables[b]

Model		Beta in	t	Sig.	Partial correlation	Collinearity statistics Tolerance	Collinearity statistics VIF	Minimum tolerance
1	Salary	–.011[a]	–.044	.965	–.011	.948	1.054	.923
	Value congruence	.573[a]	2.321	.034	.502	.683	1.464	.677

[a] Predictors in the model: (constant), gender, age.
[b] Dependent variable: job satisfaction.

Collinearity diagnostics[a]

Model	Dimension	Eigenvalue	Condition index	Variance proportions (Constant)	Age	Gender	Salary	Value congruence
1	1	2.520	1.000	.00	.00	.06		
	2	.463	2.334	.01	.01	.93		
	3	1.685E–02	12.230	.98	.99	.01		
2	1	4.341	1.000	.00	.00	.01	.00	.00
	2	.556	2.795	.00	.00	.84	.00	.01
	3	7.879E–02	7.423	.02	.00	.07	.02	.73
	4	1.763E–02	15.692	.03	.94	.07	.12	.22
	5	6.514E–03	25.816	.95	.05	.00	.85	.03

[a] Dependent variable: job satisfaction.

Residual statistics[a]

	Minimum	Maximum	Mean	Std deviation	N
Predicted value	2.7447	5.6113	4.1500	.78537	20
Residual	−1.9217	2.4897	.0000	1.09618	20
Std predicted value	−1.789	1.861	.000	1.000	20
Std residual	−1.558	2.018	.000	.889	20

[a] Dependent variable: job satisfaction.

Charts

Scatterplot

Dependent variable: job satisfaction

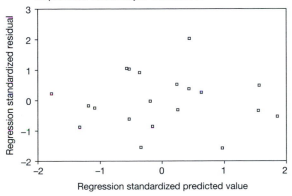

How to report the results of a hierarchical regression analysis

The results of this analysis can be reported as:

> A hierarchical multiple regression analysis was carried out to investigate whether salary and congruence between personal and organizational values made a significant contribution to the variance in job satisfaction after controlling for age and gender. No evidence of multicollinearity was found.
>
> Descriptive statistics and correlations between the variables entered into the model are presented in Table 6.14 below, and the results of the regression analysis with all four predictor variables entered is shown in Table 6.15. Table 6.14 shows the zero-order correlation between job satisfaction and value congruence to be strong, whereas it is only medium for gender and low for age and salary. The results of the full regression model show that about a third (34 per cent) of the variation in job satisfaction can be explained with the predictor variables of age, gender, salary and value congruence, but the model was not statistically significant, $F(4, 15) = 1.93$, $p = .16$. Although R^2 increased .23 (from .11 to .34) when salary and value congruence were added to the regression model, the increase in the variance explained was not significant $F(2, 15) = 2.61$, $p = .11$.

Table 6.14 Correlations between age, gender, salary, value congruence and job satisfaction

Variables	Mean	Standard deviation	1	2	3	4	5
1 Age (years)	36.7	7.03	–	.17	.21	.51*	.02
2 Gender	.40	0.50		–	−.05	−.14	−.33
3 Salary ($)	37720.5	4550.97			–	.23	.02
4 Value congruence	4.15	1.63				–	.47*
5 Job satisfaction	4.15	1.35					–

* $p < .05$

Codes: Gender: male 0, female 1.

Interpretation

See the discussion of the interpretation of the standard multiple regression. The only point to add in the case of hierarchical regression is that the emphasis in the analysis is very much on the change in the R Square (R^2) figure as each block of additional predictor variables is added, as this tells us how much better the model including the added variables is than the previous model. However, even if there is a significant difference between one regression model and the previous one, it is still important to consider whether the second model is, itself, statistically significant. If it isn't, this suggests that later variables do add something to the prediction of the dependent variable, but there is still insufficient evidence that the full model, the one containing all the variables, is a statistically significant predictor of the dependent variable.

Table 6.15 Regression of training performance on all four predictor variables

Variables	B	Beta
(Constant)	4.98	
Age (years)	−0.05	−.25
Gender	−0.54	−.21
Salary ($)	−0.00	−.08
Value congruence	0.48*	−.59

R = .58
R^2 = .34
Adjusted R^2 = .16

*$p < .05$

LOGISTIC REGRESSION

Background to logistic regression

Logistic regression is used when we wish to predict a categorical dependent variable (e.g. whether or not people leave the organization in a particular year) from two or more continuous or dichotomous predictor variables (e.g. length of service and gender). When the dependent variable has two categories we use binary logistic regression, and when it has three or more categories we use multinomial logistic regression. Here the discussion will be limited to binary logistic regression only. If you wish to use multinomial logistic regression a good source of information is Hosmer and Lemeshow (1989). From a practical point of view, logistic regression is very similar to multiple regression, the critical difference being that whereas the latter is used to predict a continuous dependent variable, logistic regression is used to predict a categorical dependent variable.

When to use logistic regression

Common uses include the following:

■ Establishing the extent to which it is possible to predict, with several predictor variables, which of two or more categories people are in.

Example: A researcher wishes to examine the extent to which it is possible to predict whether or not people are promoted from a knowledge of gender, ethnicity, training performance and appraisal scores.

■ Examining the extent to which each predictor variable uniquely predicts the dependent variable. As with multiple regression the logistic regression model enables you to consider the unique importance of each independent variable in predicting the dependent variable.

Example: After taking into account gender, training performance and appraisal scores, a researcher wishes to know the extent to which ethnicity, taken on its own, predicts who gets promoted in an organization.

Assumptions and requirements

As with multiple regression, the predictor variables may either be continuous or dichotomous. This means that, again, as with multiple regression, non-dichotomous predictor variables must be converted to dummy variables before they can be entered into the regression model. Fortunately, however, *SPSS* logistic regression has a facility which automatically creates dummy variables within the logistic regression analysis. So if you wish to enter non-dichotomous predictor variables in a logistic regression analysis, you do not have to laboriously create dummy variables using the recode command as is the case for multiple regression.

The mechanics by which multiple and logistic regression operate are quite different, and the latter makes considerably fewer assumptions. In particular, unlike multiple regression, logistic regression does not assume that each of the predictor variables has a linear relationship with the dependent variable, does not require variables to be normally distributed, and does not assume homoscedasticity.

However, as with multiple regression, multicollinearity, where one or more predictor variables are highly correlated with each other, and singularity, where predictor variables are perfectly correlated with each other, are potential problems with logistic regression. The simplest way to check for multicollinearity and singularity is to correlate all of the predictor variables prior to the analysis. If any variables are found to have perfect correlations, one of them must be deleted. If any variables have correlations less than 1 but over

.9 consider either: (a) deleting one of the variables; or (b) combining them (by adding the score each person gets on one of the variables to the score they get on the other) to create a new variable, and then entering this new variable into the regression instead of the other two. A more thorough approach is to check for multicollinearity with the multiple regression multicollinearity diagnostics. First, ensure that all non-dichotomous and categorical predictor variables are changed into dummy variables using the method described in the section on multiple regression, and then run a multiple regression analysis. Because your dependent variable is dichotomous, the overall output of the multiple regression won't be useful, but the multicollinearity diagnostics will tell you if multicollinearity is a problem with the predictor variables.

How big a sample?

It is possible to compute the exact sample sizes necessary for logistic regression, but this is relatively complicated and requires the estimation of relatively obscure parameters. In these circumstances it is recommended that the researcher uses the sample sizes set out in the previous section on multiple regression as a guide to the sample sizes that should be used for logistic regression. While this only provides a rough and ready indication of the sample sizes required with this technique, it is certainly better than having no guide at all.

A worked example

Let's say that a researcher is interested in the factors that affect whether or not individuals are promoted in an organization. Promotion is supposed to be based on an annual appraisal score, with those getting the highest appraisal rating being most eligible for promotion. However, the researcher suspects that the gender of employees might be important, with men being more likely to gain promotion than women. She decides to investigate whether gender is a statistically significant predictor of promotion after controlling for the department that people work in and their appraisal score. She collects data on 30 people, 16 of whom have recently been promoted and 14 who have not. She also collects data on the gender of these people, their annual appraisal score and the department they work in (production, finance or sales). The resulting data are shown in Table 6.16. Note that when the dependent variable is dichotomous it is coded 0 and 1 (rather than, say, 1 and 2). It is important to use zero and one in this way when using logistic regression, as it has a marked effect on the output.

To carry out the logistic regression, the first step is to enter the data in the *SPSS* Data Editor. Figure 6.27 shows what the data in Table 6.16 look like when they have been entered. The variable name of 'promot' is used for whether or not people are promoted, 'dept' for which department they work in, and 'appraise' for their appraisal score. For gender, males are coded 0 and females 1; for whether people are promoted or not, those not promoted are coded 0 and those promoted are coded 1; and for department, those in production are coded 0, those in finance 1, and those in sales 2. The *Variable View* in the *SPSS* Data Editor has been used to enter variable labels as follows: 'Promoted or not', 'Appraisal score', 'Gender' and 'Department'.

290

Table 6.16 *The gender, department, appraisal scores and promotion status of 30 employees*

Case	Whether or not promoted	Annual appraisal score	Gender	Department
1	1	1	0	0
2	0	5	1	1
3	1	6	0	0
4	1	2	1	0
5	0	4	0	1
6	0	5	0	2
7	1	2	1	2
8	1	3	1	1
9	0	6	0	0
10	1	2	1	1
11	0	5	0	2
12	0	5	0	0
13	1	3	1	0
14	1	2	1	1
15	0	2	0	2
16	1	5	0	2
17	0	2	1	1
18	1	5	0	0
19	0	1	1	0
20	1	4	1	1
21	1	4	1	0
22	0	6	0	1
23	1	3	1	0
24	1	4	1	2
25	1	6	1	2
26	0	3	0	1
27	0	4	1	0
28	1	2	1	2
29	0	5	0	1
30	0	2	0	0

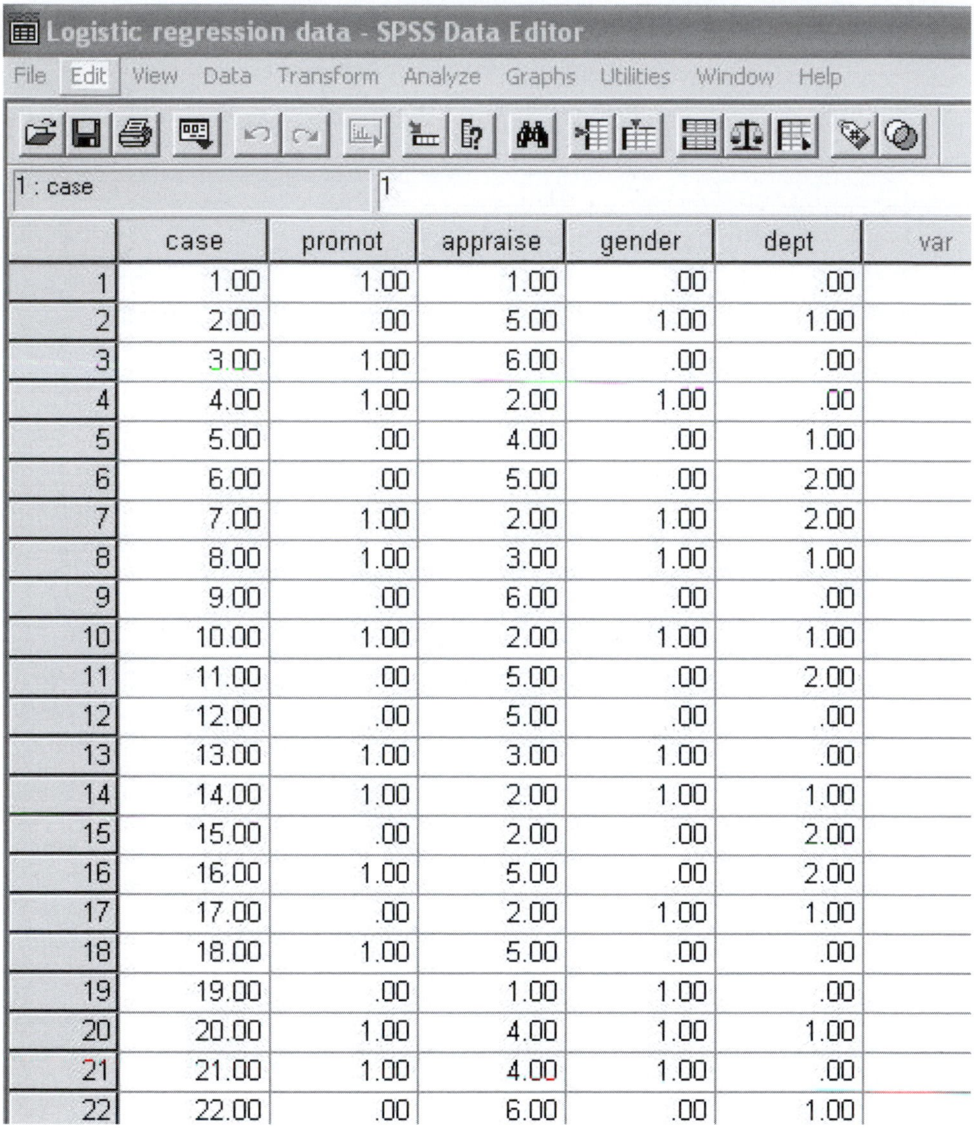

	case	promot	appraise	gender	dept	var
1	1.00	1.00	1.00	.00	.00	
2	2.00	.00	5.00	1.00	1.00	
3	3.00	1.00	6.00	.00	.00	
4	4.00	1.00	2.00	1.00	.00	
5	5.00	.00	4.00	.00	1.00	
6	6.00	.00	5.00	.00	2.00	
7	7.00	1.00	2.00	1.00	2.00	
8	8.00	1.00	3.00	1.00	1.00	
9	9.00	.00	6.00	.00	.00	
10	10.00	1.00	2.00	1.00	1.00	
11	11.00	.00	5.00	.00	2.00	
12	12.00	.00	5.00	.00	.00	
13	13.00	1.00	3.00	1.00	.00	
14	14.00	1.00	2.00	1.00	1.00	
15	15.00	.00	2.00	.00	2.00	
16	16.00	1.00	5.00	.00	2.00	
17	17.00	.00	2.00	1.00	1.00	
18	18.00	1.00	5.00	.00	.00	
19	19.00	.00	1.00	1.00	.00	
20	20.00	1.00	4.00	1.00	1.00	
21	21.00	1.00	4.00	1.00	.00	
22	22.00	.00	6.00	.00	1.00	

Figure 6.27 SPSS *Data Editor after logistic regression data are entered*

Next, run *Explore* in *SPSS* to check the data on the continuous variable(s) and *Frequencies* to check the data on the categorical variables. To do this:

> ➢ Click on **Analyze**.
> ➢ Click on **Descriptive Statistics**.
> ➢ Click on **Explore** . . . .
> ➢ A dialog box will appear with the variables in a white box on the left hand side. Click on any continuous ones and then on the black triangle to the left of the

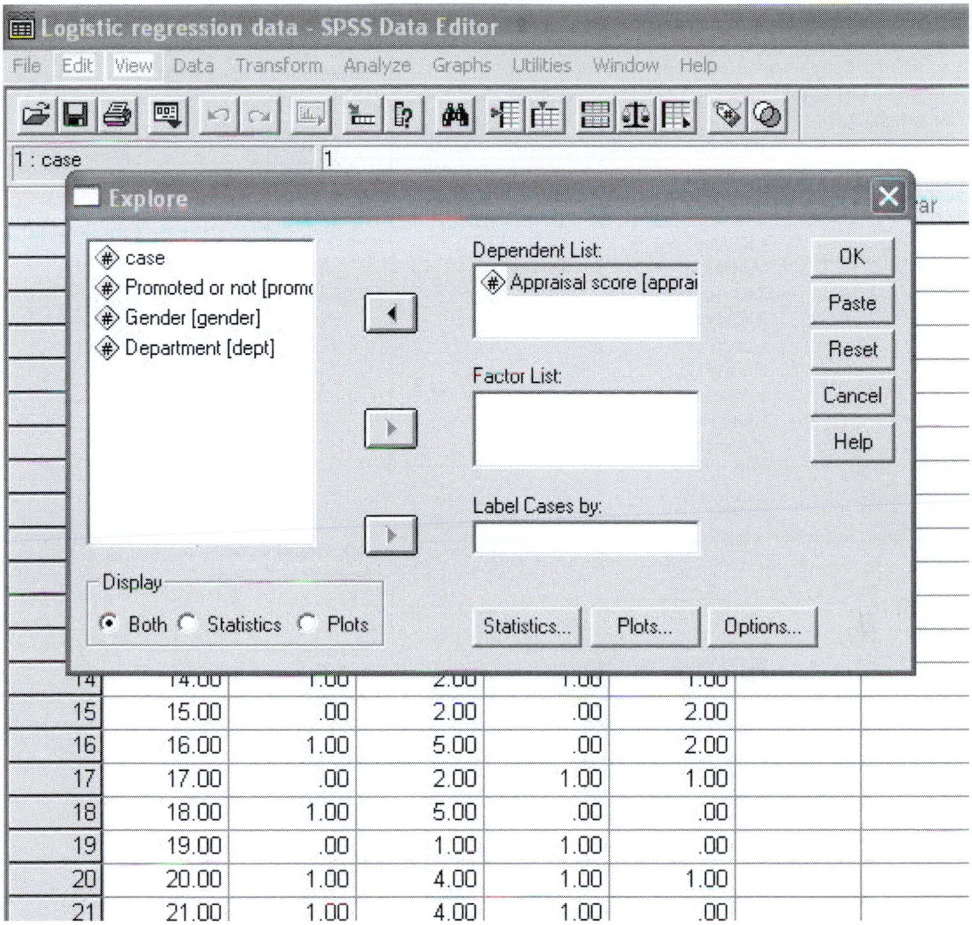

Figure 6.28 *Entering the variables when using* Explore

white box headed **Dependent List**. The variable(s) will be moved across to the
Dependent List box (see Figure 6.28).

➢ Click on **OK**.

Output in the following form will appear.

Explore

Case processing summary

	Cases					
	Valid		Missing		Total	
	N	Per cent	N	Per cent	N	Per cent
Appraisal score	30	100.0%	0	.0%	30	100.0%

Descriptives

			Statistic	Std error
Appraisal score	Mean		3.6333	.28960
	95% confidence	Lower bound	3.0410	
	interval for mean	Upper bound	4.2256	
	5% trimmed mean		3.6481	
	Median		4.0000	
	Variance		2.516	
	Std deviation		1.58622	
	Minimum		1.00	
	Maximum		6.00	
	Range		5.00	
	Interquartile range		3.0000	
	Skewness		−.012	.427
	Kurtosis		−1.302	.833

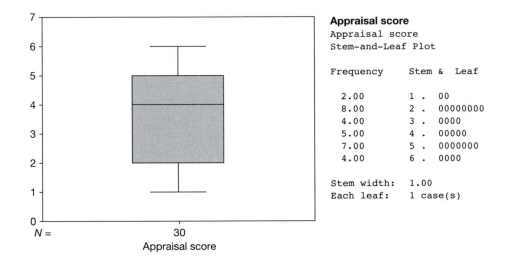

Appraisal score
Appraisal score
Stem-and-Leaf Plot

```
Frequency        Stem &  Leaf

    2.00          1 .  00
    8.00          2 .  00000000
    4.00          3 .  0000
    5.00          4 .  00000
    7.00          5 .  0000000
    4.00          6 .  0000

Stem width:   1.00
Each leaf:    1 case(s)
```

For each variable, in the table headed *Descriptives*, check that the minimum and maximum values seem correct, and in the box and whiskers plots look for any outliers or extreme scores. Details on how to do this are given on pages 90–1. If the minimum and maximum values are reasonable, and there are no outliers shown in the box and whiskers plot, follow the instructions below to perform the correlations.

If the minimum and maximum values don't look right, and/or there are outliers shown in the box and whiskers plot, check your data to make sure that the outlying or extreme values are not mistakes, and that from a research point of view it makes sense to include them in the analysis. If necessary, take steps to modify the data, and then run *Explore* again, repeating the process until you are confident that your data are sound. When you are confident that the data are acceptable, follow the instructions below to examine the frequencies of the categorical variables.

➤ Click on **Analyze.**
➤ Click on **Descriptive Statistics.**
➤ Click on **Frequencies** ....
➤ A dialog box will open. In the white box on the right hand side of the dialog box is a list of the variables. Click on a categorical variable and then on the small black triangle to the left of the white box headed **Variable(s).** The categorical variable will be moved across to the **Variables** box. Repeat this procedure for any other categorical variables you wish to examine prior to running the logistic regression analysis.
➤ Click on **OK.**

Output like the following will appear.

Frequencies

Statistics

		Promoted or not	Gender	Department
N	Valid	30	30	30
	Missing	0	0	0

Frequency table

Promoted or not

		Frequency	Per cent	Valid per cent	Cumulative per cent
Valid	Not promoted	14	46.7	46.7	46.7
	Promoted	16	53.3	53.3	100.0
	Total	30	100.0	100.0	

Gender

		Frequency	Per cent	Valid per cent	Cumulative per cent
Valid	Male	14	46.7	46.7	46.7
	Female	16	53.3	53.3	100.0
	Total	30	100.0	100.0	

Department

		Frequency	Per cent	Valid per cent	Cumulative per cent
Valid	Production	12	40.0	40.0	40.0
	Finance	10	33.3	33.3	73.3
	Sales	8	26.7	26.7	100.0
	Total	30	100.0	100.0	

Check that the frequencies are as you expect for each categorical variable. If necessary, make any required corrections.

How to run a logistic regression analysis in SPSS

To run a standard binary logistic regression:

> ➤ Click on **Analyze**.
> ➤ Click on **Regression**.
> ➤ Click on **Binary Logistic . . . .**
> ➤ A dialog box will open as in Figure 6.29. Click on the dependent variable and then on the small black triangle to the left of box headed **Dependent**. The dependent variable will be moved across to the **Dependent variable** box.
> ➤ Click on a predictor variable and then on the small black triangle to the left of the box headed **Covariates**. The predictor variable will be moved across to the

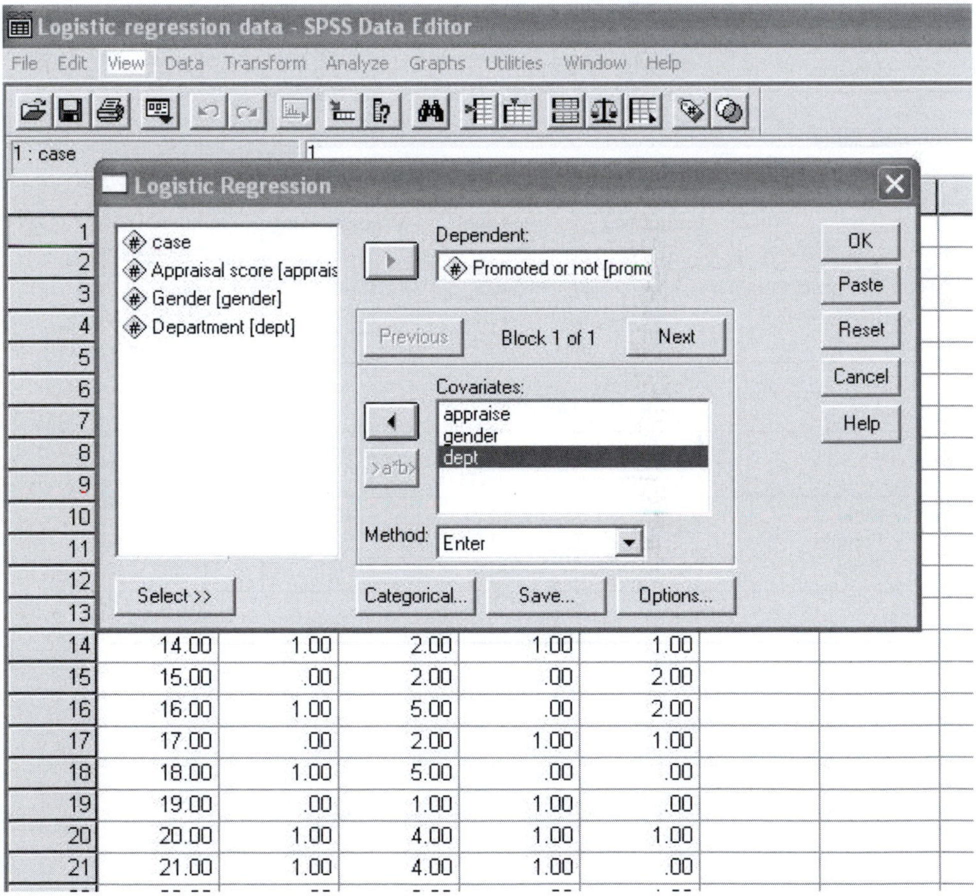

Figure 6.29 *Entering the variables in a logistic regression*

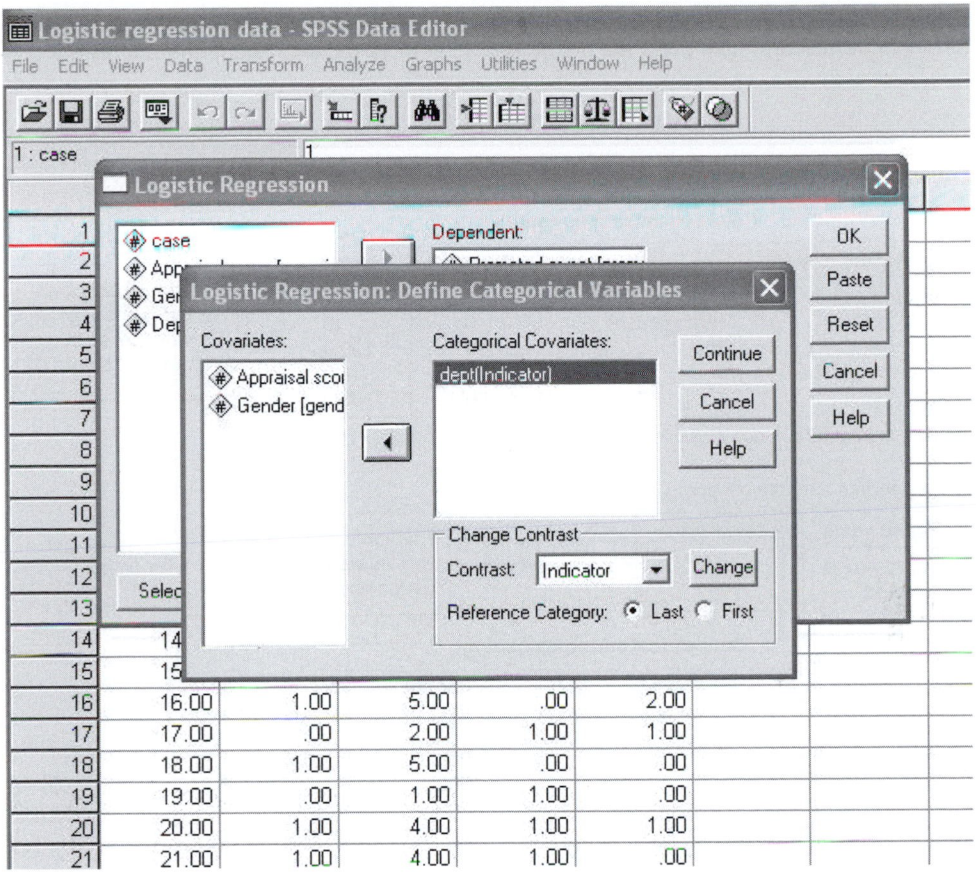

Figure 6.30 *Entering non-dichotomous categorical variables in a logistic regression*

Covariate box. Repeat this procedure for each of the remaining predictor variables.

➢ If any of the predictor variables are categorical and non-dichotomous, click on the button labelled **Categorical** . . . . A dialog box will appear as in Figure 6.30. In this example 'department' is such a variable.

➢ Click on a non-dichotomous categorical variable and then on the small black triangle to the left of the box headed **Categorical Variables**. The variable will be moved across to the **Categorical variables** box. Repeat this procedure for any other categorical variables.

➢ Click on **Continue**.

➢ Click on the **Options** button and then check the white box next to **CI for Exp(B)**.

➢ Click on **Continue**.

➢ Click on **OK**.

When the output window appears on the left hand side of the screen, click on **Block 0: Beginning Block** and then press the delete key on your keyboard. The following output will be left.

Logistic regression

Case processing summary

Unweighted cases[a]			Per cent	Per cent
Selected cases	Included in analysis	30		100.0
	Missing cases	0		.0
	Total	30		100.0
Unselected cases		0		.0
Total		30		100.0

This table shows the number of valid cases in the analysis.

[a] If weight is in effect, see classification table for the total number of cases.

Dependent variable encoding

Original value	Internal value
Not promoted	0
Promoted	1

This table shows the two values of the dependent variable.

Categorical variables codings

		Frequency	Parameter coding	
			(1)	(2)
Department	Production	12	1.000	.000
	Finance	10	.000	1.000
	Sales	8	.000	.000

This table shows the codes given to the two dummy variables created to represent the department variable. Because department has three levels, two dummy variables are created. For dummy variable 1, in the column headed (1), production is coded 1 and the other two variables are coded 0. For the second dummy variable, finance is coded 1 and the other two are coded 0. For an explanation of dummy variables see the material on them in the previous section on multiple regression.

Block 1: method = enter

Omnibus tests of model coefficients

		Chi-square	df	Sig.
Step 1	Step	8.935	4	.063
	Block	8.935	4	.063
	Model	8.935	4	.063

This table reports the result of a chi-square test designed to examine whether or not the predictor variables are able to predict how cases fall into each category of the dependent variable. Here, the chi-square value is 8.94 with 4 degrees of freedom. This is not statistically significant because .063 is greater than .05.

Model summary

Step	−2 Log likelihood	Cox & Snell R square	Nagelkerke R square
1	32.520	.258	.344

This is a psuedo R square for the model, imitating the true R square produced with multiple regression.

Classification table[a]

Observed		Predicted		
		Promoted or not		Percentage correct
		Not promoted	Promoted	
Step 1	Promoted or not	Not promoted	10	4	71.4
		Promoted	4	12	75.0
	Overall percentage				73.3

a. The cut value is .500.

This table shows the success of the logistic regression model in predicting the dependent variable.

In this example, 71.4% of those promoted were predicted to be promoted and 75% of those employees who were not promoted were predicted to be not promoted. Therefore, the model is clearly working reasonably well (though not well enough to reach statistical significance (see previous page)).

Variables in the equation

		B	S.E.	Wald	df	Sig.	Exp(B)	95.0% C.I. for EXP(B)	
								Lower	Upper
Step 1[a]	APPRAISE	.013	.296	.002	1	.965	1.013	.567	1.811
	GENDER	2.353	1.004	5.492	1	.019	10.520	1.470	75.295
	DEPT			2.001	2	.368			
	DEPT(1)	-.231	1.088	.045	1	.832	.794	.094	6.698
	DEPT(2)	-1.514	1.190	1.620	1	.203	.220	.021	2.265
	Constant	-.530	1.585	.112	1	.738	.589		

a Variable(s) entered on step 1: APPRAISE, GENDER, DEPT.

This table shows the contribution of each of the predictor variables to the logistic regression model. The Wald statistic is used to examine whether each predictor variable makes a statistically significant unique contribution to the model. In this example only gender is significant (p = .019) because the probability of every other predictor variable sig. (an abbreviation of significance), the column sixth from the left, is greater than .05.

The column labelled Exp(B) contains the odds ratios for each predictor variable and the columns to the right give the 95% confidence intervals for these ratios. Odds ratios are explained below.

To explain the concept of odds ratios, let's take an example. Imagine that there are 20 men in a department and 10 get promoted. In this case the odds (or probability) of being promoted if you are a man is 10 in 20, which equals .5 or 50 per cent. Now, let's say that there are 20 women in the department and of these only five are promoted. The odds of being promoted if you are a woman are only five in 20, which equals .25 or 25 per cent. The odds ratio in this example refers to the ratio of the odds of being promoted if you are a man to the odds of being promoted if you are a woman. So:

The odds of being promoted if you are a man = .5
The odds of being promoted if you are a woman = .25

Odds ratio = .5/.25 = 2

This means that men are twice as likely to be promoted as women. If the odds ratio had worked out at 1.5 we could say that men are 1.5 times as likely to be promoted as women. If it were 1 we would say that men and women are equally likely to be promoted. Finally, if it were less than 1 we would say that women are more likely to be promoted than men.

In the context of *SPSS* logistic regression, the Exp(B) term gives the odds ratio for a given predictor variable after controlling for the effects of the other predictor variables. So if the predictor variables are age, gender and training performance, the dependent variable is whether or not people are promoted, more men than women are promoted, and the odds ratio for gender is 1.7, we could say that after controlling for the effects of age and training performance, men are 1.7 times more likely to be promoted than women. The output also provides the 95 per cent confidence interval for the odds ratio. This confidence interval is the equivalent to the 95 per cent confidence interval for the mean discussed in Chapters 2 and 3. If the odds ratio for gender is 1.6 with a lower 95 per cent confidence limit of 1.3 and an upper 95 per cent confidence limit of 1.9, this indicates that the best estimate of the odds ratio for the population you are generalizing to is 1.6, and you can be 95 per cent confident that the correct odds ratio for this population is somewhere between 1.3 and 1.9. If the confidence interval for the odds ratio is very wide this is likely to be because the sample size is too small.

When an odds ratio is less than 1 it is more difficult to interpret. In these circumstances it is a good idea to deal with this by reversing the coding of the predictor variable. For example, imagine that you are looking at the extent to which gender affects the odds of promotion. You code males as 0 and females as 1, and obtain an odds ratio of .64. If you reverse the coding for gender, coding males as 1 and females as 0, this will result in a more easily interpretable odds ratio of over 1. It should be possible to do this within steps taken to run the logistic regression. The simplest way to do this recoding is as follows:

➢ Click on **File**.
➢ Click on **New**.
➢ Click on **Syntax**.
➢ A syntax page will be opened. On this you can enter the instructions to reverse the coding of the dependent variable. To do so you need to type

'Recode **Type the name of your dependent variable here** (1=0) (0=1).
Execute.'

So if the name of the predictor variable with an odds ratio of less than 1 was gender, with males coded 0 and females coded 1, we can reverse this coding for gender by typing in the following instruction on the syntax page:

Recode gender (1=0) (0=1).
Execute.

Remember to type this instruction in very precisely, including the full stops, or it will not work.

➢ Then, place the cursor over recode, left-click the mouse and drag the cursor down so that both the 'recode' and the 'execute' commands are highlighted.
➢ Click on the small black triangle just to the right of the binoculars at the top of the screen.

The effect of this instruction will be to recode the predictor variable, with cases which were coded 1 now coded as 0, and those which were coded as 0 coded as 1. If you do this remember to use the *Variable View* in the data editor to change the value labels for the predictor variable so that they are consistent with the new coding. You can now run the logistic regression again and you will find that where odds ratios were previously less than 1 and therefore hard to interpret, they are now greater than 1.

An odds ratio (which like *d* and the correlation coefficient, is a measure of effect size) can also be expressed as a percentage. If the ratio is 1.5 we can say that, after controlling for other predictor variables, men are 50 per cent more likely to be promoted than women, if it is 1.8 that they are 80 per cent more likely to be promoted than women, and if it is 2.2 that they are 120 per cent more likely to be promoted than women.

In the example given so far we have just dealt with categorical predictor variables but, of course, the predictor variables in logistic regression may also be continuous. In the case of such continuous predictor variables, the odds ratio tells you (after controlling for the effect of other predictor variables) the increase in the probability of getting a score of 1 rather than 0 for the dependent variable when the predictor variable increases by one unit. For example, if the continuous variable is appraisal score on a 5-point scale, the dependent variable is whether or not people are promoted, and the odds ratio is 1.5, this means the probability of being promoted, after controlling for other predictor variables, increases by 50 per cent with a one unit increase in appraisal score (e.g. an increase in appraisal score from 1 to 2, or from 3 to 4).

However the coding is organized for categorical or continuous variables, it is very important to be aware when viewing odds ratios that they are telling you how much more likely people are to have a dependent variable coded 1 than a dependent variable coded 0 when the predictor variable is *increased* by one point. It is essential when interpreting the results of a logistic regression analysis to be fully aware of what an increase from 0 to 1 in the dependent variable actually means (e.g. they are promoted or not, they are made redundant or not, they are selected for training or not, etc.), and to consider this in relation to what an increase of one point in the relevant predictor variable means (e.g. they are a year older, they are male rather than female, they are female rather than male, they have obtained one more point in their appraisal).

How to report the results of a logistic regression analysis

The results of this example might be reported as follows:

A logistic regression analysis was carried out using age, annual appraisal score and gender as predictor variables and whether or not employees are promoted as the dependent variable. A test of the full model using all predictors against a constant only model was not statistically reliable, chi-square (4, $N = 30$) = 8.94, $p = .063$, indicating that the predictor variables did not reliably predict whether or not employees were promoted. Nagelkerke's R $square$ is .34. The model correctly predicted 71 per cent of those not promoted and 75 per cent of those promoted. Regression coefficients, Wald statistics, odds ratios and the 95 per cent confidence intervals for the odds ratios are shown in Table 6.17.

Table 6.17 *Results of a logistic regression analysis in which whether or not employees are promoted is predicted with appraisal scores, gender and the department they work in*

Variable	B	Wald test	Odds ratio	95% confidence interval of odds ratio	
				Upper	Lower
Appraisal score	0.13	0.00	1.01	0.57	1.81
Gender	2.35*	5.49	10.52	1.47	75.36
Production department or not	−0.23	0.05	0.79	0.94	6.70
Finance department or not	−1.51	1.62	0.22	0.02	2.27
Constant	−0.53	0.11			

*$p < .05$

Using the Wald statistic as an indication of the unique significance of the predictor variables, only gender was statistically significant. The odds ratio for gender, at 10.52, indicates that, after controlling for the other predictor variables, men are over 10 times more likely to be promoted than women. However, the 95 per cent confidence for this odds ratio is very wide and this, coupled with the very small sample size of only 30 cases and the lack of reliability of the model, suggests that this finding should be discounted.

Comments

- The results of this logistic regression have to be treated very cautiously because the sample size is inadequate. Indeed, in real research it would not be appropriate to attempt a logistic regression with only 30 cases.
- The Wald statistics testing the unique contribution of each predictor variable should only be taken seriously if the entire model is statistically reliable (i.e. the chi-square test is statistically significant).
- The odds ratio is a good indication of the effect size of predictor variables on the dependent variable.

Interpretation

The issues raised in the interpretation of a logistic regression are similar to those for multiple regression. First, there is the issue of whether the predictor variables are collectively associated with the dependent variable. This is examined by looking at the chi-square statistic and examining whether or not it is significant. A significant chi-square indicates that the predictor variables are associated with the dependent variable.

The next issue is how strongly the predictor variables are associated with the dependent variable. This can be examined with Nagelkerke's *R square* which attempts to mimic the *R square* value in multiple regression. The greater this *R square*, the stronger the association between the predictor variables and the dependent variable. However, Nagelkerke's *R square* is not always reported, and a disadvantage it has over the *R square* value in multiple regression is that it cannot be used to express the percentage of variance in the dependent variable accounted for collectively by the predictor variables. A second way to express the strength of the relationship between the predictor variables and the dependent variable is with the information provided about the success that the logistic regression model has in predicting whether cases fall into each of the two possible categories of the dependent variable.

The final issue is the extent to which each predictor variable predicts the two possible values of the dependent variable after taking into account its relationship with other predictor variables. Here, the odds ratios are very helpful. It is generally useful to know that, after controlling for other variables, men are three times more likely to be promoted than women, or that after controlling for other variables, a one point increase in an appraisal rating means that someone is 50 per cent more likely to obtain a salary increase.

Finally, turning to the issue of causality, it is possible to use logistic regression to examine causal relationships but, as with multiple regression, this is rare in organizational research. Causality between a predictor variable and the dependent variable can only be inferred if the research is designed in such a way that there is only one explanation for the significant contribution of the predictor variable to the regression model.

FACTOR ANALYSIS AND CRONBACH'S ALPHA COEFFICIENT

When to use

Factor analysis is used when you have measured people on several continuous variables and you wish to see whether these variables can be reduced to a smaller set of variables. In areas in which there are a large number of correlated variables (e.g. personality dimensions such as calmness, extroversion, sociability, dependability, etc.) factor analysis can be used to reduce these to a smaller number of variables. The smaller number of variables identified with a factor analysis are often called hidden or latent variables, because it is only after using factor analysis that we are aware of them. Within organizational research another common use of factor analysis is to examine the structure of questionnaires. For example, it might be used to examine the evidence that a questionnaire designed to measure six different aspects of job commitment actually does so.

Background

Some of the classic uses of factor analysis have been within the field of psychology, in the study of intelligence and cognitive ability. In the case of intelligence, psychologists were interested in whether human ability boils down to just one factor. If this is the case, people who are relatively good at some things (such as tests of numerical ability) would also be good at others (such as verbal and spatial ability). In other words, human ability would be a single construct, with someone who is relatively good at one thing being relatively good at all others as well. However, if human ability is made up of several factors, being good at tests of numerical ability would not necessarily mean that someone would perform well on tests of verbal and spatial ability. Here, you would conclude that ability is made up of several factors, and that to measure someone's overall ability, you would need to assess them separately on each factor.

In the same way, psychologists used factor analysis to try to identify the basic structure of personality. They argued that there were a very large number of personality traits in the English language (caring, dogmatic, manipulative, shy, daring, etc.), and if you wanted to describe someone's personality it could be argued that you would have to measure them on every single one of these traits. However, factor analysis has shown that this plethora of specific personality traits can be reduced to a relatively small set of underlying latent variables such as extroversion–introversion. Armed with knowledge of what these latent variables are, we do not have to measure all of the specific traits on which people might vary, but just the broad underlying traits.

Factor analysis is also used in a more applied context to aid in the development of psychometric tests. Imagine that you want to develop a measure of job satisfaction, and you believe that job satisfaction may be made up of several distinct facets, such as satisfaction with a person's supervisor, satisfaction with the physical working environment, satisfaction with pay, etc. In these circumstances you might generate several questions to measure each aspect of job satisfaction, randomly distribute all of the questions generated to create a trial questionnaire, and distribute this to, say, 400 employees. Assume that this trial questionnaire has 80 items (questions). Factor analysis can be used to examine whether the pattern of responses that you obtain from the respondents indicates that each aspect of job satisfaction is, indeed, distinct from the others, and that the items you have created to measure each facet of job satisfaction are correlated reasonably highly with each other, but not with the items designed to measure other facets of job satisfaction. For example, it might be the case that the following set of four items are found to correlate highly with each other but not to correlate very highly with other items:

- 'I am dissatisfied with my basic level of pay';
- 'I am happy with the amount of bonuses I can earn';
- 'I am satisfied with the financial reward I receive';
- 'I am thinking of quitting because I am not given sufficient financial reward for my work'.

If this were the case, you would be in a position to conclude that these four items were all measuring one specific aspect of job satisfaction: satisfaction with pay.

Factor analysis can be used to identify any sets of variables that correlate well with each other but less well with other items. The sets of inter-correlated items are then viewed as factors. When factor analysis is used in this way to develop questionnaires it is often used in combination with a measure of reliability called Cronbach's alpha. The purpose of Cronbach's alpha in this context is to examine the average correlation between a set of questionnaire items, with the intention of examining how reliably the questionnaire measures a particular dimension. So, if a questionnaire is designed to measure four aspects of job satisfaction, factor analysis might be used to confirm that the questionnaire does, indeed, measure four different latent variables, and Cronbach's alpha might then be used to examine the reliability with which the questionnaire measures each set of items dealing with each of the four aspects of job satisfaction in turn.

Factor analysis is divided into two types: exploratory and confirmatory. Exploratory factor analysis, as its name suggests, is used to explore the factor structure in a set of data. Compared to confirmatory factor analysis it is a relatively straightforward procedure, and the one available in *SPSS*. Confirmatory factor analysis is a more complex procedure used to test specific theories about the nature of hidden processes. It is usually carried out with structural equation modelling, a technique which is briefly discussed later in this chapter.

Let's use another example to consider factor analysis in a little more detail. Imagine that you took a series of measurements from 1,000 randomly selected adults in the US. To keep things simple, assume that you used just four items, and that these were designed to measure just four things: satisfaction with life outside work, satisfaction with life at work, job performance and training performance. Now imagine that you correlated responses to each of these four dimensions with all of the others. You could represent the results of your work with a correlation matrix like the one shown in Table 6.18.

The correlation matrix presented in Table 6.18 shows that the correlation between job performance and training performance is 0.88, the correlation between job performance and satisfaction with life outside work is 0.05, and so on.

305

Table 6.18 *Correlations between job performance, training performance, satisfaction with life outside work and satisfaction with work*

	Job performance	Training performance	Satisfaction with life outside work	Satisfaction with work
Job performance	–	0.88	0.05	−0.11
Training performance		–	0.13	0.03
Satisfaction with life outside work			–	0.74
Satisfaction with work				–

Factor extraction

How does factor analysis identify sets of inter-correlated items? It does so by using a process called factor extraction, and this is best explained by using some very simple geometry. It is possible to represent the degree of correlation between any two variables you measure as an angle. When two variables are not correlated at all (when the correlation coefficient is 0.0) they have an angle of 90 degrees to each other. As the degree to which they are positively correlated increases so the angle decreases and, in the extreme case of two variables which are perfectly positively correlated, there would be an exact overlap between them. When the correlation between two variables is negative, the angle is greater than 90 degrees, and in the case of a perfect negative correlation it is 180 degrees.

If you represent the correlations between the four variables shown in the correlation matrix in Table 6.18 as angles, you can see that job performance and training performance have a narrow angle between them (because they are highly correlated) and satisfaction with life outside work and satisfaction with work would also have a narrow angle (because they are highly correlated with each other as well). However, as the other four pairs have quite weak correlations, the angle between the variables in each pair would be quite large (close to 90 degrees), as the pairs are not very highly correlated with each other. Such a geometrical relationship between the four dimensions is shown in Figure 6.31. As you can see, job performance and training performance are separated by a relatively narrow angle (because they are quite highly correlated with each other), and satisfaction with life outside work and satisfaction with work are also separated by a small angle (for the same reason). Because job performance has a low correlation with satisfaction with life outside work, and with satisfaction with work, the angles between these are quite large.

In factor extraction, *hypothetical* variables are placed in the best position to capture the pattern of inter-correlations in the correlation matrix. First, all the people about whom you have collected data are given a score on a newly created variable, called a factor. The factor is selected in such a way that it correlates as highly as possible with all of the other variables, the ones you have actually measured. Once this has been done, the correlation between this factor and all the other variables is eliminated (technically, 'partialled out') from the correlation matrix. This produces a new correlation matrix between the variables,

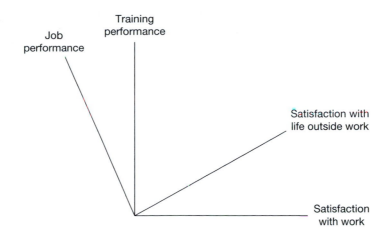

Figure 6.31 *A geometrical representation of the correlation between job performance, training performance, satisfaction with life outside work and satisfaction with work*

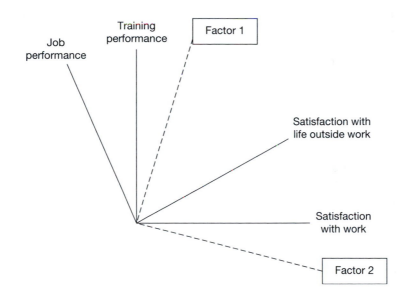

Figure 6.32 *Factor extraction: Factors 1 and 2*

one in which the variables do not correlate at all with the factor. A second factor is then created from this new correlation matrix, and the correlation between this second factor is then eliminated, producing a third correlation matrix, from which a third factor is created, and so on.

In Figure 6.32 two factors have been extracted, Factor 1 and Factor 2. The angle between each factor and the measured variables indicates the degree of correlation between them. So Factor 1 correlates relatively highly with training performance because the angle between them is small, but relatively poorly with satisfaction with life outside work as the angle this time is quite large.

307

Correlations with factors are called factor loadings. So, the factor loadings of job performance and training performance are relatively high on Factor 1, but low on Factor 2. Similarly, the factor loadings for satisfaction with work and satisfaction with life outside work are relatively high for Factor 2, but low for Factor 1.

Factor rotation

The final step in factor analysis is called factor rotation. For mathematical reasons, at the factor extraction stage factors are not placed in the best position to enable you to interpret the data. Therefore, they have to be *rotated* so that they are in the best possible position to enable you to interpret the results with ease. There are two principal ways of rotating the factors:

- orthogonal;
- oblique.

In the case of orthogonal rotation the factors are forced to be independent (not correlated) with each other whereas in oblique rotation the factors may correlate with each other.

Figure 6.33 shows the likely position of the factors after rotation. As you can see, the rotation of the factors has maximized the loadings of job performance and training performance on Factor 1, and minimized the loadings of satisfaction with life and satisfaction with work on that factor. Similarly, the loadings of satisfaction with life and satisfaction with life at work have been maximized on Factor 2, and minimized on Factor 1. This step makes it considerably easier to interpret the results of the factor analysis.

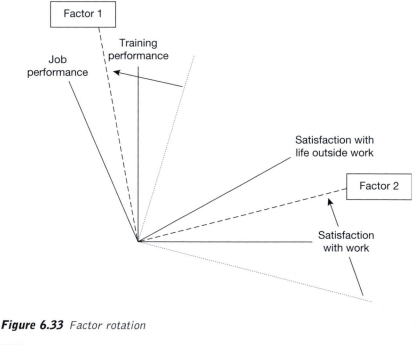

Figure 6.33 *Factor rotation*

Table 6.19 *Factor loadings, after factor rotation, of job performance, training performance, satisfaction with life and satisfaction with work*

	Factor loading	
	Factor 1	Factor 2
Job performance	0.79	0.03
Training performance	0.68	0.06
Satisfaction with life	0.12	0.77
Satisfaction with work	0.14	0.83

Interpreting the results of the analysis

The results of the factor analysis indicate the amount of the variance between the variables that each factor accounts for, and provides loadings of all the variables on each factor. A table like that shown in Table 6.19 is produced showing the loading of each variable on each factor.

Table 6.19 indicates that the loadings for Factor 1 are .79 for job performance, .68 for training performance, and so on. The convention is to take seriously any loading that is equal to or greater than .32. According to Comrey and Lee (1992) factor loadings of over .71 can be considered excellent, .63 to .70 very good, .55 to .62 good, .45 to .54 fair, and .32 to .44 poor. So, here, we have Factor 1, which is comprised of job performance and training performance (with very good factor loadings), and Factor 2, which refers to satisfaction with life and satisfaction with work (with two excellent factor loadings). The last step is to label the factors. This is an entirely subjective step. Principal components analysis and factor analysis can identify sets of inter-correlated variables, but it is up to the researcher to interpret what these sets are, and to give them a name. In the example here this should be quite straightforward. The first factor clearly seems to be concerned with performance, and the second factor with satisfaction – so you could simply label Factor 1 'performance', and Factor 2 'satisfaction'.

Although the example above sets out the essential steps in factor analysis, it is very much a simplified account because, in reality, the number of items is likely to be 40 or more rather than just 4. Nevertheless, even with 100 items the steps are essentially the same: creating a correlation matrix, factor extraction, factor rotation and, then, interpreting the results of the analysis.

The nature of factor (and component) extraction

In the above discussion it was explained that factors can be extracted from correlation matrices. However, nothing was said about how this is done. In fact, there are several ways to extract factors, and of these the most important distinction is between extraction of principal components and other ways of extracting factors. In fact, when the principal components method is used, this is technically an example of principal components analysis rather than factor analysis, although it is often referred to as factor analysis just the same.

Factor analysis and principal components analysis (PCA) each produce something different: PCA produces components, while factor analysis produces factors. The main difference between the production of components and the production of factors is in the way that the variance between the variables is analysed. With PCA *all* the variance between the variables is analysed, whereas with factor analysis only the variance *shared* by the variables is analysed.

Factor analysis is used if the purpose of the research is to understand the theoretical relationship between the variables. It is typically used when researchers want to develop (exploratory factor analysis) or test (confirmatory factor analysis) a theory about the causes of variation in scores on the variables measured: this idea is that the identified factors are viewed as causing this variation. So it would be appropriate for an examination of the nature of personality, or the nature of human ability because, here, you are interested in the theoretical relationships between the various aspects of personality and ability. PCA, on the other hand, is used when you want a complete empirical summary of the data set.

Just as there are several ways to extract factors, so there are also a variety of methods to rotate them. As you have already seen, these can be divided into two basic types: orthogonal and oblique. An orthogonal rotation is used when, for theoretical reasons, you do not expect the factors to be related to each other at all. In contrast, an oblique rotation is used when it would appear that the factors will be inter-correlated. So, if you assume that the factors that underlie personalities (such as extroversion, agreeableness, conscientiousness, etc.) are themselves correlated, you would choose an oblique rotation. If you believe the factors to be independent of each other (for example, knowing how conscientious someone is, is no indication at all of how extroverted or agreeable they are) an orthogonal rotation would be used. It should be noted, however, that with a large sample size, and robust underlying dimensions being measured, there is likely to be little difference between the outcomes of an orthogonal and an oblique rotation.

Interpretation

In examining the pattern of factor loadings, it is important to look at how 'cleanly' the items load on the various factors. Ideally, each item should load satisfactorily (i.e. with a value of 0.32 or more) on just one factor, and if it is found that a substantial proportion of items load on two or more factors, this suggests a messy factor solution. Also it is, of course, important to check that the items loading on a given factor all appear to be measuring the same thing. For example, if a factor is composed of items which measure all sorts of disparate aspects of job satisfaction, it will not be possible to conclude that this factor has successfully identified a particular aspect of job satisfaction such as satisfaction with pay, with management, or whatever.

Assumptions and requirements

Factor analysis is designed for the analysis of continuous variables. Although the distribution shape of these variables is not critical, better solutions are possible if they are normally distributed. Because factor analysis deals with correlations, and correlations express the linear relationship between two variables (see the earlier section on correlations for a discussion of this) relatively poor factor solutions will be produced when the relations between the variables are curvilinear rather than linear.

How big a sample?

Statisticians have proposed a variety of answers to the question of how large a sample size is required in order to run factor analyses. Although some have argued that a sample size as low as 100 may be adequate in certain situations (Gorsuch 1983), Comrey and Lee's (1992) suggestion that a minimum of about 300 cases is necessary to provide a good factor solution is more sound (they describe 100 cases as poor and 1,000 as excellent). The sensible approach in most circumstances is to say that 300 cases should be the minimum, and anything more than this is a good thing.

A worked example: questionnaire development

Factor analysis is different from the statistical methods discussed so far in Chapters 5 and 6 in a number of respects: it is concerned not with testing hypotheses but with reducing large numbers of variables to a smaller number of variables; there are many different ways of carrying it out (i.e. a variety of methods of factor extraction and factor rotation); and there is less than universal consensus about which of these possible techniques should be employed in a particular circumstance. Furthermore, researchers using factor analysis to investigate the structure of domains (e.g. the structure of personality or mental ability) typically analyse their data several times, varying the exact nature of the analysis on each occasion in pursuit of the ideal factor solution. For these reasons, it is not possible to deal with all of the theoretical and practical issues that arise in factor analysis in this book and the reader who wishes to get to grips with the issues involved should read the excellent account given by Tabachnick and Fidell (2001).

However, in organizational research, factor analysis is more commonly used to examine whether a questionnaire is measuring what it is supposed to measure, and this is the purpose that will be covered here. In fact, this worked example will draw not only on factor analysis but also on the other statistical technique widely used in questionnaire development: Cronbach's alpha coefficient.

A simple questionnaire in organizational research might consist of around 12 questions. Of this 12, there might be three sets of four questions, with each set measuring a different element of the construct in question. Let's imagine that a questionnaire is designed to measure job satisfaction, and that this construct is broken down into three elements: satisfaction with the job itself, satisfaction with salary and satisfaction with opportunity for development. The researcher designs a 12-item questionnaire, with four items for each of these three elements of job satisfaction. Each item consists of a statement (e.g. I am happy with my annual salary), and respondents indicate the extent to which they agree or disagree with it on a 5-point scale.

If the three elements of job satisfaction are to some extent independent, and if the four questions measuring each element are working properly, we would expect:

311

- the correlations between the four items measuring a particular element of job satisfaction (e.g. satisfaction with salary) to be relatively high; and
- the correlation of the four items measuring a particular element of job satisfaction with items measuring other elements of job satisfaction to be relatively low.

In these circumstances a factor analysis of responses to the questionnaire should produce three major factors. On one of these should load only the items concerned with satisfaction, on another only the items concerned with satisfaction with pay, and on the third only the items concerned with opportunities for development. This could be examined by using the principal components method of factor extraction and the varimax method of orthogonal rotation.

Although technically, as explained earlier, principal components analysis and factor analysis are different procedures, we will keep things simple here by using factor analysis as an umbrella term to include both factor analysis and principal components analysis, and the output of both principal components analysis and factor analysis as factors.

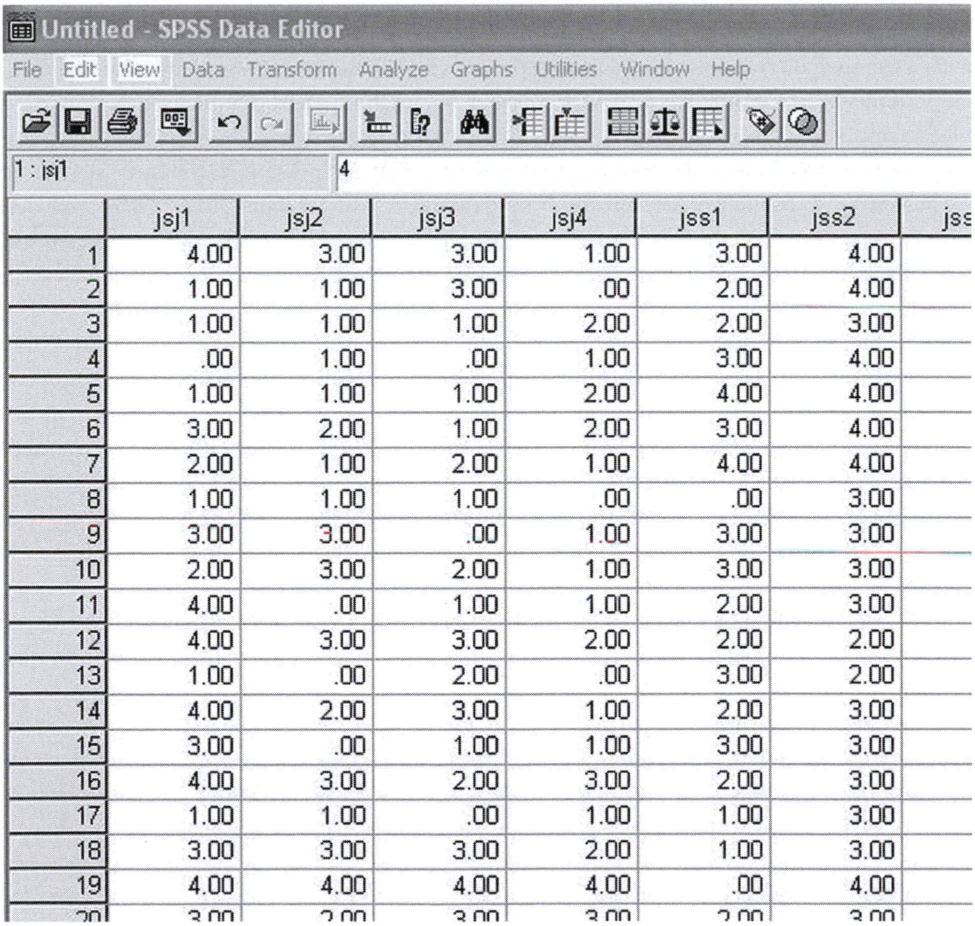

	jsj1	jsj2	jsj3	jsj4	jss1	jss2	jss
1	4.00	3.00	3.00	1.00	3.00	4.00	
2	1.00	1.00	3.00	.00	2.00	4.00	
3	1.00	1.00	1.00	2.00	2.00	3.00	
4	.00	1.00	.00	1.00	3.00	4.00	
5	1.00	1.00	1.00	2.00	4.00	4.00	
6	3.00	2.00	1.00	2.00	3.00	4.00	
7	2.00	1.00	2.00	1.00	4.00	4.00	
8	1.00	1.00	1.00	.00	.00	3.00	
9	3.00	3.00	.00	1.00	3.00	3.00	
10	2.00	3.00	2.00	1.00	3.00	3.00	
11	4.00	.00	1.00	1.00	2.00	3.00	
12	4.00	3.00	3.00	2.00	2.00	2.00	
13	1.00	.00	2.00	.00	3.00	2.00	
14	4.00	2.00	3.00	1.00	2.00	3.00	
15	3.00	.00	1.00	1.00	3.00	3.00	
16	4.00	3.00	2.00	3.00	2.00	3.00	
17	1.00	1.00	.00	1.00	1.00	3.00	
18	3.00	3.00	3.00	2.00	1.00	3.00	
19	4.00	4.00	4.00	4.00	.00	4.00	
20	3.00	2.00	3.00	3.00	2.00	3.00	

Untitled - SPSS Data Editor
File Edit View Data Transform Analyze Graphs Utilities Window Help
1 : jsj1   4

Figure 6.34 SPSS *Data Editor after principal components analysis data are entered*

Returning to the development of the questionnaire, let's say that the researcher distributes it to 100 people, and 86 of these complete it. Eighty-six is a very small sample size for factor analysis, but will suffice as an example here. She enters the data in *SPSS* as shown in Figure 6.34. You can download this data at www.dewberry-statistics.com.

The 12 variables are named as follows:

— items measuring satisfaction with the job: 'JSJ1' to 'JSJ4';
— items measuring satisfaction with salary: 'JSS1' to 'JSS4';
— items measuring satisfaction with opportunities for development: 'JSD1' to 'JSD4'.

The researcher decides to use principal components analysis to examine whether three distinct components emerge from the data (one for each of the three elements of job satisfaction), with the four items measuring each element loading on each one. This is achieved as follows.

How to run a principal components analysis in SPSS

➢ Click on **Analyze**.
➢ Click on **Data Reduction**.
➢ Click on **Factor** . . . .
➢ A dialog box will open. In this you will see the variables in the white rectangle to the right. Highlight the variables you wish to include in the analysis by placing the factor on the first one and then, holding down the right hand button of your mouse, dragging the cursor down until all desired variables are included, and click on the small black triangle to the left of the white rectangle headed **Variables**. Alternatively, if you want to select specific variables for the analysis, click on each one in turn and then on the black triangle to transfer each one into the **Variables** box individually (see Figure 6.35).
➢ Click on **Descriptives** . . . .
➢ A dialog box will appear. Check the boxes for **Univariate descriptives, Initial solution** and **Coefficients** (so that ticks appear in them).
➢ Click on **Continue**.
➢ Click on **Extraction** . . . .
➢ A dialog box will appear. Check the box for **Scree plot**.
➢ Click on **Continue**.
➢ Click on **Rotation** . . . .
➢ A dialog box will appear. Click on the radio button next to **Varimax**. Varimax is an orthogonal method of factor rotation, and is generally recommended as the most versatile.
➢ Click on **Continue**.
➢ Click on **OK**.

313

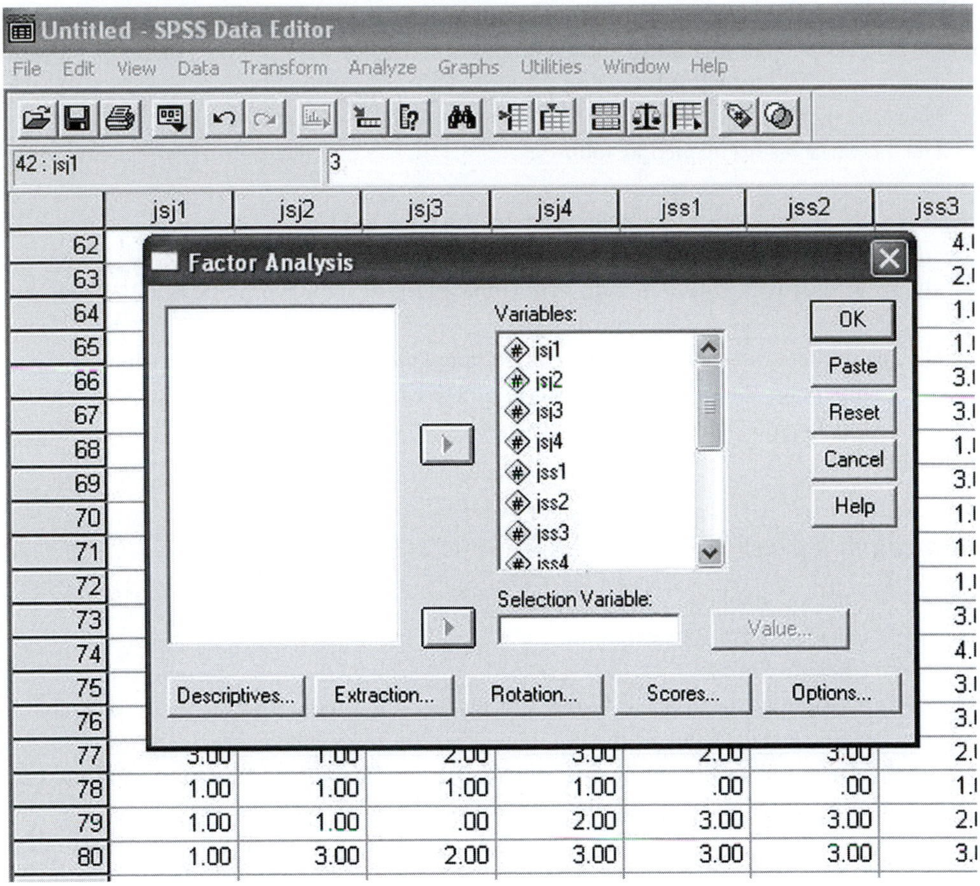

Figure 6.35 *Specifying the variables in factor analysis*

Output in the following form will appear.

Factor analysis

Descriptive statistics

	Mean	Std deviation	Analysis N
JSJ1	2.2674	1.25017	86
JSJ2	1.7558	1.19741	86
JSJ3	1.6395	1.11580	86
JSJ4	1.5581	1.04718	86
JSS1	2.3023	1.01830	86
JSS2	2.9535	.82472	86
JSS3	2.5233	.96682	86
JSS4	2.9767	.85374	86
JSD1	1.3140	1.02051	86
JSD2	1.2558	.94789	86
JSD3	1.8721	.99169	86
JSD4	2.9070	.90265	86

This table shows the mean and standard deviation for each item in the questionnaire. It also shows the number of cases for which data is available on each item.

Correlation matrix

		JSJ1	JSJ2	JSJ3	JSJ4	JSS1	JSS2	JSS3	JSS4	JSD1	JSD2	JSD3	JSD4
Correlation	JSJ1	1.000	.398	.390	.226	-.027	-.113	-.117	.028	.099	-.207	.161	.033
	JSJ2	.398	1.000	.550	.335	-.103	.048	.183	-.086	.285	-.203	-.086	.011
	JSJ3	.390	.550	1.000	.255	-.079	-.018	-.052	.078	.183	-.312	.064	.060
	JSJ4	.226	.335	.255	1.000	.016	.126	-.269	-.156	.374	-.015	.228	.143
	JSS1	-.027	-.103	-.079	.016	1.000	.241	.124	.333	-.104	.065	-.008	-.110
	JSS2	-.113	.048	-.018	.126	.241	1.000	.282	.366	.171	.015	-.094	.073
	JSS3	-.117	.183	-.052	-.269	.124	.282	1.000	.271	.034	-.032	-.199	-.119
	JSS4	.028	-.086	.078	-.156	.333	.366	.271	1.000	.062	.109	.108	.104
	JSD1	.099	.285	.183	.374	-.104	.171	.034	.062	1.000	.159	.377	.185
	JSD2	-.207	-.203	-.312	-.015	.065	.015	-.032	.109	.159	1.000	.135	.028
	JSD3	.161	-.086	.064	.228	-.008	-.094	-.199	.108	.377	.135	1.000	.249
	JSD4	.033	.011	.060	.143	-.110	.073	-.119	.104	.185	.028	.249	1.000

This correlation matrix shows the correlation of every item with every other item. If a good factor solution is to be found there should be several correlations of .32 or above.

Communalities

	Initial	Extraction
JSJ1	1.000	.604
JSJ2	1.000	.774
JSJ3	1.000	.670
JSJ4	1.000	.748
JSS1	1.000	.783
JSS2	1.000	.602
JSS3	1.000	.710
JSS4	1.000	.771
JSD1	1.000	.722
JSD2	1.000	.515
JSD3	1.000	.654
JSD4	1.000	.589

This table provides information about the extent to which the components/factors account for variance in each of the items. The figures under Extraction are the squared multiple correlation coefficients obtained by using all of the factors to predict each item score in turn (see the section on multiple correlation). For example, the figure of .60 for JSJ1 means that 60% of the variance in this item is explained by all of the factors produced in this analysis.

Extraction method: principal component analysis.

Total variance explained

Component	Initial eigenvalues			Extraction sums of squared loadings			Rotation sums of squared loadings		
	Total	% of variance	Cumulative %	Total	% of variance	Cumulative %	Total	% of variance	Cumulative %
1	2.453	20.441	20.441	2.453	20.441	20.441	2.021	16.841	16.841
2	1.851	15.424	35.865	1.851	15.424	35.865	1.688	14.063	30.904
3	1.723	14.355	50.220	1.723	14.355	50.220	1.587	13.229	44.133
4	1.109	9.242	59.462	1.109	9.242	59.462	1.446	12.054	56.187
5	1.007	8.389	67.851	1.007	8.389	67.851	1.400	11.663	67.851
6	.918	7.650	75.500						
7	.692	5.764	81.264						
8	.608	5.066	86.330						
9	.580	4.833	91.163						
10	.410	3.414	94.577						
11	.369	3.074	97.651						
12	.282	2.349	100.000						

Extraction method: principal component analysis.

In this table, the factors appear in each row. So under 'Initial eigenvalues' factor number 1 has a total of 2.453 and it accounts for 20.441% of all variance in the items. In a factor analysis, the loading of a given item on given factor represents the correlation between the item and factor. An eigenvalue for a factor is obtained by squaring the loading of every item on that factor, and then adding these sqared factor loadings together. This means that the more that all of the items load on a factor, the more variance the factor explains in the items, and the greater the eigenvalue will be. The variance of each item in a factor analysis is always standardized at 1, so here where there are 12 items the total variance to be explained is 12. To find the percentage of variance explained by a factor we divide its eigenvalue (in the case of the first factor here 2.453) by the total variance to be explained (in this case 12) and multiply by 100 (here giving a result of 20.441%).

What all this shows in this example is that the first factor explains about 20% of the variance, the second 15% and so on, with the first three factors together explaining a total of 50% of the variance (see the fourth column, Cumulative %). We are interested in the variance explained by the first three factors in this example because we are hoping that three elements of job satisfaction will emerge.

Normally only factors with eigenvalues greater than 1 are reported, as those with eigenvalues less than this are viewed as explaining an insufficient amount of variance.

Also if the factor solution is adequate we should expect the number of factors with eigenvalues over 1 to be somewhere between the number of items divided by 5 (12/5 in this case) and the number of items divided by 3 (12/3 in this case). So here we would expect 2 to 4 factors, and actually we have 5. This is a warning that a good solution may not be possible in this case.

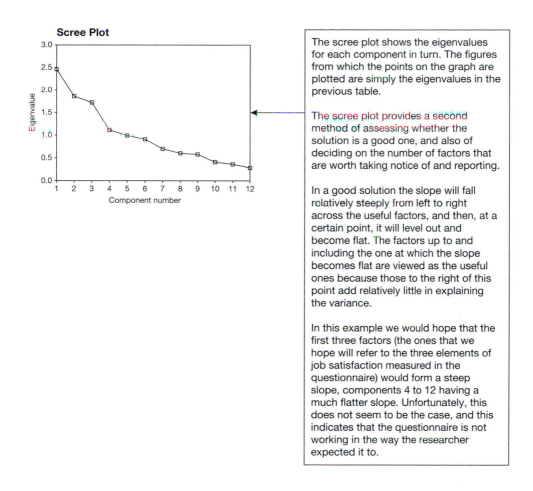

Scree Plot

The scree plot shows the eigenvalues for each component in turn. The figures from which the points on the graph are plotted are simply the eigenvalues in the previous table.

The scree plot provides a second method of assessing whether the solution is a good one, and also of deciding on the number of factors that are worth taking notice of and reporting.

In a good solution the slope will fall relatively steeply from left to right across the useful factors, and then, at a certain point, it will level out and become flat. The factors up to and including the one at which the slope becomes flat are viewed as the useful ones because those to the right of this point add relatively little in explaining the variance.

In this example we would hope that the first three factors (the ones that we hope will refer to the three elements of job satisfaction measured in the questionnaire) would form a steep slope, components 4 to 12 having a much flatter slope. Unfortunately, this does not seem to be the case, and this indicates that the questionnaire is not working in the way the researcher expected it to.

Component matrix[a]

	Component				
	1	2	3	4	5
JSJ1	.624	−5.02E−02	−.197	.415	−9.13E−03
JSJ2	.709	.117	−.427	−.270	4.856E−02
JSJ3	.713	6.198E−02	−.345	.160	−.114
JSJ4	.648	4.810E−02	.261	−.108	.496
JSS1	−.211	.520	−5.68E−02	.482	.484
JSS2	−2.82E−02	.738	−5.65E−02	−.194	.125
JSS3	−.199	.541	−.435	−.358	−.247
JSS4	−.108	.749	1.419E−02	.368	−.250
JSD1	.532	.328	.410	−.403	1.086E−02
JSD2	−.267	.169	.567	−.232	.201
JSD3	.340	8.817E−02	.660	.273	−.140
JSD4	.257	.127	.439	4.859E−02	−.559

This table shows the factor loadings before the factors are rotated.

Extraction method: principal component analysis.
[a] 5 components extracted.

Rotated component matrix[a]

	Component				
	1	2	3	4	5
JSJ1	.707	.117	−.236	.128	.137
JSJ2	.663	.443	.277	−.142	−.205
JSJ3	.787	.195	4.536E–02	9.916E–02	−2.32E–02
JSJ4	.199	.803	−.237	5.120E–04	7.839E–02
JSS1	−5.63E–02	1.773E–02	3.848E–02	−.176	.865
JSS2	−9.35E–02	.273	.612	1.183E–02	.379
JSS3	1.610E–02	−.136	.824	−.113	8.967E–03
JSS4	5.291E–02	−.183	.443	.406	.611
JSD1	3.108E–03	.717	.214	.383	−.124
JSD2	−.638	.281	−6.12E–03	.143	9.527E–02
JSD3	−2.87E–02	.271	−.313	.679	.145
JSD4	3.369E–02	2.423E–02	4.339E–02	.751	−.148

Extraction method: principal component analysis.
Rotation method: Varimax with Kaiser normalization.
[a] Rotation converged in 8 iterations.

Component transformation matrix

Component	1	2	3	4	5
1	.725	.606	−.118	.267	−.150
2	−.030	.220	.719	.243	.612
3	−.583	.356	−.373	.627	.033
4	.328	−.423	−.488	.221	.653
5	−.164	.528	−.303	−.654	.418

Extraction method: principal component analysis.
Rotation method: Varimax with Kaiser normalization.

This table shows the loadings of each item on each factor after they have been rotated (note that the factors are actually referred to more correctly as components in the *SPSS* tables because we are carrying out a principal components analysis). So the loadings on 'factor' 1 are .707 for JSJ1, .663 for JSJ2, .787 for JSJ3 and so on.

What we hope to find here is that the questionnaire items measuring a particular element of job satisfaction all load to a satisfactory extent, by which in practice we mean at least .32, on a given factor, and the other items do not. The reason that .32 is used as the criterion for a satisfactory relationship is that a loading of .32 indicates that factor accounts for 10% of the variance in the item responses. This is because factor loadings express the correlation between each item and the factor, and therefore, the percentage of variance accounted for can be worked out by squaring the correlations coefficent and multiplying by 100 (see the section on correlations). If an item explains less than 10% of the variance in a factor this is considered inadequate.

Unfortunately, this doesn't seem to be the case here, and there is no clear pattern between the factor loadings of each group of four job satisfaction items, and each factor. The best that can be said is that the job-related items (i.e. the JSJs) tend to load on factor 1, the salary-related items (the JSSs) tend to load on factor 3, and the development items (the JSDs) tend to load on factor 4. However, in general, the relation between the three sets of questionnaire items and the factor loadings is somewhat messy.

How to report the results of a factor analysis

The findings might be reported as follows:

> The 12-item questionnaire used in the study was designed to measure three elements of job satisfaction: satisfaction with the job, satisfaction with salary and satisfaction with opportunities to develop. It was distributed to 100 employees and 86 were returned. A principal components analysis with varimax rotation was used to investigate whether the items concerned with satisfaction with the job, salary and development opportunities loaded in an orderly way on three components.
>
> The eigenvalues produced in the extraction were examined on a scree plot and this failed to reveal a clear cut-off point. The five factors with eigenvalues greater than one are reported here. Factor loadings after varimax rotation are shown in Table 6.20. The three items designed to measure satisfaction with the job are named 'Job 1' to 'Job 4', those designed to measure satisfaction with salary are named 'Salary 1' to 'Salary 4' and those designed to measured satisfaction with opportunity for development are named 'Development 1' to 'Development 4'. We would hope that each set of questionnaire items loads substantially on just one factor, with one set loading on the first factor only, another set loading on the second factor only, etc. However, in this example this is clearly not the case, and the pattern of factor loadings is fairly messy. The implication of this is that the three sets of questionnaire items do not satisfactorily meaure the three aspects of job satisfaction that they were designed to measure.

Table 6.20 *Factor loadings after varimax rotation*

Items	Components				
	1	2	3	4	5
Job 1	.70	.12	−.24	.13	.14
Job 2	.66	.44	.28	−.14	−.21
Job 3	.79	.20	.05	.10	−.02
Job 4	.20	.80	−.24	.00	−.08
Salary 1	−.06	.02	.04	−.18	.87
Salary 2	−.09	.27	.61	.01	.38
Salary 3	.02	−.14	.82	−.11	.00
Salary 4	.05	−.18	.44	.41	.61
Development 1	.00	.71	.21	.39	−.12
Development 2	−.64	.28	−.06	.14	.10
Development 3	−.03	.27	−.31	.68	.15
Development 4	.03	.02	.04	.75	−.15

Comments

- In a study of this type it would be hoped that the scree plot revealed a clear break in the slope of the plotted eigenvalues, with the number of factors to the left of the break being the same as the number of sets of items in the questionnaire measuring separate domains of a construct (or different constructs).
- It would also be hoped that each set of items designed to measure a particular domain would load on a different factor, and that they would each only load on a single factor.
- When factors do emerge from a factor analysis it is always important to consider what each one is referring to. This can only be achieved by examining the nature of the items loading on each factor. If it so happens that when responses to a questionnaire are factor analysed two principal factors clearly emerge, and on one of these only items concerned with job commitment have high loadings whereas on the other only items concerned with job satisfaction load highly, it clearly makes sense to label the factors 'job commitment' and 'job satisfaction'. However, if the items that load on a factor appear to have little conceptual overlap, interpreting the meaning of the factor and naming it is not straightforward. In these circumstances, providing the factor analysis was based on reliable data and an adequate sample size, the outcome of the factor analysis would probably be to stimulate further research into the reasons for the unexpected relationships between the factors and the items loading on them.

If a researcher obtained the disappointing factor analytic results in the example used here, she would probably return to the drawing board and try to generate some better items to measure job satisfaction. However, if the results had been more positive the next step would be to examine the reliability of each of the three sets of items, and this usually involves the use of Cronbach's alpha coefficient.

Cronbach's alpha coefficient

Cronbach's alpha is a statistic used to calculate the reliability of a measurement scale. For example, imagine that you design a questionnaire to measure two variables: sociability and impulsiveness. Let us also say that you have generated three questions to measure how sociable people are, and three to measure how impulsive they are. Responses to each question are measured on a 5-point Likert scale from strongly agree to strongly disagree. In practice, you would be likely to use more than just three questions for each dimension, but in this example three will suffice.

If your three questions measuring sociability are doing their job well, we would expect them to be reasonably highly correlated. That is, if someone has high sociability, they should score highly on all three questions, whereas if they are low on sociability they should obtain low scores on all three questions. If there is little or no relationship between how people score on one of these questions, and how they score on the other two, it suggests that we cannot claim that the three questions are measuring the same construct. The same, of course, applies to impulsiveness: we expect a reasonably strong correlation between responses to the three impulsiveness questions.

The size of Cronbach's alpha is a function of two things: the average correlation between a set of items and the number of items. If we have three groups of five questionnaire items, and the mean inter-item correlation between the five items in the first set is .3, between the items in the second set .5 and the third set .7, the corresponding alphas will be .68, .83 and .92. This shows that the alpha is partly a function of the average inter-item correlation. To demonstrate that it is also a function of the number of items, imagine that we have one set of four questionnaire items, one set of six, and one set of eight, and that in all three cases the average inter-item correlation is .7. The Cronbach alphas are .80, .86 and .89 respectively.

The use of Cronbach's alpha is common when questionnaires are developed for research in organizations, and an alpha coefficient of .70 is usually taken as being the minimum level acceptable. If an alpha is less than this, the indication is that the items are unlikely to be reliably measuring the same thing.

To illustrate this we will compute the alpha for the four items measuring satisfaction with the job that were used in the factor analysis above.

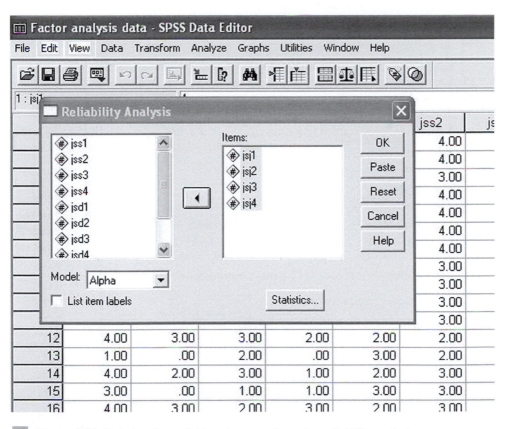

Figure 6.36 *Entering the variables when carrying out a reliability analysis*

To use Cronbach's alpha on these items:

> ➤ Click on **Analyze**.
> ➤ Click on **Scale**.
> ➤ Click in **Reliability Analysis** .... A dialog box will appear. In the white rectangle on the left hand side you will see a list of the variables. Click on each one of the variables you wish to check the reliability of and then on the black triangle to the left of the box headed **Items**. The variable will be moved across to the **Items** box. Repeat this procedure for each one of the set of items for which you wish to check the reliability (see Figure 6.36).
> ➤ Click on the **Statistics** ... button. Another dialog box will appear. Check the white boxes next to **Item**, **Scale**, **Scale if Item Deleted** and **Correlations**. Ticks will appear in the boxes (see Figure 6.37).

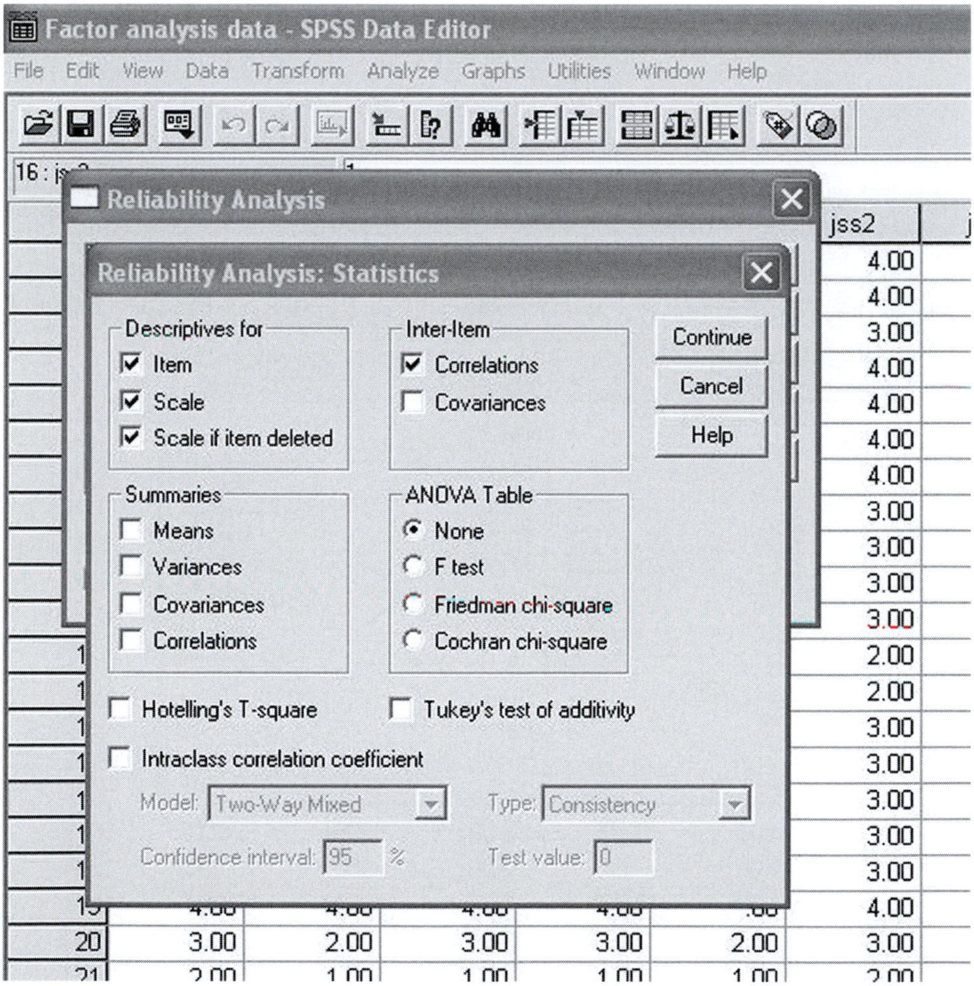

Figure 6.37 *Choosing options when carrying out a reliability analysis*

➢ Click on **Continue**.
➢ Click on **OK**.

Output in the following form will appear.

Reliability

****** Method 2 (covariance matrix) will be used for this analysis ******

—

RELIABILITY ANALYSIS - SCALE (ALPHA)

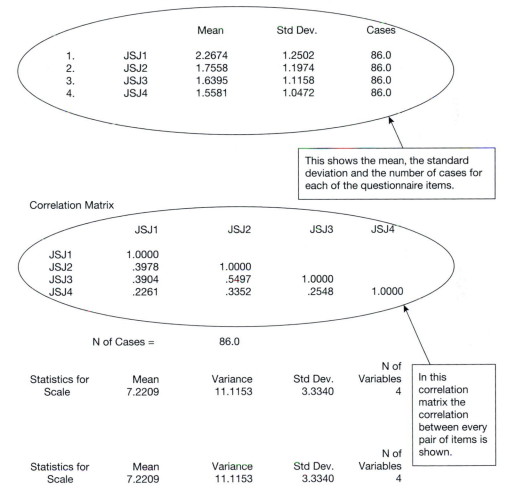

		Mean	Std Dev.	Cases
1.	JSJ1	2.2674	1.2502	86.0
2.	JSJ2	1.7558	1.1974	86.0
3.	JSJ3	1.6395	1.1158	86.0
4.	JSJ4	1.5581	1.0472	86.0

This shows the mean, the standard deviation and the number of cases for each of the questionnaire items.

Correlation Matrix

	JSJ1	JSJ2	JSJ3	JSJ4
JSJ1	1.0000			
JSJ2	.3978	1.0000		
JSJ3	.3904	.5497	1.0000	
JSJ4	.2261	.3352	.2548	1.0000

N of Cases =   86.0

Statistics for Scale	Mean	Variance	Std Dev.	N of Variables
Statistics for Scale	7.2209	11.1153	3.3340	4

In this correlation matrix the correlation between every pair of items is shown.

Statistics for Scale	Mean	Variance	Std Dev.	N of Variables
Statistics for Scale	7.2209	11.1153	3.3340	4

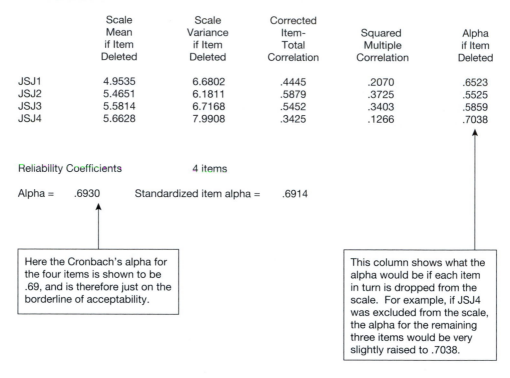

Item-total Statistics

	Scale Mean if Item Deleted	Scale Variance if Item Deleted	Corrected Item-Total Correlation	Squared Multiple Correlation	Alpha if Item Deleted
JSJ1	4.9535	6.6802	.4445	.2070	.6523
JSJ2	5.4651	6.1811	.5879	.3725	.5525
JSJ3	5.5814	6.7168	.5452	.3403	.5859
JSJ4	5.6628	7.9908	.3425	.1266	.7038

Reliability Coefficients   4 items

Alpha =   .6930   Standardized item alpha =   .6914

Here the Cronbach's alpha for the four items is shown to be .69, and is therefore just on the borderline of acceptability.

This column shows what the alpha would be if each item in turn is dropped from the scale. For example, if JSJ4 was excluded from the scale, the alpha for the remaining three items would be very slightly raised to .7038.

It is a straightforward matter to check that the alpha is above .7. If it is less than .7 (and even if it is above .7), you might consider dropping one or more items from the scale if the column labelled *Alpha if item deleted* indicates that there would be a worthwhile increase in the alpha level if particular items are dropped. Bear in mind however, that it is important to avoid what Cattell (1966) called 'bloated specifics'. These are sets of items which appear to be highly reliable because they only measure a small portion of the construct in question. For example, if the intention is for the items to measure all aspects of job commitment, but they only relate to one small component of job commitment, the items may have a high Cronbach alpha coefficient indicating that they are reliable, but this may be at the expense of providing a valid measure of the entire and complete domain of job commitment.

A BRIEF INTRODUCTION TO STRUCTURAL EQUATION MODELLING

Structural equation modelling (SEM) is a sophisticated statistical technique that enables researchers to examine quite complex relationships between variables. In a sense, it consists of a combination of multiple regression and confirmatory factor analysis. Because it is a complex procedure, and is not available in *SPSS*, it is not possible to explain how to carry out SEM here. However, because structural equation models are increasingly reported in the literature it is helpful to have a rough understanding of what they are and what to look for when they are reported.

Modelling complex relationships between variables

Previous educational success, age and the personality dimension of 'openness to experience' might be used to try to predict the performance of people on a training programme. In SEM it is possible to examine several such regression relationships simultaneously. So educational success, age and openness to experience could be used to predict training performance, and then training performance could be used along with 'number of hours worked per week' and 'years of relevant job experience' to predict job performance. These relationships are shown in Figure 6.38.

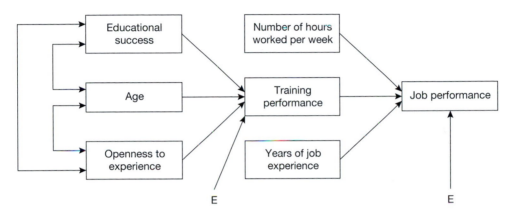

Figure 6.38 *Path diagram of a structural model involving measured variables only*

In Figure 6.38, each rectangle represents a particular variable that has been measured in the research. The proposed relationships between these variables are specified with the arrows. A line with one arrowhead indicates that a one-way relationship is proposed. The variable at the arrowhead end is the dependent variable, and the variable at the other end is the predictor variable. So, for example, 'years of job experience' is a predictor variable: it predicts the dependent variable of job performance. A line with arrowheads at both ends indicates that a correlational relationship exists between the variables, with no prediction being made about the direction of influence. So, here, a correlational relationship is proposed between educational success and age: it is not suggested that differences in age lead to more or less educational success, or that differing levels of educational success lead people to be different ages – but merely that these two variables are, for one or more reasons, related.

Note that two of the arrows, one pointing to training performance and one pointing to job performance, have an 'E' at the end. This E stands for error. The idea is that the three variables that predict training performance do not do so exactly: for example, you are not able to predict peoples' training performance precisely from a knowledge of their previous educational success, age and scores on the personality dimension of 'openness to experience'. Instead, errors of prediction are made when you try to predict in this way. In a structural equation model, all of the possible sources of variation have to be shown explicitly. Because

325

error (which, here, really stands for the variance in training performance that you cannot predict with the three predictor variables, and which could be due to all sorts of things you have not measured) is a source of variation, you have to acknowledge this.

Including factors

As well as allowing for quite complex relationships to be explored between measured variables, SEM also allows factors (sometimes called latent variables) to be included. As explained in the section on factor analysis, factors are variables that are not measured directly. They are formed from the shared variance of related variables that *are* measured. For example, you might be interested in assessment centre ability and its relationship with job performance. You cannot measure people's ability to do well in assessment centres directly, but you can do so indirectly by measuring their performance with:

- a cognitive ability test;
- a leaderless group discussion; and
- an in-tray exercise.

Similarly, you can't measure overall job performance directly either, but can do so indirectly by measuring each member of staff in terms of their boss's rating of them, a peer's ratings of them and a subordinate's ratings of them. The expected relationships are shown in Figure 6.39.

In Figure 6.39, assessment centre performance is a factor that is not directly measured but is estimated from the scores people obtained on the cognitive ability test, leaderless group discussion and an in-tray exercise. Similarly, the factor of job performance is

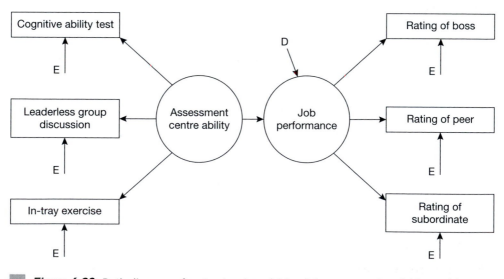

Figure 6.39 *Path diagram of a structural model involving measured variables and factors*

measured through ratings from a boss, a peer and a subordinate. Because the factor of assessment centre performance does not perfectly predict the scores that people obtain for the cognitive ability test, the leaderless group discussion and the in-tray exercise, you are, again, dealing with errors of prediction. So you say that, for example, the scores people obtain for cognitive ability are a function of both their assessment centre performance and error (in other words, all sorts of things you have not measured and do not know about). Similarly, each of the variables contributing to job performance is also associated with error, and consequently they have errors (Es) associated with them.

Finally, the model suggests that job performance is predicted by assessment centre performance. However, this prediction will not be perfect and, again, errors will occur. It is the convention to refer to the errors made when you use one factor to predict another as 'disturbances', and this is why there is a 'D' (for disturbance) associated with job performance.

Figures 6.38 and 6.39 are called path diagrams because they indicate the expected paths between variables and factors. In path diagrams, variables are represented with squares or rectangles and factors are represented with circles or ovals. A path diagram that contains only measured variables (such as Figure 6.38) is called a measurement model, while one such as 6.39 that also includes factors (sometimes referred to as latent variables) is called a structural model.

How SEM is used

Because SEM allows for the examination of complex relationships between measured variables and factors it is a powerful research tool. However, it is also very complex to carry out, something which at present requires purpose-written software such as *Lisrel* and *EQS*. Explaining in detail how to construct and test a structural equation model using *Lisrel* or *EQS* is beyond the scope of this book. However, the basic steps, as listed below, are actually quite straightforward.

1 The data are collected.
2 A path diagram is drawn to depict the expected relationships between the variables.
3 Statistical software is used to examine the extent to which the relationships hypothesized to exist between the variables, shown in the path diagram, actually do capture the relationships between the variables observed in the data. For example, with the path diagram shown in Figure 6.39, you would expect assessment centre ability to be a statistically significant predictor of job performance. The analysis would indicate whether the data actually supported this hypothesis.
4 The model is revised until a model which best fits the data is found.
5 This best-fitting model is reported and discussed.

Interpretation

When SEMs are reported, a path diagram showing the final, best-fitting model is normally reported. It is likely to look something like the model shown in Figure 6.40.

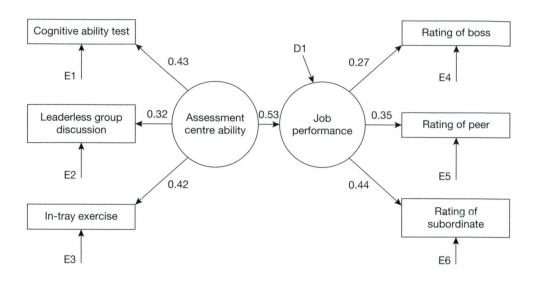

Figure 6.40 *Example of a final path diagram of a structural model involving measured variables and factors*

All variables that are associated with each other are connected with a line with either one arrowhead (indicating the direction of influence) or two arrowheads (indicating that no direction of influence is assumed). Each error and disturbance is numbered. The figures shown next to the arrow between predictor variables and dependent variables (e.g. educational success and training performance in Figure 6.38) are standardized regression coefficients. That is, they are equivalent to the beta values described in the section on multiple regression. They allow you to compare the relative contribution that each predictor variable has to explain the variance in the dependent variable. So, the higher the figure, the more variance in the dependent variable that the predictor variable explains – and, therefore, the more important it is in explaining that variance in the dependent variable. The lines between measured variables and factors are essentially factor loadings, as described in the section on factor analysis. The higher these figures, the more the factor is associated with the variable in question. Both the standardized beta coefficients and the factor loadings may have a minus sign next to them (for example, −0.28). If there is no minus sign, the variables are positively associated, but if there is a minus sign, this indicates that the variables are negatively associated.

Overall then, the model is interpreted by considering the relationships between the variables depicted in the final path diagram, and by examining which variables are relatively strongly associated, and which are less so by looking at the standardized regression coefficients and factor loadings. The direction of these associations (positive or negative) may also be important.

A BRIEF INTRODUCTION TO META-ANALYSIS

Meta-analysis is an increasingly common form of statistical analysis in organizational research, and the basic idea makes a lot of intuitive sense. Very often, organizational researchers publish research papers which present data on the strength of the relationship between variables of interest. Usually, though not always, these studies are concerned with the strength of the association between pairs of variables, and this is most often expressed with the Pearson correlation coefficient. An example is studies on the relationship between cognitive ability test scores and job performance. Since cognitive ability tests are frequently used in the selection of job candidates, we want to know how good the tests are at predicting who will perform best at work. So a validity study might be carried out on this, with the scores of a group of people who are given a cognitive ability test correlated with some measure of their job performance.

Assume that such a study involving, say, 150 employees showed the correlation between cognitive ability and job performance to be .34. How confident should you be that your correlation coefficient of .34 is an accurate estimate of the actual correlation between cognitive ability and job performance? This issue is very similar to one dealt with earlier in this book. Remember the idea, discussed in Chapter 2, that you use sample statistics (for example, the mean well-being of a sample of 100 men) to estimate population parameters (for example, the mean well-being of all men). When discussing this it was explained that the larger your sample the more confident you can be that your sample statistic is a good estimate of the population parameter you are interested in. The same logic can be applied to correlation coefficients. The larger the sample on which your correlation coefficient is based, the more confident you can be that it is a good estimate of the correlation coefficient of the population. When you ask the question, 'what is the correlation between cognitive ability test scores and job performance?' what you are really interested in is not the correlation you find in a particular study on the relationship between cognitive ability and job performance but, rather, in what is the 'actual' correlation between these two variables.

Combining the results of different empirical studies

Meta-analysis is essentially a technique for combining the results of different empirical studies concerned with a particular research question. So, if there are 20 different studies on the relationship between cognitive ability and job performance, the task of the meta-analysis is to combine the findings of these 20 individual studies. Each study will probably produce a different estimate of the correlation between cognitive ability and job performance but, by averaging the correlations across all these studies, you can obtain a correlation coefficient in which you can be relatively confident. In fact, the technique adopted is not simply to find the mean correlation coefficient but, instead, to weight the contribution that each study makes by the sample size used in it. So an individual study which involved a sample size of 1,000 employees and found a correlation of .42, will be given more weight in the computation of the overall correlation coefficient than an individual study in which the sample size is only 60.

Along with the estimate of the correlation between two variables based on the weighted mean correlations found in individual studies, the 95 per cent confidence interval for this correlation is also often given. This is very helpful because it informs you of the range of correlation coefficients within which you can be 95 per cent confident that the population correlation coefficient (the one you are really interested in) falls.

Example

A meta-analysis carried out on the correlation between personality dimensions and job performance might produce results like those shown in Table 6.21.

Table 6.21 *Results of a meta-analysis on the extent to which agreeableness and conscientiousness predict job performance*

Content area	Number of studies providing data	Total N	Average N	Sample-weighted mean r	95% confidence interval	
					Lower	Upper
Agreeableness	7	354	92	0.12	−0.27	0.32
Conscientiousness	9	569	74	0.23	0.15	0.29

The contents of the columns from left to right are:

- the personality dimension in question;
- the number of individual research studies used in the meta-analysis of that dimension;
- the total sample size across all the studies;
- the average sample size per study;
- the weighted mean correlation coefficient for these studies;
- the 95 per cent confidence interval for the mean correlation coefficient.

In the case of the personality dimension of agreeableness, seven studies were used with a total of 354 participants across all of these studies, and an average of 92 participants in each study. The mean correlation coefficient between agreeableness and work performance weighted by the sample sizes of the studies was .12, and we can be 95 per cent confident that the actual correlation between agreeableness and job performance is somewhere between −.27 and .32. Clearly, this is a very wide confidence interval, and it means that these studies do not give a very clear indication of the actual correlation between agreeableness and job performance. One reason for this might be that the correlation between agreeableness and job performance varies markedly as a function of factors such as the nature of the job someone is required to do, and that as different jobs were measured across the four studies, the correlation coefficients obtained were very different from each other. One other point worthy of note is that because the 95 per cent confidence interval includes zero, it is possible that, in fact, there is zero correlation between agreeableness and job performance. This is equivalent to the correlation coefficient not being statistically significant.

The use of meta-analysis

Meta-analyses are generally viewed as a very helpful form of statistical analysis. If done properly they can give us a valuable insight into the likely degree of association between variables; associations not just based on the results of a single study, but on the results of several studies often involving thousands of participants altogether. Furthermore, unlike so many other empirical studies in organizational research, they are implicitly concerned, not with statistical tests designed to confirm or refute a null hypothesis, but with effect sizes – usually in the form of the strength of the association between variables. The use of these effect sizes, and the confidence intervals associated with them, are of considerable help in furthering knowledge.

FURTHER READING

If you would like to learn more about statistical methods for examining associations, the book by Tabachnich and Fidell (2001) is recommended. This covers multiple regression, logistic regression, factor analysis and structural equation modelling as well as some other techniques not covered in this chapter such as discriminant function analysis and multiway frequency analysis. For more information on meta analysis see Rosenthal and DiMatteo (2001).

Answers

CHAPTER 1

1   A variable is anything that varies and can be measured. Examples in organizational research include age, and which department people work in.

2   This is categorical data. Each employee is in one of the three departments, and the figure 45 indicates that there are 45 such people in marketing. With continuous data we can say that someone has a higher score than someone else. But with categorical data like this all we can say is that someone is a member of a particular category – here, the marketing, sales or finance departments.

3   The pie chart and the bar chart.

4   A contingency table.

5   The mode, the median and the mean. The mode is used least frequently because it is based on only one piece of information about the data: the figure that occurs most often. For this reason, in most cases it does not provide as good a measure of central tendency as the median and the mean.

6   The range, the inter-quartile range, the variance and the standard deviation.

7   The mean is a measure of central tendency that may provide a misleading indication of the nature of the data measured on a continuous variable if there are one or more outliers. The variance and the standard deviation are measures of dispersion that may do so.

8   The standard deviation is the square root of the variance (and the variance is the square of the standard deviation).

9   (a) negatively skewed; (b) bimodal; (c) symmetrical; (d) positively skewed.

10 Lowest extreme, lower fourth, median, upper fourth and upper extreme.

CHAPTER 2

1   (b)

2   (b)

3   (a)

4   The sample size and the sample variance.

5   (b)

6   (b)

7 (a)

8 False

9 A measure of effect size for associations is the correlation coefficient. A measure of the effect size for the difference between two means is *d*.

10 Subtract one mean from the other and then divide by the standard deviation.

11 For associations *r* approximately equals .1 for a small effect, .3 for a medium effect and .5 and over for a large effect. For differences between means, *d* equals .2 for a small effect, .5 for a medium effect and .8 or more for a large effect.

12 Statistical power refers to the ability of statistical tests to reject null hypotheses when they are false. The amount of statistical power is a function of the level of significance used, the population effect size and the sample size.

CHAPTER 3

1 True

2 (a) 7.62; (b) 3.81.

3 (a) 47.6 per cent; (b) 24.8 per cent.

4 (a) 2.5 per cent; (b) 2.5 per cent.

5 The sampling distribution of means is the distribution of mean scores we would obtain if we took an infinite number of samples of a particular size from a population.

6 (a)

7 True

8 (b)

Appendix

STATISTICAL TECHNIQUES FOR EXAMINING DIFFERENCES

Categorical versus continuous dependent variable	Number of independent variables	Number of levels of the independent variables	Independent samples versus repeated measures or matched samples	Statistical technique
Categorical	One	Two or more	Independent samples	Chi square*
Continuous	One	Two	Independent samples	Independent samples *t*-test
Continuous	One	Two	Repeated measures or matched samples	Related samples *t*-test
Continuous	One	Three or more	Independent samples	Independent samples one-way ANOVA
Continuous	Two or more	Three or more	Independent samples	Independent samples factorial ANOVA
Continuous	Two or more	Three or more	Repeated measures or matched samples	Related samples factorial ANOVA
Continuous	Two or more	Three or more	Mixture of independent samples and repeated measures/matched samples	Mixed measures factorial ANOVA

*Whilst the Chi square test actually examines association, it is equivalent to a test of difference in proportions.

STATISTICAL TECHNIQUES FOR EXAMINING ASSOCIATIONS

Purpose	Number of variables	Technique
Examine the strength of the association between two continuous variables, or between one continuous variable and one dichotomous variable	Two	Correlation coefficient
Use scores on a continuous, or dichotomous, predictor variable to predict scores on a continuous dependent variable	One predictor variable and one dependent variable	Simple regression
Examine the relationship between a set of predictor variables and a continuous dependent variable, or examine the unique contribution of one or more predictor variables to variance in the dependent variable	Two or more predictor variables and one dependent variable	Standard multiple regression
Examine the relationship between a set of predictor variables and a continuous dependent variable after controlling for the effect of another set of predictor variables	Two or more predictor variables and one dependent variable	Hierarchical multiple regression
Use scores on two or more predictor variables to predict scores on a categorical (dichotomous) dependent variable or examine the unique contribution of a predictor variable in predicting outcomes on the categorical dependent variable	Two or more predictor variables and one dichotomous dependent variable	Logistic regression
Reduce a large number of continuous variables to a smaller number of continuous variables	Three or more	Principal components analysis, or factor analysis
Examine the average association between questionnaire items	Three or more	Cronbach's alpha coefficient
Examine the averaged findings of two or more different research studies	Varies	Meta-analysis
Examine complex relationships between several variables and/or factors	Varies	Structural equation modelling

References

Anderson, D. R., K. P. Burnham and W. L. Thompson (2000) 'Null hypothesis testing: problems, prevalence and an alternative'. *Journal of Wildlife Management* 64(4): 912–23.

Baron, R. M. and D. A. Kenny (1986) 'The moderator-mediator variable distinction in social psychological research: conceptual, strategic and statistical considerations'. *Journal of Personality and Social Psychology* 51: 1173–82.

Bausell, B. R. and Y.-F. Li (2002) *Power Analysis for Experimental Research*. Cambridge, Cambridge University Press.

Bayes, T. (1763) 'An essay towards solving a problem in the doctrine of chances'. *Philosophical Transactions of the Royal Society of London* 53: 370–418.

Berger, J. O. (2003) 'Could Fisher, Jeffreys and Neyman have agreed on testing?'. *Statistical Science* 18(1): 1–32.

Carver, R. P. (1978) 'The case against statistical significance testing'. *Harvard Educational Review* 48: 378–99.

Cattell, R. B. (1966) 'Psychological theory and scientific method', in R. B. Cattell *Handbook of Multivariate Experimental Psychology*. Chicago, Rand McNally.

Cohen, J. (1988) *Statistical Power Analysis for the Behavioral Sciences*, 2nd edn. Hillsdale, NJ, Lawrence Erlbaum Associates.

Cohen, J. (1994) 'The Earth Is Round ($p<.05$)'. *American Psychologist* 49(12): 997–1003.

Cohen, J. and P. Cohen (1975) *Applied Multiple Regression/Correlation Analysis for the Behavioural Sciences*. New York, Lawrence Erlbaum Associates.

Collis, J. and R. Hussey (2003) *Business Research*. New York, Palgrave Macmillan.

Comrey, A. L. and H. B. Lee (1992) *A First Course in Factor Analysis*. Hillsdale, NJ, Erlbaum.

Fisher, R. A. (1925) *Statistical Methods for Research Workers*. Edinburgh, Oliver and Boyd.

Fisher, R. A. (1935) 'The logic of inductive inference (with discussion)'. *Journal of the Royal Statistical Society* 98: 39–82.

Fisher, R. A. (1955) 'Statistical methods and scientific induction'. *Journal of the Royal Statistical Society* 17: 69–78.

Gigerenzer, G. (1993) 'The Superego, the Ego and the Id in statistical reasoning', in G. Keren and C. Lewis (eds) *A Handbook for Data Analysis in the Behavioral Sciences: Methodological Issues*. Hillsdale, NJ, Lawrence Erlbaum Associates.

Gorsuch, R. L. (1983) *Factor Analysis*. Hillsdale, NJ, Erlbaum.

Hosmer, D. W. and S. Lemeshow (1989) *Applied Logistic Regression*. New York, Wiley.

Howell, D. C. (1997) *Statistical Methods for Psychology*. London, Duxbury Press.

Howell, D. C. (2002) *Statistical Methods for Psychology*, 5th edn. London, Duxbury Press.

Jeffreys, H. (1961) *Theory of Probability*, 3rd edn. Oxford, Oxford University Press.

Lord, F. (1953) 'On the statistical treatment of football numbers'. *American Psychologist* 8: 750–1.

Nester, M. R. (1996) 'An applied statistician's creed'. *Applied Statistics* 45: 401–10.

Neyman, J. (1961) 'Silver jubilee of my dispute with Fisher'. *Journal of the Operations Research Society of Japan* 3: 145–54.

Neyman, J. (1977) 'Frequentist probability and frequentist statistics'. *Synthese* 36: 97–131.

Neyman, J. and E. S. Pearson (1933) 'On the problem of the most efficient tests of statistical hypotheses'. *Philosophical Transactions of the Royal Society* 231(A:): 289–337.

Rosenthal, R. and M. R. DiMatteo (2001) 'Meta-analysis: recent developments in quantitative methods for literature reviews'. *Annual Review of Psychology* 52: 59–82.

Saunders, M. N. K., P. Lewis and A. Thornhill (2002) *Research Methods for Business Students*. Harlow, Prentice Hall.

Stevens, S. S. (1946) 'On the theory of scales of measurement'. *Science* 161: 677–80.

Stevens, S. S. (1951) 'Mathematics, measurement, and psychophysics', in S. S. Stevens *Handbook of Experimental Psychology*. New York, John Wiley.

Tabachnick, B. G. and L. S. Fidell (2001) *Using Multivariate Statistics*. Boston, Allyn and Bacon.

Velleman, P. and L. Wilkinson (1993) 'Nominal, ordinal, and ratio typologies are misleading'. *The American Statistician* 47(1): 65–72.

Welch, B. L. (1951) 'On the comparison of several mean values: an alternative approach'. *Biometrika* 38: 320–36.

Wilkinson, L. and the Task Force on Statistical Inference (APA Board of Scientific Affairs) (1999) 'Statistical methods in psychology journals: guidelines and explanations'. *American Psychologist* 54(8): 594–604.

Index

339

eBooks – at www.eBookstore.tandf.co.uk

A library at your fingertips!

eBooks are electronic versions of printed books. You can store them on your PC/laptop or browse them online.

They have advantages for anyone needing rapid access to a wide variety of published, copyright information.

eBooks can help your research by enabling you to bookmark chapters, annotate text and use instant searches to find specific words or phrases. Several eBook files would fit on even a small laptop or PDA.

NEW: Save money by eSubscribing: cheap, online access to any eBook for as long as you need it.

Annual subscription packages

We now offer special low-cost bulk subscriptions to packages of eBooks in certain subject areas. These are available to libraries or to individuals.

For more information please contact webmaster.ebooks@tandf.co.uk

We're continually developing the eBook concept, so keep up to date by visiting the website.

www.eBookstore.tandf.co.uk